Lecture Notes in Computer Science   ~~3112~~

Commenced Publication in 1973
Founding and Former Series Editors:
Gerhard Goos, Juris Hartmanis, and Jan van Leeuwen

Springer
Berlin
Heidelberg
New York
Hong Kong
London
Milan
Paris
Tokyo

Howard Williams   Lachlan MacKinnon (Eds.)

Key Technologies
for Data Management

21st British National Conference on Databases, BNCOD 21
Edinburgh, UK, July 7-9, 2004
Proceedings

 Springer

Volume Editors

Howard Williams
Lachlan MacKinnon
Heriot-Watt University
School of Mathematical and Computer Sciences
Riccarton, Edinburgh EH14 4AS, UK
E-mail: {mhw, lachlan}@macs.hw.ac.uk

Library of Congress Control Number: 2004108031

CR Subject Classification (1998): H.2, H.3, H.4

ISSN 0302-9743
ISBN 3-540-22382-7 Springer-Verlag Berlin Heidelberg New York

Springer-Verlag is a part of Springer Science+Business Media

springeronline.com

© Springer-Verlag Berlin Heidelberg 2004
Printed in Germany

Typesetting: Camera-ready by author, data conversion by PTP-Berlin, Protago-TeX-Production GmbH
Printed on acid-free paper   SPIN: 11017479   06/3142   5 4 3 2 1 0

Preface

This year marked the coming of age of the British National Conference on Databases with its 21st conference held at Heriot-Watt University, Edinburgh, in July 2004. To mark the occasion the general theme of the conference was "When Data Is Key", reflecting not only the traditional key awarded on a 21st birthday, but also the ever-growing importance of electronic data management in every aspect of our modern lives. The conference was run as part of DAMMS (Data Analysis, Manipulation, Management and Storage) Week, which included a number of co-located and complementary conferences and workshops, including the 2nd Workshop on Teaching, Learning and Assessment in Databases (TLAD2), the BNCOD BioInformatics Workshop, and the 1st International Conference on the Future of Consumer Insight Developments in Retail Banking. The aim of this co-location was to develop synergies between the teaching, research and commercial communities involved in all aspects of database activities, and to use BNCOD as a focus for future synergies and developments within these communities.

Although this is entitled the British National Conference on Databases, BNCOD has always had an international focus, and this year more than most, with the majority of the papers submitted and accepted coming from outwith the UK. We were fortunate in attracting over 70 paper submissions for the conference, of which 18 were accepted, reflecting a stringent and quality-driven peer-review process and maintaining the reputation of BNCOD as a conference reporting high-quality research to the community. However, in our aim to extend the inclusivity of the conference, we also introduced an application paper stream to encourage submissions less focused on research (this stream appears in Vol. 2 of the proceedings), and at the end of this volume you will find the three best papers from TLAD2, as identified by the reviewers for that workshop.

The conference itself reflected the ever-growing diversity of the database community, with papers reflecting traditional database research concerns, through XML to multimedia, but we have strongly resisted the temptation to diversify away from our core concerns. In particular, the importance of database research was reflected in the subjects raised by the two keynote speakers. Both of these subjects are of massive international significance and have achieved the kind of universal importance that permits them to be identified with the definite article – The GRID and The Web.

Our first keynote speaker, Domenico Laforenza, is Technology Director of the Information Science and Technologies Institute (ISTI) of the Italian National Research Council (CNR). An active researcher and promoter of high-performance computing and GRID technologies, he has been deeply involved at both national and European level in the development of GRID infrastructures in Europe and the oversight of future directions for that development. His keynote address "Towards a Next Generation Grid" considered the developments in GRID research and technology that have brought us to the present situation, and elaborated on Next Generation Grid(s) in 2005–2010, and the research opportunities that will result from them, with a particular emphasis on the convergence of multi-disciplinary research.

Our second keynote speaker, Michael Wilson, is Manager of the W3C Office in the UK and Ireland, and a Member of the EU IST programme Advisory Group (ISTAG). His role as Manager in W3C is to help achieve the goal of leading the Web to full potential through ensuring the interoperability of different proprietary systems. As an active researcher in knowledge engineering, HCI, multimedia and VR, he has the background and pedigree to undertake this daunting and complex task. His keynote address "The Future of the World Wide Web" brought together a number of key concepts for this conference, the use of Web services and the Semantic Web, and the relationship between Web and GRID technologies, and he also introduced the issue of trust as a key concept in the future development of all these services.

As identified earlier, we were fortunate in attracting high-quality papers across a range of related topics. The first set of contributed papers were concerned with the processing of queries applied to data streams. Qingchun Jiang and Sharma Chakravarthy introduced novel scheduling strategies to minimize tuple latency and total memory requirements, and presented experimental results on their efficiency and effectiveness. Dan Olteanu, Tim Furche and Francois Bry were concerned with an evaluator (SPEX) for querying XML streams for which the complexity results are polynomial in the sizes of the data and queries, compared to most other methods, which are exponential in the size of the queries.

In the area of integrating data from a set of heterogeneous databases, one problem that needs to be dealt with is that of multiple query languages. Damir Becarevic and Mark Roantree described the EQL language for querying OO and object-relational database schemas in a database- and platform-independent manner. A system that is being developed to perform data integration based on a schema transformation approach is called AutoMed; Lucas Zamboulis described how the integration of XML data sources is accomplished through graph restructuring of their schemas in AutoMed. Kajal Claypool and Elke Rundensteiner focused on the problem of change over time in a database and its effect on the mapping of one data model to another.

In data analytics/manipulations one type of query that would be very useful for data mining is the path query, which determines the relationships between entities in a database. Rachel Hamill and Nigel Martin described one way of extending conventional database technology to support this type of query. Weifeng Chen and Kevin Lu discussed how agent technology has been integrated with conventional data mining techniques to realize a system for financial data mining. In order to limit the damage caused by malicious attacks on a database, Indrakshi Ray et al considered two techniques for rapid damage assessment and proposed a new one that improves on them.

XML was the focus of much of the work here. With it there was interest in new query languages and query processing techniques. G. Subramanyam and P. Sreenivasa Kumar presented a technique for multiple structural joins and showed that it performs better than existing join algorithms. Jung Kee Park and Hyunchul Kang were concerned with the use of caches to provide efficient support for XML queries, and focused on the problem of XML updates and the effect on cache answerability. Alison Cawsey et al. discussed the use of transformation constraints placed on XML documents by the information provider to constrain transformations applied to it, e.g., in personalization. On a different tack Richard Wheeldon, Mark

Levene and Kevin Keenoy were concerned with keyword search in relational databases and presented a novel algorithm for join discovery.

At the interface with the user, the automatic generation of data entry interfaces to databases usually follows a simplistic approach with limited constraints on data captured. However, Alan Cannon et al. described a semi-automatic tool for generating interfaces, which uses a domain ontology to reflect the semantics of the data, and improve the quality of the captured data. Linas Bukauskas and Michel Bohlen addressed the problem of scalability of visualization systems for large databases when data is extracted from a database and stored in a scene tree. They introduced two new data structures that improve scalability by eliminating the data bottleneck. Images may be stored in a multimedia database as sequences of editing operations. Leonard Brown and Le Gruenwald presented algorithms for performing color-based similarity searches on sets of images stored in this way.

The final session was on spatial databases and there were three papers on this theme. The performance of the M-tree, a data structure to support access to spatial data, depends on the degree of overlap between spatial regions. Alan Sexton and Richard Swinbank presented a new bulk loading algorithm to improve the performance of the M-tree and introduce a variant of it called the SM-tree. Another spatial data problem, the Obstructed Nearest Neighbour, is concerned with finding the nearest neighbours to a point in the presence of obstacles. Chengyi Xia, David Hsu and Anthony Tung presented an efficient algorithm for solving this problem. Despite much research on spatio-temporal data types, data models and query languages, little work has been done on complete spatio-temporal database systems. Tony Griffiths et al. addressed the latter problem with work on support for database programming in the spatio-temporal OODBMS Tripod.

Acknowledgements

We are deeply indebted to a number of different people and organizations without whom BNCOD21 would not have been possible. In particular we would like to thank:

- The members of the programme committee who gave willingly of their time and expertise and were most helpful, especially in having to deal with more papers than anticipated, and in managing to keep to the tight deadlines imposed on us.
- The invited speakers and authors who presented papers at BNCOD as well as those who submitted papers but were not successful. Without you there would have been no conference.
- The sponsors and exhibitors at the workshops and conferences during the whole week; your contributions, be they financial or in time and service, helped to enhance the quality of the experience for the delegates.
- The organizing committee who worked hard behind the scenes to ensure the success of the conference.

May 2004   Howard Williams and Lachlan MacKinnon

Conference Committees

Organizing Committee

L.M. MacKinnon	(Chair)	Heriot-Watt University
A.G. Burger	(BioInformatics Workshop)	Heriot-Watt University
E. Dempster	(Logistics)	Heriot-Watt University
R.G. Dewar	(Publicity, Website)	Heriot-Watt University
P.M.D. Gray	(Competition)	Aberdeen University
D. Lanc	(Data Financials Workshop)	Heriot-Watt University
P.W.Trinder	(Posters, Tutorials)	Heriot-Watt University

Programme Committee

Howard Williams (Chair)	Heriot-Watt University
David Bell	Queen's University, Belfast
Albert Burger	Heriot-Watt University
Richard Connor	Strathclyde University
Richard Cooper	University of Glasgow
Barry Eaglestone	University of Sheffield
Wenfei Fan	University of Edinburgh
Alvaro Fernandes	University of Manchester
Alex Gray	University of Wales, Cardiff
Peter Gray	University of Aberdeen
Mike Jackson	University of Wolverhampton
Anne James	Coventry University
Keith Jeffery	CLRC, Rutherford Appleton Laboratory
Jessie Kennedy	Napier University
Brian Lings	University of Exeter
Lachlan MacKinnon	Heriot-Watt University
Nigel Martin	Birkbeck College, University of London
Ken Moody	University of Cambridge
Werner Nutt	Heriot-Watt University
Norman Paton	University of Manchester
Alex Poulovassilis	Birkbeck College, University of London
Stratis Viglas	University of Edinburgh
Peter Wood	Birkbeck College, University of London

Steering Committee

Brian Lings (Chair)	University of Exeter
Barry Eaglestone	University of Sheffield
Alex Gray	University of Wales, Cardiff
Anne James	Coventry University
Keith Jeffery	CLRC, Rutherford Appleton Laboratory
Roger Johnson	Birkbeck College, University of London

Table of Contents

Interface/Visualization

Spatial Data

TLAD Workshop

Towards a Next Generation Grid

Domenico Laforenza

High Performance Computing Laboratory, ISTI, CNR, Via G. Moruzzi 1,
56126 Pisa, Italy
domenico.laforenza@isti.cnr.it

Extended Abstract

This paper aims to present the outcome of a group of independent experts convened
by the European Commission with the objective to identify potential European Research priorities for Next Generation Grid(s) in 2005 – 2010 [1].

The first part will be focused on the Grid Evolution. In fact, in order to discuss
"what is a Next Generation Grid", it is important to determine "with respect to what".
Distinct phases in the evolution of Grids are observable. At the beginning of the 90's,
in order to tackle huge scientific problems, in several important research centres tests
were conducted on the cooperative use of geographically distributed resources, con-
ceived as a single powerful computer. In 1992, Charlie Catlett and Larry Smarr
coined the term "Metacomputing" to describe this innovative computational approach
[2].

The term Grid Computing [3] was introduced by Foster and Kesselman a few
years later, and in the meanwhile several other words were used to describe this new
computational approach, such as Heterogeneous Computing, Networked Virtual
Supercomputing, Heterogeneous Supercomputing, Seamless Computing, etc., Metacomputing could be considered as the 1st generation of Grid Computing, some kind of
"proto-Grid".

The Second Grid Computing generation starts around 2001, when Foster at al.
proposed Grid Computing as *"an important new field, distinguished from conventional distributed computing by its focus on large-scale resource sharing, innovative
applications, and, in some cases, high-performance orientation"* [4].

A Grid provides an abstraction for resource sharing and collaboration across
multiple administrative domains. The term resource covers a wide range of concepts
including physical resources (computation, communication, storage), informational
resources (databases, archives, instruments), individuals (people and the expertise
they represent), capabilities (software packages, brokering and scheduling services)
and frameworks for access and control of these resources.

With the advent of multiple different Grid technologies the creativity of the re-
search community was further stimulated, and several Grid projects were proposed
worldwide. But soon a new question about how to guarantee interoperability among
Grids was raised. In fact, the Grid Community, mainly created around the Global Grid
Forum (GGF) [5], perceived the real risk that the far-reaching vision offered by Grid
Computing could be obscured by the lack of interoperability standards among the cur-

H. Williams and L. MacKinnon (Eds.): BNCOD 2004, LNCS 3112, pp. 1–3, 2004.

rent Grid technologies. Interoperability is paramount for problem solving; in fact, there is no single Grid environment because data sources, software sources, compute and storage resources, network resources and detection equipment resources are heterogeneous and distributed by nature.

The marriage of the Web Services technologies [6] with the Second Generation Grid technology led to the valuable GGF Open Grid Services Architecture (OGSA) [7], and to the creation of the Grid Service concept and specification (Open Grid Service Infrastructure - OGSI). OGSA can be considered the milestone architecture to build Third Generation Grids. Although not new, an important ongoing process in the Grid evolution is the concept of "virtualization" of Grid resources. Virtualization is a way to expose only high-level functionalities in a standard and interoperable way hiding the implementation details.

The second part of this paper is focused on the "Next Generation Grids". Starting from the Expert Group's opinion that current Grid implementations lack many essential capabilities, which would enable the vision of complete resource virtualization, NGG is seen as something that goes over the above mentioned Third Generation Grids. The Next Generation Grid Properties ("The NGG Wish List") will be presented. The current Grid implementations do not individually possess all of these properties. However, future Grids not possessing them are unlikely to be of significant use and, therefore, inadequate from both research and commercial perspectives.

As reported in [1], NGG will be "*a virtual, pervasive organisation with specific computational semantics. It performs a computation, solves a problem, or provides service to one single client or to millions of clients*". NGG will consist of millions of interconnected nodes and will pervade into everyday life.

Nowadays, the Grid programmers have to mastermind the usage of different kinds of geographically dispersed resources; all the intricacies related to resource allocation and scheduling, data movement, synchronisation, error handling, load balancing, etc. must be transparent to users and developers. Future generations Grids should be programmed through generic and problem-specific abstractions, supported by an appropriate programming environment. This requires both the needs to study and adapt existing programming models to the Grid context, as well as the definition of new programming models, combining parallel and distributed programming practices in a coherent way.

In order to realise the NGG vision much research is needed. During the last few years, several new terms such as Global Computing, Ubiquitous Computing, Utility Computing, Pervasive Computing, On-demand Computing, Autonomic Computing, Ambient Intelligence [8], etc., have been coined. In some cases, these terms describe very similar computational approaches. The term Ambient Intelligence (AmI), for instance, stems from the convergence of three key technologies: Ubiquitous Computing, Ubiquitous Communication, and Intelligent User Friendly Interfaces. It is not easy in much of the general literature on technology futures to see clearly how AmI is distinguished from older concepts such as Pervasive Computing or Ubiquitous Computing, the latter being first described more than a decade ago.

Consequently, some people are raising the following questions: Are these computational approaches facets of the same medal? What is their relationship with Grid? Moreover, for each of these approaches, we are assisting with the creation of quite disjoint "schools of thought", having very few cultural interactions with each other.

Often these communities use different languages and terminology just to emphasize the importance of their own technical contributions. A great deal of disagreement exists as to the individual definitions of each of the terms. Sometimes the same term is used to indicate different things, or different terms are used to indicate the same thing. This situation is not necessarily problematic "per se", although it may be somewhat confusing for people who are looking for more precise definitions of each term. In order to reduce the risk to re-invent the wheel, terms, concepts and definitions need to be standardized.

The realisation of the NGG vision requires much research (and funds), and the real problem that could derive from a persistent situation of apparently confusing and unclarified overlapping of those research areas is the fact that there could be some concrete risks to waste intellectual and physical (e.g. public and private funds) resources in mere "religious" wars. This will not be beneficial for anybody.

In conclusion, paraphrasing Charles Darwin, the idea that each species has been independently created is erroneous, and a stronger convergence of R&D actions among those exciting research fields seems to be absolutely required.

References

1. EU Expert Group Report, Next Generation Grid(s) 2005 – 2010, Brussels, June 2003, ftp://ftp.cordis.lu/pub/ist/docs/ngg_eg_final.pdf .
2. Smarr, L., Catlett, C.: Metacomputing, Communications of the ACM **35**(6) (1992) 45-52
3. Foster, I., Kesselman, C. (Editors), The Grid: Blueprint for a Future Computing Infrastructure, Morgan Kaufmann Publishers, USA (1999)
4. Foster, I., Kesselman, C., Tuecke, S.: The Anatomy of the Grid: Enabling Scalable Virtual Organizations, Int. Journal of High Performance Computing Applications **15**(3) (2001) 200–222
5. Global Grid Forum, www.ggf.org
6. W3C Consortium. www.w3c.org
7. Foster, I., Kesselman, C., Nick, J., Tuecke, S.: The Physiology of the Grid: An Open Grid Services Architecture for Distributed Systems Integration (2002)
8. Aarts, E., Bourlard, H., Burgelman, J-C., Filip, F., Ferrate, G., Hermenegildo, M., Hvannberg, E., McAra-McWilliam, I., Langer, J., Lagasse, P., Mehring, P., Nicolai, A., Spirakis, P., Svendsen, B., Uusitalo, M., Van Rijsbergen, K., Ayre, J.: Ambient Intelligence: from vision to reality. IST Advisory Group (ISTAG) in FP6: WG116/9/2003 (2003) Final Report.

The Future of the World Wide Web?

Michael Wilson and Brian Matthews

W3C Office in the UK and Ireland
CCLRC Rutherford Appleton Laboratory,
Chilton, Didcot, OX11 0QX, UK
{M.D.Wilson, B.M.Matthews}@rl.ac.uk
http://www.w3c.rl.ac.uk

Abstract. The Web started as a simple and very usable distributed system that was rapidly adopted. The Web protocols then passed through a period of rationalization and development to separate content from presentation in order to promote the re-usability of content on different devices. Today the developments in Web technologies are addressing new opportunities in Web Services and the Semantic Web, as well as the growing cultural diversity of the Web. These developments unite in the issue of *trust*, of content and services available on the Web, but also in access by others to the content and services that users may own. While the Web has been rationalizing, the Grid has developed to provide academic science with easier access to services and content. The Grid is now moving to exploit the robust interoperable commodity Web Services instead of maintaining its own middle level infrastructure. As Web Services, the Grid and the Semantic Web develop they will become increasingly interdependent on each other, and indistinguishable from the mainstream Web.

1 The Past

In 1991 Tim Berners-Lee, Robert Cailliau and Nicola Pellow from CERN released a portable line mode browser which could access documents held on distributed servers written in the HyperText Mark-up Language (HTML), through the HyperText Transport Protocol (HTTP), FTP or other protocols from a single address space within which each had a unique Universal Resource Location (URL).

The first major change to HTML came in 1993 when Marc Andreessen and Eric Bina from NCSA wrote the Mosaic browser and allowed in-line colour images through the introduction of the <IMG> tag.

A major addition to the overall Web architecture was also made in 1993 when Matthew Gray at MIT developed his World Wide Web Wanderer which was the first robot on the Web designed to count and index the Web servers. Initially, it only counted the available Web servers, but shortly after its introduction, it started to capture URLs as it went along. The database of captured URLs became the first Web database - the Wandex.

By 1993 these major components of the Web architecture were available from research organisations. The subsequent growth in Web pages and servers, and the

H. Williams and L. MacKinnon (Eds.): BNCOD 2004, LNCS 3112, pp. 4–15, 2004.

development of commercial tools, which will not be recounted here. Such growth and commercial involvement show that the Web was a practical success that was becoming prey to competitive commercial interests. In 1994, as a result of concerns that fragmentation of Web standards would destroy the interoperability that the Web had achieved, Tim Berners-Lee and the Laboratory for Computer Science of MIT started the World Wide Web Consortium (W3C) to direct future developments for the Web.

The technologies which constitute the Web, although practical and successful, were technically crude. HTML combined the description of the content of a page with a description of the presentation of the page, which limited the re-usability of the content, and included no type system to support static checking. There was no mechanism to present or compose time-based media such as sound or video. The HTTP transport protocol was not optimized to the resource transfer usage of the Web. There was even confusion about what a URL could point to – files, but what of other resources such as devices (e.g. printers) and even people. However, these limitations allowed an accessible conceptual model and easy interaction without which it is unlikely that the Web would have been adopted.

W3C entered into a programme of work to reform these protocols, to overcome these problems, and incorporate technologies that would facilitate extensibility. To do this the simple architecture of URL, HTML and HTTP alone had to be sacrificed for a more complex one, where the new protocols and languages would no longer be easy to write in generic text editors, but would require specialized editors.

W3C addresses the core Web technologies that build on the transport layer standardized by the IETF and which are, in turn, built on by application specific standards that require a less rigorous process. Once a W3C working group is established to create a standard, or recommendation as W3C calls them, it usually takes two to three years before it is completed and officially published. Some groups have been terminated before completion when the motivation for standardization has dissipated or stakeholder consensus cannot be reached. The protocols published so far as recommendations by W3C are shown in Table 1.

2   The Present

The main four concerns of W3C today are listed below, while the architecture as it has evolved to meet them is shown in Figure 1.

Ensure access to the Web by many devices – The Web is becoming accessible from a wide range of devices including cellular phones, TV, digital cameras, and in-car computers. Interaction with resources on the Web can be achieved through a key pad, mouse, voice, stylus or other input devices. W3C has activities addressing device independence and multimodal interaction to contribute to W3C's goal of universal access.

Account for cultural diversity – To ensure access to the Web by people speaking different languages, with different writing conventions, and having different cultural backgrounds. In 1999, approximately half of all public Web sites were associated with entities located in the United States, whereas by March 2003 only 35.2% of Web pages were in English, with 22.2% in Chinese or Japanese.

Web Services – the Web started as a tool for users to view documents. It is now moving to be a tool for computers to communicate with each other, on services provided by each other in a peer-to-peer manner rather than only in a browser to server one.

Table 1. Recommendations issued by W3C before March 2004

1996	1997	1998	1999	2000	2001	2002	2003	2004
PICS Rating	PICSRules	PICS DSig	Name spaces	DOM 2 Core	XHTML M12n	P3P 1.0	SVG 1.1	DOM 3 Validation
PICS Labels	HTML 3.2	CSS 2	CSS 1	ATAG 1.0	Canonical XML	XML Signature	DOM 2 HTML	CC/PP
		SMIL 1.0	WCAG 1.0	DOM 2 Events	Schema Primer	XML Canonicalization	SVG Mobile	Infoset (2nd)
		DOM 1	Style Sheets Pl	DOM 2 Style	Schema Struct.	XHTML 1.0	XPTR Element	Namespaces 1.1
			MathML 1.01	DOM2T raversal	Schema Types Ruby	XPath Filter	XPTR Framewk	XML 1.0 (3rd)
			XPath 1.0	DOM 2Views		Decrypt Transform	XPTR Xmlns	XML 1.1
			XSLT 1.0	XHTML Basic	XHTML 1.1	XML Encription	SOAP Adjuncts	OWL Guide
			HTML 4.01		XLink 1.0	UAAG1.0	SOAP Framewk	OWL Overview
					XML Base		SOAP Primer	OWL Reference
					SMIL 2.0		SOAP Tests	OWL Semantics
					SMIL Anim.		XForms 1.0	OWL Tests
					XSL 1.0		XML Events	OWL Use Cases
					WebCGM		MathML 2.0	RDF Concepts
							PNG (2nd)	RDF Primer
								RDF Schema
								RDF Semantics
								RDF Test Cases
								RDF/XML
								Speech Recognition
								VoiceXML 2.0

Semantic Web – as the data and service servers become more common on the Web, the data and services that they provide need to be described in a machine understandable way in order to be discovered, evaluated for fitness to a user's purpose and then called. The Web also needs to provide an environment in which contracts for the use of data and services can be established, and trust relationships defined to limit the growing incidence of cybercrime. To support machine dialogues in these areas, richer representations of ontologies, rules, and inference are required which are collectively termed the Semantic Web.

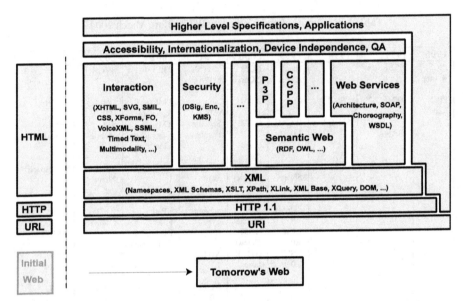

Fig. 1. The evolution of the architecture of the protocols in the World Wide Web

3 Web Services

Web Services have a long ancestry in distributed computing going back to remote procedure calls. The XML Protocol Activity which became the Web Services protocol or SOAP layer in the Web Services architecture was initiated in September 2000 in W3C following the observations that "distributed object oriented systems such as CORBA, DCOM and RMI exist with distinct functionality and distinct from the Web address space causes a certain tension, counter to the concept of a single space"[1]. As shown in Table 1, it was 2003 before any parts of SOAP reached the final recommendation form of publication.

In 2002 IBM and Microsoft agreed the main structure of the Web Services Architecture shown in Figure 2 (after [2]) which incorporated the Web Services Security component that is enlarged in Figure 3 (after [3]) since it has been so subdivided. These figures show the overall approach of a transport layer (HTTP) carrying messages (SOAP) between machines to invoke services. These services must describe their functionality (WSDL) and such descriptions can be registered in a directory (UDDI) to ease resource discovery. Privacy issues are still awaiting clarification, but most of the others have at least been proposed in pre-standardised forms. It took about 18 months for the various proposals for a Web Services Flow Language (WSFL) from IBM, Web Services Choreography Interface (WSCI) from BEA, Open Management Interface (OMI) from HP and WebMethods, to coalesce into BPEL4WS, and that is still not openly standardised, only supported by inter-company agreements. Similar time scales can be expected for any proposals for methods and interface languages higher up the stack as they pass through the development, standardization adoption and assimilation cycle.

One vision for motivating Web Services is that users will be able to use graphical business modeling tools to describe business models in terms of available services, with the desired quality and cost constraints on them. These services will be composed into the overall business that is being created in a language such as BPEL4WS, and meet various assurances and constraints on them, which can be described in other languages. The business can then be created and operated through the tool.

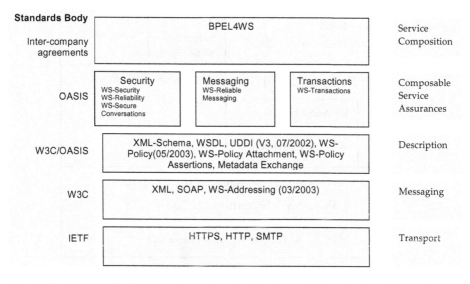

Fig. 2. The interoperable Web Services protocol architecture with the role of each layer shown on the right, and the standards body responsible on the left

The first generation of such Web Service composition tools are already available; for example, Triana from Cardiff University is an open source problem solving environment where the desired tools can be dragged to a work surface and wired together to create a workflow in BPEL4WS. It is too generic to yet include the specialised risk analysis tools and economic models to simulate whether prospective businesses would be profitable after composition, however it does support the basic composition and calling of Web Services through BPEL4WS. Such tools will become more specialized, and progressively incorporate resource discovery, trust and contract management components as they become available, adopted and assimilated.

Although there are commercial Business Process Management (BPM) tools available from many vendors, including IBM's CrossWorlds eBusiness Integration

Suite, Microsoft's Biztalk Orchestrator and SAP's Business Workflow, there are still technical and interoperability problems with BPM over Web Services that many consider are not resolved in BPEL4WS alone. To address the service composition concerns W3C has recently initiated a Web Services Choreography Working Group with 32 participating organizations. The problems are exemplified by the number of alternative languages proposed by other consortia which do not relate cleanly to BPEL4WS, including XML Process Definition Language (XPDL) and Workflow-XML (Wf-XML) from the Workflow Management Coalition; Business Process Modelling Language (BPML) and Business Process Query Language (BPQL) from BMPI.

One of the general problems in service description and discovery is in the classic data and information retrieval problem of describing the thing to be discovered in a way compatible with the target's description. Along with the details of how to describe the quality of service and other constraints on the Web Service, this is addressed by the Semantic Web.

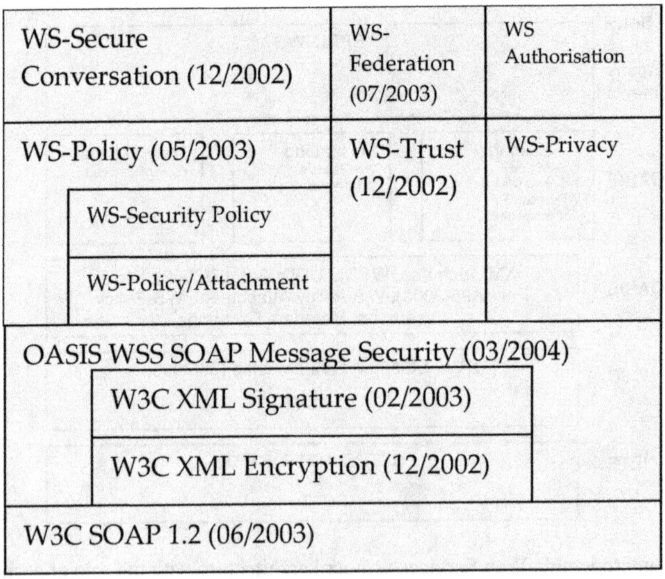

WS-Secure Conversation (12/2002)		WS-Federation (07/2003)	WS Authorisation
WS-Policy (05/2003)		WS-Trust (12/2002)	WS-Privacy
	WS-Security Policy		
	WS-Policy/Attachment		
OASIS WSS SOAP Message Security (03/2004)			
	W3C XML Signature (02/2003)		
	W3C XML Encryption (12/2002)		
W3C SOAP 1.2 (06/2003)			

Fig. 3. Web Services Security Roadmap

4   The Semantic Web

One simple problem used to motivate the Semantic Web has been the need to discover resources on the Web, not only from their content as search engines do, but from descriptions of them. The problem is exemplified by the frustration in finding articles published by an author, rather than those which include the author's name. In response to the query "Time Berners-Lee" a search engine will respond with all the papers including that phrase, a subset of which will be authored by Tim Berners-Lee, but most of which will cite or refer to him – as this paper does. The Semantic Web should allow each resource on the Web to be described in metadata that states for data and information who its author was, when it was created, what its content is, etc., and for services, what they do, what they cost and what quality measures apply to them. To do this it is necessary to define the structure of the metadata and a restricted, and machine interpretable, vocabulary in which to describe it. In turn, it is then necessary to define a language to express these two. The language initially proposed by W3C was the Resource Description Framework (RDF). A common metadata format for Web resources was also proposed in the form of the Dublin Core [4], which defines 15 elements of metadata, so that both the Dublin Core elements and the content can be stated in RDF.

Unfortunately the solution is not that simple. The use of RDF and Dublin Core for resource discovery is analogous to the use of HTML and HTTP for the Web in 1993. It is superficially attractive, and appears to solve the immediate resource discovery problem, but it does not address all the issues that the specialists in knowledge acquisition and ontology management, maintenance and reasoning raise about simple lists of words. A more elaborate architecture is required to address these problems that immediately arise as is shown in Figure 4 – after [5].

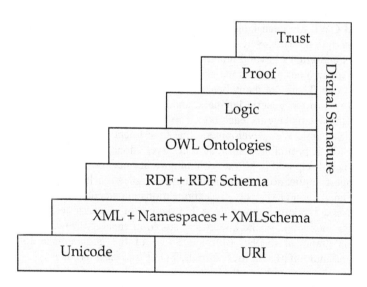

Fig. 4. The Semantic Web Architecture.

When RDF and Dublin Core alone are used for the creation of metadata an one's own Web pages the two main problems are with the creation, maintenance and interoperability of the vocabulary used, and with the trustworthiness of the metadata. The vocabulary cannot be reasoned over or proven to be complete or consistent to any rules. If the vocabulary is stated in an Ontology language such as OWL, then tools can apply Description Logic [6] to test its internal consistency and identify combinations of properties for which no terms exist. The second problem is harder to overcome - why should a resource discovery tool trust the metadata a Web page author states on their own page since many sites will place every possible term to attract the most potential readers or users of the service? The lack of accessible vocabularies and the trust problem have prevented the take up of metadata for resource description so far.

RDF and RDF Schema have been released as recommendations by W3C this year, and several robust tool sets exist for using them which should foster their use. For example the Jena toolkit from Hewlett Packard supports the creation and query of RDF knowledge bases, as well as several different inference engines that can reason over the knowledge. Equally work is underway to provide easy migration from existing vocabulary resources such as thesauri into RDF so that they can be supported by generic Semantic Web tools. RDF query which is supported by such tools has just started its path through the standardization process at W3C.

Similarly, OWL has become a recommendation this year, with the result that various vocabularies that have been created in its precursors can now be used in a standard representation, which should motivate the development of robust OWL based tools for ontology creation and management. One example is the DAML-S vocabulary to define quality measures on Web Services [7]. The standardization of an agreed OWL-S based on this is being considered by W3C at present. This would allow a standard language to be used by Web Service composition tools for properties of Web Services.

RDF and OWL are each languages that fulfill specific purposes in resource and service description. However, RDF is also a generic language for defining vocabularies and graphs beyond hierarchies, which XML describes. Therefore it can be used for many other applications, and the tools for it become generic as those for XML have done. There are many benefits in this for the users of the languages who only need to learn the generic language and tools for a wide range of applications rather than a new language for each one. This benefit is consistent with the approach taken to the Semantic Web development, that investment in each layer of the pyramid should provide a profitable return at that layer alone, so that a single massive investment is not required in all the technologies at once. For example, RDF itself is used to support applications such as the news syndication language RSS, a person networking language FOAF, as well as applications in calendar management. Each of these is addressed by other applications, but the use of a generic technology and tool set allows the interaction of the knowledge stored in each application to provide, for example, the graphical display (through SVG) of the geographical location and timeline representation of activities from the FOAF and calendar data.

Further up the pyramid are the logic and proof layers where there are several proposals for rule languages based on RDF such as RuleML [8] and N3 [9]. These are developing demonstration applications to illustrate and test their structure and tool support, but they have not yet been widely adopted, nor do they yet approach standardization. One of the problems with this layer is that it raises the specter of artificial intelligence which many business investors consider either to be too long term an investment, or have memories of losing their investment in the 1980's expert system boom which they do not wish to repeat. One important issue to be overcome before these fears can be allayed is that of the liability for actions taken by rules in distributed systems. There is concern that until distributed rule based systems are sufficiently established and contracts applying to them are standard practice based upon accepted legal precedent, then anybody in the development and use chains could be liable for compensation claims following errors.

The final layer in the pyramid addresses these issues of trust and the legal contracts that apply across the Semantic Web and Web Services.

5 Trust and Contracts

Trust and legal contract management are issues where Web Services and the Semantic Web meet, and are only now being addressed within this integrated approach.

Trust between parties (e.g. buyer and seller) in turn introduces a wider context of the contract or relationship in which the trust exists. The trust will apply to an entity in a contract to fulfill a role. To extend the Web Services architecture upwards, trust policies can be imposed on the business process management layer to constrain the lower security layer in the light of a contract, which itself is established to implement a business model in the context of the prevailing law of the country or international situation. This is illustrated in Figure 5. However, given what was said above about the current standardization and interoperability of business process management, clearly any edifice built upon it is unstable at present and still a research topic.

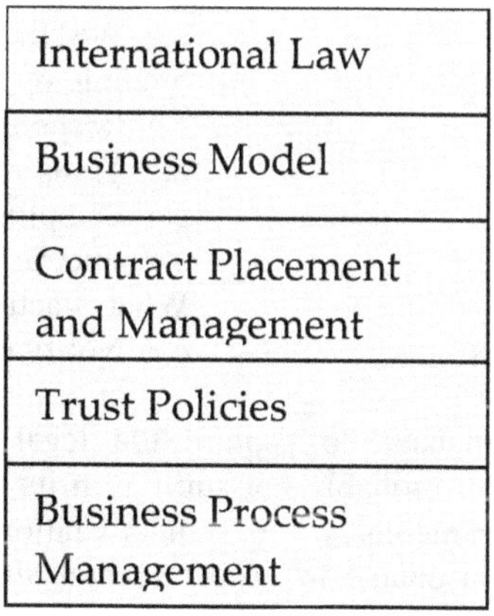

International Law
Business Model
Contract Placement and Management
Trust Policies
Business Process Management

Fig. 5. The Trust Stack.

Trust judgments can be made on individuals or organizations (trustees) using Semantic Web technologies to model and reason about them. The basis of trust judgments are the trustor's experience of the trustee and any available recommendations from others as to their trustworthiness; which may themselves be based on experience. There is a body of work on the process or collecting evidence for, and making such judgments using Subjective Logic based on the established Dempster Shaffer evidence theory [10], which is being incorporated into the Semantic Web technologies. There are also demonstrator systems for managing access control to information, data, and computational resources which include trust based authorization decisions (e.g. [11]) that can apply over the roles represented in the business process management (BPM) layer to propagate constraints to the security layer to authorize access to data and use of services and other resources. This research is also starting to introduce the delegation of obligations resulting from contracts, although this is still at a very early stage, and does not yet include the refinement of responsibilities to action plans during delegation between roles in the BPM, although it does address the concomitant delegation of authority.

The most significant recent development at the contract layer itself is the Web Services Service Level Agreement language – WSLA [12]. This requires a range of vocabularies used in WSDL that should be maintained with Semantic Web technologies. It applies them to Web Services, but is not an integral part of the Web services protocol architecture, fitting more easily into the higher level trust stack since it applies a clear legal contract to each Web Service transaction.

The WSLA language elements include those that normally occur in contracts to define liability and binding complex terms and conditions for operations with their quality of service and computational assurances as well as price :

Parties	e.g. Service provider, consumer
Action Interfaces	Interface descriptions
Sponsors	e.g. Measurement Service
Service Description	Common view of the service
Service Objects, refer to	Specification, link to serv. descr.
- WSDL	e.g. WSDL service, port,
- BPEL, ...	binding, operation
SLA Parameters	e.g. Response time
Metrics	e.g. Transaction counter
Measurement Directives	e.g. Sampling interval
Functions	e.g. (metric1 + metric2) /2
Obligations	What is actually promised
SLOs, ActionGuarantees	e.g. Notify management service

WSLA is the first language to capture the legal contractual terms from a mainstream supplier. It will probably not survive in its present form to widespread adoption but given the timescales for standardization and adoption mentioned previously, it would be reasonable to expect several alternative proposals over the next two years when a standardization process could start, completing in about five years.

6 The Web and the Grid

While the Web has been developing, the demands of scientists for sharing supercomputers, using the spare compute cycles on the many desktop machines in universities, and passing vast amounts of experimental data have lead to the development of the Grid [13]. The fundamental difference between the Grid and the Web has been that each transaction in the Web is discrete, in that the connection between client and server is broken and the only way to maintain the state of the dialogue is to deposit a copy of it (e.g. as a cookie) with the client. In contrast the

Grid calls services and maintains the state of the dialogue so that the progress being made to the objective of the service can be monitored (e.g. report on how far a computation has progressed). Recent design decisions in the GGF who standardize the GRID, have been to move to an Open Grid Services Architecture (OGSA) based on Web Services, but including the ability to model stateful resources- WS-Resource Framework (WSRF). WS-Resource [14] has been introduced recently to support the declaration and implementation of the association between a Web Service and one or more named, typed state components. WS-Resource models state as stateful resources and codifies the relationship between Web Services and stateful resources in terms of the implied resource pattern - a set of conventions on Web Services technologies, in particular WS-Addressing. When a stateful resource participates in the implied resource pattern, it is referred to as a WS-Resource. A WS-Resource is defined and associated with the description of a Web service interface while its properties are made accessible through the Web Service interface that can be managed throughout the WS-Resource's lifetime. With the introduction of OGSA and WSRF the advances made for science in Grid computing can be made available on top of the generic commodity Web Services, while freeing up the scientific development community to focus on their needs instead of developing the security, trust and semantic components for the Grid independently, since they are available at the underlying levels. As the Semantic Web and Web Services interact and are moving to a single Web, so the Grid is moving to be a layer on top of Web Services rather than a separate distributed technology.

7 Conclusion

Although the Web is a successful commodity that has millions of active users, it is not set in an unchanging form. Advances are expected in Web Services, the Semantic Web and the integration of the Web and the Grid. These should provide a basis for the creation of businesses from Web Services drawing on the vocabularies available through the Semantic Web, suitable to meet the legal requirements of national and international law. The encoding, and enforcement of legal contracts has only just begun, but it will be an active area of research with a clear financial benefit to many parties, which also requires advances in many areas of computer science. More advanced topics such as the agent-based negotiation of contracts with trustworthy, or untrustworthy, actors that are dependent on these (e.g. [15]) remain still further along the Web Roadmap (see [16]).

References

Details of the W3C recommendations mentioned in the text are available online at http://www.w3.org

1.   Berners-Lee, T.: Web Architecture from 50,000 feet.
      http://www.w3.org/DesignIssues/Architecture (1998)

2. Ferguson, D.F., Storey, A., Lovering, B., Schewchuk, J.: Secure Reliable, Transacted Web Service: Architecture and Composition. http://msdn.microsoft.com/library/default.asp?-url=/library/enus/dnwebsrv/html/wsoverview.asp (2003)
3. IBM and Microsoft, 2002 Security in a Web Services World: A Proposed Architecture and Roadmap – http://www-106.ibm.com/developerworks/webservices/library/ws-secmap/
4. DublinCore: The Dublin Core Metadata Initiative - http://dublincore.org/ (1995)
5. Berners-Lee, T., Hendler, J., Lassila, O.: The Semantic Web. Scientific American, May 2001
6. Decker, S., Fensel, D., van Harmelen, F., Horrocks, I., Melnik, S., Klein, M., Broekstra, J.: Knowledge representation on the web. In Proc. of the 2000 Description Logic Workshop (DL 2000) (2000) 89-98
7. OWL-S Coalition: OWL-S 1.0 Release http://www.daml.org/services/owl-s/1.0/ (2003)
8. Michael Schroeder and Gerd Wagner (Eds.): Proceedings of the International Workshop on Rule Markup Languages for Business Rules on the Semantic Web. Sardinia, Italy, June 14, 2002. CEUR-WS Publication Vol-60. - http://www.ruleml.org
9. Berners-Lee, T.: Notation 3: An RDF Language for the Semantic Web. http://www.w3.org/DesignIssues/Notation3.html (1998)
10. Josang. An algebra for assessing trust in certification chains. In J. Kochmar, editor, Proceedings of the Network and Distributed Systems Security Symposium (NDSS'99). The Internet Society, 1999.
11. Grandison, T., Sloman, M.: SULTAN -- A Language for Trust Specification and Analysis. Proceedings of 8th Annual Workshop HP OpenView University Association (HP-OVUA) Berlin, Germany June 24-27 2001
12. Dan, A. et. al.: Web Services on Demand: WSLA-Driven automated Management, IBM Systems Journal 43(1) (2004) http://www.hpovua.org/PUBLICATIONS/PROCEEDINGS/8_HPOVUAWS/Papers/Paper01.2-Grandison-Sultan.pdf
13. Foster, I., Kesselman, C.: Globus: A Metacomputing Infrastructure Toolkit. Intl J. Supercomputer Applications 11(2) (1997) 115-128
14. Global Grid Forum, The WS-Resource Framework (March 2004) http://www-106.ibm.com/developerworks/library/ws-resource/ws-wsrf.pdf
15. Fatima, S.S, Wooldridge, M., Jennings M.R.: An Agenda based framework for multi-issue negotiation. Artificial Intelligence (2003)
16. Berners-Lee, T, Connelly, D.: W3C Roadmap Diagrams – http://www.w3.org/2001/04/roadmap/ (2001)

Scheduling Strategies for Processing Continuous Queries over Streams*

Qingchun Jiang and Sharma Chakravarthy

Department of Computer Science and Engineering
The University of Texas at Arlington
{jiang,sharma}@cse.uta.edu

Abstract. Stream data processing poses many challenges. Two important characteristics of stream data processing - bursty arrival rates and the need for near real-time performance requirement - challenge the allocation of limited resources in the system. Several scheduling algorithms (e.g., Chain strategy) have been proposed for minimizing the maximal memory requirements in the literature. In this paper, we propose novel scheduling strategies to minimize tuple latency as well as total memory requirement. We first introduce a path capacity strategy (PCS) with the goal of minimizing tuple latency. We then compare the PCS and the Chain strategy to identify their limitations and propose additional scheduling strategies that improve upon them. Specifically, we introduce a segment strategy (SS) with the goal of minimizing the memory requirement, and its simplified version. In addition, we introduce a hybrid strategy, termed the threshold strategy (TS), to addresses the combined optimization of both tuple latency and memory requirement. Finally, we present the results of a wide range of experiments conducted to evaluate the efficiency and the effectiveness of the proposed scheduling strategies.

1 Introduction

Stream data processing differs from a traditional query processing system in several ways: (*i*) operates on high volume streaming data, with intermittent bursty mode input, (*ii*) queries are long-running continuous queries (CQs), and (*iii*) stream applications have to make near real-time decisions. These characteristics, which are unique to data stream management systems (DSMSs) and are different from traditional database management systems (DBMSs), motivate us to develop new techniques that are efficient and effective for DSMSs. Representative applications of DSMSs include network traffic engineering, fraud detection, financial monitoring, and sensor data processing, to name a few. These applications have motivated a considerable body of research ranging from algorithms and architectures for stream processing to a full-fledged data stream processing system such as Telegraph [1], STREAM [2], Aurora [3], Niagara [4], Tapestry [5], and Tribeca [6]. In this paper, we focus on the scheduling problem in a DSMS.

The scheduling problem in a DSMS is an important and complicated one. First, it has a significant impact on the performance metrics of the system, such as tuple latency and system throughput, among others. Second, although the resources such as memory size

---

* This work was supported, in part, by NSF grants IIS-0123730 and ITR-0121297

H. Williams and L. MacKinnon (Eds.): BNCOD 2004, LNCS 3112, pp. 16–30, 2004.

and CPU speed are fixed, scheduling can be highly dynamic. Third, various predefined Quality of Service (QoS) requirements for a query add additional constraints to an already complex problem. In this paper, we introduce several scheduling strategies: *1*) the PCS to achieve the best tuple latency; *2*) the SS to achieve lower memory requirement than the PCS; *3*) the simplified SS, which requires a slightly more memory but much smaller tuple latency than the SS; *4*) the TS, which is a hybrid of the PCS and the simplified SS. These strategies provide a suite of scheduling choices for achieving the desired overall performance of a DSMS. The predefined QoS requirements of a query have not been incorporated into these strategies, which is part of our future work.

The rest of the paper is organized as follows. Section 2 provides an overview of query processing over streaming data. In section 3, we first propose the PCS, and then compare the PCS with the Chain strategy [7]. We further discuss the SS, its variant (the simplified SS) and the TS. Section 4 further presents our quantitative experimental results. The related work and conclusion are presented in sections 5 and 6, respectively.

2   Stream Query Processing Strategies

In a DSMS, a CQ plan is decomposed into a set of operators (as in a traditional DBMS) such as `project`, `select`, `join`, and other aggregate operators. The difference lies in that each operator in a DSMS has to work in a non-blocking mode. As a consequence, some operators have to work in a window-based manner such as a window-based `join`. The output of one operator is buffered in a queue, which consequently acts as the input source to another operator, if it is not the final operator. Therefore, from a scheduling point of view, the query processing system over streaming data consists of a set of basic operators and queues. The system can be conceptualized as a directed acyclic graph (DAG). In such a DAG, a node represents a pipelined operator; while the directed edge between two nodes represents the queue connecting those two operators. Directed edges also determine the input and output relationship between those two operators. Each input stream is represented as a special source node, while all the upper level applications are represented as a root node. Therefore, the edges originating from source nodes represent the earliest input queues that buffer the external inputs, while the edges terminating at the root node represent the final output queues. In this DAG, each tuple originates from a source node, and then passes a series of operators until it reaches the root node or is consumed by an intermediate operator. We refer to the path from a source node to the root node excluding the source node and the root node as an `operator path` (OP), and the bottom node of an OP as a `leaf node`.

2.1   Assumptions and Notations

To facilitate our analysis, we use the following notations.

- *Operator processing capacity* $C_{O_i}^P$: the number of tuples that can be processed within one time unit at operator O_i.
- *Operator memory release capacity* $C_{O_i}^M$: the number of memory units such as bytes (or pages) that can be released within one time unit by operator O_i. $C_{O_i}^M =$

$C_{O_i}^P(InputTupleSize - T_i\sigma_i)$. Where T_i is the size of the tuple output from operator O_i; in case of an operator with multiple inputs (e.g., join), it is mean size.

- *Operator path (or segment) processing capacity* $C_{P_i}^P$: the number of tuples that can be consumed within one time unit by the operator path (OP) P_i. Therefore, the OP processing capacity depends not only on the processing capacity of an individual operator, but also on the selectivity of these operators and the number of operators in the path. For an OP P_i with k operators, its processing capacity can be derived from the processing capacities of the operators that are along its path, as follows:

$$C_{P_i}^P = \frac{1}{\frac{1}{C_{O_1}^P} + \frac{\sigma_1}{C_{O_2}^P} + \cdots + \frac{\prod_{j=1}^{k-1} \sigma_j}{C_{O_k}^P}} \tag{1}$$

where $O_l, 1 \leq l \leq k$ is the l_{th} operator along P_i starting from the leaf node. The denominator in (1) is the total service time for the path P_i to serve one tuple; and the general item $(\prod_{j=1}^{h} \sigma_j)/C_{O_k}^P$ is the service time at the $(h+1)^{th}$ operator to serve the output part of the tuple from the hth operator.

- *Path memory release capacity* $C_{P_i}^M$: the number of memory units can be released within one time unit by the path P_i. Again, in this paper, we assume that all the output tuples from a query are consumed immediately by its applications. Therefore, no memory is required to buffer the *final* output results.

$$C_{P_i}^M = C_{P_i}^P InputTupleSize \tag{2}$$

From (2), we know that the processing capacity and the memory release capacity of an OP differs with only a constant factor. Therefore, we assume that the partial order between the processing capacities of two paths is the same as the partial order between their memory release capacities. Although the sizes of all input tuples for an application may not be exactly the same, their differences are not large enough to change the relative partial orders of their OPs. Hereafter, we use the path capacity to refer to both the processing capacity and the memory release capacity.

In this paper, we make the following assumptions:

1. The root node consumes its inputs immediately after they enter queues. Therefore, there is no tuple waiting in the input queues of the root node.
2. The selectivity and the service time of an operator are known. They can be learned by collecting statistics over a period during the execution of an operator.

2.2   Preliminary Scheduling Strategies

If the input rate of each stream in a DSMS is trackable, which amounts to knowing how many tuples will be arriving in future time slots, we can find an optimal scheduling strategy that can achieve the best performance by using the minimized resources. However, in most cases, the input rate of a data stream is unpredictable, and highly bursty, which makes it harder, or even impossible to find such a feasible, optimal scheduling strategy. In practice, heuristic-based or near-optimal strategies are usually used. And these strategies have different impact on the performance and the usage of the system

Fig. 1. A query execution plan

Table 1. Operator properties

Operator Id	1	2	3
Selectivity	0.2	0.2	0.8
Processing capacity	1	1	0.2

resources. The Chain strategy [7] is a near optimal scheduling strategy in terms of total internal queue size. However, the tuple latency and the memory requirement are equally important for a CQ processing system. And they are especially important for a DSMS where its applications have to respond to an event in a near real-time manner. In the rest of this section, we use the First-In-First-Out (FIFO) strategy and the Chain strategy to show how a strategy impacts the queue size, the tuple latency, and the throughput of a CQ processing system.

FIFO Strategy: *Tuples are processed in the order of their arrival. Once a tuple is scheduled, it is processed by the operators along its OP until it is consumed by an intermediate operator or output to the root node. Then the next oldest tuple is scheduled.*

Chain Strategy: *At any time, consider all tuples that are currently in the system; of these, schedule a single time unit for the tuple that lies on the segment with the steepest slope in its lowest envelope simulation. If there are multiple such tuples, select the tuple which has the earliest arrival time.*

Let us consider a simple query plan illustrated in Fig. 1, which is a common query plan that contains both `select` and `join` operators. The processing capacity and selectivity of the operators are listed in Table 1. The input streams are highly bursty, which is the case in most stream query processing systems. Table 2 shows the total internal queue size, tuple latency, and throughput of the query plan under both the FIFO and the Chain strategy for the given input patterns.

The results clearly show that the Chain strategy performs much better than the FIFO strategy for the total internal queue size. However, it performs much worse than the FIFO strategy in terms of tuple latency and throughput. Clearly, The FIFO strategy maintains

Table 2. Performance(F:FIFO, C:Chain)

Time	Input 1	Input 2	Queue Size F	Queue Size C	Tuple Latency F	Tuple Latency C	Throughput F	Throughput C
1	1	0	1.0	1.0	-	-	0	0
2	0	1	1.2	1.2	-	-	0.0	0
3	1	1	3.0	2.4	2	-	0.16	0
4	0	0	2.2	1.6	-	-	0	0
5	0	0	2.0	0.8	3	-	0.16	0
6	0	0	1.2	0.6	-	5	0	0.16
7	0	0	1.0	0.4	4	5	0.16	0.16
8	0	0	0.2	0.2	-	5	0	0.16
9	0	0	0	0	6	6	0.16	0.16
10	1	0	1.0	1.0	-	-	0	0

its entire backlog of unprocessed tuples at the beginning of each OP. It does not consider the inherent properties of an operator such as selectivity, processing rate, which causes the total internal queue size to be bigger under the FIFO strategy than under the Chain strategy. In contrast, as the Chain strategy pushes the tuples from the bottom, it inherits the bursty property of the input streams. If the input streams are highly bursty in nature, the output of the query processing system under the Chain strategy demonstrates highly bursty property as well.

It is worth noting that the total internal queue size is much lower than the amount of memory needed to maintain the status information at some operators in order to compute results correctly. For example, a join operator has to maintain a number of tuples in its window(s) in order to compute the correct answers. Considering an input stream with a bursty period of 1M tuples and its input rate faster than the processing rate, how long do we have to wait to get the first result in a query processing system which has the maximal ability to completely process[1] 10000 input tuples per second? Under the Chain strategy, it is almost 100 seconds! Of course, the total internal queue size is much less than 1M tuples, which is the difference between the input rate and processing rate times the length of the bursty period without considering the changes of tuple size in the system. Based on this observation, we develop the PCS, which takes the tuple latency and the throughput as its primary priorities, and the total internal queue size as its secondary priority.

3   Proposed Scheduling Strategies

In this section, we first present the PCS, and then provide a thorough comparison with the Chain strategy. To overcome the large memory requirement of PCS, we further propose the SS and its variant – the simplified SS. Finally, we discuss the TS, which is a hybrid of the PCS and the simplified SS.

3.1   Path Capacity Strategy

From 2.2, we observe that the FIFO strategy has two promising properties: reasonable tuple latency and throughput. But it does not consider the characteristics of an OP such as processing capacity and memory release capacity. Also as it schedules one tuple each time, the scheduling overhead is considerably high. This motivates us to develop the PCS which improves upon the high memory requirement of the FIFO strategy, and has even better tuple latency and throughput than the FIFO strategy.

Path Capacity Strategy: *At any time instant, consider all the OPs that have input tuples waiting in their queues in the system, schedule a single time unit for the OP with a maximal processing capacity to serve until its input queue is empty or there exists an OP which has non-null input queue and a bigger processing capacity than the currently scheduled one. If there are multiple such paths, select the one which has the oldest tuple in its input queue. The following internal scheduling strategy is used to schedule the operators of the chosen path.*

---

[1] We mean the computation from reading in the input tuples to output the final results.

Internal scheduling strategy: Once an OP is chosen, a bottom up approach [2] is employed to schedule all the operators along the chosen path. The maximal number of tuples served during one round is exactly its processing capacity.

The PCS is a static priority scheduling strategy, and the priority of an OP is its processing capacity, which does not change over time until we revise the selectivity of operators. Therefore, the scheduling cost is minimized and can be negligible. Most importantly, the PCS has the following two optimal properties that are critical for a multiple CQ processing system.

Theorem 1. *The PCS is an optimal one in terms of the total tuple latency or the average tuple latency among all scheduling strategies.*

Proof. First, OP-based scheduling strategies have a better tuple latency than those which do not use an OP as a scheduling unit. In [8], we showed that if the operators of two query plans or OPs are scheduled in an interleaved manner, the overall tuple latency becomes worse. The operators of two OPs under the PCS are not scheduled as an interleaved manner and therefore, the PCS has a better tuple latency than any non-path based scheduling strategy. Second, the PCS has minimal tuple latency among all path based scheduling strategies. At any time instant, consider k OPs $p_1, p_2, \cdots, p_k$, which have $N_i \geq 1, i = 1, 2, 3, \cdots, k$ tuples in their input queues in the system, with their capacities $C_1, C_2, \cdots, C_k$ respectively. Without loss of generality, we assume that $C_1 \geq C_2 \geq \cdots \geq C_k$. The PCS has a schedule of $p_1, p_2, \cdots, p_k$, that is to serve the N_1 tuple of OP p_1, following the N_2 tuple of OP p_2, and so on. In the simplest case where $N_i = 1, i = 1, 2, 3, \cdots, k$, the total tuple latency

$$T = k\frac{1}{C_1} + (k-1)\frac{1}{C_2} + \cdots + (k-g+1)\frac{1}{C_g} + \cdots + (k-h+1)\frac{1}{C_h} + \cdots + \frac{1}{C_k},$$

where $(k-i)\frac{1}{C_i}, i = 0, 1, \cdots, k-1$ is the total waiting time of all the tuples in the system due to processing the tuple at operator O_i. If we switch any two tuples (two paths), say g, h, where $g < h$, in the PCS, then the total tuple latency

$$T' = k\frac{1}{C_1} + (k-1)\frac{1}{C_2} + \cdots + (k-g+1)\frac{1}{C_h} + \cdots + (k-h+1)\frac{1}{C_g} + \cdots + \frac{1}{C_k}.$$

The difference of two tuple latency $\Delta = T - T' = (h-g)\left(\frac{1}{C_g} - \frac{1}{C_h}\right) \leq 0$ because of $g < h$ and $C_g \geq C_h$. Similarly, for the general case, by switching any two tuples in two input queues of these k OPs, we still have $\Delta \leq 0$. Therefore, any other scheduling strategy causes at least the same total tuple latency or mean delay that the PCS causes.

Theorem 2. *Any other path-based scheduling strategy requires at least as much memory as that required by the PCS at any time instant in the system.*

Proof sketch. At any time instant, the PCS schedules the tuples waiting in the input queue of the OP which has the biggest capacity among all the paths with non-empty input queue in the system. Within one time unit, the path scheduled by the PCS consumes the maximal number of tuples because it has the biggest capacity. Any other path based scheduling strategy which does not schedule the tuples waiting in the input queue of the OP with the biggest capacity at that time instant consumes less number of tuples.

---

[2] Work on pipelined strategies are being investigated.

Therefore, any other path based scheduling strategy requires at least the same amount of memory required by the PCS.   □

Theorem 1 clearly shows that the PCS performs much better than the FIFO strategy and the Chain strategy for tuple latency. Theorem 2 shows that the PCS performs better than the FIFO strategy, but not as well as the Chain strategy in terms of memory requirement although it requires the least memory among all path-based strategies.

3.2   Critique of the Two Scheduling Strategies

In this section, we will do a comprehensive comparison and show how the above two scheduling strategies impact various performance metrics of a CQ processing system. A quantitative experimental study for these two strategies is presented in section 4.

Tuple latency & throughput: The PCS can achieve the optimal tuple latency compared with any other scheduling strategy. It also has a much smoother output rate than the Chain scheduling strategy. The main reason for the large tuple latency in Chain strategy is that the leaf nodes usually have a much bigger capacity than the other nodes of a query plan, which causes the Chain strategy gradually to push all the tuple from the leaf nodes toward the root node, and a large amount of tuples are buffered in the middle of an OP. This situation becomes even worse during a temporary overload period in which the input rates are temporarily in excess of the processing capacity of the system. All the computational resource is allocated to the operators at the bottom of the query plans and there is almost no throughput from the system. On the other hand, the throughput is surprisingly high immediately after a bursty period because there are not too many tuples waiting at leaf nodes, and most of the computational resources are used by the operators in the upper side of the query plans where a large amount of partially processed tuples wait. As a result, the Chain strategy not only has a bad tuple latency, but also a bursty output rate if the input streams are bursty in nature. Its bursty output rates may cancel out part of its saved memory because the consumed rates of applications cannot keep up with the bursty output rates.

Memory requirement: Both strategies have an optimal property in terms of the memory requirement. But the optimal property of the PCS is a relative one among all path-based scheduling algorithms, while the optimal property of the Chain scheduling strategy is a global optimal property. Under non-overload conditions, the amount of memory required by these two strategies is similar, and there are not too many tuples buffered in the queues. However, during the bursty input periods, the Chain strategy performs better than the PCS.

Starvation problem: Both strategies have the starvation problem in which some operators or OPs may never be served because both of them depend on a set of static priorities. Under heavy load situations, the Chain strategy spends all its computation resource on the operators with a bigger capacity, and since most of operators in the upper side of an OP (closer to the root) have less capacity, they starve; while the PCS spends all its computation resource on these OPs with a bigger path processing capacity, the OPs with less capacity will starve. The difference is that the Chain strategy has a very small or even no throughput at all during the heavy load situations, whereas the PCS still has reasonable throughput during heavy load periods.

Scheduling overhead: Clearly, both strategies have very small scheduling overhead because they are static priority strategies. But the scheduling overhead incurred by the PCS is less than that incurred by the Chain strategy because the number of OPs in a system is less than the number of operators.

3.3   Segment Strategy and Its Variant

Although the PCS has optimal memory requirement among all path-based scheduling strategies, it still buffers all unprocessed tuples at the beginning of an OP. In a CQ processing system with a shortage of main memory, a trade off exists between the tuple latency and the total internal queue size. Therefore, we develop SS which has a much smaller total internal queue size requirement than the PCS, and a smaller tuple latency than the Chain strategy. Furthermore, we introduce the simplified SS which further improves its tuple latency with a little larger memory requirement than the SS.

Operator scheduling and path scheduling can be seen as two ends of the spectrum, whereas segment scheduling covers the points in between. Instead of buffering the unprocessed tuples at the beginning of an OP, we partition an OP into a few segments, so that some partially processed tuples can be buffered at the beginning of a segment. This allows the system to take advantage of the lower selectivity and fast service rate of bottom side operators of a query execution plan.

The segment construction algorithm: The construction algorithm consists of two main steps. First, it partitions an OP into a few segments. Second, it prunes the current system segment list, which is initially empty, and then adds the new segments into the list. For each OP in the system, we repeat the following procedure: Consider an OP with m operators $O_1, O_2, \cdots, O_m$ from bottom to top. Starting from O_1, a segment of the OP is defined as a set of consecutive operators $\{O_k, O_{k+1}, \cdots, O_{k+i}\}$ where $k \geq 1$, such that $\forall j, k \leq j < k + i, C^M_{O_j} \leq C^M_{O_{j+1}}$. Once such a segment is constructed, we start the construction procedure again from O_{k+i+1} until all the operators along the OP have been processed. In the pruning procedure, a new segment is added to the segment link list only if: (*i*) any of its subset is already in the list; we remove all its subsets from the segment list, and then add the new segment into the list; (*ii*) none of its supersets is in the list; we add it to the list; otherwise, the new segment is discarded.

The order in which we partition an OP does not matter because the final segment list will be the same for a set of query plans, and the order of a segment in the segment list does not affect its priority. We only need to run the above algorithm once in order to construct the segment list. Later on, when a new query plan is registered into the system, we need to run the algorithm for the OPs of the newly registered query plan. When a query plan is unregistered from the system, we have to delete all the segments belonging to that query plan. In a multiple query processing system, as one segment may be shared by two or more query plans, we have to add a count field to each operator of a segment to indicate how many query plans are using it. Once a segment is deleted from the system, we decrease the value in the count field by one for each operator that belongs to the segment. When the count value of an operator reaches zero, it can be deleted from the segment.

Since CQ plans in a stream processing system are long-running queries, the number of queries that will be registered into a system or unregistered from a system is not likely to be too large (typically no more than a few per hour). Therefore, the cost of the algorithm has very little impact on system performance.

The SS schedules employs an idea similar to that of a PCS. It schedules the operator segment with a maximal memory release capacity, rather than the OP with the maximal processing capacity in PCS.

The SS is also a static priority driven strategy. The SS shares the same operator segment concept used by the Chain strategy [7] and the Train strategy [9] in Aurora. However, it is unclear how a segment is constructed in [9]. On the other hand, it is different from the Chain strategy in that: (a) the segments used in those two strategies are different. The segments used in the Chain strategy have steepest slope in its lower envelope, while the segments used in SS consist of consecutive operators that have an increasing memory release capacity. Therefore, the Chain strategy can achieve the minimal internal queue size requirement, while SS has a slightly larger internal queue size requirement, but it achieves better tuple latency, (b) SS clusters a set of operators as a scheduling unit, and hence there are no partially processed tuples buffered in the middle of an operator segment by the end of each time unit in contrast to the Chain strategy, and (c) SS has a smaller scheduling overhead than the Chain strategy. The Chain strategy is an operator-based strategy where all the operators along a segment have the same priority, while the SS is a segment-based strategy. In a general query processing system, as the number of segments is less than the number of operators, the scheduling overhead is lower for the SS.

The SS decreases the memory requirement as compared to the PCS, but it still causes longer tuple latency than the PCS because it separates one OP into multiple segments. The paper [8] shows that the overall tuple latency of the tuples from an OP increases significantly if other operators are scheduled in an interleaved manner with the operators along the OP. In order to decrease the interleaving of the operators of two segments, we propose the following simplified SS.

Simplified Segment Scheduling Strategy: Simplified SS differs from SS in that it employs a different segment construction algorithm. In a practical multiple query processing system, we observe that: (a) the number of segments constructed by the segment construction algorithm is not significantly less than the number of operators presented in the query processing system and (b) the leaf nodes are the operators that have faster processing capacities and less selectivity in the system; all other operators in a query plan have a much slower processing rate than the leaf nodes. Based on these observations, we partition an OP into at most two segments, rather than a few segments. The first segment includes the leaf node and its consecutive operators such that $\forall i, C_{O_{i+1}}^M / C_{O_i}^M \geq \gamma$, where γ is a similarity factor. In the previous segment construction algorithm, it implicitly states $\gamma = 1$. In the simplified SS, the value of γ used is less than 1 in order to decrease the number of segments. In our system, we have used $\gamma = 3/4$ in our experiments. The remaining operators along that OP, if any, forms the second segment. The simplified SS has the following advantages: (i) its memory requirement is only slightly larger than the SS because the first segment of an OP releases the most of the amount of memory that can be released by the OP, (ii) the tuple latency significantly decreases because the number of times a tuple is buffered along an OP is at most two, (iii) the scheduling overhead significantly decreases as well due to the decrease in the number of segments, and (*iv*) it is less sensitive to the selectivity and service time of an operator due to the similarity factor, which makes it more applicable.

3.4 Threshold Strategy

The TS is a dynamic strategy and is a hybrid of the PCS and the simplified SS. The principle behind it is that the PCS is used to minimize the tuple latency when the memory is not a bottleneck; otherwise, the simplified SS (or the Chain strategy) is used to decrease the total memory requirement. Therefore, this one combines the properties of these two strategies, which makes it more appropriate for a DSMS.

Threshold Strategy: *Given a query processing system with a maximal available queue memory*[3] M, *the maximal threshold* T_{max} *and the minimal threshold* T_{min}, *where* $T_{min} < T_{max} < M$, *at any time instant, when the current total queue memory consumed* $M_c \geq T_{max}$, *the system enters its memory saving mode in which the simplified SS (or Chain) is employed. The system transits from the saving mode to the normal mode in which the path scheduling strategy is employed when* $M_c \leq T_{min}$.

The values of the maximal threshold T_{max} and the minimal threshold T_{min} mainly depend on the load of the system and the length of the bursty periods; and they can be obtained heuristically or experimentally. Given that the mean total queue memory consumed by a query processing system is $\bar{M}$ memory units, we define the values of these threshold parameters in our system as

$$
\begin{cases}
T_{max} = min\left(\frac{1+\alpha}{2}M, \beta M\right); \; \alpha = \frac{\bar{M}}{M} \\
T_{min} = min\left(\bar{M}, \beta T_{max}\right); \quad 0.5 < \beta < 1
\end{cases}
\tag{3}
$$

In (3), β is a safety factor that guarantees a minimal memory buffer zone between the normal mode and the saving mode, which prevents a system from frequently oscillating between these two models. A smaller value of β causes a longer tuple latency. Therefore, its value need to be in the range of 0.5 to 1.0. α is used to adjust the threshold values as the system load changes. The mean total queue size increases as the system load increases, which causes α to increase. When α approaches 1, the $\frac{1+\alpha}{2}M$ factor approaches the maximal available queue memory M. That is why we need βM to guarantee that there is a minimal buffer between the T_{max} and M. We use $\beta = 0.9$ in our system. Our experiments show these parameters work well in general.

4   Experimental Validation

We have implemented the proposed scheduling strategies as part of the prototype of a QoS aware DSMS. In this section, we discuss the results of various experiments that we have conducted in order to compare the performance of these scheduling strategies.

---

[3] The queue memory here refers to the memory available for input queues, not including the memory consumed by maintaining the status information of an operator.

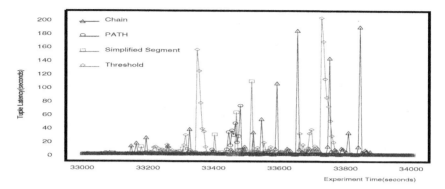

Fig. 2. Tuple latency vs. time

4.1 Setup

We are implementing a general purpose DSMS with its main goal as guaranteed satisfaction of predefined QoS requirements of each individual query. Currently, a set of basic operators such as `project`, `select`, and `join` have been implemented. And the system is capable of processing various Select-Project-Join queries over data streams. The scheduling strategies we have implemented are: the PCS, the Chain strategy, the simplified SS, the Threshold strategy, and various round-robin strategies. We use the following data streams and CQs in our experiments.

Input data streams: The input data streams generated are highly bursty streams that have the so-called self-similarity property, which we believe resembles the situation in real-life applications.

Experimental query plans: All of our queries are CQs that consist of `select`, `project`, and `symmetric hash join` operators. To mimic a real application, we run 16 actual CQs with 116 operators over 5 different data streams in our system.

The prototype is implemented in C++, and all the experiments were run on a dedicated dual processor Alpha machine with 2GB of RAM. One of the processors was used to collect experiment results while the other processor was used for query processing.

4.2 Performance Evaluation

Due to the fact that the CQs are also long running queries and that the scheduling strategies demonstrate different performance during different system load periods, we run each experiment for more than 24 hours (including the statistics collection period), and each experiment consists of multiple phases. In each phase, we intentionally increased the average input rates of data streams in order to study and validate the performance characteristics of a scheduling strategy under different system loads. We only present a portion of our experimental data (from a few phases), rather than a full range of results due to limited space. For TS, we set the maximal threshold $\mathcal{T}_{max}$ to 10M bytes, which means it employs the PCS when its total queue size is less than 10Mbytes, otherwise, it employs the Chain strategy to decrease total queue size requirement.

Tuple latency: The tuple latency of an output tuple is computed by taking the difference of its arrival time-stamp and its departure time-stamp when it leaves the query

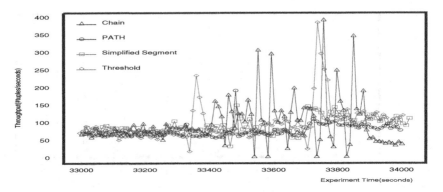

Fig. 3. Throughput vs. time

processing system. The tuple latency shown in Fig. 2 is the average tuple latency of all output tuples within every 1 second. From the results, we observe that the overall tuple latency is much better under the PCS than under the simplified SS and the Chain strategy. The Chain strategy performs worst among them. Furthermore, the overall tuple latency increases as the system load increases, but the difference among them becomes much sharper as the system load increases. The TS has a tuple latency as good as the PCS when total queue size is less than 10M bytes (i.e., from 33200 to 33300). However it performs as bad as the Chain strategy during heavy bursty periods (i.e., from 33600 to 33800). It is worth noting that during light load periods (i.e., the first 200 seconds), all of them have a reasonable tuple latency except that the Chain has a few spikes. When the system load increases, the tuple latency increases sharply during the highly bursty input periods for both the simplified SS and the Chain strategy. As we explained earlier, the high tuple latency under both strategies are because of their buffered tuples in the middle of an OP. The simplified SS performs better than the Chain strategy because it buffers a tuple for a lesser amount of time along an OP than the Chain strategy.

Throughput: The total throughput of a query processing system under any scheduling strategy should be the same because it should output the same number of output tuples no matter what scheduling strategy it employs. However, the output patterns are likely to be dramatically different under different scheduling strategies. Fig. 3 shows the output patterns under four different strategies. The PCS and the simplified SS have a much smoother output rate than the Chain strategy, and the TS has the characteristics of both the PCS and the Chain strategy. The PCS performs best among them in terms of the bursty output. The output rate for all four strategies increases as the input rates increases when the system load is moderate, which is the first 300 seconds, and their output patterns do not differ with each other too much. After the system enters the high load periods, the PCS and the simplified SS have a much smoother throughput than the other two during the high bursty input periods which are the periods from 10400 second to 11000 second and from 12400 second to 12800 second, but the Chain strategy has a lower throughput there. In contrast, the Chain strategy has a very low throughput, even no throughput during heavy load periods. On the other hand, it has a surprisingly high throughput immediately when system load decreases. Its highest output rate is almost 4 times its average output rate. The situation becomes worse when the system load or the length of the highly bursty input periods increases. This highly bursty output rate is not desirable because of the amount of partial results that have to be buffered in the system temporarily, which consumes unnecessary memory.

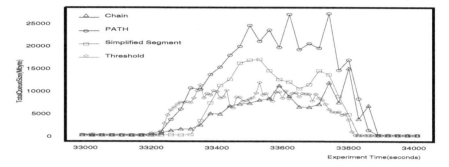

Fig. 4. Total memory requirement vs. time

Memory requirement: We study the total memory requirement of a query processing system under different scheduling strategies given an input pattern. From the results presented in Fig. 4, we observe that the Chain strategy performs better than the others. The Chain strategy and the simplified SS can absorb the extra memory requirement during the bursty input periods when system load is not high. Although the PCS has the capability to absorb the temporary high bursty input, its ability is much less than the other two strategies. The reason, as we mentioned earlier, is that the leaf nodes have a much bigger memory release capacity than the other nodes of a query plan, and that the memory release capacity of an OP is much less than that of a leaf node. As the system load or the length of a bursty period increases, the PCS requires much more memory to temporarily buffer the unprocessed tuples than the other two. The simplified SS requires a little more memory than the Chain strategy during the highly bursty periods because it only takes the benefit of the bigger memory release capacities of the leaf nodes that are major part of the operators with a bigger memory release capacity in a CQ processing system, but not all of them behave like the Chain strategy. The TS has a similar memory requirement as that of PCS during the first 300 seconds. It then switches to Chain strategy and maintains its total memory requirement around 10M bytes, which is comparable to the Chain strategy.

5   Related Work

Various scheduling problems have been studied extensively in the literature. Research directly related to our work is on the scheduling strategies for a stream query processing system. The Chain scheduling strategy [7] has been proposed with a goal of minimizing the total internal queue size. As a complement to that, the PCS proposed in this paper minimizes the tuple latency. The Aurora project employs a two-level scheduling approach

[9]: the first level handles the scheduling of superboxes which are a set of operators, and the second level decides how to schedule a box within a superbox. They have discussed their strategy to decrease the average tuple latency based on superbox traversal. However, we have used a different approach and have proved that our PCS is optimal in terms of overall tuple latency. Although their tuple batching - termed train processing - uses a similar concept used in the Chain strategy and our segment strategies, no algorithm has been provided to construct those superboxes. Furthermore, we provide a more pragmatic scheduling strategy – TS, which has the advantages of both the PCS and the Chain strategy. The rate-based optimization framework proposed by Viglas and Naughton [10] has the goal of maximizing the throughput of a query. However, they do not take the tuple latency and memory requirement into consideration. Earlier work related to improving the response time of a query includes the dynamic query operator scheduling of Amsaleg [11] and the Xjoin operator of Urban and Franklin [12].

Finally, the scheduling work is part of our QoS control and management framework for a DSMS [13] and extends our earlier work of modeling CQ plan [8,14], which address the effective estimation of the tuple latency and the internal queue size under a dynamic CQ processing system. Our results can be used to guide a scheduling strategy to incorporate QoS requirement of an application, and to predict overload situations.

6   Conclusions and Future Work

In this paper, we have proposed a suite of scheduling strategies for a DSMS and investigated them both theoretically and experimentally. We showed how a scheduling strategy impacts/affects the performance metrics such as tuple latency, throughput, and memory requirement of a CQ processing system. We proved that the PCS can achieve the overall minimal tuple latency. The simplified segment capacity strategy partially inherits the minimal memory requirement of the SS, and demonstrates a much better tuple latency and throughput than the Chain strategy. Furthermore, the TS inherits the properties of both the PCS and the simplified segment capacity strategy, which makes it more applicable to a DSMS.

References

1. Hellerstein, J., Franklin, M., et al: Adaptive query processing: Technology in evolution. IEEE Data Engineering Bulletin **23** (2000) 7—-18
2. Motwani, R., Widom, J., et al.: Query processing, approximation, and resource management in a data stream management system. In Proc. First Biennial Conf. on Innovative Data Systems Research (2003)
3. Carney, D., Cetintemel, U., Cherniack, M., Convey, C., Lee, S., Seidman, G., Stonebraker, M., TatbuL, N., Zdonik, S.: Monitoring streams - a new class of data management applications. Proc. Of the 2002 Intl. Conf. On VLDB (2002)
4. Chen, J., Dewitt, D., Tian, F., Wang, Y.: Niagaracq: A scalable continuous query system for internet databases. Proc. of the 2000 ACM SIGMOD (2000) 379–390
5. Terry, D., Goldberg, D., Nichols, D., Oki, B.: Continuous queries over append-only databases. Proc. of the 1992 ACM SIGMOD (1992) 321–330

6. Sullivan, M.: Tribeca: A stream database manager for network traffic analysis. Proc. of the 1996 Intl. Conf. on Very Large Data Bases (1996) 594
7. Babcock, B., Babu, S., Datar, M., Motwani, R.: Chain: Operator scheduling for memory minimization in stream systems. Proc. of the 2003 ACM SIGMOD (2003)
8. Jiang, Q., Chakravarthy, S.: Analysis and validation of continuous queries over data streams. http://itlab.uta.edu/sharma/Projects/MavHome/files/QA-SPJQueries2.pdf (2003)
9. Carney, D., Çetintemel, U., Rasin, A., Zdonik, S., Cherniack, M., Stonebraker, M.: Operator scheduling in a data stream manager. Proc. Of the 2003 Intl. Conf. On VLDB (2003)
10. Viglas, S., Naughton, J.: Rate-based query optimization for streaming information sources. Proc. of the 2002 ACM SIGMOD (2002)
11. Amsaleg, L., Franklin, M., Tomasic, A.: Dynamic query operator scheduling for wide-area remote access. Journal of Distributed and Parallel Databases **3** (1998)
12. Urhan, T., Franklin, M.: Xjoin: A reactively-scheduled pipelined join operator. IEEE Data Engineering Bulletin **23** (2000) 27—33
13. Jiang, Q., Chakravarthy, S.: Data stream management system for mavhome. In: Proc. of the 19th ACM SAC'04. (2004)
14. Jiang, Q., Chakravarthy, S.: Queueing analysis of relational operators for continuous data streams. Proc. of 12th Intl. Conf. on Information and Knowledge Management (2003)

Evaluating Complex Queries Against XML Streams with Polynomial Combined Complexity

Dan Olteanu, Tim Furche, and François Bry

Institute for Informatics, University of Munich
{olteanu,timfu,bry}@pms.ifi.lmu.de

Abstract. Querying XML streams is receiving much attention due to its growing range of applications from traffic monitoring to routing of media streams. Existing approaches to querying XML streams consider restricted query language fragments, in most cases with exponential worst-case complexity in the size of the query. This paper gives correctness and complexity results for a query evaluator against XML streams called SPEX [8]. Its combined complexity is shown to be polynomial in the size of the data and the query. Extensive experimental evaluation with a prototype confirms the theoretical complexity results.

1 Introduction

Querying data streams is receiving an increasing attention due to emerging applications such as publish-subscribe systems, data monitoring applications like sensor networks [6], financial or traffic monitoring [3], and routing of media streams [10]. Such applications call for novel methods to evaluate complex queries against data streams. Data streams are preferred over data stored in memory for several reasons: (1) the data might be too large or volatile, or (2) a standard approach based on data parsing and storing might be too time consuming. For some applications, such as publish-subscribe systems or news distribution, streams of XML and semi-structured data are more appropriate than streams of relational data, as XML gives rise to trees with recursive structure definition and unbounded, yet finite depths. Recently, several approaches to querying streams of XML have been proposed, e.g., [1,2,5]. These approaches are restricted to rather weak query languages, but with efficient average-case complexity.

Contribution. This paper first reports on the query evaluator against XML streams called SPEX [8] and gives for it correctness and complexity results.

The query language used in the following, called RPQ, extends the XPath fragments for which streamed evaluations have been proposed, e.g., [1,2,5]. RPQ provides the core concepts of existing query languages for XML and provides support for the XPath axes child, descendant, following-sibling and their reverses parent, ancestor, and preceding-sibling, path, tree, and DAG queries. Although SPEX can process general DAG queries, this paper treats a restricted form of DAG queries, called single-join DAG queries, that can be efficiently evaluated. A single-join DAG is a DAG composed of two single-join DAGs or tree queries sharing at most one node. Many queries encountered in practice can be expressed as single-join DAG queries.

H. Williams and L. MacKinnon (Eds.): BNCOD 2004, LNCS 3112, pp. 31–44, 2004.

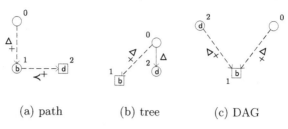

(a) path   (b) tree   (c) DAG

Fig. 1. RPQ Queries

The time and space complexities for RPQ query evaluation with SPEX are shown to be polynomial in both the query and the stream size, and in fact near the theoretical optimum [4] for in-memory evaluation of an XPath fragment included in RPQ. Extensive experimental evaluation confirms the theoretical results and demonstrates almost constant memory use in practical cases.

The remainder of this paper is organized as follows. Section 2 recalls the stream data model and introduces RPQ. Section 3 presents the RPQ query evaluation by means of SPEX networks, and their complexity analysis is shaped in Section 4. Section 5 provides experimental results performed with a SPEX prototype on various streams and queries. Section 6 concludes the paper.

2   Preliminaries

XML Streams. SPEX [8] is designed to evaluate queries against XML streams conveying tree-shaped data with labels on nodes, where an a-node of the tree is represented in the stream by a pair of opening and closing XML tags $\langle a \rangle$ and $\langle /a \rangle$. For the sake of simplicity, only element nodes are supported.

Regular Path Queries (RPQ). For querying trees-shaped data, we use an abstraction of the navigational features of XPath called RPQ. The basic constructs of RPQ are binary relations. There are two base relations: the child relation $\lhd$ associating a node to its children, and the next-sibling relation $\prec$ associating a node to its immediate next sibling. For each base relation an inverse relation is defined, and for each base and inverse relation its transitive closure is defined as well. The grammar for full RPQ is specified next:

$RPQ ::= Identifier(Var) :\text{-} Expr.$

$Expr ::= Expr \wedge Expr \mid Expr \vee Expr \mid (Expr) \mid Var\ Relation\ Var \mid Label(Var).$

$Relation ::= Base \mid Inverse \mid Base^{+} \mid Inverse^{+}. \quad Base ::= \lhd \mid \prec. \quad Inverse ::= \rhd \mid \succ.$

A relation expression $v\ r\ w$ associates two sets of nodes identified by the source variable v and the sink variable w that stand in relation r. Additionally, for each possible label there is a unary relation $Label$ specifying the set of nodes with that label, e.g., $a(v)$ restricts the set of nodes identified by v to nodes with label a. An RPQ query is an expression of the form $Q(t) :\text{-} E$ where Q is an arbitrary identifier for the query, t is a variable occurring in E and E is an atomic expression such as $v_i \lhd v_j$ or $a(v_i)$ or built up from atomic expressions using conjunctions or disjunctions. t is called the head variable, all other variables occurring in E are body variables.

Inverse relations are not explicitly considered in the following, for rewriting each expression $v \; \bar{r} \; w$, where $\bar{r}$ is the inverse to a base relation r, to $w \; r \; v$ yields an equivalent RPQ without that inverse relation. The equivalent RPQ is a single-join DAG query, where the variable v appears as sink of two expressions. Previous work of the authors [9] describes more sophisticated rewritings of queries with inverse relations yielding tree queries. Tree and single-join DAG queries are introduced below.

A path query is a query $Q(t)$:- E where in E (1) the head is the only non-source variable, (2) there is exactly one non-sink variable, (3) each variable occurs at most once as source and at most once as sink variable, and (4) there is no subset of atomic expressions such that source and sink of a conjunction of these atomic expressions are the same variable. RPQ paths correspond to XPath path expressions without predicates. Fig. 1(a) shows the path query $Q(v_2)$:- $v_0 \lhd^+ v_1 \wedge b(v_1) \wedge v_1 \prec^+ v_2 \wedge d(v_2)$.

A tree query is a path query $Q(t)$:- E where the first restriction is dropped and the third one is eased: each variable may occur in E at most once as sink but might occur several times as source of expressions. Hence, a tree query allows multi-source variables but no multi-sink variables. Tree queries correspond to XPath expressions with structural predicates. Fig. 1(b) shows the tree query $Q(v_1)$:- $v_0 \lhd^+ v_1 \wedge b(v_1) \wedge v_0 \lhd v_2 \wedge d(v_2)$, where v_0 is a multi-source variable.

A DAG query is a general query $Q(t)$:- E. A single-join DAG is a tree query where multi-sink variables are allowed and there are no two distinct paths in E with the same source and sink variable. Therefore, two distinct paths in E can share at most one variable. The single-join DAG query $Q(v_1)$:- $v_0 \lhd^+ v_1 \wedge b(v_1) \wedge v_2 \lhd^+ v_1 \wedge d(v_2)$, as depicted in Fig. 1(c), exemplifies a multi-sink variable v_1 occurring as sink in two relation expressions.

If only a source v_0 and a sink v_h variable from a subquery are of interest, such an expression can be abbreviated to $f(v_0, v_h)$, where f is an arbitrary identifier, e.g., $v_0 \lhd^+ v_1 \wedge b(v_1) \wedge v_1 \prec^+ v_2 \wedge d(v_2)$ can be abbreviated to $p(v_0, v_2)$.

The RPQ denotational semantics is given in the following by means of semantic mappings $\mathcal{R}$ and $\mathcal{S}$. Let n be the number of variables in an expression E and Nodes the set of nodes from a tree T conveyed by an XML stream. The set of all possible bindings for variables in E to nodes in Nodes, denoted Bindings, is the set of n-tuples Nodes^n, where each tuple contains one binding for each variable in E. For a tuple t, $t.v_i$ is the binding of the i-th variable in E. Given an expression E, the result of evaluating E against T is the subset $\mathcal{S}[\![E]\!](\beta)$ of $\beta = $ Bindings. From the result set, the bindings for the head variable v can be obtained by a simple projection, as done by $\mathcal{R}$: for a query $Q(v)$:- E, $\mathcal{R}[\![Q(v) :\text{-} E]\!]$(Bindings) is the set of bindings of the head variable v to nodes in Nodes such that E holds. A relation expression $v \; r \; w$ retains only those tuples, where the binding for w is in $\mathcal{A}[\![r]\!](v)$. The function $\mathcal{A}$ maps each node in Nodes

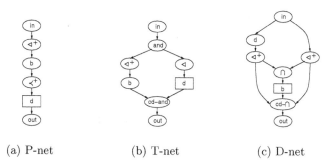

(a) P-net   (b) T-net   (c) D-net

Fig. 2. Example of SPEX Networks

to the set of nodes in Nodes related to it under the relation r. The function $\mathcal{L}$ specifies for each label s the set of nodes in Nodes with that label.

$$\mathcal{R} : \text{Query} \to \text{Bindings} \to \text{Nodes}$$
$$\mathcal{R}[\![Q(v) :\text{-} E]\!](\beta) = \pi_v(\mathcal{S}[\![E]\!](\beta))$$
$$\mathcal{S} : \text{Expression} \to \text{Bindings} \to \text{Bindings}$$
$$\mathcal{S}[\![E_1 \wedge E_2]\!](\beta) = \mathcal{S}[\![E_1]\!](\beta) \cap \mathcal{S}[\![E_2]\!](\beta) = \mathcal{S}[\![E_1]\!](\mathcal{S}[\![E_2]\!](\beta)) = \mathcal{S}[\![E_2]\!](\mathcal{S}[\![E_1]\!](\beta))$$
$$\mathcal{S}[\![E_1 \vee E_2]\!](\beta) = \mathcal{S}[\![E_1]\!](\beta) \cup \mathcal{S}[\![E_2]\!](\beta)$$
$$\mathcal{S}[\![(E)]\!](\beta) = \mathcal{S}[\![E]\!](\beta)$$
$$\mathcal{S}[\![v_1 \ r \ v_2]\!](\beta) = \{t \in \beta \mid t.v_2 \in \mathcal{A}[\![r]\!](t.v_1)\}$$
$$\mathcal{S}[\![s(v)]\!](\beta) = \{t \in \beta \mid t.v \in \mathcal{L}[\![s]\!]\}$$

Each RPQ expression is a filter applied to the current set of tuples containing variable bindings. Disjunctions and conjunctions of RPQ expressions can be directly mapped to unions and intersections of their operands' result. Conjunctions can also be expressed as the sequential application of $\mathcal{S}$ to the operands.

SPEX Transducer Networks. A single-state deterministic pushdown transducer is a tuple $(q, \Sigma, \Gamma, \delta)$, where q is the only state, Σ the input and output alphabet, Γ the stack alphabet, and the transition function δ is canonically extended to the configuration-based transition function $\vdash: \Sigma \times \Gamma^* \to \Gamma^* \times \Sigma^*$. E.g., the transition $(\langle a \rangle, [s] \mid \gamma) \vdash (\gamma, \langle a \rangle [s])$ reads: under the input symbol $\langle a \rangle$ and with $[s]$ as the top of the stack $\mid$-separated from the rest of the stack γ, the transducer outputs first the input symbol $\langle a \rangle$ followed by the top of the stack $[s]$ that is also popped from the stack.

Processing an XML stream with pushdown transducers corresponds to a depth-first traversal of the (implicit) tree conveyed by the XML stream. Exploiting the affinity between depth-first search and stack management, the transducers use their stacks for tracking the node depth in such trees. This way, RPQ relations can be evaluated in a single pass.

A SPEX transducer network is a directed acyclic graph where nodes are pushdown transducers. An edge between two transducers in a network inforces that an input tape of the sink transducer is an output tape of the source transducer. An evaluation plan for an RPQ query is represented in SPEX as a transducer network. Corresponding to the RPQ path, tree, and single-join DAG queries, there are three kinds of SPEX (transducer) networks: P-nets for the evaluation of path queries, T-nets for the evaluation of tree queries, and D-nets for the evaluation of single-join DAG queries.

3   The SPEX Evaluator

The evaluation of RPQ queries against XML streams with SPEX consists in two steps. First, an RPQ query is compiled into a SPEX transducer network. Second, the network computes the answers to the RPQ query.

The compilation of a query is defined inductively on the query structure: (1) Each RPQ relation is compiled into a pushdown transducer. (2) Each multi-source variable induces a pair of transducers (and, cd-and), if the variable is the source of conjuncted expressions, or (or,cd-or) for disjuncted expressions. These special transducers delimit the subnetworks corresponding to the expressions having that variable as source. (3) Each multi-sink variable induces a pair of transducers (∩,cd-∩), if the variable is the sink of conjuncted expressions, or (∪,cd-∪) for disjuncted expressions. (4) At the beginning of a network there is a stream-delivering in transducer and (5) at its end an answer-delivering out transducer. Fig. 2 shows networks for the RPQ queries of Fig. 1, where the head transducers that compute bindings for the head variable are marked with square boxes. Sections 3.1 through 3.4 detail the various transducers.

A network *net* for an expression $f(v_1, v_2)$ processes the XML stream enhanced by its transducer in with input bindings for v_1 and returns progressively output bindings for v_2, provided the expression holds. In the network, each transducer processes stepwise the received stream with input bindings and transmits it enhanced with computed output bindings to its successor transducers.

A node binding consists of a node annotated with a so-called condition. An annotation to a node is stored in the XML stream after the opening tag of that node. The output bindings delivered by a network *net* that processes the stream with some input bindings, contain the conditions of these input bindings.

The conditions are created by the in, and (or), and ∩ (∪) transducers. The in transducer binds each non-sink variable to all nodes, by annotating each node with (satisfied) conditions. In contrast, the RPQ semantics binds initially each variable to all nodes. Each and (or) transducer tests whether each received input binding satisfy the predicates represented by the subnetworks rooted at that and (or) transducer. In this sense, these transducers create an output binding with a new (satisfiable) condition, say $[s]$, for each received input binding, and sends it further to their successor subnetworks. The predicates are satisfied for that input binding (hence $[s]$ is satisfied), when $[s]$ is received by a cd-and (cd-or) within output bindings of each (at least one) subnetwork rooted at the corresponding and (or) transducer. The ∩ (∪) transducer processes similarly to and (or).

We use in the following an abstraction of processing XML streams with a SPEX *net* for a query $Q(v_2)$ in terms of a function $out_Q(v_1)|_{v_2}$ that returns the bindings for v_2 constructed by *net*, when input bindings for v_1 are supplied. It is shown that (1) there is a corresponding $out_Q(v_1)|_{v_2}$ function that is actually implemented by *net*, and (2) there is an equality of $out_Q(v_1)|_{v_2}$ and $\mathcal{R}[\![Q(v_2)]\!]$.

3.1 Processing RPQ Relations

For a base relation r, a transducer $t(r)$ implements the function $out_r(v_1)|_{v_2} = \{v_2|v_1 \ r \ v_2\}$. Speaking in terms of annotations with conditions, if $t(r)$ receives a node n annotated with $[c]$ (hence a binding for v_1), then (1) it removes that annotation $[c]$ of n and stores it, (2) it identifies each node n' from the incoming stream that stands in relation r with n (hence n' is a binding for v_2), and (3) it annotates each such node n' with $[c]$. E.g., the child transducer $t(\lhd)$ annotates with $[c]$ all nodes n' that are children of n.

The equality of $out_r(v_1)|_{v_2}$ to RPQ semantics under bindings β follows by:

$$\mathcal{R}[\![Q(v_2) \ \texttt{:-} \ v_1 \ r \ v_2]\!](\beta) = \pi_{v_2}(\mathcal{S}[\![v_1 \ r \ v_2]\!](\beta)) = out_r(\pi_{v_1}(\beta))|_{v_2}.$$

A **condition** $[c]$, used to annotate nodes, follows immediately the opening tags of nodes, e.g., $\langle a \rangle[c]$. Both, the opening tag $\langle a \rangle$ and the condition $[c]$, represent a binding to that a-node. On the stacks of transducers and on the stream, conditions are expressed using (list of) integers, e.g., $[1,2]$. The operation $[c] \cup [s]$ denotes the set union of $[c]$ and $[s]$. There are two special conditions: the empty (unsatisfied) condition $[\,]$ and the true (satisfied) condition $[\top]$.

Configuration-based transitions defining the child $t(\lhd)$, descendant $t(\lhd^+)$, next-sibling $t(\prec)$, and next-siblings $t(\prec^+)$ transducers are given in the following. For all transducers, the input and output alphabet Σ consists of all opening $\langle x \rangle$ and closing $\langle /x \rangle$ tags and conditions $[c]$, and the stack alphabet Γ consists of all conditions $[c]$. Initially, an empty condition $[\,]$ is pushed on the stack of each transducer. The configurations of these transducers differ only in the first transition, which is actually a compaction of several simpler transitions that do only one stack operation. In transitions 2 and 3, x stands for any node label.

The child transducer $t(\lhd)$ is defined below. The transitions of this transducer read as follows: (1) if a condition $[c]$ is received, then $[c]$ is pushed on the stack and nothing is output; (2) if an opening tag $\langle x \rangle$ is received, then it is output followed by the condition from the top of the stack; (3) if a closing tag $\langle /x \rangle$ is received, then it is output and the top condition is popped from the stack.

$$
\begin{aligned}
&1.\ ([c] \quad , \qquad \gamma) \vdash ([c] \mid \gamma, \qquad \varepsilon) \\
&2.\ (\langle x \rangle \ , \ [s] \mid \gamma) \vdash ([s] \mid \gamma, \ \langle x \rangle [s]) \\
&3.\ (\langle /x \rangle, \ [s] \mid \gamma) \vdash (\qquad \gamma, \ \langle /x \rangle)
\end{aligned}
$$

Lemma 1 ($t(\lhd)$ **Correctness**). *Transducer $t(\lhd)$ implements $out_\lhd(v_1)|_{v_2}$.*

Proof. When receiving a node n annotated with a condition $[c]$, $[c]$ is pushed on the stack. The following cases can then appear: (1) the closing tag of n is received, and $[c]$ is popped from the stack, for there are no other child nodes of n left in the incoming stream; (2) the opening tag of a child node n' of n is received, and it is output followed by $[c]$ (hence child nodes n' are annotated correctly with $[c]$). In the latter case another condition $[c']$ is received afterwards, pushed on the stack, and used to annotate child nodes of n'. Only when the closing tag of n' is received, $[c']$ is popped and $[c]$ becomes again the top of the stack. At this time, siblings of n' can be received and annotated with $[c]$ (the above case 2), or the closing tag of n is received (the above case 1). $\square$

The descendant transducer $t(\lhd^+)$ is defined below. The missing transitions 2 and 3 are like for $t(\lhd)$. In the first transition, $t(\lhd^+)$ pushes on the stack the received condition $[c]$ together with the top condition $[s]$: $[c]\cup[s]$. The difference to $t(\lhd)$ is that also conditions that annotate the ancestors n_a of n are used to annotate child nodes n' of n, for the nodes n' are descendants of nodes n_a.

$$1.\ ([c],\ [s]\ |\ \gamma) \vdash ([c]\cup[s]\ |\ [s]\ |\ \gamma,\ \varepsilon)$$

Lemma 2 $(t(\lhd^+)$ **Correctness**$)$. Transducer $t(\lhd^+)$ implements $out_{\lhd^+}(v_1)|_{v_2}$.

Proof. When receiving a node n annotated with a condition $[c]$, $[c]$ is pushed on the stack together with the current top $[s]$: $[c]\cup[s]$. The following cases can then appear: (1) the closing tag of n is received, and $[c]\cup[s]$ is popped from the stack, as there are no other descendants of n left in the incoming stream; (2) the opening tag of a child node n' of n is received, and it is output followed by $[c]\cup[s]$ (hence descendant nodes n' are annotated correctly). In the latter case another condition $[c']$ is received afterwards, the condition $[c']\cup[c]\cup[s]$ is pushed on the stack and used to annotate child nodes of n'. Only when the closing tag of n' is received, $[c']\cup[c]\cup[s]$ is popped and $[c]\cup[s]$ becomes again the top of the stack. At this time, siblings of n' can be received and annotated with $[c]\cup[s]$ (the above case 2), or the closing tag of n is received (the above case 1). $\qquad\square$

The next-sibling transducer $t(\prec)$ is defined below. The missing transitions 2 and 3 are like for $t(\lhd)$. In the first transition, $t(\prec)$ replaces the top of the stack $[s]$ with the received condition $[c]$ and pushes an empty condition $[\,]$. The condition $[\,]$ is then used to annotate child nodes n' of the received node n annotated with $[c]$. When the closing tag of n is received, the condition $[\,]$ is popped and the next sibling node of n is annotated with the top condition $[c]$.

$$1.\ ([c],\ [s]\ |\ \gamma) \vdash ([\,]\ |\ [c]\ |\ \gamma,\ \varepsilon)$$

The next-siblings transducer $t(\prec^+)$ is defined below. The missing transitions 2 and 3 are like for $t(\lhd)$. In the first transition, $t(\prec^+)$ adds to the top of the stack $[s]$ the received condition $[c]$ that annotated a node n, and pushes a condition $[\,]$. The difference to $t(\prec)$ is that the top of the stack $[s]$ is kept together with the received condition $[c]$: $[c]\cup[s]$. In this way, conditions that annotated the preceding siblings of n (like $[s]$) are used to annotate the following siblings of n.

$$1.\ ([c],\ [s]\ |\ \gamma) \vdash ([\,]\ |\ [c]\cup[s]\ |\ \gamma,\ \varepsilon)$$

Analogous to Lemmas 1 and 2, the $t(\prec)$ transducer implements $out_{\prec}(v_1)|_{v_2}$ and the $t(\prec^+)$ transducer implements $out_{\prec^+}(v_1)|_{v_2}$.

The label transducer $t(\mathsf{a})$ for a label a acts like a binding filter: the input bindings with node labels matched by the transducer parameter a are output, the other ones are filtered out, i.e., their conditions are replaced with the empty condition $[\,]$. The label matching can be here extended to regular expression matching. It is easy to see that $\mathcal{R}[\![Q(v_1) :\!\!-\ \mathsf{a}(v_1)]\!](\beta) = out_{\mathsf{a}}(\pi_{v_1}(\beta))|_{v_1}$.

3.2   Processing Path Queries

A path query is a sequence of relations such that for two consecutive relations there is a unique variable that is the sink of the first and the source of the second relation. SPEX compiles a path query into a P-net that is a sequence of connected transducers. A connection between two transducers consists in having the second transducer processing the output of the first one. The answers computed by a P-net are the nodes annotated by its last but one transducer. Fig. 2(a) shows the P-net for the query $P(v_2)$:- $v_0 \lhd^+ v_1 \wedge b(v_1) \wedge v_1 \prec^+ v_2 \wedge d(v_2)$ from Fig. 1(a) and Example 1 shows stepwise its processing.

The P-net $t(P) = [t(r_1), \ldots, t(r_n)]$ for a general path query $P(v_n)$:- $v_0 \ r_1 \ v_1 \wedge \cdots \wedge v_{n-1} \ r_n \ v_n$ is an implementation of $out_P(v_0)|_{v_n} = out_{r_n}(..(out_{r_1}(v_0)|_{v_1})..)|_{v_n}$: for given input bindings v_0, out_P returns output bindings v_n, such that for every $1 \leq i \leq n$ the relation $v_{i-1} \ r_i \ v_i$ holds. For a set of bindings β, it follows that:

$$\mathcal{R}[\![P(v_n) \text{ :- } v_0 \ r_1 \ v_1 \wedge \ldots \wedge v_{n-1} \ r_n \ v_n]\!](\beta) =$$
$$= \pi_{v_n}(\mathcal{S}[\![v_{n-1} \ r_n \ v_n]\!](\ldots(\mathcal{S}[\![v_0 \ r_1 \ v_1]\!](\beta))\ldots))$$
$$= out_{r_n}(\ldots(out_{r_2}(\pi_{v_1}(\mathcal{S}[\![v_0 \ r_1 \ v_1]\!](\beta)))|_{v_2})\ldots)|_{v_n}$$
$$= out_{r_n}(\ldots(out_{r_2}(\pi_{v_1}(out_{r_1}(\pi_{v_0}(\beta))|_{v_1}))|_{v_2})\ldots)|_{v_n}$$
$$= out_{r_n}(\ldots(out_{r_1}(\pi_{v_0}(\beta))|_{v_1})\ldots)|_{v_n} = out_P(\pi_{v_0}(\beta))|_{v_n}.$$

The correctness of a P-net $t(P)$ implementation of $out_P(v_0)|_{v_n}$, where $t(r_i)$ implements $out_{r_i}(v_{i-1})|_{v_i}$, $(1 \leq i \leq n)$, follows from the observation that the output of each transducer from P-net is streamed in the next transducer.

Example 1. Consider the path query $P(v_2)$:- $v_0 \lhd^+ v_1 \wedge b(v_1) \wedge v_1 \prec^+ v_2 \wedge d(v_2)$ from Fig. 1(a), which selects the next-siblings d-nodes of every b-node. The corresponding P-net is $t(P) = [t(\lhd^+), t(b), t(\prec^+), t(d)]$, as shown in Fig. 2(a). Table 1 gives a stream fragment *in* annotated with conditions, the intermediate and result output streams generated by the transducers in the P-net $t(P)$. Note that the intermediary output streams are created progressively and not stored. Thus, following the evaluation process corresponds to reading entire columns from left to right.

Recall that the stack of each transducer is initialized with the empty condition [ ]. The transducers do the following stack and output operations for processing the first two opening tags and two conditions:

On receiving $\langle a \rangle[1]$, the first transducer in $t(P)$, i.e., $t(\lhd^+)$, outputs $\langle a \rangle$ and its top condition [ ], and pushes the received condition [1]. The next transducer $t(b)$ receives $\langle a \rangle[\,]$ and sends it further to $t(\prec^+)$, which outputs $\langle a \rangle$ followed by its top condition [ ], adds later on the received condition [ ] to the top condition [ ], and pushes an empty condition [ ]. The next transducer $t(d)$ receives then $\langle a \rangle[\,]$ and sends it further.

On receiving $\langle b \rangle[2]$, $t(\lhd^+)$ outputs $\langle b \rangle$ and its top condition [1], and pushes [1,2]. Next, $t(b)$ receives $\langle b \rangle[1]$ and sends it further to $t(\prec^+)$, which outputs $\langle b \rangle$ followed by its top condition [ ], adds later on the received condition [1] to the top condition [ ], and pushes an empty condition [ ]. The next transducer $t(d)$ receives then $\langle b \rangle[\,]$ and sends it further.

Table 1. Processing Example with P-net

in	$\langle a \rangle$[1]	$\langle b \rangle$[2]	$\langle b \rangle$[3]	$\langle /b \rangle$	$\langle /b \rangle$	$\langle d \rangle$[4]	$\langle /d \rangle$	$\langle /a \rangle$
$out_{\lhd^+}$	$\langle a \rangle$[ ]	$\langle b \rangle$[1]	$\langle b \rangle$[1,2]	$\langle /b \rangle$	$\langle /b \rangle$	$\langle d \rangle$[1]	$\langle /d \rangle$	$\langle /a \rangle$
out_{b}	$\langle a \rangle$[ ]	$\langle b \rangle$[1]	$\langle b \rangle$[1,2]	$\langle /b \rangle$	$\langle /b \rangle$	$\langle d \rangle$[ ]	$\langle /d \rangle$	$\langle /a \rangle$
$out_{\prec^+}$	$\langle a \rangle$[ ]	$\langle b \rangle$[ ]	$\langle b \rangle$[ ]	$\langle /b \rangle$	$\langle /b \rangle$	$\langle d \rangle$[1]	$\langle /d \rangle$	$\langle /a \rangle$
out_{d}	$\langle a \rangle$[ ]	$\langle b \rangle$[ ]	$\langle b \rangle$[ ]	$\langle /b \rangle$	$\langle /b \rangle$	$\langle d \rangle$[1]	$\langle /d \rangle$	$\langle /a \rangle$

3.3 Processing Tree Queries

A tree query is a path query extended with multi-source variables. There is one path in a tree query that leads from a non-sink variable to the head variable, called the head path, the other non-head paths are called predicates. SPEX compiles a tree query into a T-net. Each multi-source variable introduces a pair of special transducers (and, cd-and), if that variable is source of conjuncted expressions, or (or,cd-or) for disjuncted expressions. These transducers delimit the subnetworks corresponding to the expressions having that variable as source. Fig. 2(b) shows the T-net for the query $T(v_1)$:- $v_0 \lhd^+ v_1 \wedge b(v_1) \wedge v_0 \lhd v_2 \wedge d(v_2)$ from Fig. 1(b).

The answers computed by a T-net are among the nodes annotated by its head. These nodes are potential answers, as they may depend on a downstream satisfaction of T-net predicates. The predicate satisfaction is conveyed in the T-net by conditions that annotate nodes. Until the predicate satisfaction is decided, the potential answers are buffered by the last transducer out in the T-net. Consider, e.g., the evaluation of the tree query $T(v_1)$:- $v_0 \lhd^+ v_1 \wedge a(v_1) \wedge v_1 \lhd v_2 \wedge b(v_2)$. When encountering in the XML stream an opening tag $\langle a \rangle$ marking the beginning of an a-node, it is not yet known whether this node has a b-node child, i.e., whether it is an answer or not. Indeed, by definition of XML streams, such a child can only appear downstream. This might remain unknown until the corresponding closing tag $\langle /a \rangle$ is processed. At this point, it is impossible for the a-node to have further b-node children. Thus, the stream fragment corresponding to a potential answer has to be buffered as long as it is not known whether predicates that might apply are satisfied or not, but no longer.

A non-empty condition [c] annotating a node n is replaced by an and (or) transducer with a new condition [q], where q is the stack size of that transducer. The transducer also pushes [q] on its stack, and forwards to its condition determinant transducer cd (cd-and or cd-or) the condition mapping [c]→[q]. Each subnetwork routed at that and (or) transducer receives [q] and when [q] is received from all (at least one) ingoing edges of the cd-and (cd-or), [q] is considered satisfied. Using the condition mapping [c]→[q], the cd transducer forwards [c] to the cd transducer corresponding to the preceding and (or) transducer that created [c], or of the out transducer corresponding to the in transducer. However, as soon as it is known that [q] can no longer be satisfied, [q] is considered unsatisfied and the nodes annotated with [q] by the head and buffered by the out transducer are discarded.

The condition mapping $[c] \to [q]$ is discarded when the cd transducer receives (1) the closing tag of n, or (2) the closing tag of the parent node of n. The former applies for and/or transducers followed by subnetworks that start with $t(\lhd)$ or $t(\lhd^+)$, as $t(\lhd)$ or $t(\lhd^+)$ and their subsequents in the subnetworks can create output bindings with $[q]$ only within the subtree rooted by the node n (and hence enclosed within the opening and closing tags of n). The latter applies for and/or transducers followed by subnetworks that start with $t(\prec)$ or $t(\prec^+)$, as they can create output bindings with $[q]$ only within the stream fragment starting with the closing tag of n and ending with the closing tag of the parent of n. The lifetime of a condition mapping, i.e., the time between its creation and its discarding, influences the number of condition mappings alive at a time. In the former above case, there can be at most d condition mappings alive at a time, where d is the depth of the tree conveyed by the input stream, whereas in the latter above case, there can be at most $d + b$ condition mappings alive at a time, where b is the breadth of the tree conveyed by the input stream.

Condition mappings are indispensable for representing condition scopes in the network's computation. A network for a query with p multi-source variables has p (and/or, cd) pairs, hence p condition scopes. Consider the condition mappings $[c_i] \to [c_{i+1}]$ $(1 \le i \le p)$ created by a transducer network with p condition scopes, where each mapping corresponds to a scope. If the head has annotated nodes with $[c_h]$, then they become answers only when $[c_h]$ is satisfied and from each other scope i $(1 \le i \le p, i \ne h)$ at least one condition $[c_i]$ that is mapped directly or indirectly to $[c_h]$ is also satisfied. As soon as they become answers, they are output and removed from the buffer.

Let us consider the correctness of T-nets for tree queries with conjunctions. For tree queries with disjunctions similar treatment can be applied. A tree query $T(v_h) :\!\!- h(v_0, v_h) \wedge q_i(v_j, v_i)$ with path $h(v_0, v_h)$, which leads to the head variable v_h via intermediate variables v_j $(0 \le j \le h)$, and predicates $q_i(v_j, v_i)$ $(h < i \le m)$ is compiled into a T-net network $t(T) = (t(h), t(q_i))$ with a head P-net $t(h)$ and predicate P-nets $t(q_i)$. The T-net $t(b)$ is an implementation of a function $out_b(v_0)|_{v_h} = \{out_h(v_0)|_{v_h} \mid \forall h < i \le m, \exists v_i \in out_{q_i}(v_j)|_{v_i}, 0 \le j \le h\}$: for given input bindings v_0, it returns output bindings for v_h, such that the path $h(v_0, v_h)$ holds and there exists a binding of v_i for each $q_i(v_j, v_i)$. It follows that:

$$\mathcal{R}[\![T(v_h) :\!\!- h(v_0, v_h) \wedge q_i(v_j, v_i)]\!](\beta) = \pi_{v_h}(\mathcal{S}[\![h(v_0, v_h)]\!](\beta) \cap \mathcal{S}[\![q_i(v_j, v_i)]\!](\beta))$$

$$= \pi_{v_h}(\{t \mid t \in \mathcal{S}[\![h(v_0, v_h)]\!](\beta), t \in \mathcal{S}[\![q_i(v_j, v_i)]\!](\beta)\})$$

$$= \{t.v_h \mid t.v_h \in out_h(\pi_{v_0}(\beta))|_{v_h}, \exists t.v_i \in out_{q_i}(\pi_{v_j}(\beta))|_{v_i}\} = out_T(\pi_{v_0}(\beta))|_{v_h}.$$

The correctness of a T-net $t(T) = (t(h), t(q_i))$ implementation of $out_T(v_0)|_{v_h}$, where h and q_i implement $out_h(v_j)|_{v_h}$ and $out_{q_i}(v_0)|_{v_i}$ $(h < i \le m, 0 \le j \le h)$ follows from the above characterizations of and and cd-and.

3.4   Processing Single-Join DAG Queries

A single-join DAG query consists of several subqueries that share only one variable. SPEX compiles such queries into D-nets. Each multi-sink variable introduces a pair of special transducers ($\cup$, cd-$\cup$), if the variable is the sink of disjuncted expressions, or $(\cap, \text{cd-}\cap)$ for conjuncted expressions. Fig. 2(c) shows the D-net for the query $D(v_1) :\!-\, v_0 \vartriangleleft^+ v_1 \wedge b(v_1) \wedge v_2 \vartriangleleft^+ v_1 \wedge d(v_2)$ from Fig. 1(c).

The transducers $\cap/\cup$ are similar to the and/or transducers. However, as set operations are defined for $k \geq 2$ operands, these transducers have k ingoing edges and their cd transducers have $k + 1$ incoming edges, one edge for each subnetwork implementing an operand and one edge for the subnetwork enclosed. For each node, a set transducer receives also a condition $[c_i]$ $(1 \leq i \leq k)$ from each ingoing edge and possibly creates a mapping $[c_i] \rightarrow [q]$. The $\cap/\cup$ transducer creates the new condition $[q]$ only if all (at least one) $[c_i]$ conditions are non-empty. If potential answers are annotated with $[q']$, then they become answers only when $[q']$ is satisfied, one condition that is mapped directly or indirectly to $[q']$ from each condition scope is satisfied, and for the $\cap/\cup$ transducer all (at least one) $[c_i]$ conditions are satisfied.

The correctness of D-nets can be proven similarly to P-nets and T-nets.

4   Analytical Complexity

The evaluation of RPQ with SPEX has a polynomial combined complexity in the stream and the query size, near the optimum [4] for in-memory evaluation of the XPath fragment included in RPQ. We assume that the tree conveyed by the XML stream has depth d, breadth b, and size s. We define four RPQ classes: RPQ_1 contains path queries and their conjunctions and disjunctions, RPQ_2 contains queries without closure relations, RPQ_3 contains RPQ_2 and the $\vartriangleleft^+$ relation, and RPQ_4 contains RPQ_3 and the $\prec^+$ relation.

Theorem 1. The time T_i and space S_i complexities for processing RPQ_i are:

1. $T_1 = O(q \times s)$ and $S_1 = O(q \times d)$.
2. $T_2 = O(q \times s)$ and $S_2 = O(q \times d + s)$.
3. $T_3 = O(q \times d \times s)$ and $S_3 = O(q \times d^2 + s)$.
4. $T_4 = O(q \times \max(d, b) \times s)$ and $S_4 = O(q \times d \times \max(d, b) + s)$.

Proof. The size of a network for a RPQ query is linear in the size of the query. A stack can have d entries, for every opening tag brings a condition that is pushed on the stack, and its corresponding closing tag pops a condition. For evaluating queries with multi-source variables, i.e., with predicates, the extra space s can be needed for buffering potential answers. This buffering is independent of SPEX and in some cases unavoidable. The entire space s is needed only in pathological cases, e.g., when the entire XML stream is a potential answer that depends on a condition satisfaction which can be decided only at the end of the XML stream.

(1) In a network for a query without multi-source variables, only the in transducer creates new conditions, which are in fact satisfied conditions $[\top]$. Hence, the condition unions done by transducers for closure relations yield always satisfied conditions of constant size. Thus, the entries on any transducer stack have constant size. The time needed to read/write a tag or condition is constant.

(2) No closure relations in the query means no transducers in the network to compute unions of conditions and consequently conditions of constant size. Processing queries with multi-source variables can require extra space s.

(3) The $t(\lhd^+)$ transducer computes condition unions. As there can be d condition mappings created at a time within a condition scope and stored on stacks, a condition union has maximum size d. The stacks have d entries, hence the size of a stack can be d^2. To read/write a condition can take d time.

(4) The $t(\prec^+)$ transducer computes condition unions. An and/or can store $b+d$ condition mappings at a time, if a $t(\prec^+)$ immediately follows it. Otherwise, case (3) applies. A condition can have $\max(d, b)$ size.   □

The extra space s that can add to the worst-case space complexity of processing queries of RPQ_i ($i \geq 2$) classes with SPEX is not necessary for the evaluation of queries with multi-source variables that have their predicates always being evaluated before the head transducer annotates potential answers. In this case, it is already known whether the conditions used by the head transducer for annotation are satisfied. E.g., in the evaluation of the query $T(v_2)$:- $v_0 \lhd^+ v_1 \wedge b(v_1) \wedge v_0 \prec^+ v_2 \wedge d(v_2)$, the predicate $b(v_1)$:- $v_0 \lhd^+ v_1 \wedge b(v_1)$ is always evaluated before the head path $h(v_2)$:- $v_0 \prec^+ v_2 \wedge d(v_2)$, because the nodes bound to v_1 are among the descendants of the nodes bound to v_0, whereas the nodes bound to v_2 are among the following siblings of the nodes bound to v_0 and therefore are encountered later in the stream. The class RPQ_5 of queries, the evaluation of which does not require to buffer stream fragments:

$$RPQ_5 = RPQ_1 \cup \{Q(v_1) :- f_0(v_0, x) \wedge f_1(x, v_1) \wedge f_i(x, v_i) \mid$$
$$f_1(x, v_1) = x \ (\prec|\prec^+) \ v_1' \wedge f_1'(v_1', v_1), f_i(x, v_i) = x \ (\lhd|\lhd^+) \ v_i' \wedge f_i'(v_i', v_i),$$
$$f_0(v_0, x) \in RPQ_5, f_1'(v_1', v_1) \in RPQ_5, f_i'(v_i', v_i) \in RPQ, i \geq 2\}.$$

5   Experimental Evaluation

The theoretical results of Section 4 are verified by an extensive experimental evaluation conducted on a prototype implementation of SPEX in Java (Sun Hotspot JRE 1.4.1) on a Pentium 1.5 GHz with 500 MB under Linux 2.4.

XML Streams. The effect of varying the stream size s on evaluation time is considered for two XML stream sets. The first set [7] provides real-life XML streams, ranging in size from 21 to 21 million elements and in depth from 3 to 36. The second set provides synthetic XML streams with a slightly more complex structure that allows more precise variations in the workload parameters. The synthetic data is generated from information about the currently running processes on computer networks and allows the specification of both the size and the maximum depth of the generated data.

Queries. Only RPQ queries that are "schema-aware" are considered, i.e., that express structures compatible with the schema of the XML streams considered. Their generation has been tuned with the query size q and several probabilities: $p_{\prec}$ and p_+ for next-sibling, resp. closure relations, p_λ and $p_\curlyvee$ for a branch, resp. a join, and p_* for the probability that a variable has a label relation. E.g., a path query has $p_\lambda = p_\curlyvee = 0$ and a tree query $p_\curlyvee = 0$. For each parameter setting, 10–30 queries have been tested , totaling about 1200 queries.

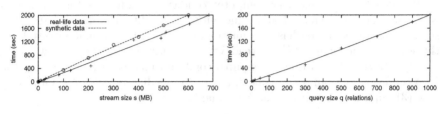

(a) Varying stream size s ($q = 10$, $3 \leq d \leq 32$)

(b) Varying query size q ($s = 244$ kB, $d = 32$)

Fig. 3. Scalability ($p_* = p_+ = p_\prec = p_\lambda = p_\curlyvee = 0.5$)

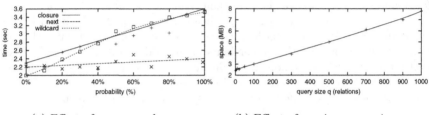

(a) Effect of p_*, p_+, and $p_\prec$

(b) Effect of varying query size q

Fig. 4. If not varied, $s = 244$ kB, $d = 32$, $q = 10$, $p_* = p_+ = p_\prec = p_\lambda = p_\curlyvee = 0.5$

Scalability. Scalability results are only presented for stream and query size. In all cases, the depth is bounded in a rather small constant ($d \leq 36$) and its influence on processing time showed to be considerably smaller than of the stream and query size. Fig. 3 emphasizes the theoretical results: Query processing time increases linearly with the stream size as well as with the query size. The effect is visible in both the real-life and the synthetic data set, with a slightly higher increase in the synthetic data due to the more complex structure.

Varying the query characteristics. Fig. 4(a) shows an increase of the evaluation time by a factor of less than 2 when p_* and p_+ increase from 0 to 100%. It also suggests that the evaluation times for $\prec$ and $\lhd$ are comparable. Further experiments have shown that the evaluation of tree and DAG queries operations is slightly more expensive than the evaluation of simple path queries.

The **memory usage** is almost constant over the full range of the previous tests. Cf. Fig. 4(b), an increase of the query size q from 1 to 1000 leads to an increase from 2 to 8 MB of the memory for the network and for its processing. The memory use is measured by inspecting the properties of the Java virtual machine (e.g., using `Runtime.totalMemory()` and `Runtime.freeMemory()`).

6   Conclusion

This paper gives correctness and complexity results for the SPEX [8] query evaluator against XML streams. SPEX evaluates XPath-like queries, i.e., path, tree, and single-join DAG queries, with polynomial time and space complexity. The complexity results are confirmed by extensive experimental evaluation.

Acknowledgments. We thank the anonymous reviewers and Holger Meuss that made many helpful suggestions on the penultimate draft.

References

1. M. Altinel and M. J. Franklin. Efficient filtering of XML documents for selective dissemination of information. In *Proc. of VLDB*, pages 53–64, 2000.
2. C.-Y. Chan, P. Felber, M. Garofalakis, and R. Rastogi. Efficient filtering of XML documents with XPath expressions. In *Proc. of ICDE*, pages 235–244, 2002.
3. Cisco Systems. Cisco IOS netflow, 2000.
   `http://www.cisco.com/warp/public/cc/pd/iosw/prodlit/iosnf_ds.pdf`.
4. G. Gottlob, C. Koch, and R. Pichler. The complexity of XPath query evaluation. In *Proc. of PODS*, pages 179–190, 2003.
5. T. J. Green, G. Miklau, M. Onizuka, and D. Suciu. Processing XML streams with deterministic automata. In *Proc. of ICDT*, pages 173–189, 2003.
6. S. Madden and M. J. Franklin. Fjording the stream: An architecture for queries over streaming sensor data. In *Proc. of ICDE*, pages 555–566, 2002.
7. G. Miklau. XMLData repository, Univ. of Washington, 2003.
   `http://www.cs.washington.edu/research/xmldatasets`.
8. D. Olteanu, T. Furche, and F. Bry. An Efficient Single-Pass Query Evaluator for XML Data Streams. In *Proc. of ACM SAC*, pages 627–631, 2004.
9. D. Olteanu, H. Meuss, T. Furche, and F. Bry. XPath: Looking forward. In *Proc. of EDBT Workshop XMLDM*, pages 109–127, 2002. LNCS 2490.
10. D. Rogers, J. Hunter, and D. Kosovic. The TV-trawler project. *J. of Imaging Systems and Technology*, pages 289–296, 2003.

The EGTV Query Language*

Damir Bećarević and Mark Roantree

Interoperable Systems Group, Dublin City University, Glasnevin, Dublin 9, Ireland.
{Damir.Becarevic, Mark.Roantree}@computing.dcu.ie

Abstract. When storing data in heterogeneous databases, one of the top-down design issues concerns the usage of multiple query languages. A common language enables querying of database schemas in a platform independent format. This is particularly useful in federated database systems when newly added databases may be both numerous and heterogeneous. As the existing query language standards are generally incompatible and translation between them is not trivial, a new query language has been developed. The EQL language facilitates querying of object-oriented and object-relational database schemas in a database and platform independent manner. The EQL language also provides an orthogonal type system, the ability to define simple views, and updatability at the object level. EQL is supported with formally defined object algebra and specified semantics of query evaluation.

1 Introduction

The Físchlár system [9] provides a large centralised repository of multimedia files. As expansion is very difficult and different user groups have a requirement to define their own schemas, the EGTV (**E**fficient **G**lobal **T**ransactions for **V**ideo) project was established to examine how the distribution of this database could be managed. This project is primarily aimed at providing efficient query and update capabilities for this potentially large distributed repository of multimedia objects. The individual repositories take the form of databases, independently designed and supplied by different vendors, thus heterogeneous in terms of data model and schema design. This assumes a federated database approach [12], although it is unusual in that it takes a top-down strategy for design. In this project, it is presumed that participating databases are capable of storing objects, and presently two standards exist: object-oriented databases with the ODMG standard [3] and object-relational (O-R) databases with the SQL:1999 standard [6].

The ODMG standard [3] specifies the Object Query Language (OQL) for querying object database schemas. The language is based on the ODMG data model and its type system. The main problem with this type system is the different semantics used for representing object types and literals. As a consequence, the semantics of OQL is complex and inputs to and output from the query language are not orthogonal. This results in an ambiguous semantics of nested queries

---

* Supported by Enterprise Ireland Research Grant IF-2001-305

H. Williams and L. MacKinnon (Eds.): BNCOD 2004, LNCS 3112, pp. 45–56, 2004.

and makes the process of query evaluation more difficult. The OQL language does not support updates of database objects.

The SQL:1999 specification defines a standard for querying O-R databases by extending an existing relational query language with object features. Since the backward compatibility to relational model is preserved, the syntax and semantics of added object extensions is very complex and non-intuitive. The SQL:1999 type system adds User-Defined Types (UDT), collections and a reference type to an existing set of atomic literals, thus making query inputs and results non-orthogonal.

Since ODMG OQL and SQL:1999 SQL are two different and incompatible standards for database schema querying, query translation is not trivial. Also, both O-R and ODMG models lack the ability to define efficient operators for multimedia types. These problems motivated us to define a new query language (EQL) that can be applied to provide an efficient interface to both O-R an O-O databases in our multimedia federation. The EQL language is supported with a formally specified algebra and a defined semantics of the process for query evaluation. Due to the space limitations we restrict this discussion to key language and algebraic features only. A more complete version of this paper is provided in [1].

The remainder of this paper is structured as follows: §2 describes our EQL query language; EQL algebra is presented in §3, while semantics of query evaluation is defined in §4; related research is presented in §5; prototype is discussed in §6, and finally, in §7 conclusions are made.

2   Language Overview

The EGTV Query Language (EQL) provides querying and updating for (distributed) EGTV multimedia database schemas. This language modifies the ODMG OQL [3] by providing full orthogonality between query input and output in the form of classes, where a class is defined as a pair: `<metadata, object extent>`. Metadata defines the structure of the class and the types of its properties. It is represented in the EGTV metamodel format [10] and stored in the EGTV Schema Repository. Object extent contains all objects instantiated from the class. Input to an EQL query is a set of classes, and the result of query evaluation is a single virtual class. This is different to OQL whereby each query can return either an object identifier, atomic value, structure or collection. Other language improvements include: support for updates, creates and deletes with fully updatable query results; ability to define custom operators and overload behaviour of existing ones; orthogonality of data types; and the ability to define simple views as stored queries.

The language is described through a series of examples based on the Multimedia Recording System illustrated in ◘gure 1.

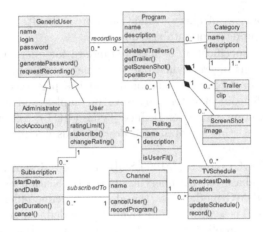

Fig. 1. Database Schema for Multimedia Recording System.

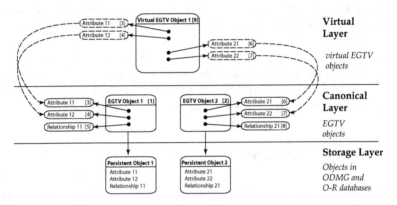

Fig. 2. The EGTV Model.

2.1 Data Model

The EQL query language is built upon the EGTV data model [7] illustrated in ◘gure 2. The model provides a common interface to objects stored in ODMG or object-relational databases and is specifically designed to facilitate global updates. It uses classes as templates for the instantiation of objects. A class defines properties (attributes and relationships) that belong to the object and a set of operations that can be applied against the object. Classes can also define generalisation relationships with other classes in the schema, where multiple inheritance is possible. It is important to note that the EGTV model does not provide object storage itself, but acts as a wrapper for O-O and O-R models. Unlike many other object-oriented models, properties of an object are not contained in the object. Rather, they are independent objects, referenced from their parent object. Properties contain the actual values of the corresponding persistent object's properties. Using object-oriented modelling terminology, the EGTV model replaces all containments with aggregations, not affecting the expressiveness of the model. An advantage of this approach is that both objects and their properties can be directly referenced using the same type of reference.

Figure 2 illustrates a representation of a join, where two EGTV objects are joined to form a virtual one. Persistent objects are first transformed to EGTV objects (at the Canonical Layer) and later joined (at the Virtual Layer). Object identities are shown in square brackets with their values generated by the system. Persistent objects are stored in an external database (at the Storage Layer), and can only be manipulated through an EGTV wrapper object. For each persistent object, a single EGTV object is materialised, forming a canonical representation of the persistent object. This EGTV object has a new object identity, which is bound to the identity of their original object for the lifetime of the EGTV object. The properties of all EGTV objects have object identities of their own, which are also immutable.

Virtual objects are materialised at the Virtual Layer as query results or views. An object identifier is generated for all virtual objects and thus, the materialisation of query objects uses an object generating semantics. The properties of virtual objects retain the identifiers of the EGTV properties upon which they are based. In figure 2, they are shown as dashed elements, with dashed arrows pointing to EGTV properties. This approach benefits in updatable virtual objects, as updates to their properties are directly propagated to base and persistent objects.

2.2   Query Structure

Each query consists of a projection specification (select clause), a source specification (from clause) and an optional restriction specification (where clause). A query can also contain two or more subqueries to which a set operation (union, intersection, and difference) is applied. This is illustrated in Definition 1.

Definition 1. *EQL_Query ::=* ***select*** *<attribute_list>*
                      from   *<source_predicate>*
                      (***where*** *<predicate>)**
                      /
                      (Query1 <setop> Query2)+

The structure of an EGTV query result extent is identical to the structure of class extent, which is a set of objects belonging to a single class. This identical structure facilitates easy subquerying (nesting queries). Also, client applications manipulate query extents and objects using the same interface (as both are of type set). This is distinct from the semantics of nested ODMG queries which are unclear, as the class extent is different in structure to the query extent. It also provides a simple view mechanism whereby views are represented as stored EQL queries.

EQL supports the type system defined in the EGTV model where types are categorised as built-in and user-defined. Built-in types are those already provided by the model, while a user-defined type is effectively a class. An important feature of our type system is orthogonality between built-in and user defined types. Contrary to ODMG, O-R, and some other database models, instances of EGTV built-in types are not literals, but objects with OIDs. Objects instantiated from built-in types can be directly referenced and are manipulated by EQL in the same manner as user-defined classes, thus providing full orthogonality and reducing the complexity of the type system. The other advantage of this approach is the ability to define type specific operators and methods (i.e. string comparison, date conversions). We commonly refer to the built-in types and user-defined classes as types.

Unlike other query languages, EQL operators are not hard-wired to the query language, but are associated with types. Each EQL operator invokes the appropriate operator defined within the type. The behaviour of built-in types is part of the model itself and cannot be changed. Operators in user-defined classes are defined by the class designer, where for some operations, the default behaviour is provided. This default behaviour can be overridden and thus modified by the class designer. EQL operators are classified as comparison (=, <, >, <=, =>,!=, identical), arithmetic (*, /, +, -), logic (and, or, not), assignment (:=), aggregate (max, min, avg, sum, count) and set (union, unionall, intersection, difference, inset, distinct) operators. In addition to these, new aggregate operators can be defined. For example, the length aggregate operator can be defined for class VideoClip to return the total length in seconds of all video clips.

2.3   Joins

EQL defines two join operators: property join which defines the standard inner join operator, and navigational join. Navigational Join creates a join-like result that spans two interconnected classes using path navigation. This operator is not defined in OQL, but is found in other object-oriented query languages [13]. The result set produced by the navigational join is a set of pairs containing the start and the end points of the navigation path. EQL introduces a new operator connect which denotes the navigational join operation. For example, consider the query where a list of programs marked for recording should be retrieved for each user. This query uses a navigational join to connect instances of User and Program classes as is illustrated in Example 1.

```
select User.name as uName, Program.name as pName
from Program connect User on User.recordings;
```

Example 1. Navigational join example.

2.4 Updates

OQL does not support create, update and delete operations on database objects. These operations can be performed only through user-defined methods. This provides limited update functionality and as the operation invocation semantics is vaguely defined, the effect of such an operation invoked within a query remains unclear. The EQL language extends OQL with support for update operations. EQL defines only projection, source and optional restriction specification, with no special language elements provided for updates. This maintains a syntax that is both simple and consistent.

Create. New objects are created by invoking an object constructor in the projection specification. This is illustrated in Example 2 where a new object of the class User is created by invoking a constructor method in the select clause.

```
select User( "Tom", "tom67", "passwrd", nil, nil, ratingRef )
from User, Rating as ratingRef
where Rating.name = "all";
```

Example 2. Create example.

Parameters of the constructor are provided in the order specified in the Schema Repository definition of the constructor method. The effect of this query is that an EGTV object is materialised, and the corresponding persistent object in the Storage Layer is created. The query returns a virtual class containing a newly materialised object.

Delete. Objects are deleted by invoking their destructor method. Delete is represented in the EQL syntax by assigning nil to the object. This invokes a destructor on the object and releases the reference.

Update. Updates in the EQL are specified using ':=' to assign new values to the properties of the selected object or to the object itself. These modifications are then propagated to persistent objects in the database. To maintain orthogonality, the result returned by the query is a virtual class containing updated objects. This result set can be used as an input to the other queries or to the parent subquery in the nested query. The database can also be updated by methods invoked in the EQL query, thus producing possible side effects, discussed in [8].

The query in Example 3 illustrates an update where the TV schedule with the maximum duration is first selected and then its duration is increased by 10.

```
select max(duration) := max(duration) + 10
from TVSchedule;
```

Example 3. Update example.

3   EQL Algebra

The EQL algebra is defined as a set of high level operators for manipulating EGTV classes. Algebraic operators have the same input and output as queries, so each EQL query can be easily transformed to an algebraic representation. This is illustrated in Definition 2. This is consistent with the closure rules defined for relational algebraic operators [5] and orthogonality of the EQL language.

Definition 2.

egtvClass $\leftarrow$ *EQLQuery* ({egtvClass}$^{1..*}$, queryExpression)

egtvClass $\leftarrow$ *algebraicOperator* ({egtvClass}$^{1..2}$, {expression}$^{0..1}$)

All EGTV operators are classified into two categories: general and set operators. General operators are: projection, filter, cartesian product, path, navigational join, property join, and rename. Set operators define mathematical set operations on sets of EGTV objects and include union, unionall, intersection, difference, inset, and distinct. All other EQL operators (comparison, logic, arithmetic, aggregate, and assignment) are not part of the algebra, since they are defined as behaviour of built-in types or user-defined classes. Operators and methods defined in types can be accessed and invoked from within EQL algebra. EQL algebraic operators are not type dependant and can be applied to EGTV objects of any type.

3.1   General Operators

This group of operators comprise the core of the EQL algebra and facilitates the high level operations of the query language. Operators can manipulate class metadata, objects or both.

Filter (ϕ). Filter is a unary operator that filters unwanted objects from the input class C_1 using the boolean predicate condition commonly specified in the **where** clause of the EQL query. The result is a new virtual class C_2.

Definition 3. $C_2 (p_{11} .. p_{1n}) \leftarrow \phi_{predicate} C_1 (p_{11} .. p_{1n})$

Projection (π). Projection is used to project properties into a new class. Input is a class C_1 and an expression in the form of property list. Property list corresponds to the **select** clause of the EQL query and defines the attributes of the result class C_2. For each object in the extent C_1, one object in the extent C_2 is generated.

Definition 4. $C_2 (p_{21} .. p_{2m}) \leftarrow \pi_{propertyList} C_1 (p_{11} .. p_{1n})$

Cartesian Product ($\times$). This is a binary operator which generates the result as a cartesian product of two input classes. The cartesian product operator is never used directly, and it is required only for construction of more complex join operators.

Definition 5. $C_3 (p_{11} .. p_{1n}, p_{21} .. p_{2m}) \leftarrow C_1 (p_{11} .. p_{1n}) \times C_2 (p_{21} .. p_{2m})$

The C_1 and C_2 are classes defining two object extents. Result is a virtual class C_3 which has all the properties of both C_1 and C_2 and its extent contains all combinations of C_1 and C_2 object pairs.

Path ($\vdash$). Path operator takes as an input one class and a path expression. For each object in the class extent C_1, a path expression is evaluated to an C_2 object or to a set of C_2 objects located one nesting level below.

Definition 6. $C_2\left(p_{21} .. p_{2m}\right) \leftarrow \vdash_{pathExpression} C_1\left(p_{11} .. p_{1n}\right)$

Property join ($\bowtie$). Property join is a binary operator which takes two classes (C_1 and C_2) as input and a predicate defining the joining criterion. The result is a new virtual class C_3 containing the properties of both input classes and a new extent.

Definition 7.

$$C_3\left(p_{11} .. p_{1n}, p_{21} .. p_{2m}\right) \leftarrow C_1\left(p_{11} .. p_{1n}\right) \bowtie_{predicate} C_2\left(p_{21} .. p_{2m}\right) \Leftrightarrow$$
$$\phi_{predicate}\left(C_1\left(p_{11} .. p_{1n}\right) \times C_2\left(p_{21} .. p_{2m}\right)\right)$$

The operator can be formally expressed as the cartesian product of C_1 and C_2 classes to which is then applied a filter operator with the `predicate` condition.

Navigational join ($\bowtie$). This algebraic operator maps directly to the `connect` operation in the EQL. This is a binary operator which takes two classes (C_1 and C_2) as input and creates a join-like result C_3 based on the relationship defined between them. The joining condition is specified as the name of the relationship.

Definition 8.

$$C_3\left(p_{11} .. p_{1n}, p_{21} .. p_{2m}\right) \leftarrow C_1\left(p_{11} .. p_{1n}\right) \bowtie_{pathExpression} C_2\left(p_{21} .. p_{2m}\right) \Leftrightarrow$$
$$\phi \,_{\exists pathExpression}\left(C_1\left(p_{11} .. p_{1n}\right) \times C_2\left(p_{21} .. p_{2m}\right)\right)$$

The navigational join operator is formally represented as the cartesian product of the classes C_1 and C_2, to which is then applied the filter operator to remove all objects not satisfying the **path expression** condition. The result is a new virtual class C_3.

Rename (R). Rename is a unary operator that can change class name or names of its properties.

Definition 9.

$$C_2(p_{11} .. p_{1n}) \leftarrow R_{renameExpression} \; C_1(p_{11} .. p_{1n}) \Leftrightarrow \pi_{propertyList} \; C_1(p_{11} .. p_{1n})$$
$$rename \; expression := \{ \; (\; old\_name, \; new\_name \;) \; \}^{1..*}$$
$$name := old\_name - new\_name$$
$$property \; list := \{ \; name \; \}^{1..*}$$

Rename can be formally represented as the special case of projection operator, where all properties are projected to the equivalent ones, only with different names.

3.2   Set Operators

Set operators in the EQL algebra provide set operations on the EGTV classes. Set operators include: union, unionall, intersection, difference, inset and distinct. The semantics of each operator is straightforward and described in [7]. Set operators are the only operators of the EQL query language explicitly defined in the algebra, and not as the behaviour of the built-in types and user-defined classes. This is because the query processor applies set operators only to dynamically created virtual classes (resulting from two subqueries) which do not have any behaviour defined or included from input classes. For this reason, set operators must be supported at the EQL algebra level as global operators. All other operators of the EQL language are always mapped to the existing behaviour in the built-in types or user-defined classes.

3.3   Mapping Operators

The operator set defined in the EQL algebra can be used to formally represent any EQL query. Algebraic operators are directly mapped to algorithms in the query execution tree, where each algorithm defines one stage of the query processing. However, since the EGTV model is a canonical model and effectively a wrapper for persistent objects stored elsewhere, two additional operators have been defined. Their role is to provide on-demand materialisation of EGTV object extents and behaviour invocation. These operators are referred to as mapping operators, they are not part of the formal algebra and are defined as algorithms in the query execution tree. These two operators are `extent`, and `eval`.

extent. `extent` is an unary operator whose role is to materialise EGTV objects and retrieve their metadata. This is then used as input to other operators in the query execution tree. The `extent` operator is always invoked at the start of query processing as it facilitates direct interaction with the EGTV model and the EGTV Schema Repository.

eval. The role of this operator is to provide an invocation interface for behaviour (methods and operators) defined in the built-in types and user-defined classes. Thus, this operator effectively acts as a wrapper for behaviour defined in EGTV model types. Behaviour is outside the scope of this research and is covered elsewhere [8].

4   Query Processing

The processing of an EQL query can be divided into three stages: query parsing, execution tree construction and result materialisation.

In the first stage of processing, an EQL query string is parsed to the syntactic tree representation. The nodes of the tree are class, property and operation names grouped in three branches: `select`, `from`, and `where`. During the construction of the tree, the query is syntactically validated. The result of the parsing stage is an EQL syntactic tree.

In the second stage of processing, the query in the syntactic tree is transformed to its algebraic representation. In this process the whole syntactic tree is traversed and all EQL syntactic elements (select, from, where, path navigation, join, and behaviour invocations) are transformed to algebraic operators and represented as the query execution tree. This effectively performs semantic validation of the query to check if types used in the query exist in the Schema Repository and if operations are compatible with these types.

In the materialisation phase, the execution tree is processed and a query result generated. The processing starts with materialisation of all class extents required as inputs for algebraic operators. Then, operations defined in the execution tree are sequentially applied to create the final result. During this process, temporary objects can be created as intermediary results. This is because each algebraic operator returns a result as a virtual class which subsequently becomes an input for other operators. However, when the final result is generated, all intermediary results (temporary objects) are closed.

5   Related Research

The LOQIS database system [13] introduces the concept of references which are used to access both properties and objects. This is conceptually similar to our EGTV data model, as it provides the full orthogonality of query inputs and outputs. LOQIS expressions are specified using the Stack-Based Query Language (SBQL) and they return a reference to an object containing the result of an expression, with the effect that the generated object can be used to update the base object. Queries are a form of expressions, procedures are series of expressions with some control statements and views are results of the procedure execution, thus their results are updatable. EQL extends LOQIS by addressing issues of interoperability of heterogeneous data sources and global schema construction. Furthermore, as SBQL presents a low-level programming language type approach, we replace it with EQL, a high-level OQL-like query language.

COCOON [11] employs a proprietary functional model where objects are manipulated using functions only. Functions are divided into properties and methods, where methods modify objects and properties do not. A result of a query is set of properties and methods, but only methods can update the objects used to construct the query result. New methods and properties can be defined for a query. The query, when the definition is stored within the database is a view. A schema contains multiple views, where relationships between views can be defined. In the EGTV model, the objects which are generated as a result of an EQL query can be used to update the base objects on which they are formed.

The MOOD database system [4] derives its model from the C++ object model. The MOOD SQL is an "objectised" version of SQL which facilitates method invocation within queries. METU Interoperable DBMS (MIND) is a multidatabase system that integrates multiple MOOD databases into a four layer federation, similar to [12]. The federated schema is constructed using simple views specified in an extended ODMG ODL language. The view extent is defined as a MOOD SQL query, while ODL extensions specify mapping rules to base classes. Unlike the MOOD which is based on proprietary data model, the EGTV architecture utilises standard O-O and O-R databases. Contrary to views defined in MIND export and global schemas, EGTV views are fully updatable, as there is a tight mapping between ODMG and O-R databases.

The Garlic Project [2] defines an architecture for a system of interconnected multimedia data stores. It provides a global schema for multimedia data originating from different data repositories by extending the ODMG-93 object-oriented model [3]. The query language for Garlic is based on SQL-92 and extended with object-oriented features like references, collections, path expressions and method invocation. All queries are read-only and data modification is not possible. Our approach extends ODMG OQL as it is more suited to querying an object-oriented data model than SQL. However, our reference model requires a re-specification of OQL in order to exploit data distribution and updatability of views. Thus, while employing an OQL like syntax, the semantics are different.

6   Prototype Description

To test the use of EQL in meaningful database operations, multiple test systems were developed. In terms of platform, Versant (ODMG) and Oracle 9i databases were used on both Windows XP and Linux. Five separate database users designed schemas according to their different goals and design patterns: multimedia recording system, multimedia editing system, TV news archive, sports database, and Irish language news database. The multimedia content was mainly drawn from the Físchlár system, although once stored locally, it was possible for users to manipulate the data set according to their own needs.

The prototype was built in the C++ programming language and ported to Windows and Linux platforms. An object manager was developed for both Oracle 9i and Versant databases. Oracle interface is implemented using the Oracle C++ Call Interface (OCCI) which allows direct access to database objects, thus bypassing SQL. The Versant interface is standard ODMG API defined in the ODMG mapping for C++. Since the query processing relies heavily on metadata information, we developed a specialised metadata service for easy retrieval of class metadata from the EGTV Schema Repository.

7   Conclusions

The EGTV project involves the top-down design of a federated database system of text-based and multimedia data. The top-down approach allowed us to choose target database systems and models, but the heterogeneity across the standard for O-O and O-R databases meant that neither language met the requirements of a canonical query interface. Thus, we developed a new language and processor using conventional syntax but with different semantics for specific query types. This paper concentrated on the query and update semantics for the EGTV Query Language. Specifically, we provide syntax, semantics and a description of processing functionality. Its contribution is the clear semantics in terms of query input and output (over existing language standards); the provision of an algebra for query evaluation; the update capabilities (supported by the model) and the open specification of the query processing semantics (in the form of a tree) to later optimisation techniques. The current focus is on the optimisation of both the object materialisation strategy (described in earlier work), and the query evaluation methodology described here, as both can be refined in order to improve query performance. The management of behaviour is crucial to the performance of multimedia queries and although its discussion is not within the scope of this paper, EQL fully supports the invocation of operations as defined in EGTV classes.

References

1. D. Bećarević. Querying Heterogeneous Data Sources. *Technical Report ISG-04-01 www.computing.dcu.ie/˜isg*, pages 1–25, 2004.
2. M. Carey, L. Haas, P. Schwarz, M. Arya, W. Cody, R. Fagin, M. Flickner, A. Luniewski, W. Niblack, D. Petkovic, J. Thomas, J. Williams, and E. Wimmers. Towards Heterogeneous Multimedia Information Systems: The Garlic Approach. In *Proceedings of the Fifth International Workshop on Research Issues in Data Engineering (RIDE): Distributed Object Management*, pages 124–131. IEEE-CS, 1995.
3. R. Catell and D. Barry. *The Object Data Standard: ODMG 3.0*. Morgan Kaufmann, 1999.
4. A. Dogac, C. Ozkan, B. Arpinar, and T. Okay. METU object-oriented DBMS. In *On Object-Oriented Database Systems*, pages 513–541. Springer Verlag, 1994.
5. R. Elmasri and S. Navathe. *Fundamentals of Database Systems*. Addison Wesley, 1994.
6. P. Gulutzan and T. Pelzer. *SQL-99 Complete, Really*. R&D Books, 1999.
7. D. Kambur, D. Bećarević, and M. Roantree. An Object Model Interface for Supporting Method Storage. *In proceedings of the 7th East European Conference on Advances in Databases and Information Systems ADBIS*, 2003.
8. D. Kambur and M. Roantree. Storage of complex business rules in object databases. *5th International Conference on Enterprise Information Systems (ICEIS 2003)*, 2003.
9. H. Lee, A. Smeaton, C. O'Toole, N. Murphy, S. Marlow, and N. O'Connor. The Físchlár Digital Video Recording, Analysis, and Browsing System. In *Proceedings of the RIAO 2000 - Content-based Multimedia Information Access*, pages 1390–1399, 2000.
10. M. Roantree and D. Bećarević. Metadata Usage in Multimedia Federations. In *First International Meta informatics Symposium (MIS 2002)*, pages 132–147, 2002.
11. M. Scholl, C. Laasch, C. Rich, H. Schek, and M. Tresch. The COCOON object model. *Technical Report 211*, Dept of Computer Science, ETH Zurich, 1994.
12. A. Sheth and J. Larson. Federated Database Systems for Managing Distributed, heterogeneous and Autonomous Databases. 22(3):183–226, 1990.
13. K. Subieta, C. Beeri, F. Matthes, and J. Schmidt. A Stack-Based Approach to Query Languages. In *Proceedings of the Second International East/West Workshop*, pages 159–180. Springer Verlag, 1994.

XML Data Integration by Graph Restructuring

Lucas Zamboulis

School of Computer Science and Information Systems,
Birkbeck College, University of London, London WC1E 7HX
lucas@dcs.bbk.ac.uk

Abstract. This paper describes the integration of XML data sources within the AutoMed heterogeneous data integration system. The paper presents a description of the overall framework, as well as an overview of and comparison with related work and implemented solutions by other researchers. The main contribution of this research is an algorithm for the integration of XML data sources, based on graph restructuring of their schemas.

1 Introduction

The advent of XML as a new data format has given rise to new research issues. XML is the first step towards the realization of the Semantic Web vision. It is a markup language designed to structure and transmit data in an easy to manipulate form, however it is not the total solution — it does not do anything by itself. The second step consists of logic inference tools and tools that automate tasks which have been manual up to now. For this, well-studied research issues concerning mostly relational data need to be explored in the context of XML data. Such issues include schema matching and data integration, both virtual and materialized. In this paper we focus on the virtual integration of heterogeneous XML data sources by transforming the schemas of XML documents using graph restructuring techniques.

Section 2.1 provides an overview of the AutoMed system, and the AutoMed approach to data integration. Section 2.2 presents the schema definition language used for XML data, specifies its representation in terms of AutoMed's Common Data Model and presents the unique IDs used in our framework. Section 3 presents the schema transformation algorithm and describes the query engine and wrapper architecture. Section 4 reviews related work, while Section 5 gives our concluding remarks.

2 Our XML Data Integration Framework

2.1 Overview of AutoMed

AutoMed is a heterogeneous data integration system that supports a schema-transformation approach to data integration (see http://www.doc.ic.ac.uk/automed). Figure 1 shows the AutoMed integration approach in an XML setting.

H. Williams and L. MacKinnon (Eds.): BNCOD 2004, LNCS 3112, pp. 57–71, 2004.

Each data source is described by a data source schema, denoted by S_i, which is transformed into a union-compatible schema US_i by a series of reversible primitive transformations, thereby creating a transformation pathway between a data source schema and its respective union-compatible schema. All the union schemas[1] are syntactically identical and this is asserted by a series of id transformations between each pair US_i and US_{i+1} of union schemas. id is a special type of primitive transformation that 'matches' two syntactically identical constructs in two different union schemas, signifying their semantic equivalence. The transformation pathway containing these id transformations can be automatically generated. An arbitrary one of the union schemas can then be designated as the global schema GS, or selected for further transformation into a new schema that will become the global schema.

The transformation of a data source schema into a union schema is accomplished by applying a series of primitive transformations, each adding, deleting or renaming one schema construct. Each add and delete transformation is accompanied by a query specifying the extent of the newly added or deleted construct in terms of the other schema constructs. This query is expressed in AutoMed's Intermediate Query Language, IQL [16,8]. The query supplied with a primitive transformation provides the necessary information to make primitive transformations automatically reversible. This means that AutoMed is a **both-as-view (BAV)** data integration system [14]. It subsumes the local-as-view (LAV) global-as-view (GAV) and GLAV approaches, as it is possible to extract a definition of the global schema as a view over the data source schemas, and it is also possible to extract definitions of the data source schemas as views over the global schema [14,9].

In Figure 1, each US_i may contain information that cannot be derived from the corresponding S_i. These constructs are not inserted in the US_i through an add transformation, but rather through an extend transformation. This takes a pair of queries that specify a lower and an upper bound on the extent of the new construct. The lower bound may be Void and the upper bound may be Any, which respectively indicate no known information about the lower or upper bound of the extent of the new construct. There may also be information present in a data source schema S_i that should not be present within the corresponding US_i, and this is removed with a contract transformation, rather than with a delete transformation. Like extend, contract takes a pair of queries specifying a lower and upper bound on the extent of the deleted construct.

In our XML data integration setting, each XML data source is described by an XML DataSource Schema (a simple schema definition language presented in Section 2.2), S_i, and is transformed into an intermediate schema, I_i, by means of a series of primitive transformations that insert, remove, or rename schema constructs. The union schemas US_i are then automatically produced, and they extend each I_i with the constructs of the rest of the intermediate schemas. After that, the id transformation pathways between each pair US_i and US_{i+1} of union schemas are also automatically produced. Our XML integration framework supports both top-down and bottom-up schema integration. With the

---

[1] Henceforth we use the term 'union schema' to mean 'union-compatible schema'.

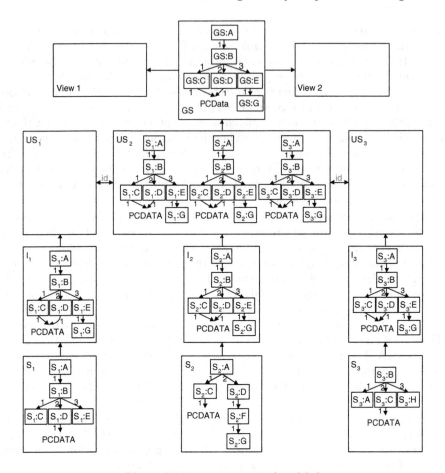

Fig. 1. XML integration in AutoMed

top-down approach, the global schema is predefined, and the data source schemas are restructured to match its structure. With the bottom-up approach, the global schema is not predefined and is automatically generated. Both approaches are described in Section 3.1.

2.2   A Schema for Representing XML Data Sources

When encoding data in XML, there two ways to enforce the intended structure and types over the XML files: DTD and XML Schema. However, as these technologies provide a complex grammar for the file, they describe the possible structure of a file, not the actual one. The structure of an XML file is very important in data integration, both for schema integration and in optimizing query processing. It is also possible that the XML file may have no referenced DTD or XML Schema. For these reasons, we introduce the XML DataSource Schema, which abstracts only the structure of an XML file, omitting information such as data types. The concept of XML DataSource Schema is similar to DataGuides [6]. However, XML DataSource Schemas are XML trees whereas DataGuides are OEM graphs.

To obtain an XML file's XML DataSource Schema, we first copy the XML file into memory, in its DOM representation. This copy will then be modified and become the XML DataSource Schema, according to the following pseudocode:

1. Get the root R. If it has child nodes, get its list of children, L.
   a) Get the first node in L, N. For every other node N' in L that has the same tag as N do:
      - copy any of the attributes of N' not present in N to N
      - copy and append the list of children of N' to the list of children of N
      - delete N' and its subtree
   b) Get the next child from the list of children and process it in the same way as the first child, L, in step (a) above.
2. Treat each one of the nodes in the new list of children of R, as R in step 1.

AutoMed has as its common data model a Hypergraph Data Model (HDM). This is a low-level data model that can represent higher-level modelling languages such as ER, relational, object-oriented and XML [12]. HDM schemas consist of nodes, edges and constraints. The selection of a low-level common data model for AutoMed was intentional, so as to be able to better represent high-level modelling languages without semantic mismatches or ambiguities.

Table 1 shows the representation of XML DataSource Schema constructs in terms of the HDM. XML DataSource Schemas consist of four constructs:

1. An element e can exist by itself and is a nodal construct. It is represented by the scheme $\langle\langle e \rangle\rangle$.
2. An attribute a belonging to an element e is a nodal-linking construct and is represented by the scheme $\langle\langle e, a \rangle\rangle$. In terms of the HDM this means that an attribute actually consists of a node representing the attribute, an edge linking the attribute node to its owner element, and a cardinality constraint.
3. The parent-child relationship between two elements e_p and e_c is a linking construct with scheme $\langle\langle e_p, e_c, i \rangle\rangle$, where i is the order of e_c in the list of children of e_p. In terms of the HDM, this is represented by an edge between e_p and e_c and a cardinality constraint.
4. Text in XML is represented by the PCDATA construct. This is a nodal construct with scheme $\langle\langle \text{PCDATA} \rangle\rangle$. In any schema, there is only one PCDATA construct. To link the PCDATA construct with an element we treat it as an element and use the nest-list construct.

Note that this is a simpler XML schema language than that given in [12]. In our model here, we make specific the ordering of children elements under a common parent in XML DataSource Schemas (the identifiers i in **NestList** schemes) whereas this was not captured by the model in [12]. Also, in that paper it was assumed that the extents of schema constructs are sets and therefore extra constructs 'order' and 'nest-set' were required, to respectively represent the ordering of children nodes under parent nodes, and parent-child relationships

Table 1. XML DataSource Schema representation in terms of HDM

Higher Level Construct	Equivalent HDM Representation
Construct: **Element** Class nodal Scheme $\langle\langle e\rangle\rangle$	Node $\langle\langle xml{:}e\rangle\rangle$
Construct: **Attribute** Class: nodal-linking, constraint Scheme: $\langle\langle e,a\rangle\rangle$	Node $\langle\langle xml{:}e{:}a\rangle\rangle$ Edge $\langle\langle \_, xml{:}e, xml{:}e{:}a\rangle\rangle$ Links $\langle\langle xml{:}e\rangle\rangle$ Cons $makeCard(\langle\langle \_, xml{:}e, xml{:}e{:}a\rangle\rangle, 0{:}1, 1{:}N)$
Construct **NestList** Class linking, constraint Scheme $\langle\langle e_p, e_c, i\rangle\rangle$	Edge $\langle\langle i, xml{:}e_p, xml{:}e_c\rangle\rangle$ Links $\langle\langle xml{:}e_p\rangle\rangle$, $\langle\langle xml{:}e_c\rangle\rangle$ Cons $makeCard(\langle\langle i, xml{:}e_p, xml{:}e_c\rangle\rangle, 0{:}N, 1{:}1)$
Construct: **PCDATA** Class nodal Scheme $\langle\langle \text{PCDATA}\rangle\rangle$	Node $\langle\langle xml{:}\text{PCDATA}\rangle\rangle$

where ordering is not significant. Here, we make use of the fact that IQL is inherently list-based, and thus use only one **NestList** construct. The nth child of a parent node can be specified by means of a query specifying the corresponding nest-list, and the requested node will be the nth item in the IQL result list.

A problem when dealing with XML DataSource Schema is that multiple XML elements can have the same name. The problem is amplified when dealing with multiple files, as in our case. To resolve such ambiguities, a unique IDs assignment technique had to be devised. For XML DataSource Schemas, the assignment technique is $\langle schemaName\rangle{:}\langle elementName\rangle{:}\langle count\rangle$, where $\langle schemaName\rangle$ is the schema name as defined in the AutoMed repository and $\langle count\rangle$ is a counter incremented every time the same $\langle elementName\rangle$ is encountered, in a depth-first traversal of the schema. As for XML documents themselves, the same technique is used, except that the unique identifiers for elements are of the form $\langle schemaName\rangle{:}\langle elementName\rangle{:}\langle count\rangle{:}\langle instance\rangle$ where $\langle instance\rangle$ is a counter incremented every time a new instance of the corresponding schema element is encountered in the document.

After a modelling language has been defined in terms of HDM via the API of AutoMed's Model Definition Repository [1], a set of primitive transformations is automatically available for the transformation of the schemas defined in the language, as discussed in Section 2.1.

3   Framework Components

Our research focuses on the development of semi-automatic methods for generating the schema transformation pathways shown in Figure 1. The first step is a schema matching [17] process, using for example data mining, or semantic mappings to ontologies. Both approaches can be used to automatically generate fragments of AutoMed transformation pathways — see for example [19]. Once this process reveals the semantic equivalences between schema constructs, the algorithm we describe in Section 3.1 integrates the XML DataSource Schemas by transforming each one into its respective union schema, using graph restructuring techniques. When several sources have been integrated, the global schema can be used for querying the data sources, as described in Section 3.2.

3.1   Schema Transformation Algorithm

Our schema transformation algorithm can be applied in two ways: top-down, where the global schema is predefined and the data source schemas are transformed to match it, regardless of any loss of information; or bottom-up, where there is no predefined global schema and the information of all the data sources is preserved. Both approaches create the transformation pathways that produce intermediate schemas with identical structure. These schemas are then automatically transformed into the union schemas US_i of Figure 1, including the id transformation pathways between them. The transformation pathway from one of the US_i to GS can then be produced in one of two ways: either automatically, using 'append' semantics, or semi-automatically, in which case the queries supplied with the transformations that specify the integration need to be supplied by the user. By 'append' semantics we mean that the extents of the constructs of GS are created by appending the extents of the corresponding constructs of $US_1, US_2, \ldots, US_n$ in turn. Thus, if the XML data sources were integrated in a different order, the extent of each construct of GS would contain the same instances, but their ordering would be different.

Top-down approach: Consider a setting where a global schema GS is given, and the data source schemas need to be conformed to it, without necessarily preserving their information capacity. Our algorithm works in two phases. In the growing phase, GS is traversed and every construct not present in a data source schema S_i is inserted. In the shrinking phase, each schema S_i is traversed and any construct not present in the global schema is removed.

The algorithm to transform an XML DataSource Schema S_1 to have the same structure as an XML DataSource Schema S_2 is specified below. This algorithm considers an element in S_1 to be equivalent to an element in S_2 if they have the same element name. As specified below, the algorithm assumes that element names in both S_1 and S_2 are unique. We discuss shortly the necessary extensions to cater for cases when this does not hold.

Growing phase: consider every element E in S_2 in a depth-first order:

1. If E does not exist in S_1:
   a) Search S_1 to find an attribute a with the same name as the name of E in S_2
      i. If such an attribute is found, **add** E to S_1 with the extent of a and **add** an edge from the element in S_1 equivalent to $owner(a, S_2)$ to E.
      ii. Otherwise, **extend** E. Then find the equivalent element of $parent(E, S_1)$ in S_2 and **add** an edge from it to E with an **extend** transformation.
      iii. In both cases, insert the attributes of E from schema S_2 as attributes to the newly inserted element E in S_1 with **add** or **extend**

transformations, depending on if it is possible to describe the extent of an attribute using the rest of the constructs of S_1. Note that one or more of these insertions might result in the transformation of an element in S_1 into an attribute.

    b) If E is linked to the PCDATA construct in S_2:

        i. If the PCDATA construct is not present in S_1, insert it with an `extend` transformation, then insert an edge from E to the PCDATA construct, also with an `extend` transformation.

        ii. Otherwise, `add` an edge from E to the PCDATA construct.

2. If E exists in S_1 and $parent(E, S_2) = parent(E, S_1)$:

    a) Insert any attributes of E in S_2 that do not appear in E in S_1, similarly to 1(a)iii.

    b) If E is linked to the PCDATA construct in S_2, do the same as in 1b.

3. If E exists in S_1 and $parent(E, S_2) \neq parent(E, S_1)$:

    a) Insert an edge from E_P to E, where E_P is the equivalent element of $parent(E, S_2)$ in S_1. This insertion can either be an `add` or an `extend` transformation, depending on the path from E_P to E. The algorithm finds the shortest path from E_P to E, and, if it includes only parent-to-child edges, then the transformation is an `add`, otherwise it is an `extend`.

    b) Insert any attributes of E in S_2 that do not appear in E in S_1, similarly to 1(a)iii.

    c) If E is linked to the PCDATA construct in S_2, do the same as in 1b.

Shrinking phase: traverse S_1 and remove any constructs not present in S_2.

Renaming phase: traverse S_1 and rename edge labels as necessary to create a contiguous ordering of identifiers.

In step 3a, the algorithm decides whether to issue an `add` or an `extend` transformation, depending on the type of edges the path from E_P to E contains. To explain this, suppose that the path contains at some point an edge (B, A), where actually, in S_1, element A is the parent of element B. It may be the case that in the data source of S_1, there are some instances of A that do not have instances of B as children. As a result, when migrating data from the data source of S_1 to schema S_2, some data will be lost, specifically those A instances without any B children. To remedy this, the `extend` transformation is issued with both a lower and an upper bound query. The first query retrieves the actual data from the data source of S_1, but perhaps losing some data because of the problem just described. The second query retrieves all the data that the first query retrieves, but also generates new instances of B (with unique IDs) in order to preserve the instances of A that the lower bound query was not able to. Such a behaviour may not always be desired, so the user has the option of telling the algorithm to just use `Any` as the upper bound query in such cases.

An example application of the algorithm is illustrated in Figure 2. The corresponding transformation pathway is shown in Table 2 and is divided into three sections. The first one illustrates the growing phase, where schema S_1 is augmented with the constructs from schema S_2. The second illustrates the shrinking phase, where the constructs of S_1 that do not appear in S_2 are removed. The first one illustrates the growing phase, the second the shrinking phase, and the third the renaming phase. The `generateElemUID` function generates element instances

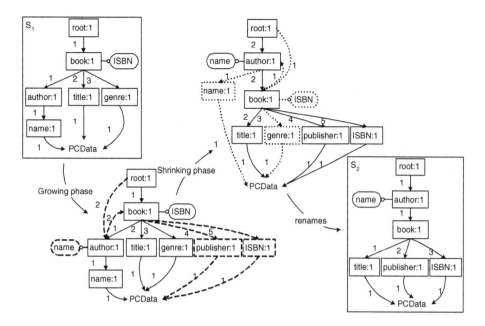

Fig. 2. Example Schema Transformation.

from attribute instances and is useful whenever an attribute is transformed into an element, and vice versa — see g_7–g_9 and s_2–s_4 in Table 2.

Combining AutoMed's insert and remove operations allows more complex transformations to be achieved. For instance, in step 1(a)i of the algorithm, an attribute is transformed into an element, e.g. see g_7 in Table 2; in step 1(a)iii, elements may be transformed into attributes, e.g. see g_2. Finally, step 3a of the algorithm simulates a move operation [3], e.g. see g_3.

The algorithm presented above assumes that element names in both S_1 and S_2 are unique. In general, this may not be the case and we may have (a) multiple occurrences of an element name in S_1 and a single occurrence in S_2, or (b) multiple occurrences of an element name in S_2 and a single occurrence in S_1, or (c) multiple occurrences of an element name in both S_1 and S_2.

For case (a), the algorithm needs to generate a query that constructs the extent of the single element in S_2 by combining the extents of all three elements from S_1. For case (b), the algorithm needs to make a choice of which of the elements from S_1 to migrate the extent of the single element in S_2 to. For this, a heuristic can be applied which favours (i) paths with the fewest **extend** steps, and (ii) the shortest of such paths. For case (c), a combination of the solutions for (a) and (b) needs to be applied.

Bottom-up approach: In this approach, a global schema GS is not present and is produced automatically from the source schemas, without loss of information. A slightly different version of the above schema transformation algorithm is applied to the data source schemas in a pairwise fashion, in order to

Table 2. Transformations for Figure 2.

g_1: $addNestList(\langle\langle root{:}1\rangle\rangle, \langle\langle author{:}1\rangle\rangle, 2, [\{r,a\}|\{r,b\} \leftarrow \langle\langle root{:}1, book{:}1, 1\rangle\rangle;$
$\qquad\qquad\qquad\qquad\qquad\qquad\qquad \{b,a\} \leftarrow \langle\langle book{:}1, author{:}1, 1\rangle\rangle])$

g_2: $addAttribute(\langle\langle author{:}1\rangle\rangle, \langle\langle author{:}1, name\rangle\rangle,$
$\qquad\qquad [\{a,p\}|\{a,n\} \leftarrow \langle\langle author{:}1, name{:}1\rangle\rangle; \{n,p\} \leftarrow \langle\langle name{:}1, PCDATA\rangle\rangle])$

g_3: $extendNestList(\langle\langle author{:}1\rangle\rangle, \langle\langle book{:}1\rangle\rangle, 2,$
$\qquad\qquad\qquad\qquad\qquad [\{a,b\}|\{b,a\} \leftarrow \langle\langle book{:}1, author{:}1, 1\rangle\rangle], Any)$

g_4: $extendElement(\langle\langle publisher{:}1\rangle\rangle, Void, Any)$

g_5: $extendNestList(\langle\langle book{:}1\rangle\rangle, \langle\langle publisher{:}1\rangle\rangle, 4, Void, Any)$

g_6: $extendNestList(\langle\langle publisher{:}1\rangle\rangle, \langle\langle PCDATA\rangle\rangle, 1, Void, Any)$

g_7: $addElement(\langle\langle ISBN{:}1\rangle\rangle,$
$\qquad [\{o\}|\{b,i\} \leftarrow \langle\langle book{:}1, ISBN\rangle\rangle; \{o\} \leftarrow generateElemUID \{b,i\} \langle\langle ISBN{:}1\rangle\rangle])$

g_8: $addNestList(\langle\langle book{:}1\rangle\rangle, \langle\langle ISBN{:}1\rangle\rangle, 5,$
$\qquad [\{b,o\}|\{b,i\} \leftarrow \langle\langle book{:}1, ISBN\rangle\rangle; \{o\} \leftarrow generateElemUID \{b,i\} \langle\langle ISBN{:}1\rangle\rangle])$

g_9: $addNestList(\langle\langle ISBN{:}1\rangle\rangle, \langle\langle PCDATA\rangle\rangle, 1,$
$\qquad [\{o,i\}|\{b,i\} \leftarrow \langle\langle book{:}1, ISBN\rangle\rangle; \{o\} \leftarrow generateElemUID \{b,i\} \langle\langle ISBN{:}1\rangle\rangle])$

s_1: $deleteNestList(\langle\langle root{:}1\rangle\rangle, \langle\langle book{:}1\rangle\rangle,$
$\qquad\qquad [\{r,b\}|\{r,a\} \leftarrow \langle\langle root{:}1, author{:}1, 2\rangle\rangle; \{a,b\} \leftarrow \langle\langle author{:}1, book{:}1, 2\rangle\rangle])$

s_2: $deleteNestList(\langle\langle author{:}1\rangle\rangle, \langle\langle name{:}1\rangle\rangle,$
$\qquad [\{a,o\}|\{a,n\} \leftarrow \langle\langle author{:}1, name\rangle\rangle; \{o\} \leftarrow generateElemUID \{a,n\} \langle\langle name{:}1\rangle\rangle])$

s_3: $deleteNestList(\langle\langle name{:}1\rangle\rangle, \langle\langle PCDATA\rangle\rangle,$
$\qquad [\{o,n\}|\{a,n\} \leftarrow \langle\langle author{:}1, name\rangle\rangle; \{o\} \leftarrow generateElemUID \{a,n\} \langle\langle name{:}1\rangle\rangle])$

s_4: $deleteElement(\langle\langle name{:}1\rangle\rangle,$
$\qquad [\{o\}|\{a,n\} \leftarrow \langle\langle author{:}1, name\rangle\rangle; \{o\} \leftarrow generateElemUID \{a,n\} \langle\langle name{:}1\rangle\rangle])$

s_5: $deleteAttribute(\langle\langle book{:}1{:}ISBN\rangle\rangle,$
$\qquad\qquad [\{o\}|\{b,i\} \leftarrow \langle\langle book{:}1, ISBN{:}1\rangle\rangle; \{i,p\} \leftarrow \langle\langle ISBN{:}1, PCDATA\rangle\rangle])$

s_6: $contractNestList(\langle\langle book{:}1\rangle\rangle, \langle\langle author{:}1\rangle\rangle,$
$\qquad\qquad\qquad\qquad\qquad [\{b,a\}|\{a,b\} \leftarrow \langle\langle author{:}1, book{:}1, 2\rangle\rangle], Any)$

s_7: $contractNestList(\langle\langle book{:}1, genre{:}1, 3\rangle\rangle, Void, Any)$

s_8: $contractNestList(\langle\langle genre{:}1, PCDATA, 1\rangle\rangle, Void, Any)$

s_9: $contractElement(\langle\langle genre{:}1\rangle\rangle, Void, Any)$

r_1: $renameNestList(\langle\langle root{:}1, author{:}1, 2\rangle\rangle, \langle\langle root{:}1, author{:}1, 1\rangle\rangle)$

r_2: $renameNestList(\langle\langle author{:}1, book{:}1, 2\rangle\rangle, \langle\langle author{:}1, book{:}1, 1\rangle\rangle)$

r_3: $renameNestList(\langle\langle book{:}1, title{:}1, 2\rangle\rangle, \langle\langle book{:}1, title{:}1, 1\rangle\rangle)$

r_4: $renameNestList(\langle\langle book{:}1, publisher{:}1, 4\rangle\rangle, \langle\langle book{:}1, publisher{:}1, 2\rangle\rangle)$

r_5: $renameNestList(\langle\langle book{:}1, ISBN{:}1, 5\rangle\rangle, \langle\langle book{:}1, ISBN{:}1, 3\rangle\rangle)$

incrementally derive each one's union-compatible schema (Figure 3). The data source schemas S_i are first transformed into intermediate schemas, IS_i. Then, the union schemas, US_i, are produced along with the id transformations. To start with, the intermediate schema of the first data source schema is itself, $S_1 = IS_1^1$. Then, the schema transformation algorithm is employed on IS_1^1 and S_2 (see annotation 1 in Figure 3) The algorithm augments IS_1^1 with the constructs from S_2 it does not contain. It also restructures S_2 to match the structure of IS_1^1, also augmenting it with the constructs from IS_1^1 it does not contain. As a result, IS_1^1 is transformed to IS_1^2, while S_2 is transformed to IS_2^1. The same process is performed between IS_2^1 and S_3, resulting in the creation of IS_2^2 and IS_3^1

(annotation 2). The algorithm is then applied between IS_1^2 and IS_2^2, resulting only in the creation of IS_1^3, since this time IS_1^2 does not have any constructs IS_2^2 does not contain (annotation 3). The remaining intermediate schemas are generated in the same manner: to produce schema IS_i, the schema transformation algorithm is employed on IS_{i-1}^1 and S_i, resulting in the creation of IS_{i-1}^2 and IS_i^1; all other intermediate schemas except IS_{i-1}^2 and IS_i^1 are then extended with the constructs of S_i they do not contain. Finally, we automatically generate the union schemas, US_i, the id transformations between them, and the global schema (by using append semantics).

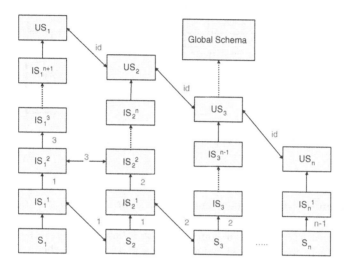

Fig. 3. XML DataSource Schema integration

3.2   Querying XML Files

AutoMed's query engine and wrapper architecture are shown in Figure 4. The `AutoMedWrapperFactory` and `AutoMedWrapper` classes are abstract classes that implement some of the abstract methods, while the `XMLWrapperFactory` and `XMLWrapper` classes implement the remaining abstract methods. Factories deal with model specific aspects, e.g. primary keys for relational databases. The XML-specific factory class contains a validating switch. When it is on, the parsing of the XML file the `XMLWrapper` object is attached to is performed by consulting the DTD/XML Schema the file references. A number of switches, e.g. a switch for collapsing whitespace, will be added in the future. As Figure 4 indicates, the architecture is extensible with wrappers for new data source models.

After the generation of transformation pathways by either top-down or bottom-up integration, queries submitted to the global schema can be evaluated.

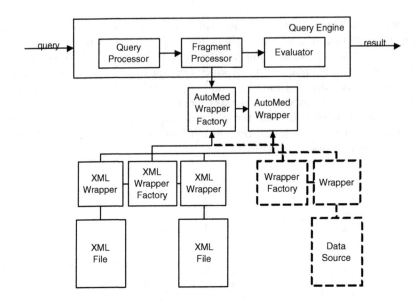

Fig. 4. AutoMed's query engine & wrapper architecture

A query submitted to the query engine is first processed by the query processor, which is responsible for reformulating it into a query that can be evaluated over the data sources. This is accomplished by following the reverse transformation pathways from the global schema to the data source schemas. Each time a `delete`, `contract` or `rename` transformation is encountered, it replaces any occurrences of the removed or renamed scheme with the query supplied with the transformation. As a result, the original query is turned into a query that can be evaluated on the data sources — see [16,9]. The fragment processor replaces IQL subqueries by XML wrapper objects. The evaluator then evaluates the query, making a call to the XML wrapper object where necessary. At present, querying of XML files is performed by translating IQL queries into XPath. Future plans include XQuery support.

As an example, suppose that schemas S_1 and S_2 of Figure 2 have been integrated into the global schema GS of Figure 5 which is the global schema in this integration scenario. In order to retrieve the title and genre of each book in the global schema, the following query is submitted to GS (for simplicity, we omit here the element counter from each element name):

$$[\{b,t\}|\{b,i\} \leftarrow \langle\langle book, title\rangle\rangle; \{i,t\} \leftarrow \langle\langle title, PCDATA\rangle\rangle] \;++$$
$$[\{b,g\}|\{b,i\} \leftarrow \langle\langle book, genre\rangle\rangle; \{i,g\} \leftarrow \langle\langle genre, PCDATA\rangle\rangle]$$

The fragments of the transformation pathways from S_1 and S_2 to GS of relevance to this query are:

$S_1 \rightarrow GS$:
$extendElement(\langle\langle publisher{:}1\rangle\rangle, Void, Any)$
$extendNestList(\langle\langle book{:}1\rangle\rangle, \langle\langle publisher{:}1\rangle\rangle, Void, Any)$
$extendNestList(\langle\langle publisher{:}1\rangle\rangle, \langle\langle \text{PCDATA}{:}1\rangle\rangle, Void, Any)$

$S_2 \rightarrow GS$:
$extendElement(\langle\langle genre{:}1\rangle\rangle, Void, Any)$
$extendNestList(\langle\langle book{:}1\rangle\rangle, \langle\langle genre{:}1\rangle\rangle, Void, Any)$
$extendNestList(\langle\langle genre{:}1\rangle\rangle, \langle\langle \text{PCDATA}{:}1\rangle\rangle, Void, Any)$

Traversing the pathways $GS \rightarrow US_1$ and $GS \rightarrow US_2$, the above query is reformulated to:

$[\{b,t\}|\{b,i\} \leftarrow (US_1{:}\langle\langle book, title\rangle\rangle \; {+}{+} \; US_2{:}\langle\langle book, title\rangle\rangle);$
$\qquad \{i,t\} \leftarrow (US_1{:}\langle\langle title, PCDATA\rangle\rangle \; {+}{+} \; US_2{:}\langle\langle title, PCDATA\rangle\rangle)] \; {+}{+}$
$[\{b,g\}|\{b,i\} \leftarrow (US_1{:}\langle\langle book, genre\rangle\rangle \; {+}{+} \; US_2{:}\langle\langle book, genre\rangle\rangle);$
$\qquad \{i,g\} \leftarrow (US_1{:}\langle\langle genre, PCDATA\rangle\rangle \; {+}{+} \; US_2{:}\langle\langle genre, PCDATA\rangle\rangle)]$

Then, traversing the pathways $US_1 \rightarrow S_1$ and $US_2 \rightarrow S_2$, we obtain:

$[\{b,t\}|\{b,i\} \leftarrow (S_1{:}\langle\langle book, title\rangle\rangle \; {+}{+} \; S_2{:}\langle\langle book, title\rangle\rangle);$
$\qquad \{i,t\} \leftarrow (S_1{:}\langle\langle title, PCDATA\rangle\rangle \; {+}{+} \; S_2{:}\langle\langle title, PCDATA\rangle\rangle)] \; {+}{+}$
$[\{b,g\}|\{b,i\} \leftarrow (S_1{:}\langle\langle book, genre\rangle\rangle \; {+}{+} \; (Void, Any));$
$\qquad \{i,g\} \leftarrow (S_1{:}\langle\langle genre, PCDATA\rangle\rangle \; {+}{+} \; (Void, Any))]$

Instances of (Void,Any) can be eliminated, using the techniques described in [9], giving the following final query:

$[\{b,t\}|\{b,i\} \leftarrow (S_1{:}\langle\langle book, title\rangle\rangle \; {+}{+} \; S_2{:}\langle\langle book, title\rangle\rangle);$
$\qquad \{i,t\} \leftarrow (S_1{:}\langle\langle title, PCDATA\rangle\rangle \; {+}{+} \; S_2{:}\langle\langle title, PCDATA\rangle\rangle)] \; {+}{+}$
$[\{b,g\}|\{b,i\} \leftarrow S_1{:}\langle\langle book, genre\rangle\rangle;$
$\qquad \{i,g\} \leftarrow S_1{:}\langle\langle genre, PCDATA\rangle\rangle]$

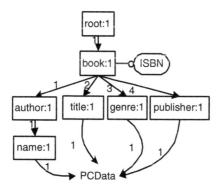

Fig. 5. Global schema GS.

4   Related Work

Schema matching is a problem well-studied in a relational database setting. A recent survey on schema matching is [17]. A machine-learning approach to schema matching is [4] and an approach using neural networks is [11]; however both approaches are semi-automatic. In [10], the schema authors provide themselves the semantics of the schema elements, by providing mappings between elements of their schemas to a global ontology.

Concerning schema integration, Clio [15] first transforms the data source schemas, XML or relational, into an internal representation. Then, after the mappings between the source and the target schemas have been semi-automatically derived, Clio materializes the target schema with the data of the source, using a set of internal rules, based on the mappings. DIXSE [20] follows a similar approach, as it transforms the DTD specifications of the source documents into an inner conceptual representation, with some heuristics to capture semantics. Most work, though, is done semi-automatically by the domain experts that augment the conceptual schema with semantics. The approach in [18] has an abstract global DTD, expressed as a tree, very similar to a global ontology. The connection between this DTD and the DTDs of the data sources is through path mappings: each path between two nodes in a source DTD is mapped to a path in the abstract DTD. Then, query rewriting is employed to query the sources.

In the context of virtual data integration, SilkRoute [5] and XPERANTO [2] are both middleware systems that use query rewriting to translate user queries submitted in XML query languages to the language of the underlying data sources. These systems are GAV. The approach in [7] on the other hand combines GAV, LAV and GLAV integration rules in a peer-to-peer setting.

The framework we have presented in this paper approaches the XML data integration problem using graph restructuring techniques. Our approach allows for the use of multiple types of schema matching methods (use of ontologies, semantics provided in RDF, data-mining), which can all serve as an input to the schema integration algorithm. The main contributions of the work presented here is the automatic integration of XML data using a purely XML solution.

5   Concluding Remarks

This paper has presented a framework for the virtual integration of XML data within the AutoMed heterogeneous data integration system. Assuming a semi-automatic schema matching process, the schema transformation algorithm succeeds in integrating XML data sources automatically. The algorithm makes use of a simple schema definition language for XML data sources and an assignment technique for unique identifiers, both developed specifically for the purposes of XML data integration. The novelty of the algorithm is the use of XML-specific graph restructuring techniques. Our framework also supports the materialization of the virtual global schema, as discussed in [21].

We note that our schema transformation algorithm can also be applied in a peer-to-peer setting. Suppose there is a peer P_T that needs to query XML data stored at a peer P_S. We can consider P_S as the peer whose XML DataSource

Schema needs to be transformed to the XML DataSource Schema of peer P_T. After the application of our algorithm, P_T can then query P_S for the data it needs via its own schema, since AutoMed's query engine can treat the schema of P_T as the 'global' schema and the schema of P_S' as the 'local schema'.

Evolution of applications or changing performance requirements may cause the schema of a data source to change. In the AutoMed project, research has already focused on the schema evolution problem in the context of virtual data integration [13,14]. For future work we will investigate the application of these general solutions specifically for XML. The main advantage of AutoMed's both-as-view approach in this context is that it is based on pathways of reversible schema transformations. This enables the development of algorithms that update the transformation pathways and the global schema, instead of regenerating them when data source schemas are modified. These algorithms can be fully automatic if the information content of a data source schema remains the same or contracts, though require domain knowledge or human intervention if it expands.

References

1. M. Boyd, P. McBrien, and N. Tong. The AutoMed Schema Integration Repository. In *Proceedings of the 19th British National Conference on Databases*, pages 42–45. Springer-Verlag, 2002.
2. M. Carey, D. Florescu, Z. Ives, Y. Lu, J. Shanmugasundaram, E. Shekita, and S. Subramanian. XPERANTO: Publishing Object-Relational Data as XML. In *WebDB (Informal Proceedings)*, pages 105–110, 2000.
3. G. Cobena, S. Abiteboul, and A. Marian. Detecting Changes in XML Documents. In *ICDE (Data Engineering, also in BDA 2001)*, 2002.
4. A. Doan, P. Domingos, and A. Halevy. Reconciling Schemas of Disparate Data Sources: A Machine-Learning Approach. In *SIGMOD Conference*, 2001.
5. M. Fernandez, A. Morishima, and D. Suciu. Efficient Evaluation of XML Middle-ware Queries. In *SIGMOD Conference*, 2001.
6. R. Goldman and J. Widom. DataGuides: Enabling Query Formulation and Optimization in Semistructured Databases. In *VLDB'97, Proceedings of 23rd International Conference on Very Large Data Bases*, pages 436–445, 1997.
7. Alon Halevy, Zachary Ives, Peter Mork, and Igor Tatarinov. Piazza: Data management infrastructure for semantic web. In *Proceedings of the Twelfth International World Wide Web Conference*, pages 556–567. ACM, May 2003.
8. E. Jasper, A. Poulovassilis, and L. Zamboulis. Processing IQL Queries and Migrating Data in the AutoMed toolkit. AutoMed Technical Report 20, June 2003.
9. E. Jasper, N. Tong, P. Brien, and A. Poulovassilis. View Generation and Optimisation in the AutoMed Data Integration Framework. AutoMed Technical Report 16, October 2003. To appear in *6th International Baltic Conference on Databases & Information Systems 2004*.
10. L. Lakshmanan and F. Sadri. XML Interoperability. In *ACM SIGMOD Workshop on Web and Databases (WebDB), San Diego, CA*, pages 19–24, June 2003.
11. W. Li and C. Clifton. SEMINT: A tool for identifying attribute correspondences in heterogeneous databases using neural networks. In *VLDB'94, Proceedings of 20th International Conference on Very Large Data Bases*, September 1994.

12. P. McBrien and A. Poulovassilis. A Semantic Approach to Integrating XML and Structured Data Sources. In *Conference on Advanced Information Systems Engineering*, pages 330–345, 2001.
13. P. McBrien and A. Poulovassilis. Schema Evolution In Heterogeneous Database Architectures, A Schema Transformation Approach. In *CAiSE*, pages 484–499, 2002.
14. P. McBrien and A. Poulovassilis. Data integration by bi-directional schema transformation rules. In *19th International Conference on Data Engineering*. ICDE, March 2003.
15. L. Popa, Y. Velegrakis, R.J. Miller, M.A. Hernandez, and R. Fagin. Translating Web Data. In *Proc. VLDB'02*, pages 598–609, 2002.
16. A. Poulovassilis. The AutoMed Intermediate Query Langauge. AutoMed Technical Report 2, June 2001.
17. E. Rahm and P. Bernstein. A survey of approaches to automatic schema matching. *VLDB Journal*, 10(4):334–350, 2001.
18. C. Reynaud, J.P. Sirot, and D. Vodislav. Semantic Integration of XML Heterogeneous Data Sources. In *IDEAS*, pages 199–208. IEEE Computer Society, 2001.
19. N. Rizopoulos. BAV Transformations on Relational Schemas Based on Semantic Relationships between Attributes. AutoMed Technical Report 22, August 2003.
20. P. Rodriguez-Gianolli and J. Mylopoulos. A Semantic Approach to XML-based Data Integration. In *ER*, volume 2224 of *Lecture Notes in Computer Science*, pages 117–132. Springer, November 2001.
21. L. Zamboulis. XML Data Integration By Graph Restructuring. AutoMed Technical Report 27, February 2004.

AUP: Adaptive Change Propagation Across Data Model Boundaries

Kajal Claypool[1] and Elke A. Rundensteiner[2]

[1] Computer Science Department, University of Massachusetts - Lowell
[2] Computer Science Department, Worcester Polytechnic Institute
kajal@cs.uml.edu, rundenst@cs.wpi.edu

Abstract. Although databases focus on the longevity of data, rarely is this data or its structure static. This is particularly true in some domains such as the protein databases that have seen and continue to see an exponential growth rate. Managing the effects of change on derived information (views, web pages) and on applications has been recognized as an important problem. Previous research efforts have developed techniques to both propagate sources changes to views as well as techniques to hide the change from the views and other dependent applications. While this continues to be an active area of research, the problem of management of the effects of change is further compounded by the semantic and the structural heterogeneity that in practice often exists between the source and the derived target information. In this work we now examine and address the problem of change propagation across these semantic and structural heterogeneity barriers. This work is based on our previous work Sangam, which provides explicit modeling of the mapping of one data model to another in the middle-layer. In this work, we now present an adaptive propagation algorithm that can incrementally propagate both schema and data changes from the source to the target in a data model independent manner using the Sangam framework as enabling technology. We present a case study of the maintenance of relational views of XML sources to illustrate our approach.

Keywords: Cross Model Mapping Algebra, Heterogeneous System Integration, Schema Transformation

1 Introduction

A fundamental aspect of information that DBMSs must deal with is that of change. Not only is it difficult to pre-determine the database schema for many complex applications during the first pass, but worse yet application requirements typically change over time. Such changes often manifest themselves as changes in the data as well as changes in the structure, i.e., the schema. This is in particular true of molecular biology databases that are currently experiencing an exponential growth rate [2]. For this reason, commercial database systems [11] provide support for schema evolution as well as for the specification of data changes. However, beyond this basic support for change, systems must also provide adequate support to manage the effect of change on derived information and dependent applications. Two common approaches taken in previous work to address

H. Williams and L. MacKinnon (Eds.): BNCOD 2004, LNCS 3112, pp. 72–83, 2004.

this are *change propagation* [18,15,10] wherein the change in the source schema or data is propagated directly to the derived information, a view in most cases; and *transparent propagation* [14] wherein the system attempts to *hide* the change when possible thereby causing little to no interruption in the working of the dependent applications.

In current electronic environments where information or subsets of information are often published in many different forms and formats, maintenance of this published information in the face of source changes is an especially challenging problem. Current research focused on the publishing of XML views for relational sources [16] has looked at the maintenance [17] of both the XML views in light of relational changes, and maintenance of relational sources with XML view changes [17]. Tatarinov et al. [17] have presented data update primitives and an algorithm that translates data changes from XML source to the relational views. As opposed to many of the view maintenance algorithms [18,15,10] which offer a "one algorithm fits all view definitions", the propagation of change across data model boundaries as presented in [17] is tightly coupled to the algorithmic mapping of the source information to the target. In these approaches propagation of change typically implies the apriori translation of the source change to a target change, possibly a set of target changes, based on the mapping used to transform the source schema and data to the target schema and data. Thus, to handle change propagation in today's heterogeneous environment, we would need to provide change translations for each set of possible mappings between each pair of possible data models, a rather tedious task!

In this paper, we now move away from the change translation work that has been done to date to provide an *adaptable* solution to handle the propagation of source changes to the target across data model boundaries. Our work is based on the hypothesis that an adaptable solution to change propagation across data model boundaries must necessarily loosen the tight coupling of the change and the mapping between the source and the target. We thus propose a *middle-layer* based solution wherein first the change in the local database is translated to a sequence of changes in the middle-layer; next each change in the middle-layer is propagated through an algebraic representation of the translation between the source and the target; and finally the net-change is translated to a set of changes that are then applied to the target.

In this work, we use the *Sangam* framework [6,5,7] as our middle-layer. *Sangam*, a meta-modeling approach [1,13] to schema and data integration, is a *transformation environment* that provides a *uniform model* for the representation of linear translations, thereby treating translations as first-class citizens. To facilitate the adaptive propagation, we (1) provide a well-defined set of primitive data and schema update operations for the data model in the middle-layer; (2) show how local changes in the relational or the XML model can be mapped to the primitive update operations; and (3) develop an *adaptive propagation algorithm* that incrementally pushes the change through the modeled transformation to the target.

A unique feature of the *adaptive propagation algorithm* that fundamentally sets it apart from past view maintenance work on SQL [10] and SchemaSQL views [12], is its handling of in situ structural changes to the modeled transformations during the propagation process. Operators in modeled transformations (or mappings) by their very nature exist at the finer granularity of an individual node or edge, unlike SQL or SchemaSQL views where the algebra operators operate on entire sets of data. A change such as the deletion of an attribute, may thus result in the deletion of the node modeling its mapping therein causing an update to the overall structure of the modeled transformation. This is in contrast to view maintenance algorithms that have been presented for SQL views [10] or SchemaSQL views [12] where changes are made in-place on the individual algebra operators with no effect on the overall structure of the algebra tree. The *adaptive propagation algorithm* must thus now also take into account the effect of the change on the overall structure of the modeled transformation. To address this, in this paper we present a unique 2-pass *adaptive propagation algorithm* that adapts the modeled transformation to any structural changes that may occur as a side effect of the update propagation process.

Road-map: The rest of the paper is organized as follows. In Section 2 we present our middle-layer framework, Sangam. Section 3 briefly presents the set of operations defined for updating our graph model, and shows how local relational and XML changes can be translated into changes in the middle-layer. Section 4 presents our incremental propagation algorithm. We conclude in Section 5.

2   Sangam Framework – The Translation Layer

In this section, we briefly describe the two fundamental concepts of the Sangam middle-layer, namely the middle-layer schema model and the uniform model for the translation representation. Due to space constraints, we present these models based on examples, while full details can be found in [6].

2.1   Schema Model

We assume, as in previous modeling approaches [1,13], that schemas from different data models are represented in one common data model. Our middle-layer schema model, called the *Sangam* graph model (SGM), is based on the XML Schema model and can represent schemas from the XML, relational and object models[1].

An instance of the Sangam graph model is called a *Sangam graph*. A Sangam graph $G = (N, E, \lambda)$ is a directed graph of nodes N and edges E, and a set of labels λ. Each node $n \in N$ is either *complex* representing a *user-defined type*; or *atomic* representing a *literal type* such as a *String* or an *integer*. Each node n is assigned a label $l \in \lambda$, and has associated with it an extent of objects, termed *nodeObjects*, where each nodeObject is a pair $< o, v >$, where o is a unique object identifier, and v the data value. Each edge e exists between a parent and a child node, and is annotated with a set of constraints. The constraints include a *local order*, that gives a monotonically increasing, relative local ordering for all outgoing edges from a given node n; and *quantifier* that specifies the minimum and maximum occurrences of the data instances. Each edge also has an associated extent of edgeObjects, where each edgeObject is a four-tuple $< oid, o_1, o_2, ord >$ where oid is a unique identifier, o_1 and o_2 are object identifiers such that o_1 and o_2 are in the extent of the parent and the child node respectively, and ord is the ordinal that denotes the local ordering of the objects of a given parent object o_1.

---

[1] Inheritance in object models is handled via flattening of the hierarchy.

2.2 The Translation Model

The Translation Model $TM = (\mathcal{O}p, \mathcal{C}p)$ represents the set of all possible modeled transformations of a Sangam graph. Here $\mathcal{O}p$ is the set of nodes representing the four basic linear transformation operators [8] namely cross, connect, smooth, and subdivide; and $\mathcal{C}p$ is the set of edge types representing two ways of composing, context dependency and derivation, the transformation operators.

The cross operator, graphically represented by $\otimes$, takes as input a node n in the input Sangam graph G and produces as output a node n' in the output Sangam graph G'. The cross operator is a total mapping, i.e., the nodeObjects in the extent of n given by I (n) are mapped one-to-one to the nodeObjects in the extent of n', I (n') in the output Sangam graph G'. The connect operator, graphically represented by $\ominus$, corresponds to an edge creation in the output graph G'. It takes as input an edge e between two nodes n_1 and n_2 in the input graph G and produces an edge e' between two nodes n_1' and n_2' in G'. All edgeObjects o $\in$ I (e), where I (e) is the extent of e, are also copied as part of this process. The connect operator preserves the annotations of the edge e, i.e., the output edge e' will have the same quantifier and local ordering annotation as the input edge e. The smooth operator, graphically represented by $\ominus$, models the combination of two relationships in G to form one relationship in G'. Let G be a Sangam graph with three nodes n_1, n_2, and n_3, and the two relationships represented by edges e1:$< n_1, n_2 >$ and e2:$< n_2, n_3 >$. The smooth ($\ominus$) operator replaces the relationships represented by edges e1 and e2 in G with a new relationship represented by edge e':$< n_1', n_3' >$ in G'. The *local order* annotation on the edge e' is set to the *local order* annotation of the edge e1. However, as the edge e' has a larger information capacity than the edges e1 and e2, the *quantifier* annotation of the edge e' is given as the combined quantifier of the two input edges e1 and e2. The edgeObjects of e1 and e2 are transformed similarly to form new edgeObjects for the edge e'. The subdivide operator, graphically represented as $\oslash$, intuitively performs the inverse operation of the smooth operator, i.e., it splits a given relationship into two relationships connected via a node. Let G have two nodes n_1 and n_3 and edge e:$< n_1, n_3 >$. The subdivide operator introduces a new node n_2' in G' such that the edge e in G is replaced by two edges e1':$<n_1$', n_2'> and e2':$<n_2$', n_3'> in G'. The local order annotation for the edge e1':$< n_1', n_2' >$ is the same as the local order annotation of the edge e as $\otimes(n_1) = n_1$'. The edge e2' is the only edge added for the node n_2' and thus has a local order annotation of 1. To preserve the extent I (e), the edges e1' and e2' are assigned quantifier annotations as follows. If min(quantifier(e)) = 0, then the quantifier range for e1' is given as $[0 : 1]$, else it is always set to $[1 : 1]$. The quantifier of edge e2' is set equal to the quantifier of edge e.

Two or more linear transformation operators can be connected via two edge types ($\mathcal{C}p$), namely context dependency and derivation. Context dependency, enables several algebra operators to collaborate and jointly operate on sub-graphs to produce one combined output graph. The outputs of all operators connected by the context dependency edges are visible in the final output Sangam graph. Derivation composition enables the nesting of several algebra operators wherein the output of one or more operators becomes the input of another operator. The final output in this case is the output of the parent operator that consumes the inputs of the children operators.

An instance of the Translation Model, a *cross algebra tree* (CAT), is a graph $T = (N, E)$ where op $\in N$ is one of the four linear transformation operators, and e $\in E$ is either a context dependency edge or a derivation edge. An algebraic expression where context dependency edge is represented by ',', and a derivation edge by a pair of '(', ')' provides an alternative representation of the cross algebra tree.

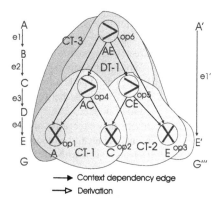

Fig. 1. An Example Cross Algebra Graph.

Figure 1 gives an example of a cross algebra tree that transforms the input graph G to the output graph G'. Here, the operators op1 and op3 produce the output nodes A' and E' respectively, while the operator op6 incrementally transforms the edges e1, e2, e3 and e4 to the edge e1' in the output graph G' through a nested sequence of smooth ($\ominus$) operators. The algebraic expression for this is given as:(CAT3 = DT1, (op1$_{A'}$(A) $\circ$ op3$_{E'}$(E))).

3   Taxonomy of Sangam Graph Changes

Information is not static, rather it changes over time. In most database systems this change is made through a set of data update primitives and schema evolution primitives, the semantics of which define the precise change. In this section, we present a taxonomy of schema and data change primitives that can be applied in the middle-layer on a Sangam graph and data graph respectively resulting in a modified Sangam graph or data graph. Changes in the local data models, such as the XML and relational model, can be translated into a set of Sangam primitive changes thereby eventually enabling the propagation of change from one local data model to another.

3.1   Change Primitives

To modify a Sangam graph, we have defined five change operations, namely insert-Node, deleteNode, insertEdge, deleteEdge and rename, to insert and delete a node, insert and delete an edge, and to rename both the node as well as an edge respectively. Table 1 gives a brief description of these operations.

Table 1. Taxonomy of Sangam Graph Graph Change Primitives.

Schema Change Primitive	Description
insertNode $(\text{ln}, \tau, \text{m}, \text{l}, \text{q})$	Creates new node with label ln and inserts it as child of node m
insertNodeAt $(\text{ln}, \tau, \text{m}, \text{l}, \text{q}, \text{pos})$	Creates new node with label ln and inserts it as child of node m at position pos
deleteNode (m, n)	Deletes child node n from parent m
insertEdge $(\text{m}, \text{n}, \text{l}, \text{q})$	Inserts new edge between nodes m and n, making n child of node m
insertEdgeAt $(\text{m}, \text{n}, \text{l}, \text{q}, \text{pos})$	Inserts new edge at position pos between nodes m and n, making n child of node m
deleteEdge (m, l)	Deletes edge e with label l from the node m
rename (n, l')	Modifies label of node n to l'

In addition to these, we also define four operations to enable modifications on the Sangam data graph, that is to allow insertion and deletion of nodeObjects into and from the extent I (n) of a node n, and the insertion and deletion edgeObjects into and from the extent R (e) of an edge e. Table 2 gives a brief description of these Sangam data graph modification operations. It can be shown that the Sangam graph change primitives as well as the Sangam data graph change primitives are both minimal and correct [3].

Table 2. Taxonomy of Sangam Graph Data Graph Change Primitives.

Data Modification Primitive	Description
addObject (v, n)	Creates new object o with data value v. Inserts object o into extent I (n) of node n
deleteObject (o,n)	Removes object o from extent I (n) of node n based on either the object id or the value
addEdgeObject (o_1, o_2, e)	Creates new edgeObject $(o_e: <o_1, o_2>, \text{ord})$. Inserts the edge-Object o_e into the extent R (e) of edge e:$<\text{m}, \text{n}>$ at position ord
deleteEdgeObject (o_e, e)	Removes object o_e from extent R (e) of edge e:$<\text{m}, \text{n}>$ based on either the object id or the value

4   The Adaptive Update Propagation Strategy

Once a local change has been translated into a set of changes on the Sangam graph in the middle-layer, it must then be translated into a set of changes on the target Sangam graph.

This is done by propagating the change through the cross algebra tree that represents the transformation of the source Sangam graph to the target Sangam graph. The goal of the propagation algorithm is to produce as output a set of incremental changes that can be applied on the target schema. In this section we describe an adaptive propagation strategy for pushing a change from an input Sangam graph to an output Sangam graph.

4.1 Updates on Cross Algebra Trees

Definition 1 (Valid Update). *Let SC denote the set of all operations on a Sangam graph as defined in Section 3. An operation* $c \in SC$ *on a node* n *or an edge* e *is* **defined** *for the Sangam graph G if* n *(or* e*) either exists and/or is reachable by the specified path (for delete operations) or does not exist and/or is not reachable by the specified path (for add operations).*

A local schema change, i.e., a change on the XML DTD or a relational schema, often results in a sequence of changes on the Sangam graph. To meet our primary goal of propagating a local schema change from the input to the output and hence eventually to the output application schema, we must thus consider the propagation of a sequence of changes through the cross algebra tree. We define a valid update sequence as follows.

Definition 2 (Valid Update Sequence). *A sequence* $u_1, u_2, \ldots u_i \ldots u_n$ *(1 < i ≤ n) with* $u_i \in SC$*, denoted by* δG*, is valid for Sangam graph G if* u_i *is defined for the Sangam graph* G^{i-1} *that was obtained by applying* $u_1, u_2, \ldots u_{i-1}$ *to G .*

4.2 Overall Propagation Strategy

For SQL views, many incremental update strategies have been proposed [10,9]. Their focus is the calculation of the extent difference between the old V and new view V' by adding or subtracting tuples from the extent of the view V. In these works, the schemas of V and V' were assumed to stay the same. In the scenario when schema changes are considered [12] as in update propagation through SchemaSQL views by Koeller et al., the changes are made in-place on the individual algebra operators in the algebra tree with no resulting modifications to the structure of the algebra tree.

However, when propagating Sangam graph changes through a cross algebra tree not only is the old output Sangam graph G different from the modified output Sangam graph G' , but also the structure of the cross algebra tree itself may be affected. New algebra nodes may be added as a result of an insertion and/or existing algebra nodes may be removed as a result of deletion. Moreover, we find that although data modification and deletion operations can be propagated through the cross algebra tree using the same propagation algorithm, we are unable to handle the insertion schema operations with the same. This is primarily due to the fact that any additional node or edge created in the input Sangam graph can be mapped to the output Sangam graph in many different ways or perhaps not at all. While ideally, the mapping of the new node or edge in the input Sangam graph must be done in accordance to the existing modeled transformation, we do provide default propagation and hence default mappings for handling the insertion operations. Due to space constraints, we only present the *AUP* algorithm to handle data updates and deletion schema operations. Details on the *AUP_Insert* algorithm to handle the insertion operations can be found in [4].

Table 3. Brief Description of Functions Used in Algorithms of Figures 2 and 4.

Function	Description
op.*toBeDeleted*()	Returns true if one of the inputs of operator op have become invalid
op.*markForDeletion*()	Returns true and marks the operator op for deletion in the cleanup pass of *AUP*
op.*generateUpdate* (u)	Generates and returns an update u' based on the input update u .
op.*isAffectedBy*(u)	Returns true if the operator op is affected by u)
op.*contexts*()	Returns the number of parent operations for operator op, such that e:$<$op$_p$, op$>$ == *context dependency*
op.*derivations*()	Returns the number of parent operations for operator op, such that e:$<$op$_p$, op$>$ == *derivation*
op.*removeEdge*(e)	Removes the specified edge e outgoing from op
op.*children*()	Returns the number of children operators of the operator op. This includes all operators op$_i$ that op derives from, and all op$_i$ with which op is in context dependency relationship.
up$_i$.*getUpdate*()	Returns u , the update component of the update pair up$_i$
up$_i$.*getOperator*()	Returns op, the operator that generated the update u$_i$ in the update pair up$_i$

The *AUP* Algorithm

The First Pass: Propagating the Update. The Adaptive Update Propagation (*AUP*) algorithm works as a two-step process. The first pass of the algorithm performs a post-order traversal of the algebra tree. This ensures that each operator processes the input updates after all its children have already computed their output. A cross algebra tree is connected and cycle-free (refer [6]). Hence all operators will be visited exactly once. After all operators have been visited, the output of the algorithm, an update sequence δ, will be produced.

Figure 2 depicts the first pass of the *AUP* algorithm. Table 3 lists the functions and their brief descriptions as used in Figure 2. Here, each node in the algebra tree is aware of the algebra operator it represents. At any given time, an operator op$_i$ can accept *one* input update u$_i$, where u$_i \in$ SC , and will generate as output *one* update u$_i$' to be applied to the output Sangam graph G' . The output update for each operator is recorded as a pair $<$u$_i$', op$_i>$ in a local *update sequence* δ, where u$_i$' is the output update and op$_i$ is the operator to which the input update u$_i$ was applied to produce u$_i$'. The updates u$_i$ and u$_i$' are Sangam change operations and are specified with all their parameters. We assume that given an update operation, an algebra operator can detect whether or not it is affected by the change. If it is not affected, it will simply return the input update u$_i$ as its output.

After all the updates u$_i$ for the children of an operator op$_p$ have been computed and collected in a sequence (denoted by variable δ in the algorithm), each update u$_i \in \delta$ is propagated through op$_p$, irrespective of if the child op$_i$ is related to op$_p$ via derivation or context dependency. In either case, a new update u$_i$' will be produced by the parent operator op$_p$ if the operator op$_p$ is affected by the update u$_i$ produced by the child

function List *AUP* (Update u_p ,
  Operator op_p) {
  List inSequence ← ∅,
  List δ ← ∅, *//Updates from children*
  List δ' ← ∅ *// Update seq. of parent*
  UpdatePair up , up_i
  Boolean updateApplied
  if (op_p is leaf)
    up ← *applyUpdate* (u_p , op_p)
    δ.*append* (up)
  else
    //If not a leaf, then recursively invoke
    //AUP for all children
    for (*all children* op_i *of* op_p)
      δ.*append*(AUP (u_p , op_i))
      // δ = updates of children of op_p
      // Cal. effect of each update on op
      // Generate parent's update seq. δ'
      for (*all updatePairs* $up_i ∈ δ$) {
        δ' ← *calculateUpdate* (up_i, op)
    }
    return δ';
}

function List *calculateUpdate*(UpdatePair
  up_i, Operator op) {
  List δ' ← ∅ u_i ← up_i.*getUpdate*()
  up_i' ← *applyUpdate* (u_i ,op_p)
  //Decide if up_i *and* up_i' *must be*
  //appended to parent's sequence δ' of if
  // up_i must be discarded
  op_i ← up_i.*getOperator*()
  if ((e:<op,op_i) == *contextDependency*)
    // Calculate effect of the original update
    // Check if update applied before
    if (!updateApplied)
      up ← *applyUpdate* (u_p , op_p)
      updateApplied ← **true**
    δ'.*append*(up_i)
    δ'.*append*(up)
    δ'.*append*(up_i')
  elseif ((e:<op, op_i>) == *derivation*)
    δ'.*append*(up_i')
  return δ'

Fig. 2. First Pass of Cross Algebra Tree Target Maintenance Algorithm.

operator op_i. This update u_i' is recorded as an update pair (u_i', op_p) and is appended to the update sequence δ' produced by the operator op_p.

function UpdatePair *applyUpdate* (Update u_p , Operator op_p)
{   **if** (op_p.*isAffectedBy*(u_p))
    u_p' ← op_p.*generateUpdate* (u_p)
    if (op_p.*toBeDeleted*())
      op_p.*markForDeletion*()
    up ← (u_p' ,op_p)
  return up
}

Fig. 3. First Pass of Cross Algebra Tree Target Maintenance Algorithm - The UpdatePair Function.

The edge, context dependency or derivation, between the parent and the child operator affects the parent operator in two ways: (1) in deciding whether the original update u must be applied to the parent operator op_p; and (2) in deciding whether the update sequence generated by the child operator must be propagated up, i.e., should be included in the update sequence generated by the parent operator.

In general, a parent operator op_p is not affected by the original update u if none of its children are affected by the same update u and *all* the children are related to the parent operator by derivation. If however the parent is related to a child operator by a context dependency edge then the parent may be affected by the update u even if the child operator is not affected. Hence, the original update u must be applied to the parent operator op_p. If the operator op_p is affected by the update u, then a new update u' and a corresponding update pair up' is generated. The update pair up' is appended to the update sequence δ' outputted by op_p. While, the original update u is not appended to the output update sequence δ' generated by an operator, it is stored as a *global update* as it may need to be applied to other parent nodes that are in a context dependency relationship with the children operators. This propagation of the update u is indicated in the *AUP* algorithm (Figure 2) by up ← *applyUpdate* (u_p, op_p).

We next consider the effect of the type of edge that exists between op_p and op_i on the generation of the update sequence δ' produced by the parent operator op_p. In a derivation tree only the output of the root operator is visible in the final output produced by the tree. It therefore follows that if there exists a derivation relationship between op_p and op_i, only the update u_i' generated by op_p will appear in the update sequence δ' generated by op_p. Hence, after producing the update u_i', the update pair (u_i, op_i) is discarded, and the update pair (u_i', op_p) is appended to the update sequence δ'[2] generated by the parent operator op_p. This is given by: δ'.*append*(up$_i$') in the *AUP* algorithm depicted in Figure 2. On the other hand, in a context dependency tree the outputs of all children operators and the root operator appear in the final output produced by the tree. Thus, if there exists a context dependency edge between the parent operator op_p and the child operator op_i, then the update pair (u_i, op_i) is appended to the update sequence δ' produced by the parent operator op_p. To maintain the dependency between the parent and the child operator, the update pair (u_i', op_p) is appended after the update pair (u_i, op_i) in the update sequence δ'. This is given by the pair of statements: δ'.*append* (up$_i$'), δ'.*append*(up$_i$), in the *AUP* algorithm depicted in Figure 2.

For any operator op_i if the update u_i is such that it removes the input of the operator op_i, then the operator op_i is marked for deletion. The actual removal of the operator from the CAG occurs in the second pass, *AUP_Clean*, of the *AUP* algorithm.

The Second Pass: Cleaning Up. Structural change operations, i.e., the schema operations, on the input Sangam graph may render some of the cross algebra operators non-functional as their input no longer exists in the input Sangam graph. The purpose of the second pass is to remove from the cross algebra tree any such non-functional operators, and if needed to modify the update sequence δ' produced by the first pass of the algorithm to reflect the effects of the removal. Figure 4 gives the second pass of the *AUP* algorithm called *AUP_Clean*. The algebra tree is traversed in-order as the deletion of a parent operator may affect the child operator. In the second pass *AUP_Clean*, for each operator op_p marked for deletion in the first pass *AUP*, if the operator op_p has children operators op_i connected via derivation, then all non-shared operators op_i are also marked for deletion. If the operator op_i is shared, then the derivation edge between op_p and op_i is marked for deletion. If the operator op_p has children operators op_i connected via context dependency, then the children operators op_i remain unaffected. Once all children of an operator are visited and marked for deletion where appropriate, all children (and

---

[2] Initially the update sequence δ' is empty.

edges) marked for deletion are removed as well as the parent (if marked for deletion). The final update sequence δ' is then applied to the output Sangam graph G'.

function *AUP_Clean* (Operator op)

if (op.*markForDeletion* ())
   // *Propagate markForDeletion to all*
   // *derivation children*
   for (*all children* op$_i$ *of op*)
      if ((e:<op, op$_i$) == *derivation*)
         if (op$_i$ is not shared)
         // *Mark the child operator for deletion.*
          op$_i$.*markForDeletion*()
         else
         // *Mark the derivation edge for deletion.*
          e.*markForDeletion*()

//*Recursively invoke algorithm*
for (*all children* op$_i$ *of op*)
   AUP_Clean (op$_i$)

// *Remove the operator*
if (op.*markForDeletion* ())
   delete (op)

return

Fig. 4. Second Pass - Clean Up of Cross Algebra Tree Target Maintenance Algorithm.

4.3   Example: Propagating Change

To illustrate the working of the *AUP* algorithm, consider that the Sangam graph change primitive u = deleteEdge (D, e4) is applied to the input Sangam graph G given in Figure 1, deleting the edge e4 outgoing from the node D. Propagating the update u through the cross algebra tree (Figure 1, we find that the cross operators op1, op2 and op3 are not affected by the change. Hence, the update sequences δ_1, δ_2 and δ_3 produced by the three operators respectively is null. The original update u is then applied to the operators op4 and op5 as they are in context dependency relationship with the operators op1, op2 and op3. The update u has a direct effect on the operator op5 as one of its inputs (edge e4) has been deleted. As a consequence the output of the operator op5, a temporary edge e3' that combines the edges e3 and e4 must be deleted resulting in the update u' = deleteEdge (C', E'). The update sequence produced by the operator op5 is thus: δ_5 = < u', op5 >. The operator op4 is not effected by the update. As both operators op4 and op5 are in derivation relation with the operator op6, the original update u is no longer applied to the operator op6. Rather only the update sequence δ_5 is applied resulting in the final update sequence δ_6 that contains the update u'' = deleteEdge (A', e1'). The final update sequence δ_6, applied to the output graph G'' results in a graph with two disconnected nodes A' and E'. The cross algebra tree itself is also modified via the second-pass of the algorithm resulting in only operators op1 and op3.

5   Conclusions

In conclusion, our approach provides an incremental propagation algorithm for pushing a change from the source to the target, using our *Sangam* [6,5] middle layer as enabling technology. It therefore provides propagation of data and schema changes from a source to a target independent of the data models and independent of the transformations applied to produce the target schema and data from the source.

References

1. P. Atzeni and R. Torlone. Management of Multiple Models in an Extensible Database Design Tool. In P. M. G. Apers and et al., editors, *Advances in Database Technology - EDBT'96, Avignon, France, March 25-29,* LNCS. Springer, 1996.
2. F. Bry and P. Kroger. A Computational Biology Database Digest: Data, Data Analysis, and Data Management. *International Journal on Distributed and Parallel Databases, special issue on Bioinformatics (to appear),* 2002.
3. K. Claypool and E. Rundensteiner. Evolving Sangam Graphs: A Taxonomy of Primitives. Technical Report UML-CS-TR-02-09, UMass-Lowell, November 2002.
4. K. Claypool and E. Rundensteiner. Propagating Change Through Sangam Transformation Models. Technical Report UML-CS-TR-02-10, UMass-Lowell, November 2002.
5. K. Claypool and E. Rundensteiner. Sangam: A Framework for Modeling Hetergoeneous Database Transformations. In *Fifth International Conference on Enterprise Information Systems,* 2003.
6. K. Claypool and E. Rundensteiner. Sangam: A Transformation Modeling Framework. In *8th International Conf. on Database Systems for Advanced Applications,* pages 47–54, 2003.
7. K. Claypool, E. Rundensteiner, X. Zhang, and H. e. a. Su. SANGAM: A Solution to Support Multiple Data Models, Their Mappings and Maintenance. In *Demo Session Proceedings of SIGMOD'01,* 2001.
8. J. Gross and J. Yellen. *Graph Theory and it Applications.* CRC Press, 1998.
9. A. Gupta and J. Blakeley. Using Partial Information to Update Materialized Views. *Information Systems,* 20(8):641–662, 1995.
10. A. Keller. Updates to Relational Database Through Views Involving Joins. In *Scheuermann,* 1982.
11. G. Koch and K. Loney. *Oracle: The Complete Reference.* Oracle Press, Osborne-McGraw Hill, 1995.
12. A. Koeller and E. Rundensteiner. Incremental Maintenance of Schema-Restructuring Views. In *Int. Conference on Extending Database Technology (EDBT),* page to appear, 2002.
13. S. Melnik, E. Rahm, and P. Bernstein. Rondo: A Programming Platform for Generic Model Management. In *SIGMOD,* pages 193–204, 2003.
14. Y. G. Ra and E. A. Rundensteiner. A Transparent Schema Evolution System Based on Object-Oriented View Technology. *IEEE Transactions on Knowledge and Data Engineering,* 9(4):600–624, September 1997.
15. E. A. Rundensteiner, A. J. Lee, and A. Nica. On Preserving Views in Evolving Environments. In *Proceedings of 4th Int. Workshop on Knowledge Representation Meets Databases (KRDB'97): Intelligent Access to Heterogeneous Information,* pages 13.1–13.11, Athens, Greece, August 1997.
16. J. Shanmugasundaram, G. He, K. Tufte, C. Zhang, D. DeWitt, and J. Naughton. Relational Databases for Querying XML Documents: Limitations and Opportunities. In *Proceedings of 25th International Conference on Very Large Data Bases (VLDB'99),* pages 302–314, 1999.
17. T. Tatarinov, Z. G. Ives, A. Halevy, and D. Weld. Updating XML. In *SIGMOD,* 2001.
18. Y. Zhuge, H. Garcia-Molina, J. Hammer, and J. Widom. View Maintenance in a Warehousing Environment. In *SIGMOD,* pages 316–327, May 1995.

Database Support for Path Query Functions

Rachel Hamill and Nigel Martin

School of Computer Science and Information Systems, Birkbeck College
University of London, Malet Street, London WC1E 7HX
{rachel, nigel}@dcs.bbk.ac.uk

Abstract. Extending relational database functionality to include data mining primitives is one step towards the greater goal of more closely integrated database and mining systems. This paper describes one such extension, where database technology is used to implement path queries over a graph view of relational data. Partial-path information is pre-computed and stored in a compressed binary format in an SQL data type. Path querying is implemented using SQL table functions, thus enabling the retrieved path tables to be manipulated within SQL queries in the same way as standard relational tables. The functions are evaluated with particular reference to response time, storage requirements and shortest-path optimality, using road system data representing relationships between over 2.8 million entities.

1 Introduction

Conventional relational database designs do not support path queries, that is, queries that return a representation of the relationship between two entities in terms of other entities and relationships in the database. However, there are many potential applications of server-side implementations of path algorithms as data-mining primitives used by more complex mining operations. In particular, the ability to search over join paths is important in the field of multi-relational data mining [1]. This paper describes one method of extending database functionality to provide path-query support using adaptations of shortest-path algorithms described in the literature. We focus on two variants of this problem: the single-pair and single-source algorithms. Given an input graph, a source node and a destination node, the single-pair algorithm returns a path between the two nodes through the graph. The single-source shortest-path algorithm, takes as its input a graph, a source node and an integer n and returns all nodes reachable from the source node via a path no longer than n. Note that in each case the input graph can be generated from ordinary relational data: nodes correspond to entities in the database and edges to foreign-key relationships.

We based this path-finding functionality on modified versions of Jing, Huang and Rundensteiner's Hierarchical Encoded Path View (HEPV) approach [2] and Chan and Zhang's disk-based Dijkstra's (*diskSP)* algorithm [3]. Both these algorithms have a pre-processing and a querying phase. The pre-processing phase materializes partial-path information which is then used in the querying phase to accelerate path process-

H. Williams and L. MacKinnon (Eds.): BNCOD 2004, LNCS 3112, pp. 84–99, 2004.

ing. Thus they aim to provide reasonable response times without incurring unacceptably high storage costs.

As these algorithms were to be implemented in a database context, potentially to be used as mining primitives, we took the view that achieving good response times was more important than the ability to retrieve optimal shortest paths. Whereas finding shortest paths is useful in applications such as route finding, we were more concerned with using database structures to discover relationships between entities in any given database. Therefore we were prepared to compromise the optimality of the solution in favour of rapid response times. We modified HEPV and *diskSP* in accordance with these priorities (for convenience we refer to the modified versions of these algorithms as *mHEPV* and *mdiskSP* respectively). We also investigated two hybrid versions of the algorithms. These were designed to provide optimality for relatively short paths while providing a better approximation of the shortest path than *mHEPV* for longer paths.

The rest of this paper is organised as follows. Section 2 places this paper in the context of related work. Section 3 contains a brief description of each of the path-finding algorithms implemented. In Section 4 we describe how relational database functionality was used to implement each of these algorithms and experimental results are given in Section 5.

2 Related Work

Various approaches to the problem of extending database functionality to handle queries about relationships between entities are described in the literature. Jagadish describes a compression technique to materialize the transitive closure of a relation [4]. He argues for the importance of the ability of a database to answer queries regarding the existence of a path between two nodes in a graph underlying a database relation. However, the graphs used are very small (up to 1000 nodes) and the technique does not maintain path information, only reachability information. Another approach is to implement a query language capable of expressing such queries. For example, Ayres and King extend a functional database language with 'associational facilities' to allow users to pose queries about relations between entities in the database [5]. Again, however, there is a question mark over the scalability of the technique, which is applied to databases of a few hundred entities.

Chaudhuri addresses the more general issue of database support for data mining operations in [6]. He argues the case for adding primitive functionality that can be exploited by many mining algorithms rather than implementing specific mining algorithms in their entirety. Our work follows this idea. An analysis of the definition and implementation of several data-mining operators in database systems can be found in [7]. Examples of the use of table functions to implement mining primitives in databases can be found in Sattler and Dunemann's work on decision tree classifiers [8] and Sarawagi et al.'s experiments using association rule mining [9].

A complementary approach is the specification of application programming interfaces for the integration of data mining with the database engine. For example, the International Organisation for Standardization (ISO) has recently developed an extension to SQL, known as SQL/MM [10], as part of the SQL:1999 standard. The SQL/MM Data Mining package provides an interface to data mining algorithms that can be layered on top of any object-relational database system. The standard provides support for rule, clustering, regression and classification models, therefore offering different functionality to that described in this paper. The OLE DB for Data Mining is another example of an API designed to support operations on data-mining models within database systems [11].

Several commercial data mining systems that incorporate database technology have been developed. DBMiner combines database, OLAP and data mining technologies in a system that implements a variety of data mining functions including characterization, association, classification and clustering [12]. DB2 Intelligent Miner for Scoring integrates the IBM Intelligent Miner with the DB2 Universal Database. It provides functions such as clustering, regression, neural networks and decision trees as database extensions [13]. To our knowledge, neither of these systems provides a path-querying facility.

There have been many approaches to path finding in large graphs using partially materialized path information to speed up query processing [2,3,14,15]. Their implementation in a database context, however, has not been discussed.

3   Path Algorithms

This section outlines the path algorithms implemented. All the algorithms described have a pre-processing phase involving the partitioning of the original graph. The method chosen was based on Karypis and Kumar's graph-partitioning algorithm [16]. This aims to partition a graph into fragments of roughly equal size in such a way that the number of edges connecting nodes in different fragments is minimized. Further details of this partitioning method and implementation of the path-finding algorithms can be found in [17].

3.1   Single-Pair Algorithms

mHEPV. This is a modified version of Jing et al.'s Hierarchical Encoded Path View (HEPV) approach [2]. We simplified the hierarchical representation of the graph created in the pre-processing stage in order to accommodate a less complex querying algorithm (originally exponential in the number of levels of the hierarchy). As a result, the algorithm is not optimal. The modifications are explained more fully in [17].

The pre-processing phase constructs a hierarchy of progressively smaller graphs, ending with a graph small enough to fit into main memory. It begins by partitioning the original, or flat, graph into a number of fragments. In Jing et al.'s approach, the border nodes of the partition become the nodes of the graph at the next highest level. In *mHEPV*, the fragments themselves constitute the graph at the next highest level. As the number of fragments in a partitioned graph is generally a lot smaller than the number of border nodes, *mHEPV* should produce smaller graphs at each level, ultimately reducing the number of levels necessary before a graph is found that can fit in memory. For each fragment, at each level of the hierarchy, all-pairs shortest path information is computed and stored. For each pair in each fragment, the path length and identifier of an intermediate node in the path, known as the *next hop* node, are held. The *next hop* information enables the recursive reconstruction of the shortest path at run time.

Jing et al.'s querying algorithm involves an exhaustive comparison of paths recursively through the hierarchy. While this is feasible for graphs consisting of a few thousand nodes, we hoped for good response times when searching graphs with millions of nodes. We therefore modified the algorithm as follows. Consider finding the shortest path between two nodes s and d in fragments S_1 and D_1 respectively (as illustrated in Fig. 1). If $S_1 = D_1$ then we simply find the shortest path using the all-pairs shortest-path information stored for that fragment. Otherwise, we query the next highest level to find the fragments containing S_1 and D_1, S_2 and D_2 respectively, and so on until we reach a level l where $S_l = D_l$. Using the all-pairs shortest path information stored for S_l, we find the path between S_{l-1} and D_{l-1}. We then use the all-pairs shortest path information stored for each node in the l-1 path to construct the l-2 path, and so on until a flat-graph path is found. The cost of avoiding this exhaustive comparison of paths is that, unlike the original HEPV algorithm, the paths obtained are not necessarily the shortest.

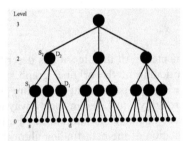

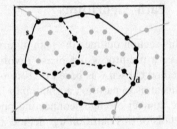

Fig. 1. A four-level hierarchy constructed during the pre-processing stage of *mHEPV*

Fig. 2. A super-graph fragment with level-1 fragments outlined by dashed lines

mdiskSP. Our modifications to Chan and Zhang's *diskSP* algorithm [3] did not affect the optimality of the algorithm. Instead more information was pre-computed and stored than required by the original algorithm in order to accelerate the querying process.

Like HEPV, *diskSP* has a pre-processing and a querying phase. During the pre-processing stage, a two-level hierarchy is constructed from the original flat graph in the following way. The flat graph is partitioned into a number of fragments. For each fragment, a *distance matrix* stores the distances between all border nodes in the fragment. The *distance matrices* implicitly represent the graph at the next-highest level, or super graph. In an attempt to accelerate path querying, *mdiskSP* adds an intermediate level to the hierarchy so that each super-graph fragment contains one or more fragments from the intermediate level. All-pairs shortest-path weight and *next hop* values were stored for each intermediate fragment in exactly the same way as for *mHEPV*. *mdiskSP*'s hierarchy therefore has three levels, the level 0 graph corresponding to the flat graph, level 2 corresponding to *diskSP*'s super graph and level 1, the intermediate level.

Chan and Zhang's querying algorithm begins by merging the fragments containing the source and destination nodes with the super graph. By applying Dijkstra's algorithm to the resulting graph, a *skeleton* shortest path is obtained, that is, a path containing *skeleton* edges that link super-graph nodes. A *skeleton* edge is expanded to become a flat-graph path by applying Dijkstra's algorithm to the super-graph fragment over which the *skeleton* edge crosses. It is at this stage of the querying process that *mdiskSP*'s level-1 graph is used. Dijkstra's algorithm is applied to the border nodes of the level-1 fragments contained in the relevant super-graph fragment. This results in another *skeleton* path, whose edges represent paths across level-1 fragments. Filling in these edges, however, is just a matter of accessing the appropriate level-1 fragment and looking up the path stored there. Fig. 2 shows a possible *skeleton* edge linking the super-graph nodes **s** and **d**. *mdiskSP* expands this edge by applying Dijkstra's to the level-1 border nodes (here coloured black), then using the pre-computed information for the level-1 fragments to retrieve the flat-graph path.

Hybrid Algorithms. We investigated different hybrid versions of the two algorithms described above. Our hybrid algorithms used the hierarchy as built for *mHEPV*, but only after attempting to obtain an optimal path using Dijkstra's algorithm. These algorithms were therefore designed to return optimal paths for relatively short paths while providing a better approximation of the shortest path than *mHEPV* for longer paths. The optimal stage of both algorithms is exactly the same; they only differ in the approximation method used.

The Optimal Stage. The optimal stage of both algorithms attempts to find an optimal path using Dijkstra's algorithm. This stage takes as its input a source node, a destination node, a max_opt parameter and the hierarchical structure built in the preprocessing stage of mHEPV. max_opt indicates the maximum weight of optimal paths returned by the algorithms. Any path whose weight exceeds this value is not guaranteed to be optimal. To ensure the symmetry of the algorithms, two instances of Dijkstra's algorithm run concurrently, one with the source node as input and the other with the destination node. In each case Dijkstra's is applied to the graph consisting of the border nodes of the level 1 fragments to create skeleton paths. If a skeleton path linking the source and destination nodes is found, it is filled in using the encoded-path information as described for diskSP. If the optimal stage fails to discover the shortest path, the partial-path information obtained can be passed to the approximation stage. The optimal stage runs until a shortest path is found or all possibilities of finding a path with weight not greater than max_opt have been exhausted.

The Approximation Stage. If no path is found during the optimal stage, a means of approximating the path is employed. We experimented with two different approximation methods.

i) hybrid. The first method is based on mHEPV. However, instead of taking as input one source and one destination node, it takes as input two sets of nodes. These sets are provided as the output of the optimal stage of the algorithm. The source set contains those nodes reachable via a path of length max_opt/2 from the source node and the destination set comprises those nodes at max_opt/2 from the destination node. Given these sets, the algorithm searches for the lowest level in the hierarchy where at least one fragment contains at least one node from each set. It then works back down the hierarchy to establish a flat-graph path in a similar way to *mHEPV*. Because there are multiple source and destination nodes, there may be a choice of paths at each level, in which case the shortest is chosen.

ii) hierDijk. The second method can be viewed as a hierarchical implementation of Dijkstra's algorithm. If the optimal stage fails to produce a path, Dijkstra's algorithm is run again using the same max_opt parameter to constrain the search, only substituting level-1 fragments for level-0 nodes. Instead of the source and destination nodes, it takes as input the level-1 fragments containing the source and destination nodes. For each level-1 fragment accessed in the optimal stage, the average distance of its constituent nodes from the source (or destination) node is calculated. This is used to provide an initial ordering of fragments for the second run of Dijkstra's algorithm. If this second run fails to produce a path the process is repeated for level-2 fragments and so on until a fragment path is found. A flat-graph path is then produced by working back down through the hierarchy using the encoded-path views of each fragment at each level.

3.2 Single-Source Algorithm

nconnected. The single-source shortest-path algorithm, known as *n-connected*, is simply Dijkstra's algorithm adapted to take advantage of the pre-computed path information stored for HEPV. Instead of requiring that the entire graph be loaded into memory before searching for the requested paths, the algorithm reads in one fragment of the graph at a time, taking advantage of the incremental nature of Dijkstra's algorithm.

nconnected requires a two-level hierarchical graph with all-pairs shortest path information recorded for each fragment. Given a source node and an integer n, it returns all nodes reachable from the source node via a path no longer than n. When processing a node, if it is found to be adjacent to a node in another fragment, that entire fragment can be read into memory at once. If the fragment already exists in memory, the precomputed-path weights can be used to update path weights from the source node efficiently. The algorithm terminates when all nodes at path-weight n from the source have been found or all nodes in the graph have been processed.

4 Relational Database Implementation

Relational database functionality was used both in the pre-processing and querying phases of the algorithms. Path information constitutes by far the greatest storage requirement of the pre-processing stage. We were able to compress this data by storing it in a BLOB (Binary Large OBject), an SQL data type that holds up to 4GB of binary data in the *Oracle* implementation. The path-querying functionality was wrapped up inside an SQL function. This function returns a user-defined table that can be manipulated by relational operators in the same way as any standard relational table.

This section describes the relational representation of the graph, the structures built in the pre-processing stage and the SQL functions used to query the database.

4.1 The Graph

We constructed our graph using Tiger/Line data. Tiger/Line files are extracts from the US Census Bureau's TIGER (Topologically Integrated Geographic Encoding and Referencing) database [18]. They include information on road systems for each county in the United States. The graph was stored in an *Oracle 9i* database in a binary relation. In many applications edges have associated weights and directions. For example, in road system data an edge weight might represent the distance between two points while the edge direction indicates the direction of traffic flow between them. However, for the purposes of this experiment, we assumed the graph was undirected and all edge weights were equal. Therefore each tuple in the relation represented two edges in the graph, one from the source node to the destination and one from destination to source.

4.2 The Pre-processing Stage

Path Encoding of Fragments. The algorithms described in section 3 all require the storage of all-pairs shortest-path information for each fragment in at least one level of the hierarchy constructed during pre-processing. For each path in the fragment two pieces of information are stored - the weight of the path and the identifier of one of the intermediate nodes in the path, known as the *next hop* node. The *next hop* information allows the recursive reconstruction of the shortest path during the querying phase. This information was generated by calculating the transitive closure of the adjacency matrix representation of each fragment. To keep storage requirements to a minimum the data is compressed into a binary format and stored in the database as a Binary Large OBject (BLOB). With the maximum number of nodes in each fragment set to 1024, the maximum size of each BLOB is 1.25Mb. Fig. 3 describes the path encoding of a fragment.

The level-2 fragments required for *mdiskSP* were encoded in a similar way. As the algorithm only requires border-to-border-node path-weight information at this level, no *next hop* data or means of identifying the fragment's border nodes need be stored. The maximum size of level-2 fragments was set to 20,000 and the maximum number of border nodes in each fragment was set to 1024.

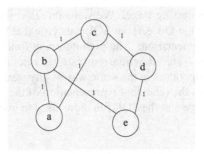

Fig. 3a. The Fragment

	a		b		c		d		e	
	Next Hop	Wght	Next Hop	Wght	Next Hop	Wght	Next Hop	Wght	Next Hop	Wght
a	a	0	a	1	a	1	c	2	b	2
b	b	1	b	0	b	1	e	2	b	1
c	c	1	c	1	c	0	c	1	d	2
d	c	2	e	2	d	1	d	0	d	1
e	b	2	e	1	d	2	e	1	e	0

Fig. 3b. The transitive closure of (a) with path information

B **L** **O** **B**	No. of nodes in fragment	a	b	c	d	e	Number of edge bytes.	Border node data	0	1	0	1	2	2	1	2	1	1	...
	In this case 5.		Node labels.				The number of bytes used to store edge data	A bitmap describing which nodes are attached to inter-fragment edges.	Edge information. The shaded section corresponds to the shaded section in (b). Instead of labels, offsets are stored. For example, a is at offset 0, b at 1 etc. The maximum fragment size was set to 1024. Therefore, only 10 bits were required to store each *next hop* and weight value in the BLOB.										

Fig. 3c. The BLOB representation of the Fragment

Fig. 3. A Fragment, its transitive closure and BLOB representation

Relational Representation of the *mHEPV*, *hybrid*, *hierDijk* and *nconnected* Hierarchy. The following shows the tables necessary to represent one level in the hierarchy built in the pre-processing stage of *mHEPV*. The two hybrid algorithms use the same hierarchical structure as *mHEPV*. *nconnected* requires only a two-level hierarchy.

frag_n	frag_n+1

This encodes the hierarchical structure as depicted in Fig. 1 by associating each fragment label (or node label if n is 0) at level n of the hierarchy with a fragment label at level $n+1$ of the hierarchy.

s_frag_n	s_frag_n+1	d_frag_n	d_frag_n+1

This contains information on inter-fragment edges. Each inter-fragment edge at level $n+1$ of the hierarchy is described in terms of the inter-fragment edges at level n. For example, if n is 0, s_frag_n and d_frag_n represent two adjacent flat-graph nodes that have been grouped into different level-1 fragments, s_frag_n+1 and d_frag_n+1 respectively.

frag	bin

This associates each fragment label with the BLOB (such as that depicted in Fig. 3) holding path information for that fragment.

Relational Representation of the *mdiskSP* hierarchy. The database representation of the *mdiskSP* three-level hierarchy is described below.

node_0	frag_1	frag_2	bound_2

This represents the hierarchical graph structure by associating each node in the graph with a level-1 and level-2 fragment label. *bound_2* is a flag indicating whether that node is a boundary node in the level-2 graph.

s_node_0	s_frag_1	d_node_0	d_frag_1		s_node_0	s_frag_2	d_node_0	d_frag_2

These contain information on the inter-fragment edges at levels 1 and 2 of the hierarchy. Each inter-fragment edge is described in terms of level-0 nodes. The first table holds adjacent flat-graph nodes, s_node_0 and d_node_0, that have been grouped into different level-1 fragments, s_frag_1 and d_frag_1 respectively. The second holds the same information for level-2 fragments.

frag	bin

This associates each fragment label with a BLOB holding path information for that fragment. At level 1, all-pairs shortest path information is held. At level 2, only boundary-to-boundary node path-length information is stored.

4.3   The Querying Stage

Single-Pair SQL Functions. The path-querying methods were written in C++ and published as SQL functions in an *Oracle* database. Each returns a user-defined type, a table of user-defined objects. Each object in the table contains two fields, a label identifying the node and a number identifying that node's place in the path sequence. The table can be manipulated by relational operators in the same way as any standard relational table. For example, the following SQL query finds a path between two nodes in the Tiger/Line graph. Each node in this graph represents a road intersection and each edge, a segment of road between two intersections. It performs a self-join on the user-defined table returned by the 'path' stored procedure to display the path as a table of edges. It also joins with the 'feature' table, which stores the feature name of each edge in the Tiger/Line graph.

```
SELECT table_1.step, feature.source, feature.dest,
feature.name
FROM
TABLE(CAST path((83933522,83933733) AS PATHTABLE)) table_1,
TABLE(CAST path((83933522,83933733) AS PATHTABLE)) table_2,
feature
WHERE table_2.step = table_1.step + 1
AND table_1.label = feature.source
AND table_2.label = feature.dest
ORDER BY table_1.step;
```

STEP	SOURCE	DEST	NAME
1	83933522	83933524	Broadway
2	83933524	83933526	Conant St
3	83933526	83933558	Conant St
4	83933558	83933560	Conant St
5	83933560	83933563	Jackson Hill Rd
6	83933563	83933567	Jackson Hill Rd
7	83933567	83933569	Jackson Hill Rd
8	83933569	83933733	Intervale Rd

n-connected **SQL Function.** For any given path weight the volume of data returned by *n-connected* can be significantly larger than that returned by a single-pair path method. It was therefore necessary to implement the *n-connected* function as a pipelined table function so that results could be returned as a collection of subsets, reducing the amount of memory required to cache the results.

The following example query joins the table returned by the 'nconnected' function with the 'county_state' table to display the counties and states neighbouring the input node.

```
SELECT t.step, t.label, cs.state, cs.county
FROM  TABLE(CAST(nconnected(81658105,  2)  AS  PATHTABLE))  t,
      county_state cs
WHERE t.label = cs.label
ORDER BY t.step;
```

```
        STEP       LABEL ST COUNTY
---------- ---------- -- ----------
         0   81658105 MA Middlesex
         1   81658102 MA Middlesex
         1   81658106 MA Middlesex
         1   81658109 MA Worcester
         1   83905758 MA Worcester
         2   81658086 MA Middlesex
         2   81658100 MA Middlesex
         2   81658110 MA Middlesex
         2   81658112 MA Middlesex
         2   83905760 MA Worcester
         2   83905781 MA Worcester
         2   83905785 MA Worcester
```

5 Evaluation

We tested our algorithms on a graph constructed from the Tiger/Line files. 206 Mb of this data was extracted and stored in a relational database incorporating tables that support a graph view of the data. Each algorithm was evaluated according to response time, optimality and storage requirements.

5.1 Storage Requirements

We compare the storage requirements for *mHEPV* and *mdiskSP*. *n-connected, hybrid* and *hierDijk* use the same pre-processed structures as *mHEPV*.

Table 1. Tiger/Line storage requirements

	No. of levels in hierarchy	Lob segments (Mb)	Other tables and indexes (Mb)	Total storage (Mb)
mHEPV	3	2688	104	2792
mdiskSP	2	2697	159	2856

As illustrated in Table 1, the path information stored in the lob segments takes the bulk of the storage requirements for both *mHEPV* and *mdiskSP*. Although the *mdiskSP* hierarchy has only two levels compared to *mHEPV*'s three, it requires more storage due to the necessity of storing both inter-fragment edge and intra-fragment path information in terms of level 0 graph nodes at both levels of the hierarchy.

The Tiger/Line graph consists of 2,830,451 nodes and 4,007,859 edges, requiring 206 Mb when stored in a binary relation. At first sight the storage overhead for the path-finding algorithms appears large in comparison. However, we are interested in applying these functions to databases with ordinary attribute data and associated indexes as well as the graph view. This data stored for 2.8 million entities would make the additional overhead of the LOB data a reasonable percentage of the overall storage requirements.

5.2   Response Time

To analyse the response time and optimality of our algorithms, data was collected from one thousand paths generated at random.

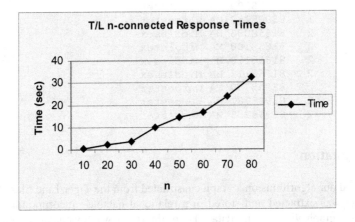

Fig. 4. Response times for single-source path algorithm in Tiger/Line data

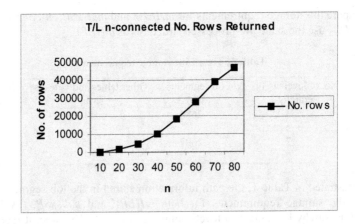

Fig. 5. No. of rows returned for different values of *n* in *n-connected* algorithm

Figs. 4 and 5 summarize the performance of the single-source path algorithm, *n-connected*. It is able to process tens of thousands of nodes reasonably quickly and returns results for (perhaps more likely) queries with smaller values of *n* within a few seconds. Its response time depends largely on the number of entities it has to process. These results provide a basis for choosing the *max_opt* parameter for the single-source algorithms *hierDijk* and *hybrid*. The optimal stage of both algorithms retrieves all paths from the source node and all paths from the destination node of length not greater than half the value of *max_opt*. We chose 50 as the value of *max_opt* as *n-connected* queries where *n* was set to 25 returned a manageable number of rows within a few seconds.

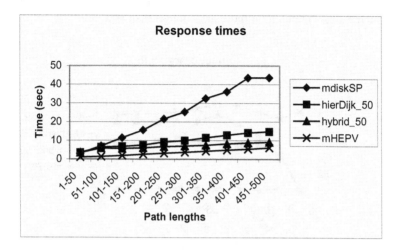

Fig. 6. Response times for single-pair path algorithms in Tiger/Line data with *max_opt* set to 50 for *hierDijk* and *hybrid*

The chart in Fig. 6 shows that *mHEPV* provides the fastest response times of the single-pair path algorithms, returning paths hundreds of nodes long in less than five seconds. This is to be expected as the querying algorithm consists mainly of a series of look-ups, with little regard to optimality. *mdiskSP*, by contrast, pays the price for optimality in slower response times. The performance of the two hybrid algorithms is much closer to that of *mHEPV* than that of *mdiskSP*. As *hybrid* reverts to *mHEPV* when it fails to find an optimal path, its response time remains within a few seconds of *mHEPV*'s. *hierDijk* is slightly slower again as it applies Dijkstra's algorithm to each level of the hierarchy until a path is found.

5.3 Optimality

We measured the optimality of our single-pair path algorithms using the *inaccuracy rate* measure defined by Huang et al. [19]. This is the difference between the length of the path returned by the algorithm and the optimal-path length as a proportion of the optimal-path length. The *max_opt* parameter of *hierDijk* and *hybrid* was set to 50 in each case.

As Fig. 7 illustrates, all implemented single-pair algorithms apart from *mHEPV* maintain optimality for paths with length less than *max_opt*. This is likely to be sufficient for most applications searching for meaningful relationships between entities. In contrast, *mHEPV*'s inaccuracy rate is poor even for short paths. On average it returns paths twice the length of the optimal one. The high level of deviation from this average (Fig. 8) makes it difficult to rely on even as an approximate measure of path length. The performance of *hybrid* tends towards that of *mHEPV* as the path lengths increase. This is to be expected as the *hybrid* algorithm reverts to *mHEPV* when it fails to find an optimal path. Although *hierDijk*'s recursive application of Dijkstra's algorithm provides better optimality performance than *hybrid* and *mHEPV*, its inaccuracy rate remains quite high for those paths longer than *max_opt*.

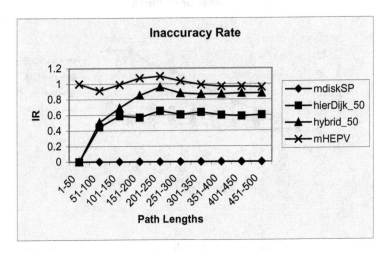

Fig. 7. Inaccuracy Rate of single-pair path algorithms in Tiger/Line data with *max_opt* set to 50 for *hierDijk* and *hybrid*

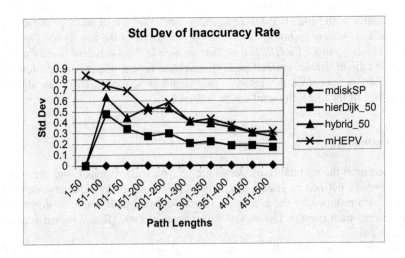

Fig. 8. Standard Deviation of Inaccuracy Rate of single-pair shortest path algorithms in Tiger/Line data with *max_opt* set to 50 for *hierDijk* and *hybrid*

6 Conclusion

We have implemented several single-pair and single-source path algorithms in a database context. The functionality runs on a database server and is callable in SQL. Our results demonstrate that it is possible to use database structures to retrieve paths quickly in relatively large graphs, but that guaranteeing optimality for longer paths comes at too high a price in terms of response time. We have also implemented triggers that automatically handle database updates. The algorithms are amenable to dynamic implementation due to the fact that as path information is stored only at the fragment level, the effects of many updates will remain localised. Changes are only propagated through the affected pre-processed structures, leaving the rest of the database untouched.

The path-query results lead to the conclusion that in any domain where fast response times are important, retrieving optimal paths is only feasible for relatively short paths. However, it could be argued that users of most path-finding applications are only interested in paths of reasonable length as these represent meaningful relationships between entities. In our experiments, we chose 50 as the maximum value for optimal-path lengths, but this parameter can be adjusted by the user to suit a particular data set or application. Restricting the length of retrieved paths, by restricting the search space, opens the possibility of introducing functionality to retrieve paths that conform to given constraints. For example, the ability to specify that the retrieved path include a node or edge of a given type would be useful in many applications.

In future, therefore, we intend to focus on augmenting the path-retrieval functionality for relatively short paths. In particular, a mechanism for specifying constraints in path queries would be useful in many database applications. Another consideration, worthy of investigation from a performance point of view, is the potential ability of the algorithms to exploit the database's parallel processing capabilities. Our eventual aim is to build up a set of database mining primitives useful to a range of more complex mining operations.

References

1. Domingos, P.: Prospects and Challenges for Multi-Relational Data Mining. ACM SIGKDD Explorations Newsletter, Vol. 5, Issue 1. ACM Press, New York (2003) 80-83
2. Jing, N., Huang, Y.-W., Rundensteiner, E.A.: Hierarchical Encoded Path Views for Path Query Processing: An Optimal Model and Its Performance Evaluation. IEEE Transactions on Knowledge and Data Engineering, Vol. 10, No. 3 (1998) 409-432
3. Chan, E.P.F., Zhang, N.: Finding Shortest Paths in Large Network Systems. In: Proceedings of the Ninth International Conference on Advances in Geographic Information Systems. ACM Press, New York (2001) 160-166
4. Jagadish, H. V. : A Compression Technique to Materialize Transitive Closure. ACM Transactions on Database Systems, Vol. 15, No. 4. (1990) 558-598
5. Ayres, R., King P.J.H.: Querying Graph Databases Using a Functional Language Extended with Second Order Facilities. In: Proceedings of the 14th British National Conference on Databases. Lecture Notes in Computer Science, Vol. 1094. Springer-Verlag, Berlin Heidelberg New York (1996) 188-203

6. Chaudhuri, S.: Data Mining and Database Systems: Where is the Intersection? Bulletin of the IEEE Computer Society Technical Committee on Data Engineering, Vol. 21, No. 1. (1998) 4-8

7. Geist, I., Sattler, K.-U.: Towards Data Mining Operators in Database Systems: Algebra and Implementation. In: Proceedings of the 2nd International Workshop on Databases, Documents and Information Fusion. (2002)

8. Sattler, K.-U., Dunemann, O.: SQL Database Primitives for Decision Tree Classifiers. In: Proceedings of the 10th International Conference on Information and Knowledge Management. ACM Press, New York (2001) 379-386

9. Sarawagi, S., Thomas, S., Agrawal, R.: Integrating Association Rule Mining with Relational Database Systems: Alternatives and Implications. In: Proceedings of the ACM Special Interest Group on the Management of Data. ACM Press, New York (1998) 343-354

10. Melton, J., Eisenberg, A.: SQL Multimedia and Application Packages (SQL/MM). The ACM SIGMOD Record, Vol. 30, No. 4 (2001) 97-102

11. Netz, A., Chaudhuri, S., Fayyad, U., Bernhardt J.: Integrating Data Mining with SQL Databases: OLE DB for Data Mining. In: Proceedings of the 17th International Conference on Data Engineering. IEEE Computer Society (2001) 379-387

12. Han, J., Chiang, J.Y., Chee, S., Chen, J., Chen, Q., Cheng, S., Gong, W., Kamber, M., Koperski, K., Liu, G., Lu, Y., Stefanovic, N., Winstone, L., Xia, B.B., Zaine, O.R., Zhang, S., Zhu, H.: DBMiner: A System for Data Mining in Relational Databases and Data Warehouses. In: Proceedings of the 1997 Conference of the Centre for Advanced Studies on Collaborative Research. IBM Press (1997) 249-260

13. IBM: IBM DB2 Intelligent Miner Scoring. Administration and Programming for DB2. Version 8.1. (2002)

14. Hutchinson, D., Maheshwari, A., Zeh, N.: An External-Memory Data Structure for Shortest Path Queries. In: Proceedings of the 5th Annual International Conference on Computing and Combinatorics. Lecture Notes in Computer Science, Vol. 1627. Springer-Verlag, Berlin Heidelberg New York (1999) 51-60

15. Jung, S., Pramanik, S.: An Efficient Path Computation Model for Hierarchically Structured Topographical Road Maps. IEEE Transactions on Knowledge and Data Engineering, Vol. 14, No. 5 (2002) 1029-1046

16. Karypis, G., Kumar, V.: Mutilevel k-way Partitioning Scheme for Irregular Graphs. Journal of Parallel and Distributed Computing, Vol. 48, No. 1 (1998) 96-129

17. Hamill, R.E.A., Martin, N. J.: The Implementation of Path-Querying Functions in a Relational Database. Technical Report BBKCS-04-01, Birkbeck College (2004)

18. www.census.gov/geo/www/tiger

19. Huang, Y.-W., Jing, N., Rundensteiner, E.A.: Hierarchical Path Views: A Model Based on Fragmentation and Transportation Road Types. In: Proceedings of the Third ACM Workshop on Geographic Information Systems. ACM Press, New York (1995) 93-100

Agent-Based Data Mining Approach for the Prediction of UK and Irish Companies Performance

Weifeng Chen and Kevin Lü

Brunel University, Uxbridge, UB8 3PH, UK
Kevin.lu@brunel.ac.uk

Abstract. The discovery of previously unknown and valuable knowledge is a key aspect of the exploitation of the enormous amount of data that stored in data sources. It has a wide range of applications, such as finance data analysis. A number of approaches for knowledge discovery and data mining have been developed for different scenarios. This paper presents our approach of integrating agent technology with conventional data mining methods to construct a system for financial data mining.

1 Introduction

Financial markets generate large volumes of data. Analysing this data to reveal valuable information and making use of the information in decision-making presents great opportunities and challenges for Data Mining (DM). Data analysis is a central issue in business and economics. In particular, it plays an important role in the realms of monetary policy, investment analysis, and risk management. In recent years, DM techniques have been increasingly applied to the financial data analysis domain. A number of DM techniques have been used in financial data mining. Hillol Kargupta [1] monitored the stock market using a *decision tree* for data classification. Agent-based data mining is a promising technique to improve the efficiency of DM. An agent is a computer system that is situated in some environment, and that is capable of autonomous action in this environment in order to meet its design objectives [2]. The autonomy of intelligent agents enables them react under unexpected condition, which is required by data mining tasks.

This paper introduces our effort on financial data mining through integrating linear regression and ANN methods with intelligent agents techniques. We have designed and implemented a prototype of an agent-based data mining system, which can be used to perform data mining in dynamic environments. Initial experiments also have been conducted, using back propagation neural networks (BPN) multiple linear regression classification methods are tested. The paper is organised as followings. The background and motivation are discussed in Session 2. Session 3 presents our approach. Results of experiments are shown in session 4. Session 5 shows our conclusion and future work.

2 Background and Motivation

DM is the process of searching for & finding valuable information from databases. It is the key element among the steps of the overall knowledge discovery process [3].

H. Williams and L. MacKinnon (Eds.): BNCOD 2004, LNCS 3112, pp. 100–105, 2004.

The method of multiple linear regression is used to predict numeric data in data mining. It allows response variable Y to be modelled as a linear function of a multidimensional feature vector [3]. An ANN is an information-processing paradigm that is inspired by the way biological nervous systems. Different types of ANN are used for data classification, clustering, and prediction. ANN involves long training times and therefore is more suitable for applications where this is feasible.

Intelligent agents are defined as software or hardware entities that perform some set of tasks on behalf of users with some degree of autonomy [4]. The main issue in the use of intelligent agents is the concept of autonomy. There may be many agents in a system, each responsible for one or many tasks, and able to cooperate with other agents. Intelligent agents play an important role in multi-agent systems because of its factors of flexibility, modularity and general applicability to a wide range of problems.

3 Framework of Agent-Based DM

Our Agent-based DM framework (ADM) is designed by J2EE (Java2 Platform, Enterprise Edition) for financial analysis (see Figure 1). It is a platform providing general agent facilities and allowing high heterogeneity in agent architectures and communication languages.

Fig. 1. Agent-based Data Mining Framework

Users request data mining services through the Task Controlling Agent. The Task Controlling Agents support the functionalities of controlling and co-ordinating various agents in the system. The Knowledge Integration Agents perform the merging and integration of results obtained from mining distributed data sources. The Data Mining Agents carry the mining algorithm to the data source and performs mining. The results obtained from Data Mining Agents are passed to the knowledge integration component of the agent control centre by means of Data Mining Result Agents. Data Mining Monitoring Agents monitor data resources in the system.

In the ADM, a BPN learning agent is treated as a DM agent, which is equipped with ANN algorithm and performs data mining tasks. Similarly, other DM algorithms could also be implemented in different DM agents.

3.1 Linear Regression

In linear regression, data are modelled using a straight line [3]. Linear regression models can be shown as $Y = \alpha + \beta X$.

Y: response variable, X: predictor variable

α, β: regression coefficients

These coefficients can be solved by the method of least squares, which minimizes the error between the actual data and the estimate of the line. Given s samples or data points of the form $(x1, y1)$, $(x2, y2)$, ... (xs, ys), then the regression coefficients can be estimated using this method with the following equations:

$$\beta = \frac{\sum_{i=1}^{s}(xi - avg(x))(yi - avg(y))}{\sum_{i=1}^{s}(xi - avg(x))^2} , \alpha = avg(y) - \beta avg(x)$$

where avg(x) is the average of $x1, x2, ... xs$, and avg(y) is the average of $y1, y2, ... ys$. The coefficient α and β often provide good approximations to other complicated regression equations.

3.2 BPN Method

Back propagation is one of the neural network architectures for supervised learning. It features a feed-forward connection topology, meaning that data flows through the network in a single direction, and uses a technique called the backward propagation of errors to adjust the connection weights [5]. It is composed of input, output, and one or more layers of hidden units. The Figure below shows a diagram of a back propagation neural network and illustrates the three major steps in the training process.

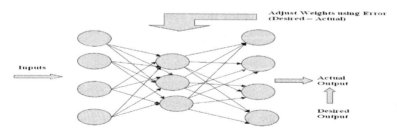

Fig. 2. Back propagation neural network

4 Financial Analysis of FAME

The dataset used in our experiments is extracted from the FAME [6], which is a database recording a variety of finance information for British companies. This dataset includes the financial information for all of the companies in the sector of manufacture of wearing apparel and dressing and fur dyeing industry in the UK. The main purpose of this experiment is to compare the predication result of our method with the real data, therefore to verify the accuracy of our approach, and to examine the feasibility of this approach. Our experiments are based on the key financial factors of these companies including: *Turnover, Profit (loss) before tax, Total assets, Current QuiScore, Current ratio, and Gearing* over the last three years.

Table 1. Financial data attributes from FAME

Variable	Definition
V1	Turnover_th_GBP_Last_Year
V2	Turnover_th_GBP_Year-1
V3	Turnover_th_GBP_Year-2
V4	Profit_before_Tax_th_GBP_Last_Year
V5	Profit_before_Tax_th_GBP_Year-1
V6	Profit_before_Tax_th_GBP_Year-2
V7	Total_Assets_th_GBP_Last_Year
V8	Total_Assets_th_GBP_Year-1
V9	Total_Assets_th_GBP_Year-2
V10	Number_of_Employees_Last_Year
V11	Number_of_Employees_Year_1
V12	Number_of_Employees_Year_2
V13	Current_QuiScore_Last_Year
V14	Current_QuiScore_Year_1
V15	Current_QuiScore_Year_2
V16	Current_Ratio_Last_Year
V17	Current_Ratio_Year_1
V18	Current_Ratio_Year_2
V19	Gearing_Last_Year
V20	Gearing_Year_1
V21	Gearing_Year_2

In Figure 4, the three dimensions indicate the financial factors (randomly chosen amongst seven factors) of each company (total 296 companies): *turnover last year* (*V1*), *profit last year* (*V4*), and *total assets last year* (*V7*). This figure demonstrates the financial status of these companies in 2003.

4.1 Linear Regression Experiment

The main purpose of this experiment is to examine the performance of a *linear regression-learning agent*. In this experiment, we used the *training and testing* process. The experiment is composed of 9 tests. Every test is used to predict one variable. In each test, 98 datasets are trained and 296 datasets are tested. Each variable is predicted by the other two years' data. For instance, *turnover of last year* (*V1*) is predicted by *turnover year –1* (*V2*) and *turn over year –2* (*V3*). The test procedures are as follows: $V1, V2 \rightarrow V3$ $V1, V3 \rightarrow V2$ $V2, V3 \rightarrow V1$

Figure 5 shows the prediction of last year's financial factors generated by a *regression-learning agent*. Comparing Figure 5 with Figure 4, the error rate of prediction in linear regression agent is reasonably high.

4.2 BPN Experiment

In the BPN experiment, the training process adjusts the parameters in the network, which are based on the input-output paired examples from the training set. In order to validate the training result, the trained network is used to predict the test set. Each training example or test case has an input vector, which comprises the seven financial factor variables and an output of error rate as a measure of prediction accuracy. This experiment uses 2 years' financial data to estimate the result of the third year. There are 3 sets of validation tests in this experiment. The procedure of this experiment is shown as

(V1, V4, V7, V10, V13, V16, V19),
(V2, V5, V8, V11, V14, V17, V20)
→ (V3, V6, V9, V12, V15, V18, V21)

(V1, V4, V7, V10, V13, V16, V19),
(V3, V6, V9, V12, V15, V18, V21)
→ (V2, V5, V8, V11, V14, V17, V20)

(V3, V6, V9, V12, V15, V18, V21),
(V2, V5, V8, V11, V14, V17, V20)
→(V1, V4, V7, V10, V13, V16, V19)

For each test, the parameters involved are shown in the Figure 3.

Learning Rate	Momentum	Training Datasets	Tested datasets
0.3	0.2	592	296

Fig. 3. Attributes in BPN experiment

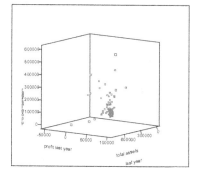

Fig. 4. 2003 Financial Status

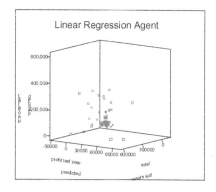

Fig. 5. Linear Regression agent's result

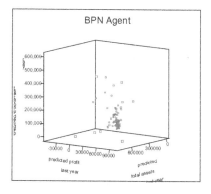

Fig. 6. Result of using BNP learning agent

Figure 6 shows the prediction of *last year*'s financial status generated by using BNP neural network agent. Comparing Figures 5 and 6, Figure 6 is closer to Figure 4 than Figure 5. Observing Figure 5 and 6, it can be found that the error rate of the linear regression agent is higher than that of the BNP agent. The BPN agent is more efficient and precise than the linear regression agent when dealing with supervised learning. This is due to adjusting the testing attributes can control the error rate of the experiment.

5 Conclusions

We have successfully constructed a prototype of an agent-based DM system (ADM). Two conventional data mining methods, namely, linear regression method and a neural networks method, have been integrated with the agent system. Initial experiments also have been conducted. Our future work will be focused on introducing multi-agent techniques into our system, so that more than one agent can be used. Another direction will be to associate a further development of distributed data mining in a multi-processor platform.

References

1. Kargupta, H., Park, B.-H.: MobiMine: Monitoring the Stock Market from a PDA, ACM **3** (2002)
2. Woodridge, M.: This is MyWorld: the logic of an agent-oriented testbed for DAI. Intelligent Agents: Theories, Architectures and Languages (eds M. Woodridge and N.R. Jennings), LNAI 890 (1995) 160-178
3. Han, J., Kamber, M.: Data Mining: Concepts and Techniques, Morgan Kaufmann (2000)
4. Maes, P.: Agents that Reduce Work and Information Overload, Communications of the ACM, **37** (1994) 31- 40
5. El Adawy, M.I., Aboul-Wafa, M.E.: A SOFT-back propagation algorithm for training neural networks Radio Science Conference (2002) 397 – 404
6. http://fame.bvdep.com/cgi
7. Fayyad, U., Piatetsky-Shapiro, G., Smyth, P., Uthurusamy, R.: Advances in Knowledge Discovery and Data Mining. AAAI Press/MIT Press (1996)
8. Witten, I. H., Frank, E.: Data Mining: Practical Machine Learning Tools and Techniques with JAVA implementations, Morgan Kaufmann Publishers (2000)

Reducing Damage Assessment Latency in Survivable Databases

Indrakshi Ray[1], Ross M. McConnell[1], Monte Lunacek[1], and Vijay Kumar[2]

[1] Department of Computer Science
Colorado State University
Fort Collins, CO 80523-1873
{iray, rmm, lunacek}@cs.colostate.edu
[2] School of Computing and Engineering
University of Missouri-Kansas City
kumarv@umkc.edu

Abstract. Traditional recovery mechanisms are not adequate in protecting databases from malicious attacks. A malicious transaction by virtue of writing on to the database can corrupt one or more data items; benign transactions reading these data items and writing on other data items can help spread the damage. To prevent the damage from spreading, it is important to assess the damage and confine it as quickly as possible. Algorithms providing fast damage assessment are needed. In this paper we look at two existing techniques for damage assessment and analyze their complexity. We also propose a new technique that improves upon the existing techniques by reducing the time required for damage assessment.

1 Introduction

Traditional recovery techniques [2] are not adequate in protecting a database from malicious attacks. A malicious transaction can write one or more data items and corrupt it. A good transaction reading corrupted data items can spread the damage to the data items that it writes. Such a good transaction is said to be *affected*. A malicious transaction together with affected transactions can corrupt a significant portion of the database.

When an attack is detected, it is important to find out which transactions and data items were affected by this attack. This process is known as *damage assessment* [1,4, 9]. Liu et al. [7,8] acknowledge that unless damage assessment proceeds at a faster rate than normal processing of transactions, it is possible that the damage assessment process will never terminate. The time interval between the detection of an attack and damage assessment is known as the *damage assessment latency*. To prevent the damage from spreading, it is important to reduce the damage assessment latency.

To assess the damage caused by a malicious transaction, there are two approaches: transactional dependency and data dependency approach In transactional dependency approach [1,6,5], all the good transactions that depend on the malicious transaction are identified. Panda and Giordano [9] realized that some of the transactions operations are innocent and may not have been affected by malicious transactions. The data dependency approach identifies only those statements within a transaction that are affected. Since

H. Williams and L. MacKinnon (Eds.): BNCOD 2004, LNCS 3112, pp. 106–111, 2004.

this method suffers from transaction integrity issues unless some other actions are taken [10], we focus on transactional dependency based approaches.

In order to repair damage, it is important to get a list of the affected transactions in an order such that, if the transactions are repaired in that order, it is always the case that when it is time to repair transaction T_j, all of the prior transactions on which it depends have already been repaired. Let us call such an ordering a *repair schedule*. An important ingredient in damage assessment is to provide a list of affected transaction, together with a suitable repair schedule.

In this paper, we analyze the asymptotic running times of Lala and Panda's algorithm [5], as well as of Ammann, et. al's [1]. We propose a damage assessment algorithm that is similar to Lala and Panda's in that the dependency information is stored in a separate data structure that represents a directed acyclic graph on the transaction. The running time of our approach improves upon theirs; ours finds the affected transactions and a suitable repair schedule in time that is proportional to the sum of sizes of the log-file records of the affected transactions.

The rest of the paper is organized as follows. Section 2 analyzes the existing damage assessment algorithms. Section 3 presents our damage assessment algorithm. Section 4 concludes our paper with some pointers to future directions.

2 Analysis of Existing Damage Assessment Algorithms

2.1 Ammann, Jajodia, and Liu's Damage Assessment

Ammann, Jajodia, and Liu have given a set of algorithms for assessment and repair. In most of these algorithms the damage assessment and repair phases are not distinct, and so we do not discuss them. We present the algorithm in which the damage assessment phase is distinct.

The algorithm begins by scanning the log backward to find the entry corresponding to the start record of the malicious transaction. Then the log is processed forward to identify all the transactions that directly or indirectly depend on the malicious transaction.

One disadvantage of this approach is that the log file is usually quite large, and is larger than conventional log files which do not record dependency information. When a malicious transaction is detected, the entire portion of the log file that comes after the malicious transaction must be scanned. If malicious activity occurs, this may not be detected for some time, and there is some urgency to repair the effects of a malicious transaction once it is discovered. If an attack involves more than one transaction, and not all of them are discovered at the same time, then fixing them all can involve multiple repeated scans of a large interval of the log file.

2.2 Damage Assessment by Lala and Panda

To assess damage faster, Lala proposes to create dependency lists and transaction information lists by analyzing the information stored in the log. The dependency list stores the dependency information of transactions. In the damage assessment phase an *affected list* is created that gives a valid repair schedule.

Specifically, let a *transaction* be an operation on the database that reads data items $R = \{r_1, r_2, ..., r_r\}$ and uses these to compute values that are written to data items $W = \{w_1, w_2, ..., w_w\}$. A transaction is *committed* if it has completed successfully and carried out its write operations on the database. A committed transaction T_j is *directly dependent* on a committed transaction T_i if R_j contains some element that was last written to by T_i.

Let $(T_1, T_2, ..., T_n)$ be the sequence of transactions in the log, in the order in which they are committed, and let the *timestamp* of T_j be denoted by j.

Initially Lala and Panda's damage algorithm for assembling an affected list consists only the malicious transaction T_j. It then iteratively removes an entry T_j from the front of the affected list, finds all the neighbors of T_j that are unmarked, and marks and inserts them to the affected list "in sorted order". That is, they maintain the invariant that the timestamps of vertices in the affected list are in ascending order, which is a valid repair schedule.

Let V be the set of affected transactions, and let $v = |V|$, and let s denote the sum of sizes of the transaction records corresponding to V in the log file. Lala and Panda do not discuss data structures for implementing the affected list. If it is implemented with a linked list, then it is easily shown that the running time of their repair algorithm is $O(v^2 + s)$. This time bound would not be practical, because of the quadratic behavior in the size of v, as v might be large. However, a fairer assessment of their running time is obtained by observing that the affected list is accessed in accordance with an abstract data type called a *priority queue*. A priority queue allows elements to be inserted into a list in $O(\log n)$ time and the minimum element to be removed in $O(\log n)$ time, where n is the size of the list.

Under this assumption, Lala and Panda's algorithm can be shown to run in $O(v \log v + s)$ worst-case time, using the most efficient implementations of priority queues known [3]. Though this is a practical time bound, because of the $\log v$ factor in the running time, this is not linear in the sum of lengths of the affected transactions. This is due to the use of a priority queue, a data type whose use we show can be eliminated from the problem altogether, improving the worst-case efficiency and simplifying the task of implementing it.

3   Our Approach

We can model direct dependencies with a directed *dependency graph* whose vertex set is the set of transactions, and whose edge set is $\{(T_i, T_j)|\ T_j$ is directly dependent on $T_i\}$. Since (T_i, T_j) is an edge only if T_j is committed after T_i, it follows that the dependency graph is a directed acyclic graph. This structure is similar to that of Lala and Panda, although we would propose using a standard adjacency-list representation of the graph [3], rather than the more cumbersome representation given in Lala and Panda's paper.

Instead of using a priority queue, we propose using *depth-first search*. This is a recursive strategy that marks a node u as *discovered* when a recursive call is made on u. The call on u then generates recursive calls on the unmarked neighbors of u. When all of these have been completed, all neighbors have been marked, u is marked as *finished* and the recursive call on u returns.

An initial call is initiated at any malicious transaction. After it returns, new calls may be initiated at unmarked transactions. It is not hard to show by induction that after all malicious transactions have been marked, so have the affected transactions.

Let us now address the question of how to produce a repair schedule. Every time a node is marked as *finished*, we prepend it to an affected list. We claim that when all malicious transactions and affected nodes have been marked, our affected list is a valid repair schedule, even though it does not necessarily list the transactions in ascending chronological order.

The reason that the repair schedule is that it constitutes a *topological sort* of the subgraph induced by the affected transactions. A topological sort is an ordering of the affected transaction such that all directed edges in the subgraph that they induce point from earlier to later elements of the ordering. It is well-known that taking vertices of a directed acyclic graph in descending order of finishing time produces a topological sort [3].

If the transactions are repaired from left to right, then when a transaction T_j is reached, all transactions on which it depends, namely, all transactions that have a directed edge to T_j, are earlier in the list, and have therefore already been repaired.

Lemma 1. *The proposed assessment algorithm produces a repair schedule in time proportional to the sum of lengths of the affected transactions.*

It remains to give asymptotic bounds for the total time spent keeping the dependency graph up-to-date as new transactions are committed and added to the log file. The transaction vertices are stored in an array, a Transaction Array; the numberings or timestamps serve as their indices into the array. The number of transactions in the array grows as new transactions are committed. When the array is full, it can be copied to a newly allocated array that is twice as large to create more room for nodes. By an *amortized analysis*, the total cost of reallocating and recopying is bounded by the number of elements in the array [3].

In addition to this, each data element of the database carries a *last-write record*, which is the index of the last transaction that wrote to it. This allows lookup of this transaction in the transaction array in $O(1)$ time.

When a new transaction T_n is added to the log file, the last-write records of the data elements read by T_n gives a multilist of transactions on which T_n belongs. This can be reduced to a a simple list, where no transaction appears more than once, by traversing the list, accessing the transactions in $O(1)$ time, marking each occurrence of an element in the list that is not already marked, and deleting any occurrences that were previously marked. This removes duplicates from the list. A second traversal of the list serves to remove the marks so that they do not interfere with later operations. An edge can then be installed from each T_j on which T_n belongs in $O(1)$ time, because we use an adjacency-list representation of the graph.

To finish updating the structure, T_n must replace the last-write records of the set of elements that it writes to with its index n. This takes time proportional to the number of elements that it writes to. The total time inserting T_n is proportional to the number of data elements that it reads and writes, which is proportional to the length of the transaction. This gives the following:

Lemma 2. *The total time to construct the dependency graph is proportional to the sum of lengths of transaction records in the log file.*

Because of this, the time to maintain the graph is on the order of the time simply to write the transaction records to the log file.

4   Conclusion

In this paper we analyzed two damage assessment algorithms and proposed a new algorithm that can reduce the time taken for damage assessment. The first algorithm [1] that we analyzed reads the log to find out the transactions that were affected by the malicious transaction. The log file, containing records of all operations of transactions, is typically very large and accessing it will involve significant disk I/Os. The second algorithm [5] that we analyzed minimizes log accesses by storing the transaction dependency information in a list structure. This information is captured while the transactions execute. We show how to store this dependency information in a data structures such that the speed for damage assessment is minimized. We also compare our approach with others and show that our approach requires the minimum time for damage assessment.

This paper looked at damage assessment algorithms based on transaction dependencies. This approach may result in a lot of false positives. Such false positives can be reduced by data dependency approaches. In future we plan to study existing data dependency approaches and improve upon them, if possible. Reducing the time taken for damage assessment is important, but it is also necessary to minimize the time taken for damage repair. In future, we also plan to optimize, if possible, existing damage repair algorithms.

References

1. P. Ammann, S. Jajodia, and P. Liu. Recovery from malicious transactions. *IEEE Transactions on Knowledge and Data Engineering*, 14(5):1167–1185, 2002.
2. P.A. Bernstein, V. Hadzilacos, and N. Goodman. *Concurrency Control and Recovery in Database Systems*. Addison–Wesley, Reading, MA, 1987.
3. T.H. Cormen, C.E. Leiserson, R.L. Rivest, and C. Stein. *Introduction to Algorithms*. McGraw Hill, Boston, 2001.
4. Sushil Jajodia, Catherine D. McCollum, and Paul Ammann. Trusted recovery: An important phase of information warfare defense. *Communications of the ACM*, 42(7):71–75, July 1999.
5. C. Lala and B. Panda. Evaluating damage from cyber attacks. *IEEE Transactions on Systems, Man and Cybernetics*, 31(4):300–310, July 2001.
6. Chandana Lala and Brajendra Panda. On achieving fast damage appraisal in case of cyber attacks. In *Proceedings of the IEEE Workshop on Information Assurance*, West Point, NY, 2000.
7. Peng Liu and Sushil Jajodia. Multi-phase damage confinement in database systems for intrusion tolerance. In *Proc. 14th IEEE Computer Security Foundations Workshop*, 2001.

8. Peng Liu, Sushil Jajodia, and Catherine D. McCollum. Intrusion confinement by isolation in information systems. In *IFIP Workshop on Database Security*, pages 3–18, 1999.
9. Brajendra Panda and Joseph Giordano. Reconstructing the database after electronic attacks. In *Proceedings of the 12th Annual Working Conference on Database Security*, Chalkidiki, Greece, 1998.
10. Brajendra Panda and Kazi Asharful Haque. Extended data dependency approach - a robust way of rebuilding database. *ACM Symposium on Applied Computing*, pages 446–452, 2002.

Efficient Processing of Multiple Structural Join Queries

G.V. Subramanyam and P. Sreenivasa Kumar

Dept of Computer Science and Engineering,
Indian Institute of Technology - Madras,
Chennai 600036, India.
{gvs, psk}@cs.iitm.ernet.in

Abstract. XML is widely used for representing and exchanging hierarchical data and queries naturally specify hierarchical patterns to select relevant parts of an XML document. These patterns have a sequence of selection predicates connected by operators representing parent-child or ancestor-descendant relationships. In this context, the operation of structural join involves discovering pairs of nodes that are in ancestor-descendant relationship from the cross product of two sets of nodes. In this paper, we propose a novel way of solving queries with multiple structural joins by maintaining an extra piece of information for each element called $nDesc$, which specifies the number of descendants having same tag name as that of the element. An extensive experimental evaluation of our algorithms with datasets of varying $nDesc$ value shows that our algorithms perform better than the currently existing join algorithms.

1   Introduction

With the ever increasing use of XML as a format for exchanging information in the World Wide Web, a lot of the research has been done in proposing new query languages and techniques for efficient query processing. As XML is represented as an ordered, rooted and node-labeled tree having elements as internal nodes and data as leaves, queries use tree-structured patterns to find matches in an XML document. The result of a query may be an entire XML document or parts of it. Many query languages have been proposed for posing such queries (e.g., [3,5, 6]). XQuery uses XPath for navigating XML document tree and qualify relevant parts that match with the given query pattern. For example, the query:

$$workshop[location = `Chennai']//part[type = `T2000']$$

selects all parts whose type is 'T2000' produced in the workshop located in 'Chennai'. This query comprises both value-based search such as $type=$ 'T2000' and structural search such as $workshop//part$. Here '//' specifies ancestor-descendant relationship where as '/' specifies parent-child relationship.

Solving queries by naive tree traversal is a costly and time consuming process. Recently proposed techniques involve computing the given query pattern

H. Williams and L. MacKinnon (Eds.): BNCOD 2004, LNCS 3112, pp. 112–123, 2004.

by splitting it into the pairs of nodes that are structurally related (ancestor-descendant or parent-child). Computing such pairs (for e.g., (*part*, *type*), (*workshop*, *part*)) involves joining list of ancestors with the list of descendants. The joining algorithms can be categorized into two types depending on whether they operate on *indexed* lists or *non-indexed* lists.

Briefly, the algorithms operating on *non-indexed* lists make sequential scans over the input element lists that are retrieved using *tag* (or element) name as a key. Examples of such algorithms are MPMGJN (multi-predicate merge join) [15] and stack-tree algorithm [1]. MPMGJN is a variant of traditional relational-style merge join process, that finds all matches that are structurally related. The stack-tree uses an in-memory stack of ancestors during join process and it guarantees that every ancestor and descendant is accessed only once unlike in MPMGJN where it makes multiple scans over the lists. The type of algorithms that assume index on the lists [4,10], can effectively skip ancestors and descendants that do not participate in the join. Though, they perform well on single join operation, they can not solve queries containing multiple structural joins effectively because index can not be assumed on the intermediate resultant lists. The stack-tree algorithms can solve query patterns containing multiple structural joins, but it sequentially scans the entire lists irrespective of the number of pairs that actually join during the process. Moreover, visiting elements that do not participate in the join process leads to unnecessary disk I/Os which results in degraded performance.

In this paper, we propose a solution that belongs to the type of algorithms that operate on *non-indexed* lists. Our algorithms can process queries containing multiple joins and can effectively skip most of the ancestor-descendants pairs that are not participating in the join. Here, we make use of the existing [1,4,15] node identification scheme (*DocID*, *start*, *end*, *level*) and add one more attribute called *nDesc*. This attribute specifies the number of descendants of same label (*tag* name) as that of the node. The *nDesc* value of a node is initially computed during the generation of the element lists and it is maintained dynamically during runtime. The following subsection summarizes our contributions in this paper.

Our Contributions

- Introducing a new attribute *nDesc* into the tuple (*DocID*, *start*, *end*, *level*), which can be utilized to skip most of the ancestors and descendants that do not participate in a join.
- An improved version of the existing stack-tree algorithm, which outputs pairs either in ancestor order or descendant order, is introduced.
- An extensive experimental evaluation of our algorithms was conducted and the results are compared with the stack-tree algorithms. We ran these algorithms with datasets of varying *nDesc*. Our comparative study shows that our algorithms perform better than the stack-tree algorithms.

The organization of this paper is as follows. We provide background material in Section 2 followed by a review on related work. We discuss our work in Section 4 where we present our algorithms and explain about the dynamic maintenance of $nDesc$. Section 5 describes performance analysis and we conclude in Section 6.

2   Background

Queries in XPath or XQuery use path expressions which are sequences of location steps to navigate through XML tree [9]. Basically, queries specify patterns that match the relevant twigs in the XML document. Since XML employs tree-structured data model for its representation, determining ancestor-descendant relationship between any pair of elements and finding all element pairs that are structurally related between the two element lists plays an important role in solving queries.

2.1   Numbering Scheme

To solve structural relationship between any two elements a numbering scheme is proposed [1,15] which is based on the region encoding of elements. In an XML document, each element is assigned with a tuple ($DocID$, $start$, end, $level$) and between any two elements (say, a and d) the relationship can be determined as follows: (i) If $a.start < d.start$ and $a.end > d.end$ then a is an ancestor of d. (ii) In addition to condition (i) if $level(a) = level(d) - 1$, then a is a parent of d. For each element, the ($start$, end) can be assigned by making a depth first traversal of an XML document tree [1,15]. If the $start$ value of a node v is η then its end value can be assigned with $\eta + count(subtree(v)) + 1$ ($+\lambda$), where $\lambda \geq 0$ provides space for future insertions with in the region encoding ($start$, end). The function $count$ returns the number of nodes in the subtree of node v.

Figure 1 shows a sample XML document tree containing nodes with start and end values. The root node a is assigned with (1, 50) and the children are (2, 11), (12, 15), (20, 31) and so on.

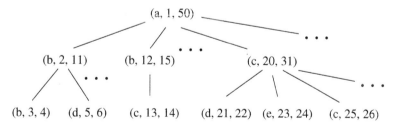

Fig. 1. A Sample XML Document

There are some other ways of identifying the node in a tree. One such approach is Dietz numbering scheme [7] which relies on the tree traversal orders. In this, each node is assigned with preorder rank as $start$ and postorder rank as end and it also satisfies region containment property. Other approach uses a path from the root node as a node-identification scheme which is referred as PID (Path ID) [11]. Using this, node a is an ancestor of d if and only if PID of

a is a prefix of PID of d. In our algorithms we use region encoding numbering scheme i.e., $(start, end)$, for effective structural matches.

2.2   Structural Joins

The basic structural relationship such as $p_1 \mathbin{//} p_2$ is computed by joining p_1-list with p_2-list. Let AList (list of candidate ancestors) be the set of all p_1-nodes and DList (list of candidate descendants) be the set of all p_2-nodes, where nodes in the candidate lists are sorted on their $(DocID, start)$ values. The goal of structural join algorithms is to find all pairs (a_i, d_j), where $a_i \in$ AList and $d_j \in$ DList, such that a_i is an ancestor of d_j. The element lists are stored in OS files in a storage structure indexed using tag (element) name as a key, which could retrieve the appropriate candidate list when the specific tag appears in the query pattern.

The evaluation process involves joining the two given lists and output all the resulting pairs (a_i, d_j) sorted either in ancestor order $(a_i.start)$ or in descendant order $(d_j.start)$. The query processor chooses the order dynamically during the evaluation process. The importance of the output order is explained in Section 4.3.

3   Related Work

Most of the query processing techniques that apply structural joins between the element lists assume tree-structured model of XML data [1,4,12,15]. There were many techniques proposed using the more popular RDBMS [13,14,15] having SQL as the querying agent. The motivation behind these techniques is that a large amount of XML data as of now and in future is expected to be stored in relational database systems. Zhang et. al. [15] propose a notion of "containment" join using multi-predicate merge join (MPMJGN) that differs from the traditional relational-style merge join algorithms. The XML documents are decomposed into relational tables having $(DocID, start, end, level)$ as the schema. Similar to this work, [12] proposes EE-join and EA-join algorithms for generating ancestor-descendant pairs by merging the two given element lists sorted on their $(DocID, start)$ values. These algorithms make multiple scans over the input lists during the join.

An improved version of MPMJGN algorithm can be found in [1], where an ancestor stack is used to guarantee that each element is accessed exactly once. We extend this work and demonstrate that by utilizing the information about the number of descendants of a node we can effectively skip most of the element pairs that do not match in the join. The idea of skipping elements is motivated from the work [4,10], that assume index on the lists such as B$^+$-tree. Particularly, [10] can skip both ancestors and descendants that do not participate in the join, whereas [4] can skip only the descendants effectively. But the disadvantage with such methods is that queries containing multiple structural joins can not be solved effectively because index is not available on intermediate element lists.

Recently, Bruno et. al [2] proposed a twig-join algorithm which is a generalization of stack-tree-algorithm [1]. It uses path stack for path expressions queries and twig-stack for tree-pattern queries. The stacks are linked according to the ancestor-descendant relationship between the elements occurring in the query pattern. This is done to avoid maintaining intermediate element lists that occur during the process of subsequent joins. Our technique can be easily embedded into these algorithms for effective query processing.

4   Structural Join Algorithms

In a multiple join query, the results are pipelined from one join to the subsequent join. So at every step of the query, effective processing of join is required. Existing state-of-art algorithms assume index on the lists. Even though they process the join effectively, they can not compute subsequent joins effectively because index is not maintained on the intermediate element lists. We address this drawback and propose a new solution by considering the nesting information of a document. For each element we add an extra piece of information $nDesc$, which specifies number of descendants of that element having same tag name as that of the element. The subtree of the XML data considered for the above definition of $nDesc$ is the one induced by the elements in the current AList and DList. The motivation behind using $nDesc$ comes from the following observations: For any two elements say a, d.

1. If d is descendant of a, then all the descendants of d are the descendants of a.
2. Similarly, if d is not a descendant of a, then none of the descendants of d is a descendant of a.
3. If a is an ancestor of d, then it is not necessary that all the descendants of a in the ancestor list are the ancestors of d. But, if a is not an ancestor of d, then none of the descendants of a in the ancestor list is an ancestor of d.

To appreciate the use of $nDesc$, consider the examples given in Figure 2a and Figure 2b. Each labeled line segment represents the region encoding of an element. Segments labeled with a correspond to elements from AList (ancestor list) and the segments labeled with d correspond to elements from DList (descendant list).

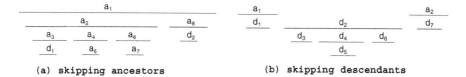

(a) skipping ancestors   (b) skipping descendants

Fig. 2. Scenario that explains the skipping of elements

During the processing of the scenario given in Figure 2a, the stack-tree procedure goes on like this: after joining d_1 with a_1, a_2 and a_3 (a_1, a_2 and a_3 would be on the stack with a_1 at the bottom and a_3 at the top), it takes d_2 and compare it with the top of stack i.e., a_3. Since a_3 and a_2 are not ancestors of d_2, it pops a_3 and a_2 from the stack. It then proceeds by pushing a_4 on to the stack and checking if a_4 is an ancestor of d_2. Since it is not, a_4 is popped too. This process of pushing and popping continues till a_8 is pushed on to the stack. Here we note that, it makes an unnecessary visit of the elements a_4-a_7 though, none of these elements are ancestors of d_2. To avoid such a visit (a_4-a_7), in our algorithm we proceed as follows: after popping a_2, we can directly seek a_8 which is $nDesc(a_2)$ elements away from a_2. Similarly in the example shown in the figure 2b, skipping all the descendants of d_2 is achieved by seeking d_7 which is $nDesc(d_2)$ elements away from d_2. S-Y Chein [4] used B$^+$-tree structure to skip ancestors by finding $a'(= a_8)$ having $a'.start ¿ a_2.end$ and descendants by finding $d'(=d_7)$ having $d'.start ¿ d_2.end$. As we mentioned before, using B$^+$-tree approach queries containing multiple joins can not be solved effectively.

Section 4.1 and 4.2 cover the description of the structural join algorithms based on $nDesc$. They take AList (candidate ancestor list) and DList (candidate descendant list) as input and output all the ancestor-descendant pairs (a_i, d_j), such that $a_i \in$ AList, $d_j \in$ DList. The output can be produced in either ancestor order or descendant order. During joining process, we can effectively skip most of the ancestors and descendants that have no matches.

4.1   Structural Join Algorithm for Descendant Order

The Algorithm shown in the Figure 4 for generating the output of the structural join in descendant order is a refinement of Stack-Tree-Desc [1] algorithm. When node a is joined with node d, we check for all the possible cases that are shown in Figure 3.

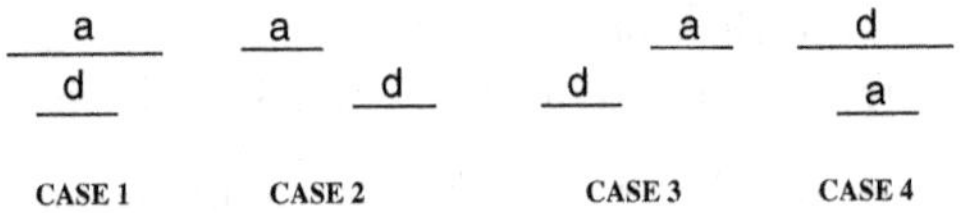

a	a		a	d
d		d	d	a

CASE 1   CASE 2   CASE 3   CASE 4

Fig. 3. Cases that occur during the join

The details are as follows: a and d act as cursors starting at the beginning of the lists and moves over AList and DList respectively until the end of one of the lists is reached. At run time, a stack of ancestors is maintained so as to join with the following descendants. In such an ancestor stack, a_i is on top of a_j only if a_j is an ancestor of a_i. The step in lines 5–8 pops out all the elements that are not ancestors of current d. This step is skipped at the beginning, because the stack is initially empty and obviously contains no ancestors to pop out. Considering case 1 dealt at line 9, a is pushed on to the stack only if a is ancestor of d. Note that, at any instance the stack contains only the elements that are ancestors of current d where as in Stack-Tree-Desc algorithm, all the elements from AList that occur before the current d are pushed on to stack, resulting in unnecessary stack operations. In the case 2 (lines 13–15), where a lies before d, we skip all

Input: AList (Set of candidate ancestors $[a_1, a_2, \ldots]$)
             DList (Set of candidate descendants $[d_1, d_2, \ldots]$)
Output: OutputList $[(a_i, d_j)]$ sorted in $d_j.start$
 1: $a = \text{first(AList)}$;
 2: $d = \text{first(DList)}$;
 3: $stack = \text{NULL}$;
 4: **while** (not end of AList and DList) **do**
 5:    **if** ($stack$ is NOT null) **then**
 6:       Pop all elements that are not ancestors of d;
 7:       Let a be the last element popped;
 8:    **end if**
 9:    **if** (a is ancestor of d) **then**
10:       /* **case 1:** when a is ancestor of d */
11:       Push a on to the $stack$;
12:       $a = $ next element in AList after a;
13:    **else if** ($a.end < d.start$) **then**
14:       /* **case 2:** a comes before d */
15:       $a = $ element in AList at $a.nDesc+1^{th}$ position from a;
16:    **else**
17:       **if** ($stack$ is NOT null) **then**
18:          /* output d with all elements on the stack */
19:          append all (a, d) pairs such that $a \in stack$, to the OutputList
20:          $d = $ next element in DList after d;
21:       **else if** ($d.end < a.start$) **then**
22:          /* **case 3:** a lies after d */
23:          $d = $ element in DList at $d.nDesc + 1^{th}$ position from d;
24:       **else**
25:          /* **case 4:** a is descendant of d */
26:          $d = $ next element in DList after d;
27:       **end if**
28:    **end if**
29: **end while**

Fig. 4. Structural Join Algorithm using $nDesc$

the descendants of a by directly seeking a' in AList which is the $a.nDesc + 1^{th}$ element from a. In case 3 (lines 21–23) where d lies before a, we can skip all the descendants of d by directly seeking d' in DList which is the $d.nDesc + 1^{th}$ element from d, provided stack is empty. Skipping descendants when stack is non-empty result in loss of some of ancestor-descendant pairs that match during the join. Lastly in case 4 (lines 24–27), when d is an ancestor of a we proceed with the next element in DList after d. Here we observe that we can't skip descendants of d because there may be some element $d' \in$ DList which is a descendant of both a and d.

4.2   Structural Join Algorithm for Ancestor Order

This technique is similar to the Stack-Tree-Anc [1] algorithm in the way we output the pairs sorted in ancestor order. The details are as follows: Let a_i be on top of a_j in the ancestor stack, if d is descendant of a_i then it is descendant of a_j

(and in fact, descendant of all the elements below a_i). Since $a_i.start > a_j.start$, we can not output a_j with the current d until a_i is popped out from the stack. This is because there may be some other element $d' \in$ DList after d which is also a descendant of a_j. Here, we associate *InheritList* and *SelfList* to each node of the ancestor stack as done in the Stack-Tree-Anc algorithm. *SelfList* of a node e is the set of all descendants from DList that were joined with e and *InheritList* of e is the set of all joined pairs (a_i, d_j) such that $a_i \in$ AList, $d_j \in$ DList and a_i was a descendant of e, but not currently on stack. When d is a descendant of the top of stack, instead of outputting d with all the nodes on the stack, we add it to the *SelfList* of all the nodes in the stack. When any other node is popped out, we append its *InheritList* to its *SelfList* and then the resultant list is appended to the *InheritList* of the node at the top of stack. When the stack is empty after a node is popped, we output its *SelfList* first and then its *InheritList*. Here, we can observe that no output is generated until the bottom most node of the stack is popped out.

4.3   Dynamic Maintenance of $nDesc$ Value

Each node in the joining lists is associated with a tuple (*DocID, start, end, nDesc, level*) and $nDesc$ plays an important role in skipping elements that do not participate in the join. Since only the subset of elements from the AList and the DList is in the output of a join, updating $nDesc$ is necessary for the processing of a query containing multiple structural joins. The modification of $nDesc$ value depends on the order (Ancestor / Descendant) the result is produced. For instance, consider a query $Q_1 : a[//b]/c$, to solve such query it is required to join a and b and output the result in an ancestor order for further processing of the join between a and c. Similarly, query $Q_2 : a//b/c$ requires the output of join (a, b) in descendant order for joining the result with c.

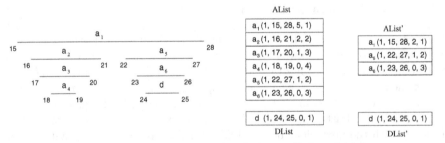

Fig. 5. An XML fragment and the lists before and after the join process

Updating $nDesc$ is needed only when the pairs are produced in ancestor order. This is based on the observation that if b is a descendant of a, then all the descendants of b are descendants of a; but, if a is an ancestor of b, then it need not be the case that all the descendants of a from AList are the ancestors of b. Figure 5 shows an XML fragment and the instances of lists that occur before join and after join process.

Table 1. DTD used for the Experiments and a set of sample queries

<!ELEMENT workshop (machine+)>   <!ELEMENT machine (part+, compon-   ent*, type)>   <!ELEMENT part (part*, component?,   name?, desc?)>   <!ELEMENT component (component*,   name?, desc?)>   <!ELEMENT name (#PCDATA)>   <!ELEMENT desc (#PCDATA)>   <!ELEMENT type (#PCDATA)>

Query	Path Expressions
Q_1	$part//name$
Q_2	$part//component$
Q_3	$component//name$
Q_4	$part//component//name$

The procedure for updating $nDesc$ is simple: In each stack node, we maintain a temporary variable called *"tmpnDesc"*. Initially, the *"tmpnDesc"* of a node is set to zero when it is pushed on to the stack, but for all the elements below it the value of *"tmpnDesc"* is incremented by one. The *"nDesc"* of a node is actually updated with *"tmpnDesc"* when we output the node to the *List*

5   Performance Study

We now explain the comparative study of our algorithms discussed in the paper with the existing stack-tree algorithms. With our results, we claim that the performance of a join can be greatly improved by considering the document nesting information. For our experiments, we used synthetic datasets so as to have control over the structure and the $nDesc$ value of each element. The generated XML documents confirm to the DTD shown in the Table 1 and each XML document is of size around 100 MB. In generated documents, we maintain the average $nDesc$ value of the elements such as *part* and *component* varying from 2 to 10. We show (in Figure 6) the performance graphs of the experiments run with the datasets having $nDesc$ values 2, 4, 6, 8, 10. We also compare the performance of join algorithms using the set of queries shown in the Table 1, in which queries Q_1, Q_2 and Q_3 are simple structural join queries and query Q_4 is a complex query containing multiple structural joins. For each query, the result is generated in ancestor order as well as in descendant order, for the purpose of comparison. The above queries are specifically selected to show that the improvement in the join performance is sensitive to the $nDesc$ value.

The experiments were conducted using Red Hat v7.2 on PIII 500 MHz processor with 256 MB RAM and 20 GB hard disk having disk page size of 4KB. The disk is locally attached to the system and is used to store XML data and the element lists. All these algorithms are coded in C++ and compiled using GNU C++ compiler. The Gnome XML parser [16] was used for parsing large XML documents.

Table 2. Number of Elements scanned (in thousands) and output cardinality with varying $nDesc$ values

(a) Q_1: part // name

nDesc	STJ	STJ+N	o/p card.
2	580	435	78
4	766	386	82
6	843	280	47
8	781	213	34
10	746	176	28

(b) Q_2: part // component

nDesc	STJ	STJ+N	o/p card.
2	1148	617	146
4	1029	491	172
6	1195	312	105
8	1196	375	195
10	1198	305	159

(c) Q_3: component // name

nDesc	STJ	STJ+N	o/p card.
2	860	609	62
4	910	396	49
6	940	311	52
8	874	238	37
10	836	194	31

(d) Q_4: part // component // name

nDesc	STJ	STJ+N	o/p card.
2	1529	987	178
4	1638	937	221
6	1650	813	155
8	1607	785	267
10	1549	656	219

5.1 Experimental Results

This subsection details the experimental evaluation and performance plots of our algorithms. We use the following notations: STA and STD for the existing Stack-Tree algorithms, STA+N and STD+N refer to the modified Stack-Tree algorithms considering $nDesc$. "A" refers to Ancestor order and "D" refers to descendant order.

The generated datasets with varying $nDesc$ are used to perform comparison among the four join algorithms. These datasets are parsed using Gnome XML parser [16] which generates element lists to the *store* and these lists are retrieved using *tag* name as a key. The *store* groups the lists into OS files and elements are accessed using primitive file operations: *read* and *seek*. Observing the plots shown in the Figure 6 carefully, we note that the performance of our join algorithms is marginally less than that of stack-Tree algorithms at lower $nDesc$ values. However, our algorithms perform much better when there is an increase in the complexity of nesting in an XML document i.e., at higher $nDesc$ values.

The metrics we adopt for measuring the performance of the join algorithms are (i) Total number of elements scanned. (ii) Elapsed time: Total time spent in joining process.

Table 2 reports the output cardinality and number of elements scanned (in thousands) by the queries Q_1, Q_2, Q_3, and Q_4. STJ represents Stack-Tree join algorithms and STJ+N represents Stack-Tree join algorithms considering $nDesc$ of an element. It can be observed that the number of elements scanned by STJ+N algorithms, at higher $nDesc$ values, is quite less compared to that of STJ algorithms.

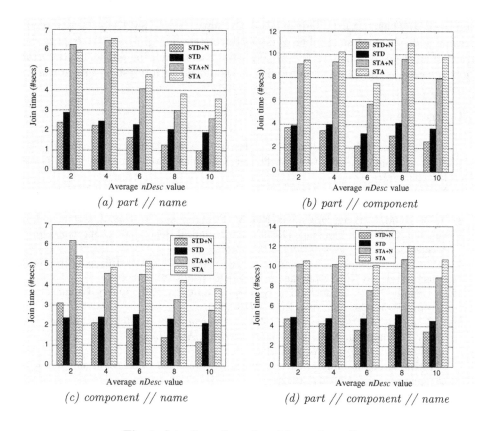

Fig. 6. Join time of queries with varying $nDesc$

To get the cache state (warm / cold) independent view of run times, the algorithms are run several times and the CPU times are averaged. Since stack-tree algorithms access all the elements, the improvement in the performance of our algorithms is due to lessening of element comparisons by skipping most of the elements that have no matches in the join.

6   Conclusions

In this paper, we mainly focused on solving queries containing multiple structural joins. Our motivation is the observation that the algorithms that operate on *indexed* lists can not solve queries containing multiple structural joins effectively. The work we discussed here can solve multiple joins using nesting information of the document i.e., $nDesc$. Using $nDesc$, we can skip most of the ancestors and descendants that do not occur in the join and it can be maintained dynamically during runtime. To the best of our knowledge concerning our related work, no work has been done on skipping elements by considering nesting information of a document. The algorithms we discussed here are the one that operate on *non-indexed* element lists. Our experiments have shown that the proposed algorithms indeed scan less number of nodes during the join process. We expect the performance to be much better on larger data sets. Devising efficient structural join algorithms for graph structured data would be an interesting future work.

References

1. S. Al-khalifa, H. V. Jagadish, N. Koudas, J. M. Patel, D. Srivastava, and Y. Wu. Structural joins: A primitive for efficient XML query processing. In *ICDE*, pages 141-152, 2002.
2. N. Bruno, N. Koudas, and D. Srivatsava. Holistic twig joins: Optimal XML pattern Matching. In *SIGMOD*. pages 310-321, 2002.
3. A. Berglund, S. Boag, D. Chamberlin, M. F. Fernandez, M. Kay, J. Robie, and J. Siméon. XML Path Language (XPath) 2.0 Technical Report, *W3C Working Draft*. Available at *http://www.w3.org/TR/XPath20/*. *2001*.
4. S-Y. Chein, Z. Vagena, D. Zhang, V. J. Tsotras, and C. Zanilo. Efficient structural joins on Indexed XML Documents. In *VLDB*. pages 263-274, 2002.
5. D. Chamberlin, J. Robie, and D. Florescu. Quilt: An XML Query Language for Heterogeneous Data Sources. In *WebDB* 2000.
6. D. Chamberlin, D. Florescu, J. Robie, J. Siméon, and M. Stefenscu. XQuery: A Query Language for XML. *W3C Working Draft*. Available at *http://www.w3.org/TR/XQuery 2001*.
7. P. F. Dietz. Maintaining order in a linked List. In *ACM Symposium on Theory of Computing*, pages 122-127, 1982.
8. D. Florescu, and D. Kossman. Storing and Querying XML data using RDBMS. *IEEE Data Engineering Bulletin*, 22(3):27-34, 1999.
9. T. Grust. Accelerating XPath Location Steps. In *SIGMOD*, pages 109-120, 2002.
10. H. Jiang, H. Lu, W. Wang, and B. C. Ooi. XR-Tree: Indexing XML Data for Efficient Structural Joins. In *ICDE*, pages 253-264, 2003.
11. Jan-Marco Bremer and Michael Gertz. An Efficient XML Node Identification and Indexing Scheme. *Technical Report CSE-2003-04*. Department of Computer Science, University of California at Davis, January *2003*
12. Q. Li and B. Moon. Indexing and Querying XML data for Regular Path Expressions. In *VLDB*, pages 361-370, 2001.
13. J. Shanmugasundaram, K. Tufte, G. He, C. Zhang, D. J. Dewit, and J. F. Naughton. Relational Databases for Querying XML Documents : Limitations and Opportunities. In *VLDB*, pages 302-314, 1999.
14. I. Tatarinov, S. Viglas, K. Beyer, J. Shanmugasundaram, E. Shekita and C. Zhang. Storing and querying ordered XML using a relational database systems. In *SIGMOD*, pages 204-215, 2002.
15. C. Zhang, J. Naughton, D. Dewit, Q.Luo, and G. Lohman. On supporting containment queries in Relational database management systems. In *SIGMOD*, pages 425-436, 2001.
16. Available at *http://www.xmlsoft.org*.

Handling Updates for Cache-Answerability of XML Queries on the Web*

Jung Kee Park and Hyunchul Kang

School of Computer Science and Engineering, Chung-Ang University,
Seoul, 156-756, Korea
{jkpark@dblab.cse.cau.ac.kr, hckang@cau.ac.kr}

Abstract. Cache-answerability of XML queries is crucial for efficient support of XML database-backed Web applications. In this paper, we deal with XML updates for cache-answerability of XML queries on the Web. We consider the multi-tier architecture for XML database-backed applications on the Web where middle-tier XML caching at the application server is provided while the XML source update takes place at the data server. Implementation where relational DBMSs are employed as XML stores for the XML source as well as its cache is described, and the results of performance evaluation through a detailed set of experiments conducted on the real Web are reported.

1 Introduction

Since the emergence of XML as a standard for data exchange on the Web, today's Web applications are to retrieve information from remote XML sources across the network. *Cache-answerability* of XML queries is thus crucial for efficient support of XML database-backed Web applications.

Let us consider *semantic caching* which is view-based query caching whereby the result of an XML query against the base XML documents in the underlying XML source is cached and maintained as a *materialized view*. In order to capitalize on the XML cache in processing XML queries, given a query, it should be possible to compute the whole or part of its result from the relevant materialized view and to rewrite the original query against the source XML documents into the one against the materialized view. There are three types of XML query processing with the materialized views, each called *MV, BD+MV*, and *BD* [1]. MV could be employed for the case where the materialized view and the query result are in complete match or the materialized view contains the query result provided query rewriting is possible. BD+MV could be employed for the case where the materialized view and the query result only partially match. Here, the query rewriting is more complicated than that of MV. The original query is decomposed into two sets of subqueries, one against the materialized view and the other against the base documents. BD is for the case where there is no

---

* This work was supported by grant No. R01-2003-000-10395-0 from the Basic Research Program of the Korea Science and Engineering Foundation.

H. Williams and L. MacKinnon (Eds.): BNCOD 2004, LNCS 3112, pp. 124–135, 2004.

match between the materialized view and the query result or query rewriting is impossible, and thus, the cache is not used.

There are three major issues that need to be dealt with in realizing cache-answerability of XML queries on the Web. (1) Rewriting an XML query with the XML cache, (2) Propagating the update done to the XML source to the cache, and (3) Integrating the partial query results obtained from the source and from the cache to produce the final result.

The first and the third issues were investigated in our earlier work [1]. In this paper, we investigate the second issue to complete a full-fledged solution to cache-answerability of XML queries on the Web, and evaluate its performance through a detailed set of experiments conducted on the real Web. We consider the multi-tier architecture for XML database-backed applications on the Web where middle-tier XML caching at the application server is provided while the XML source update takes place at the data server. Contrary to the first issue, the solution to the other two issues is closely dependent on the XML storage structures for the base documents as well as their materialized views. We employ *relational DBMSs* to store them. Since they are in dominantly wide use, storing and querying XML documents with them is of pragmatic importance and is attracting much attention.

The rest of this paper is organized as follows. Section 2 gives an overview of XML storage in our system that provides cache-answerability of XML queries on the Web. Section 3 presents the techniques for handling XML updates. Section 4 reports implementation and the results of performance evaluation. Finally, Section 5 gives some concluding remarks.

2 XML Storage

Four tables named *ELEMENT, PATH, TEXT* and *ATTRIBUTE* are used for storing the XML source documents at the data server. Such four table-based XML storage was first proposed in [2] but the schema of the four tables in this paper is newly designed with our own *XML numbering scheme*. Our numbering scheme, however, can be embedded in other alternative approaches to XML storage proposed in the literature such as the Edge table approach or the Edge/separate value table approach of [3].

When an XML document is stored, it is first assigned a unique document identifier (*Did*) and decomposed into elements. An XML document is usually modeled as a node-labeled ordered tree, and each XML element, be it leaf or non-leaf, corresponds to a node of that tree. Each element is mapped to relational tuples with a unique identifier (*Eid*), which is assigned in a monotonically increasing way from the root element to its subelements in the *preorder* traversal of the XML tree. Eid is not just the unique identifier of an element but carries the structural information among the elements (e.g., ancestor-descendant relationship) [4] and the information on the order of the elements in a document.

The PATH table stores every unique path from the root element to an element in the documents that appears at least once along with its unique path identifier assigned. The <path, id> pair is stored in columns *Epath* and *EpathId*. The TEXT table is to store the text (PCDATA) of the leaf XML elements. It consists of columns Did, Eid,

EpathId, and *Text*. Each tuple of TEXT corresponds to a leaf element. For leaf *e*, Eid stores the identifier of *e*, Text stores the text of *e*, and EpathId stores the identifier of the path from the root to *e*. The ATTRIBUTE table is to store the attribute name and value pairs, and consists of columns Did, Eid, EpathId, *AttrName*, and *AttrValue*. Each attribute of an element is mapped to a tuple of ATTRIBUTE. For attribute *a* with value *v* in element *e*, Eid stores the identifier of *e*, AttrName and AttrValue store *a* and *v*, respectively, and EpathId stores the same as in TEXT.

The rest of the information on each element is stored in the ELEMENT table, which consists of columns Did, Eid, *Ename*, EpathId, *ParentEid*, *RmdEid*, *IrmcEid*. Each tuple of ELEMENT corresponds to an element. For element *e*, Ename stores the tag name of *e*, and EpathId stores the same as in TEXT or ATTRIBUTE. ParentEid stores the identifier of the parent element of *e*, storing parent-child relationship among the elements. RmdEid stores the ancestor-descendant relationship among the elements. RmdEid along with IrmcEid is also for supporting XML updates of any type such that the Eid's of all the elements in the document are still kept in the preorder after updates without reassigning the Eid's at all. Such *update robust* XML numbering is desirable since most of the state-of-the-art XML query processing algorithms are centered around the preorder-based XML numbering schemes. RmdEid and IrmcEid play the core role in our XML numbering scheme, and their detailed explanation is given in Section 3.1.

The table schema for XML materialized views is the same as that for the source XML documents except that each of ELEMENT, TEXT, and ATTRIBUTE table schema is augmented with an additional column, view identifier (*Vid*). As for the PATH table, it could be shared among all the views. Thus, it would be better to cache the PATH table once in its entirety. We consider the XML query in *path expression* against *a collection of* XML documents. The result of path expression *q* against XML document *D* is a forest of subtrees of *D* rooted at the last element in *q* with the filter operator removed, if any. We call that element as the *target element* of *q*. For path expression *movie/reviews[review/reviewer="Jane"]*, for example, the target element is *reviews*. As such, an XML view, which is the result of an XML query, is also a forest of subtrees each of which is rooted at the target element of the query's path expression retrieved from all the source documents.

The way an XML view is cached at the application server is as follows: Given XML query *q* in path expression, it is sent to the data server and transformed into SQL expressions against the four tables. The tuples of the SQL result sets out of all the tables except PATH augmented with Vid are cached into their corresponding tables at the application server.

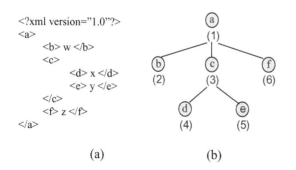

(a)   (b)

Fig. 1. Example XML Document

3 Handling XML Updates

In this section, we investigate the issue of propagating the updates done to the source XML documents at the data server to the application server to incrementally refresh the XML materialized views there. To deal with the XML updates, we first propose a update robust XML numbering scheme.

3.1 Update Robust XML Numbering Scheme

Consider the XML document in Fig. 1(a). Its tree representation excluding the text is in Fig. 1(b) where the integers in parentheses beside each node denote the Eid's assigned in the preorder traversal of the tree. Without loss of generality, in Fig. 1(b), we assume that Eid's are monotonically increased by 1 in the preorder starting at 1 from the root. Fig. 2(a) gives the RmdEid and IrmcEid values as well where the 3-tuple (i, j, k) beside each node denotes (Eid, RmdEid, IrmcEid). Intuitively speaking, for element e, RmdEid of e (denoted as RmdEid(e)) stores the identifier of the *rightmost descendant* element of e whereas IrmcEid of e (denoted as IrmcEid(e)) stores the value that would have been assigned as the Eid to the *imaginary rightmost child* element of e in the preorder traversal of the XML tree. Their formal definitions are as follows:

Definition 1 [RmdEid and IrmcEid]. For element e, RmdEid(e) stores some value z such that x $z < y$ where x and y are as follows: x is the identifier of the rightmost descendant element of e. y is the identifier of the immediate successor element of e's rightmost descendant in the preorder traversal of the XML tree if one exists. Otherwise, y is the identifier of the imaginary rightmost child of the root. IrmcEid(e) stores some value z such that RmdEid(e) $< z$ y where y is the same as above.   □

For example, RmdEid(c) in Fig. 1(b) is 5. c's rightmost descendant is e and e's immediate successor in the preorder is f. Thus, e's Eid (denoted as Eid(e)) RmdEid(c) $<$ Eid(f) (i.e., 5 RmdEid(c) < 6). RmdEid(e) is also 5. The rightmost descendant of every leaf node is itself, and thus, Eid(e) RmdEid(e) $<$ Eid(f) (i.e., 5 RmdEid(e) < 6).

Meanwhile, IrmcEid(c) in Fig. 1(b) is 6 because RmdEid(c) $<$ IrmcEid(c) Eid(f) (i.e., 5 $<$ IrmcEid(c) 6). Note that for every element p, RmdEid(p) $<$

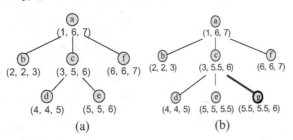

(a)   (b)

Fig. 2. Eid, RmdEid, IrmcEid

IrmcEid(p) by Definition 1. IrmcEid(e) is also 6 because RmdEid(e) $<$ IrmcEid(e) Eid(f) (i.e., 5 $<$ IrmcEid(c) 6). For a or f in Fig. 1(b), no immediate successor of their rightmost descendants in the preorder exists. In that case, the Eid of the imaginary rightmost child of the root which is 7 in the initial assignment of the Eid's in Fig. 1(b) is employed. IrmcEid(a) and IrmcEid(f) are both 7 because RmdEid(a) < IrmcEid(a)   7 (i.e., 6 < IrmcEid(a)   7) and RmdEid(f) < IrmcEid(f)   7 (i.e., 6 < IrmcEid(a)   7).

Now let us consider XML updates. We deal with the insertion or deletion of a leaf element and with modification of the text of a leaf element. More complicated types of update can be conducted with a series of these basic update operations.

Insertion of a Leaf. Suppose leaf element <g> v </g> is inserted as a child of c in the XML document of Fig. 1. Element c has already two subelements d and e. As such, in inserting g, its position matters. For ease of explanation, let us now assume that the XML document is an *unordered* one, and as suggested in [5], the new element is inserted as the rightmost child. Insertions into an ordered document are addressed afterwards.

Such an insertion requires reassigning the Eid's of all the elements in the document including the newly inserted g if the preorder is to be kept. In our XML numbering scheme, however, all the current Eid's remain unchanged, the Eid(g), RmdEid(g), and IrmcEid(g) are assigned, and just local adjustments on the relevant RmdEid's and IrmcEid's take place. Fig. 2(b) shows the result of g's insertion. 5.5, 5.5, and 6 were assigned to Eid(g), RmdEid(g), and IrmcEid(g), respectively. Accordingly, RmdEid(c) was adjusted to 5.5, and IrmcEid(e) was adjusted to 5.5. As a result, the preorder is kept. These were done as follows:

1. Eid(g), RmdEid(g), and IrmcEid(g) are set to x, x, and y, respectively where $x = $ (RmdEid(c) + IrmcEid(c))/2 and $y = $ IrmcEid(c).
2. RmdEid(c) is adjusted to (RmdEid(c) + IrmcEid(c))/2.
3. IrmcEid(e) is adjusted to (RmdEid(e) + IrmcEid(e))/2.

We call this procedure *XInsAdjust*. Note that XInsAdjust provides self-adjustability of the XML tree in the sense that RmdEid and/or IrmcEid values of each node can be adjusted using its own RmdEid and IrmcEid. Now let us examine applying XInsAdjust to an arbitrary XML document. For every element e of the XML document, we assume the following. RmdEid(e) was initialized to the identifier of the rightmost descendant element of e. As for IrmcEid(e), it was initialized to the identifier of the immediate successor element of e's rightmost descendant in the preorder traversal of the XML tree if one exists. Otherwise, it was initialized to the identifier of the imaginary rightmost child of the root. The properties that hold with XInsAdjust in an arbi-

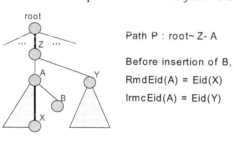

Path P : root~ Z- A

Before insertion of B,

RmdEid(A) = Eid(X)

IrmcEid(A) = Eid(Y)

Fig. 3. Leaf Element Insertion

trary XML document can be stated in the following Lemmas (refer to Fig. 3), leading to Theorem 1. All the proofs are omitted for the lack of space.

Lemma 1. For two elements p and q in XML document D, RmdEid(p) = RmdEid(q) if and only if IrmcEid(p) = IrmcEid(q).   □

Lemma 2. Consider path P whose target element is A in XML document D where the Eid's have been assigned in the preorder. Suppose leaf element B is inserted as the rightmost child of A and XInsAdjust is done. Then, the following holds:
   (1) RmdEid(A)- < Eid(B) < IrmcEid(A)- where $x(A)$- denotes A's x before insertion,
   (2) RmdEid(B) = Eid(B), and
   (3) IrmcEid(B) = IrmcEid(A)-.   □

Lemma 3. Consider path P whose target element is A in XML document D where the Eid's have been assigned in the preorder. Suppose leaf element B is inserted as the rightmost child of A and XInsAdjust is done. Then, for each element C that appears along path P *including* A such that RmdEid(C)- = RmdEid(A)-, RmdEid(C) = (RmdEid(C)- + IrmcEid(C)-)/2.   □

Lemma 4. Consider path P whose target element is A in XML document D where the Eid's have been assigned in the preorder. Suppose leaf element B is inserted as the rightmost child of A and XInsAdjust is done. Then, for each descendant element C of A *excluding* B such that IrmcEid(C)- = IrmcEid(A)-, IrmcEid(C) = (RmdEid(C)- + IrmcEid(C)-)/2.   □

Theorem 1. Consider path P whose target element is A in XML document D where the Eid's have been assigned in the preorder. Suppose leaf element B is inserted as the rightmost child of A. Then, the Eid's of all the elements in D including B could be still kept in the preorder without reassigning the Eid's at all.   □

To employ XInsAdjust, (1) Eid, RmdEid, and IrmcEid should be of type *real*, and (2) some values m, n need to be given as the Eid of the root and as the *gap* between two consecutive Eid's in the preorder, respectively when the initial assignment of the Eid's is done. (In Fig. 1(b), $m = n = 1$.)[1] To maintain Eid, RmdEid, and IrmcEid as integers or as real numbers with a small number of fractional digits, the calculation (RmdEid + IrmcEid)/2 in XInsAdjust can be refined to $\lfloor$(RmdEid + IrmcEid)/2$\rfloor$ to truncate the fractional part unless it gets equal to RmdEid.

Insertion into an Ordered XML Document. Ordering support is important for many XML applications. The procedure XInsAdjust described above can be easily extended to deal with insertions into the ordered documents. There are three cases for ordered

---

[1] In fact, n need not be constant for all of the two consecutive Eid pairs. For the pairs that expect more insertions than others, large n is desirable, whereas for those expecting little insertions, small n will do.

insertions. For element A, new leaf element B can be inserted (1) as the rightmost child of A, (2) at the right of some designated child of A, say C, but not as the rightmost one, and (3) as the leftmost child of A at the left of the former leftmost, say C.

The first case was already dealt with for unordered documents. XInsAdjust that needs to be exercised for the other two cases is very similar to that for the first case, and simpler. For the second case, $Eid(B)$, $RmdEid(B)$, and $IrmcEid(B)$ are set to x, x, and y, respectively where $x = (RmdEid(C) + IrmcEid(C))/2$ and $y = IrmcEid(C)$. The adjustment of RmdEid's is not necessary. For element e which is either C or a descendant of C such that $IrmcEid(e)$- = $IrmcEid(C)$-, $IrmcEid(e)$ is adjusted to $(RmdEid(e)$- + $IrmcEid(e)$-$)/2$. As for the third case, $Eid(B)$, $RmdEid(B)$, and $IrmcEid(B)$ are set to x, x, and y, respectively where $x = (Eid(A) + Eid(C))/2$ and $y = Eid(C)$. Neither RmdEid's nor IrmcEid's need adjustment.

Deletion or Modification of a Leaf. Contrary to the insertion of a leaf element, adjustment of RmdEid and IrmcEid against the deletion of a leaf element or the modification of the text of a leaf element is *not* necessary to keep the Eid's in the preorder. As for modification, the structure of the XML document remains intact, and thus, it is obvious that no adjustment is needed. As for deletion, though it causes structural change in the document, no adjustment does not damage the preorder of the Eid's nor correct functioning of further updates against the document due to our flexible definition of RmdEid and IrmcEid in Definition 1.

3.2 XML Update to SQL Mapping

Since the XML documents are stored in relational tables, the processing of XML updates with our XML numbering scheme should be expressed in SQL. In this section, we show that generation of such SQL expressions is possible. To simply convey how such mapping is accomplished, we assume that only *one* unordered XML document is stored in a *single* table as in the Edge table approach proposed in [3] where attributes are treated the same as elements. Below, such a single table is called *XMLOneTab*, and presumed to consist of columns Eid, Ename, Epath, Text, ParentEid, RmdEid, and IrmcEid (see Fig. 4).

For path P whose target element is A and leaf element B, say <b> xyz </b>, to insert B as the rightmost child of A, the following three SQL statements where :ename, :epath, and :text are the host variables are generated and executed in that order:

```
INSERT INTO XMLOneTab
   SELECT (RmdEid+IrmcEid)/2, :ename, :epath, :text, Eid, (RmdEid+IrmcEid)/2, IrmcEid
   FROM    XMLOneTab   WHERE   Epath = 'P'

UPDATE XMLOneTab   SET   RmdEid = (RmdEid+IrmcEid)/2
WHERE   RmdEid IN (SELECT RmdEid FROM XMLOneTab WHERE Epath = 'P')
            AND Epath NOT LIKE 'P/%'

UPDATE XMLOneTab   SET   IrmcEid = (RmdEid+IrmcEid)/2
WHERE   IrmcEid IN (SELECT IrmcEid FROM XMLOneTab WHERE Epath ='P')
```

AND Epath **LIKE** 'P/%'
AND Epath <> :epath

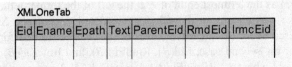

Fig. 4. Single Table Schema

The first INSERT statement is to insert a tuple for newly inserted element *B* where the host variables are assigned as :ename = '*b*', :epath = '*P/b*', and :text = '*xyz*'. It fetches the tuple for element *A* by giving condition Epath = '*P*' in the WHERE clause, comes up with the tuple for element *B*, and insert it.

The next UPDATE statement is to adjust the RmdEid's affected by the insertion of element *B*. The second condition, Epath NOT LIKE '*P/%*', in the outer WHERE clause is to exclude *A*'s descendants for adjustment. Only those elements along path *P* inclusive of *A* might be affected as far as RmdEid is concerned (refer to Lemma 3).

The last UPDATE statement is to adjust the IrmcEid's affected by the insertion of element *B*. The second condition, Epath like '*P/%*', in the outer WHERE clause is to exclude *B*'s ancestors for adjustment. Only *A*'s descendants except *B* might be affected as far as IrmcEid is concerned (refer to Lemma 4). The last condition, Epath <> :epath, is to exclude *B*.

The SQL statements to delete an element (either a leaf or a non-trivial subtree) or to modify the text of a leaf element into *new_value* are the followings where *P* is the path to the target element to be deleted or the path to the leaf whose text is to be modified:

DELETE FROM XMLOneTab **WHERE** Epath = 'P' **OR** Epath **LIKE** 'P/%'
UPDATE XMLOneTab **SET** Text = 'new_value' **WHERE** Epath = 'P'

Note that the above SQL expressions against XMLOneTab are just to show the way they could be generated for a given XML update. They are the versions considering neither multiple documents nor multiple occurrences of the same path in a document before as well as after the update. The former restriction is easily eliminated by employing column Did. Eliminating the latter one makes the above SQL expressions a little bit lengthy. It is often the case that the same path appears more than once in an XML document. Path *P* specified in the above SQL expressions might be such a one. In that case, the above SQL expressions are to update all the matched parts of the document. Such type of multiple or bulk updates may be useful in some applications. However, the XML update is usually intended against a specific one instance of path *P*, and attributes like ID and/or the text of the elements need to be used to restrict the scope of the update. As such, we need to add more conditions to the WHERE clauses.

Multiple occurrences of the same path in a document may be due to the insertion of an element. Suppose leaf element *d* is inserted at the end of path *a/b/c*. Path *a/b/c/d* may have already existed before the insertion. To deal with such a case, the last condition in the outer WHERE of the UPDATE statement to adjust IrmcEid (i.e., Epath <> :epath) needs to be changed not to exclude the preexisting element *d*'s of path *a/b/c/d* for possible adjustments. Recall that this condition is to exclude *B* in adjusting IrmcEid triggered by *B*'s insertion (refer to Lemma 4). One way is to add further conditions to distinguish the newly inserted *d* from the preexisting ones (e.g., using an attribute like ID of new *d*, if any). The other is to replace the current condition with

Eid **NOT IN** (**SELECT** RmdEid **FROM** XMLOneTab **WHERE** Epath ='P').

In our implementation described in Section 4, a module of generating SQL expressions for a given XML update was developed. Given the parameters describing an XML update such as the identifier of the document to be updated, the path to the target element for update, the conditions that need to be satisfied by the element to be updated, the element (either a leaf or a non-trivial subtree in XML) to be inserted, the new text to replace the one to be modified, and so on, the corresponding SQL statement(s) against the four tables storing the XML documents described in Section 2.1 and in Section 3.1 are generated. Multiple occurrences of the same path were also considered.

3.3   Propagation of Relevant Updates to Cache

For the XML update done at the data server, its relevance to the cache at the application server needs to be checked. This problem is similar to that of checking containment relationship between the result of an XML query and the XML cache. As such, algorithm *Check_Containment* proposed in our earlier work [1] for the latter problem is adapted for the relevance checking.

For the relevant update, its effects should be propagated to the cache. The tuples that need to be newly cached and/or the parameters for generating appropriate SQL statements are sent from the data server to the application server. There are two policies considered in this paper, *immediate* and *deferred*. For immediate propagation of updates, the execution of SQL statements could be done *in parallel* at the two servers. The data server sends the required data to the application server before it starts to execute the SQL statements against its tables. The update is completed after the application server reports completion of its part. For deferred propagation of updates, the data server *logs* the data to be sent to the application server. When the cache is to be accessed later, the log is sent at the request of the application server.

4   Implementation and Performance Evaluation

Our solution to cache-answerability of XML queries on the Web proposed in our earlier work [1] and in this paper was implemented on the real Web environment in Java. We were particularly interested in the case where the application server is accessing remote XML sources as well as the local ones. In our implementation, the application server ran in a system with Pentium IV 1.6GHz CPU and 512MB memory on Windows 2000 Server, and the remote XML data server also ran in a system with exactly the same specification. Although both of the two servers were located in Seoul, Korea, their sites were far from each other and they connected to each other through the Internet. The network bandwidth had not exceeded 1 Mbps. The RDBMS employed in each server was Oracle 9*i*. As for the SAX parser, Apache Xerces2 Java Parser 2.5.0 Release was used.

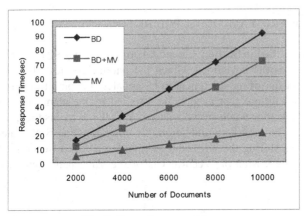

Fig. 5. Query Response Time

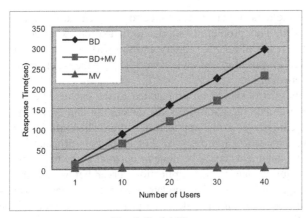

Fig. 6. Scalability

With the implemented system, we conducted a set of experiments to evaluate the performance improvement through cache-answerability as well as its overheads incurred for update propagation on the Web. The XML documents on *movies* whose average number of elements per document is about 20 were used as the source documents managed by the data server. The XML query embedded in the Web page and employed in the experiments was the one to retrieve the reviews of the movies. Let us call it *q*. The average number of elements retrieved per document for the result of *q* was about 10. At the application server, there were two materialized views. One is the result of *q*. Let us call it *v1*. The other called *v2* was the subset of the result of *q*. In processing *q*, *v1* was used in MV type of processing whereas *v2* was used in BD+MV type of processing. Contribution of *v2* to the final answer of *q* was 51% in terms of bytes excluding the white space after XML tagging, 30% in terms of the number of elements, or 34.6% in terms of the number of tuples. The experimental results were obtained by averaging 10 times of measurements conducted between 4:00 am and 9:00 am. During other time spans, the fluctuation of the network bandwidth was observed so severe.

Fig. 5 compares *q*'s response times through MV, BD+MV, and BD as the number of source documents varies 2,000 to 10,000. It was assumed that the materialized views were up-to-date when *q* was processed with them due to the immediate update propagation. As the volume of XML source got larger, performance degradation in

BD was most severe, that in BD+MV was next, whereas MV still showed acceptable performance. Fig. 6 compares *scalability* of MV, BD+MV, and BD as the number of users that issue q increases from 1 to 40. The number of source documents was set to 2,000. The materialized views were also assumed to be up-to-date when q was processed with them. It turned out that MV was very scalable whereas neither BD+MV nor BD was.

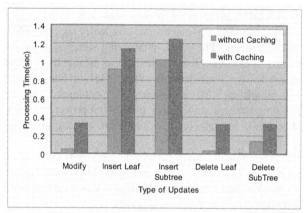

Fig. 7 measures the overhead incurred for an XML updates in maintaining $v1$ with immediate update propagation. The number of source documents was set to 2,000, and any one of them is updated. We considered five types of XML updates (leaf insertion/deletion, subtree insertion/deletion, and text modification), which are all relevant to $v1$. The

Fig. 7. Overhead in Update Processing with Immediate Update Propagation

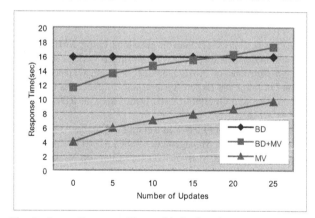

Fig. 8. Query Response Time with Deferred Update Propagation

height of the subtrees inserted or deleted was 2. The view maintenance overhead was not small for deletion and modification compared with the time it took to process the update only at the data server. However, the maximum overhead was less than about 0.3 sec for all types of the update experimented, which is negligible to human users on the Web. It is due to the parallel processing of source update and cache refresh as described in Section 3.3. Fig. 8 compares q's response times through MV and BD+MV with deferred update propagation with that through BD depicted in Fig. 5 as the number of logged updates increases from 0 to 25. The number of source documents was set to 2,000, and the five types of updates in Fig. 7 were uniformly done. Despite the overhead incurred in refreshing the materialized views to be used in processing q, deferred update propagation turned out to be also a viable policy as long as the update log is not too long.

5   Concluding Remarks

Cache-answerability of XML queries is crucial for efficient support of XML database-backed Web applications. In this paper, we proposed a solution to the issue of *handling XML updates* in realizing such functionality. Combined with the result of our earlier work on *query rewriting* and *partial result integration* [1], now a full-fledged solution to cache-answerability of XML queries on the Web is provided.

Our XML numbering scheme proposed in this paper can efficiently support XML query processing as well as XML updates. The XML numbering schemes have received hot attention in recent years. They were mainly devised to efficiently process XML queries. Just a few of them, however, considered handling XML updates as well [6-10]. Our scheme considerably simplifies XML update handling compared with the previous ones while not undermining the structural query processing power. We also showed that our scheme could be easily implemented with an RDBMS employed for XML storage.

As reported in Section 4, MV type of XML query processing greatly benefits from the cache but that is not necessarily the case when it comes to BD+MV type. Extending BD+MV type processing so that multiple relevant materialized views may be used to further enhance query performance is now under investigation.

References

1.   Moon, C., Kim, S., Kang, H.: Processing XML Path Expressions Using XML Material-
     ized Views. Lecture Notes in Computer Science, Vol. 2712. Springer-Verlag (2003) 19-37
2.   Shimura, T. et al.: Storage and Retrieval of XML Documents Using Object-Relational
     Databases. Proc. Int'l Conf. on Database and Expert Systems and Applications (1999)
3.   Florescu, D., Kossmann, D.: Storing and Querying XML Data Using an RDBMS. IEEE
     Data Eng. Bulletin 22(3) (1999) 27-34
4.   Zhang, C. et al.: On Supporting Containment Queries in Relational Database Management
     Systems. Proc. ACM SIGMOD Int'l Conf. on Management of Data. (2001) 425-436
5.   Tatarinov, I. et al.: Updating XML. Proc. ACM SIGMOD Int'l Conf. on Management of
     Data (2001) 413-424
6.   Amagasa, T. et al.: QRS: A Robust Numbering Scheme for XML Documents. Proc. Int'l
     Conf. on Data Eng. (2003) 705-707
7.   Chien, S. et al.: Storing and Querying Multiversion XML Documents using Durable Node
     Numbers. Proc. 2nd Int'l Conf. on Web Information Systems Eng. (2001) 232-241
8.   Cohen, E. et al.: Labeling Dynamic XML Trees. Proc. of ACM Int'l Symp. on PODS
     (2002) 271-281
9.   Li, Q., Moon, B.: Indexing and Querying XML Data for Regular Path Expressions. Proc.
     Int'l Conf. on VLDB (2001) 361-370
10. Tatarinov, I. et al.: Storing and Querying Ordered XML Using a Relational Database
     System. Proc. ACM SIGMOD Int'l Conf. on Management of Data (2002) 204-215

Constraining XML Transformations for Personalised Information Presentation

Alison Cawsey, Euan Dempster, Daniel Pacey, Howard Williams, David Marwick, and Lachlan MacKinnon

School of Mathematical and Computer Sciences, Heriot-Watt University, Edinburgh EH14 4AS
{alison, euan, ceedp, mhw, dhm, lachlan}@macs.hw.ac.uk

Abstract. Through the use of different stylesheets it is possible to transform the information contained in XML documents and present it in different ways, for example to create personalised presentations. However, in doing so there is a danger that the transformation may result in a presentation, which fails to carry the essential message intended by the provider of the source document. We believe that the Information Provider should be able to provide constraints on permitted transformations of their document, stating for example which elements are mandatory, which must not be changed, which must have the order preserved. This paper discusses the need for such transformation constraints, and proposes a simple metadata annotation expressing the required constraints. We consider the adequacy of the proposed approach, and alternative ways to constrain transformations.

1 Introduction

As more and more documents are marked up in XML, unique opportunities are available to present the information contained in them in different forms, depending on the individual user, his/her context, and the goals of the information provider. Stylesheet languages (such as XSLT [1]) have been developed for transforming XML and presenting the information contained in XML documents, and allowing radically different presentations of the same content. This may be used by the information provider to maximize the effect on the end user (e.g. to increase sales) or by a third party to allow improved "added value" services, such as personalised news feeders. Our concern in this paper is with third party transformations.

Personalisation may involve filtering the information set to remove information that does not fit with user's interests or preferences, or customizing it to present it in a different order or style. Transformations applied may delete sections of information or re-order them. Such re-structuring may inadvertently result in misleading or even dangerous presentations, where information is presented in a manner not intended by the author. This may result in incorrect conclusions being drawn by the reader.

Nevertheless, such transformations are likely to become increasingly important. For example, they may enable disabled users, or people using small mobile devices,

H. Williams and L. MacKinnon (Eds.): BNCOD 2004, LNCS 3112, pp. 136–143, 2004.

easier access to data, or may be used to generate personalised summaries based on interest profiles. They play an important role in the development of context-aware and personalised services, and adapting presentations to different user groups and hardware, both of which are established research areas [2, 3] that are now feeding into commercial systems [4]. Yet there has been very little research done on the potential problems that may arise from automatic document transformation, or into how to preserve essential properties of a document.

As an example, consider a situation in which one has an online catalogue of pharmaceutical drugs returned as an XML file. The data includes the name, price, main use and comments on a range of drugs. Using style sheets an intermediate provider might extract a subset of this information and present it to the user. However, in doing so it might omit part of the drug information e.g. the comments field (which may contain serious warnings) or disclaimers. Information (such as instructions) may be re-ordered in a way that distorts its meaning.

It is therefore important that the authors of XML documents (or suppliers of information in XML) should be able to retain some degree of control over those aspects of their document that they regard as important, while permitting transformations by third parties that might provide added value for particular users or groups. We have already reported on our initial analysis of this problem [5], which focused on medical documents. Based on an analysis of problems in this domain we proposed a number of simple constraints that an author or owner of a document might want to provide, delimiting what transformations are legitimate and likely to maintain the coherence and essential content of the document. Certain relations between elements of the document could be asserted as metadata .

We now report the next stage of this work. We consider XML constraint languages to see if they provide a well-founded basis for these sorts of constraints. We describe our transformation constraint notation, and data provenance assertions. As the problem is very difficult in the general case, we propose a framework where, given cooperative authors of documents and constraints, we may check validity. Finally we discuss the limitations of this approach and future directions.

2   XML Constraints

In considering how to formalise constraints on transformations work on XML constraints offers an obvious starting point. XML constraints adapt the notion of integrity constraints in databases, where assertions may be made about the integrity of the data. These assertions often concern the primary and foreign keys fundamental to database design, but may also include checks that no nonsensical data is present. Several researchers have argued that these notions are equally relevant in XML, especially given the common use of XML as a data interchange language, exchanging data between, in some cases, heterogeneous databases. Constraint languages, and extensions to DTDs and Schemas have been proposed [6-9].

These schema and constraint languages allow one to express certain classifications of constraint concerned with the integrity of the data in an individual document. However, none of these approaches appears to be sufficient to handle the problem addressed here. We are concerned with expressing constraints on the relationships between two documents, including both their content and structure. While conventional constraint languages cover some of the types of constraints required here, they do not cover those which relate content and order of information in one document to content and order in another. Consider the case of a list of items in some particular priority order that the author of a document wishes to preserve. Schemas or integrity constraints will not be sufficient to assert that this ordering relation should be maintained across the transformation. In general two types of constraint are therefore needed: conventional document constraints and transformation constraints. See figure 1.

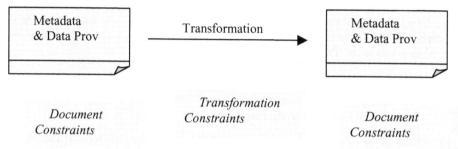

Fig. 1. Conventional document constraints and transformation constraints

3   Constraints on Transformations

Additional to traditional constraints as captured by Schemas plus integrity constraints, there is a role for transformation constraints. These constraints can be encoded as part of the metadata associated with a resource. Transformation constraint metadata can be added by the owner/author, and used to validate transformed structures.

Through these transformation constraints, it is essential to be able to express various kinds of relationships that must hold between elements or between documents that are being selected for a presentation. As in general a source document may be subject to a succession of transformations (and hence revisions) it is important to be able to link this constraint metadata to data provenance metadata, and ensure that constraints are propagated appropriately to transformed documents.

The analysis of potential problematic transformations suggests the following elementary constraints may be required.

- Element X is mandatory.

- Element X must not be altered.

- If Element X is included/omitted Element Y must be included/omitted too.

- Element X and Y must occur as adjacent elements.

- Ordering of an element group must be maintained across the transformation.

"Element" may refer to either a specific identifiable element within one document, normally identified using its ID, or to a whole document. We consider constraints that may be specific to a particular document, and not just those that generalize across a document type. To handle such constraints using conventional approaches, such as XML schema, can become very complex and in some cases impossible.

Most of the constraints listed refer implicitly or explicitly to the relationship between one document and another. For example, the order constraint above may apply to a set of *step* elements. Suppose that these list steps to be carried out in some medical procedure. Putting them in the wrong order could be crucial. It is necessary to be able to assert that the original order (and perhaps content) must be maintained.

In order to capture these different constraints across source and target documents we define *group* and *part* metadata elements, which allow the relevant relations to be defined. A group element has attributes that allow one to express constraints and relations on its parts. The attributes include:

- Order – allowing one to assert that the order of the parts must be maintained.

- Split – allowing one to assert that the set of parts must not be split (i.e., another element should not be inserted between them).

Condition – allowing one to express the fact the first part must occur if the second part does, and variations of this.

```
<group order="yes" split="no" condition="if-yes">

        <part IDREF="a1" alter="yes" mandatory="no "
/>

        <part IDREF="a2" alter="no" mandatory="no"/>

</group>

...

<data>

        <info ID="a1"> Some Information </info>

        <disclaimer ID="a2"> A disclaimer
</disclaimer>

</data>
```

Fig. 2. Transformation Constraint Metadata and Content Fragment

The *part* element may have an *alter* attribute, which is used to express the constraint that an element must remain unchanged in the transformation, and a *mandatory* attribute that is used to state that the element must exist in the transformed document, but may undergo changes.

Figure 2 shows an example of *group* metadata and associated content. This asserts that two named elements must remain in the given order, and may not have other elements placed between them i.e. may not be split. If the first part occurs, so must the second (although they are not individually mandatory), although the second could appear without the first. While one constituent must not be altered, the other may.

In this example it might be reasonable to apply this constraint to all information/disclaimer examples in documents of a particular type. In other examples the constraint might be specific to a particular document instance.

Note that a small extension to our constraint notation allows us to express more general and powerful rules. We replace document IDs with general Xpath expressions, allowing us to specify rules, which refer to specific document structures and content (e.g., to make mandatory the "comments" field of a drug if it includes the word "fatal"!).

These constraints may be asserted in source document metadata, and copied into target document metadata. In order to verify that these constraints hold one must have access to the source document. This is accessed via the data provenance metadata added to the target, described briefly below.

4   Data Provenance

In order to manage document transformations, whether or not the contributing authors and owners retain some degree of control, it is essential that data provenance is tracked. One needs to know where and how the information was produced, who has corrected it and how old it is. Also, if one is interested in intellectual property issues, data provenance is an essential part of understanding the ownership of data. [10] describes an approach to computing provenance when the data of interest has been created by a database query. A syntactic approach is adopted and results are presented for a general data model that applies to relational databases as well as to hierarchical data such as XML. A novel aspect of this work is a distinction between "why" provenance (refers to the source data that had some influence on the existence of the data) and "where" provenance (refers to the location(s) in the source databases from which the data was extracted). Data provenance - sometimes called "lineage" or "pedigree" [11, 12] - is the description of the origins of a piece of data and the process by which it arrived in a database.

To take account of data provenance for our problem we require a basic data provenance *stamp* on all data, such as shown in figure 3.

This specifies the creator of the document, date created and source site(s) from which it originated. It also states, with <IPchangeable/>, that the Information Provider has allowed changes to be made to this document. When a document is transformed a new data provenance stamp must be added to the transformed document, with a link to the source site, allowing us to track back to find all source documents and their transformation constraints.

```
<provenance>

        <creator>Euan</creator>

        <date-created> 31/12/89</date-created>

        <source-sites>

          <site>http://www.euan.co.uk

          </site>

        </source-sites>

        <IPchangeable/>

</provenance>
```

Fig. 3. Data Provenance Stamp

5   An Initial Framework for Constrained Transformations

Our current approach to transformation constraints only works if authors of both source documents and transformations obey certain rules. The author of the source documents must:

- Provide metadata to state constraints on allowable transformations.
- Provide element IDs for all elements mentioned in constraints.

The authors of any transformations of these documents must:

- Preserve element IDs across the transformation.
- Add a data provenance stamp allowing access to source document(s) and constraints.

They may, if they choose, add constraints on further transformations as metadata on the new transformed document.

The output of the transformations can then be validated. We can use the data provenance stamp to access the source document and its constraints. We can then use a general validation tool to check that the transformed documents obey the constraints in the source.

It is important to note that this approach can, in principle at least, generalize to the case where a sequence of transformations is applied to a document, perhaps each transformation written by a different author. The data provenance stamp is used to track back and collect constraints asserted by either source document authors or constraints asserted at earlier stages in transformation (on an intermediate document). This collection of constraints provides the context for the final transformation. This is illustrated in figure 4, where the dotted lines indicate data provenance links back.

We currently have a simple demonstrator implementation of a validation tool that works with a single set of constraints. We perform an explicit comparison with the source (using XSLT as the language for the validator). We plan to extend this to the case where we have multiple source documents and a sequence of transformations. The details of our metadata notation and validator are somewhat arbitrary. Our aim is simply to illustrate the problem, and demonstrate one direction for a solution.

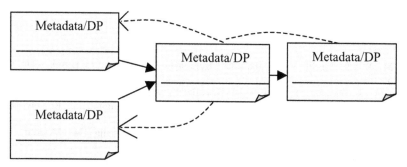

Fig. 4. Data Provenance Links

6   Conclusions and Further Work

This work only scratches the surface of a difficult but important problem – how to allow document transformations that are constrained in certain well-defined ways.

Our initial approach focuses on constraints applying to specific instances of source and transformed documents. We need to explore how best to integrate this with constraints that apply to all documents of a given type (e.g., in documents giving descriptions of drugs, never omit the side-effect if they are included in the source). Many of these could be expressed as integrity constraints. However, certain constraints still require special treatment, for example, constraints on order – the order of all child elements of this element must always be retained. When dealing with general constraints on documents of a given type it would be preferable to validate the transformation itself (e.g., XSLT stylesheet) rather than doing a source/target comparison. With a transformation language such as XSLT this is very difficult to check. However, preliminary analysis suggests that strongly typed transformation languages such as CDUCE [13] would be amenable to constraints and proofs of the kind required.

Clearly much more work is required. Here we have argued for the importance of transformation constraints, presented some simple but useful kinds of constraint that should be handled, and given some rather tentative suggestions as to how these can be formalised as metadata and validated by comparison of source and target documents against constraints. In general the problem is extremely difficult, yet if we *can* define the rules under which data and document transformations can occur, this opens up opportunities for knowledge and information re-use in different contexts while reducing the danger of confusion in resulting sources.

Acknowledgements. This work has been funded by the Engineering and Physical Science Research Council, grant reference GR/N22229/01 Dynamic Information Presentation, and we gratefully acknowledge their support.

References

1. Kay, M.: XSLT 2nd Edition - Programmer's Reference. Wrox Press Ltd, Birmingham, UK, (2001).
2. Kobsa, A., Koenemann, J., Pohl, W.: Personalized Hypermedia Presentation Techniques for Improving Online Customer Relationships. Knowledge Engineering Review **16**(2) (2001) 111-155
3. Brusilovsky, P.: Methods and Techniques of Adaptive Hypermedia. User Modeling and User-Adapted Interaction **6**(2-3) (1996) 87-129
4. Manber, U., Patel, A., Robison, J.: Experience with personalization on Yahoo! Comm ACM **43**(8) (2000) 35-39
5. Cawsey, A., Dempster, E., Bental, D., Pacey, D., Williams, H., MacKinnon, L., Marwick, D.: Preventing Misleading Presentations of XML Documents: Some Initial Proposals. Proc 2nd International Conference on Adaptive Hypermedia (2002) 492-496
6. Benedikt, M., Chan, C-Y., Fan, W., Freire, J., Rastogi, R.: Capturing both Types and Constraints in Data Integration. Proc ACM SIGMOD Conference on Management of Data (SIGMOD) (2003) 277-288
7. Buneman, P., Davidson, S., Fan, W., Hara C., Tan, W.: Keys for XML. Computer Networks **39** (2002) 473-487
8. Fan, W., Simeon, J.: Integrity Constraints for XML. In Proc ACM PODS, Dallas, TX (2000) 23-34
9. Fan, W., Kuper, G., Siméon, J.: Unified Constraint Model for XML. Computer Networks **39** (2002) 489 – 505
10. Buneman, P., Khanna, S., Tan, W.: Why and Where: A Characterization of Data Provenance. Proc International Conference on Database Theory (ICDT) (2001) 316-330
11. Woodruff, A., Stonebraker, M.: Supporting fine-grained data lineage in a database visualization environment. Proc Thirteenth Int. Conf on Data Engineering (ICDE'97) (1997) 91-102
12. Cui, Y., Widom. J.: Practical lineage tracing in data warehouses. Proc. ICDE 2000 (2000) 367-378
13. Benzaken, V., Castagna, G., Frisch, A.: Cduce, An XML-Centric General-Purpose Language. Proc. ACM International Conference on Functional Programming (2003) 51-63

DbSurfer: A Search and Navigation Tool for Relational Databases

Richard Wheeldon, Mark Levene, and Kevin Keenoy

School of Computer Science and Information Systems
Birkbeck University of London
Malet St, London
WC1E 7HX, United Kingdom
{richard,mark,kevin}@dcs.bbk.ac.uk

Abstract. We present a new application for keyword search within relational databases, which uses a novel algorithm to solve the join discovery problem by finding Memex-like trails through the graph of foreign key dependencies. It differs from previous efforts in the algorithms used, in the presentation mechanism and in the use of primary-key only database queries at query-time to maintain a fast response for users.

Keywords: Relational Databases, Hidden Web, Search, Navigation, Memex, Trails, DbSurfer, Join Discovery, XML

1   Introduction

"Future users of large data banks must be protected from having to know how the data is organized in the machine (the internal representation)."

E. F. Codd [4]

We consider that for many users of modern systems, being protected from the internal structures of pointers and hashes is insufficient. They also need to be spared the requirement of knowing the logical structures of a company or of its databases. For example, customers searching for information on a particular product should not be expected to know the address at which the relevant data is held. But neither should they be expected to know part numbers or table names in order to access this data, as required when using SQL.

In 1945, Vannevar Bush envisaged a future machine called Memex which would help the user build a "web of trails". His seminal paper "As We May Think" [3] first suggested the concept of a trail as a sequence of connected pages. This concept is now well established in the hypertext community.

We have previously developed tools which automate trail discovery for providing users with navigational assistance and search facilities within web sites and Javadocs [12]. These tools have been shown to enable users to find information in less time, with fewer clicks, and with a higher degree of satisfaction [9].

H. Williams and L. MacKinnon (Eds.): BNCOD 2004, LNCS 3112, pp. 144–149, 2004.
© Springer-Verlag Berlin Heidelberg 2004

Building on this work we have developed a tool called DbSurfer, which provides an interface for extracting data from relational databases. This data is extracted in the form of an inverted index and a graph, which can together be used to construct trails of information, allowing free text search on the contents. The free text search and database navigation facilities can be used directly, or can be used as the foundation for a customized interface.

Recent work at Microsoft Research [1], the Indian Institute of Technology[7,11] and the University of California [6] has resulted in several systems similar in many ways to our own. However, the system we describe here differs greatly in the design of the algorithms and in the style of the returned results. Our system also offers the opportunity for integrating both web site and database content with a common interface and for searching both simultaneously.

The rest of the paper is organized as follows. In Section 2 we describe our methods of indexing relational databases for keyword search. In Section 3 we describe the algorithms for extending this to compute joins by building trails, and give examples of the results achieved. Section 4 gives an overview of the system's architecture and Section 5 discusses the query options and syntax available to users of DbSurfer. An extended version of this paper [14] gives further details on the algorithm architecture. Further discussion of the metrics used and the alternative applications of the trail metaphor can be found in the first author's thesis [12].

2   Indexing a Relational Database

A single relation (or table) is a set of rows each of which can be addressed by some primary key. To index these rows we extract the data from each row in turn and construct a virtual document or web page, which is indexed by our parser. Since a relational database can be viewed as a special case of a more general model of semistructured data and XML, it might not be suprising that we can handle XML data using DbSurfer. Indeed that is all DbSurfer does! The virtual documents are XML representations of relational tuples, compatible with the emerging SQL/XML standard [5]. By combining the database reader with our web crawler, XML documents discovered on web sites can be automatically recognized as such and indexed in the same way, as can XML documents stored in the database, thus increasing coverage. The entries in the posting lists provide references to a servlet which produces a customized page for each row entry by rebuilding the virtual document and applying an XLST stylesheet. The textual content of each document is extracted and stored in an inverted file, such that the posting lists contain normalized tf.idf entries as prescibed by Salton [10]. Attribute names are also indexed as individual keywords so that, for example, the query "Anatomy of a search engine author" should return trails from the Google anatomy paper [2] to the entries for Sergey Brin and Larry Page.

Answers to users' queries may be spread over several tables, which must be joined together. We can answer such queries with the help of a link graph. We have shown how we can create an inverted file containing URLs, some of which reference traditional web pages and some of which reference servlets which return customized views of database content. All these URLs are assigned a separate 32-bit number which identifies them. It is these numbers which are stored in the inverted file, and it is these numbers which are stored in the link graph. The link graph is constructed by examining the foreign key constraints of the database (either by accessing the data dictionary table or via the JDBC APIs) and the data entries themselves. Each matching set of (*table*, *attribute*) pairs where there is a recognized referential constraint generates a bi-directional link.

3   Computing Joins with Trails

Given a suitable link graph, we can utilise our navigation engine approach to construct join sequences as trails. The navigation engine works in 4 stages. The first stage is to calculate scores for each of the nodes matching one or more of the keywords in the query, and isolate a small number of these for future expansion. The second stage is to construct the trails using the Best Trail algorithm [13,12]. The third stage involves filtering the trails to remove redundant information. In the fourth and final stage, the navigation engine computes small summaries of each page or row and formats the results for display in a web browser.

Selection of starting points is done by combining the $tf.idf$ scores for each node with a ranking metric called potential gain, which rates the navigation potential of a node in a graph based upon the number of trails available from it. The Best Trail algorithm takes the set of starting nodes as input and builds a set of navigation trees, using each starting point as the root node. Two series of iterations are employed for each tree using two different methods of probabilistic node selection. Once a sufficient number of nodes have been expanded, the highest ranked trail from each tree is selected. The subsequent set of trails is then filtered and sorted. With appropriate choice of parameters, the Best Trail algorithm can emulate the simpler best-first algorithm.

Trails are scored according to two simple metrics: the sum of the unique scores of the nodes in the trail divided by the length plus a constant, and the weighted sum of node scores, where weights are determined by the position in the trail, and the number of repetitions of that node. These functions encourage non-trivial trails, whilst discouraging redundant nodes.

Filtering takes place using a greedy algorithm and removes any sequences of redundant nodes which may be present in the trail. Redundant nodes are nodes which are either deemed to be of no relevance to the query or replicate content found in other nodes.

Once they have been filtered and sorted, the trails are returned to the user and presented in our NavSearch interface, the two main elements of which are a navigation toolbar comprising of a sequence of URLs (the "best trail") and a navigation tree window with the details of all the trails. Figure 1 shows how trails would be presented in the navigation tree window as a response to the question "vannevar bush" on a database generated from the DBLP data set. The content of any row can be examined in an adjacent frame by clicking on any likely looking entry or by examining the summary data in the enhanced tooltips.

As a preliminary evaluation of DbSurfer's performance, we ran two experiments on the DBLP corpus. In the first experiment, we selected 20 papers from the DBLP corpus, and constructed 20 queries by taking the surname of the first author and 1, 2 or 3 significant keywords with which a user might expect to identify that paper. We submitted these queries to DbSurfer for evaluation. We also submitted them to BANKS (Browsing ANd Keyword Search in relational databases) [7] and CiteSeer [8] for comparison. The key result found was that DbSurfer performed well (and outperformed BANKS and Citeseer) in finding requested references. The second experiment provided a closer analysis of the times taken is computing the results. Computing scores for nodes takes around 50% of the total processing time, with the trail finding taking around 30%, computing the text summaries around 15% and filtering redundant information around 2%, with the remainder being taken up by system overhead, XML transformation and presen-

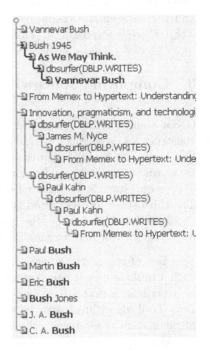

Fig. 1. Trails given by DbSurfer for the query "vannevar bush".

tation. Increasing the number of keywords causes a limited increase in the time to compute page scores, but this impact is dwarfed by other factors. One other interesting result is that as the number of keywords increases so does the fraction of nodes in the returned trails which are distinct within the entire trailset. Only extensive user testing will confirm whether this is a positive feature.

4   Architecture

Conventional web search engines usually use an architecture pattern comprising three components - a robot or crawler, an indexer and a query engine. We extend this design by augmenting the information retrieval engine with our trail finding system. and combining the crawler with the database reader. A key difference betweeen the DbSurfer and a conventional search engine is that a search engine traditionally returns links to pages which are logically and physically separated from the pages of the servers performing the query operations, whereas the links returned by the DbSurfer refer mostly to the row display servlet we have described.

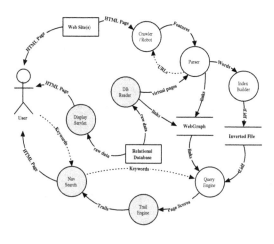

Fig. 2. Architecture of DbSurfer.

Figure 2 shows the basic architecture. The database content is retrieved by the DB Reader when the index is built and by the display servlet when examining the constructed trails. The DB Reader selects all the accessible tables and views, and asks the administrator which of these should be indexed. The program then extracts the referential constraints for all of the selected tables and generates a lookup table. This is kept separate from the main index and is used by both the DB Reader and the display servlet.

5   Query Expressiveness

We have extended the search engine style query syntax to support an attribute container operation using the "=" sign. The construct $x = y$ means that an attribute y must be contained in an XML tag x. For example, the query "Simon" might return publications relating to Simon's probabilistic model as well as articles by authors named Simon. The query `author=simon` would restrict the returned entries to those contained in an XML attribute ⟨author⟩, which translates to those in the author table. i.e. publications written by authors named Simon. The search engine query operations such as +, - and `link:` still remain supported with this extension. By default, we provide trails which answer disjunctive queries, with preference for results containing as many keywords as possible (conjunctive).

6   Concluding Remarks

We have presented DbSurfer - a system for keyword search and navigation through relational databases. DbSurfer's unique feature is a novel join discovery algorithm which discovers Memex-like trails though the graph of foreign-to-primary key dependencies. DbSurfer allows queries to be answered efficiently, providing relevant results without relying on a translation to SQL. We hope that the work will be continued by improving the user interface, allowing effective handling of numerical queries and addressing the security implications of the current architecture.

References

1. Sanjay Agrawal, Surajit Chaudhuri, and Gautam Das. Dbxplorer: A system for keyword-based search over relational databases. In *Proceedings of IEEE International Conference on Data Engineering*, pages 5–16, 2002.
2. S. Brin and L. Page. The anatomy of a large-scale hypertextual web search engine. In *Proceedings of International World Wide Web Conference*, pages 107–117, Brisbane, 1998.
3. Vannevar Bush. As we may think. *Atlantic Monthly*, 76:101–108, 1945.
4. E. F. Codd. A relational model of data for large shared data banks. *Communications of the ACM*, 13(6):377–387, 1970.
5. Andrew Eisenberg and Jim Melton. SQL/XML is making good progress. *SIGMOD Record*, 31(2):101–108, 2002.
6. Vagelis Hristidis and Yannis Papakonstantinou. Discover: Keyword search in relational databases. In *Proceedings of the 28th VLDB Conference*, Hong Kong, 2002.
7. Arvind Hulgeri, Gaurav Bhaltoia, Charuta Nakhe, Soumen Chakrabarti, and S. Sudarshan. Keyword search in databases. *Bulletin of the Technical Committee on Data Engineering. Special Issue on Imprecise Queries*, 24(3):22–32, 2001.
8. Steve Lawrence, Kurt Bollacker, and C. Lee Giles. Indexing and retrieval of scientific literature. In *Eighth International Conference on Information and Knowledge Management, CIKM 99*, pages 139–146, Kansas City, Missouri, November 1999.
9. Mazlita Mat-Hassan and Mark Levene. Can navigational assistance improve search experience: A user study. *First Monday*, 6(9), 2001.
10. Gerard Salton and Chris Buckley. Term weighting approaches in automatic text retrieval. *Information Processing and Management*, 24:513–523, 1998.
11. N. L. Sarda and Ankur Jain. Mragyati : A system for keyword-based searching in databases. *Computing Research Repository*, cs.DB/0110052, 2001.
12. Richard Wheeldon. *A Web of Trails*. PhD thesis, Birkbeck University of London, October 2003.
13. Richard Wheeldon and Mark Levene. The best trail algorithm for adaptive navigation in the world-wide-web. In *Proceedings of 1st Latin American Web Congress*, Santiago, Chile, November 2003.
14. Richard Wheeldon, Mark Levene, and Kevin Keenoy. Search and navigation in relational databases. *Computing Research Repository*, cs.DB/0307073, July 2003.

Ontology-Driven Automated Generation of Data Entry Interfaces to Databases

Alan Cannon[1], Jessie B. Kennedy[1], Trevor Paterson[1], and Mark F. Watson[2]

[1]School of Computing, Napier University, Edinburgh, EH10 5DT, U.K.
{a.cannon, j.kennedy, t.paterson}@napier.ac.uk
[2]Royal Botanic Garden, Edinburgh, EH3 5LR, U.K.
m.watson@rbge.org.uk

Abstract. This paper discusses an ontology based approach for the automatic generation of data entry interfaces to databases. An existing domain ontology is mapped to a system domain model, which a domain expert can then specialise using their domain expertise, for their data entry needs as required for individual projects. Based on this specialised domain knowledge, the system automatically generates appropriate data entry interfaces with the aid of a presentation model. By constraining the data entered to a term definition ontology and utilising appropriate defined domain terminology the quality of the collected data can be improved. Compared with traditional model-based user automatic interface development environments, this approach also has the potential to reduce the labour requirements for the expert developer.

1 Introduction

Designing data entry interfaces which allow the capture of high quality data to databases without overburdening users remains a significant challenge in database and user interface research. It is common to present forms-based user interfaces to allow data entry to the database. These forms, whilst often automatically generated, are generally simplistic, being designed to conform to the structure of database tables (or views) and can only constrain data entered to conform to the system data type associated with the table attributes. In most databases many attributes are stored as character strings, for which it is difficult to ensure consistent use or data quality, especially in terms of their semantics related to the domain of the attribute. In order for data to be meaningful in the long term and to allow data integration across databases, it is important that the semantics of the data are captured along with the actual data. However, achieving this without placing undue requirements on users has proven difficult. In this paper we present a semi-automatic data entry interface generation tool to help improve the quality of data entry to databases. The system generates an interface that reflects the semantics of the data as captured in a domain ontology.

A domain in which the problem of capturing semantically well-defined data is important is that of biological taxonomy, the branch of biology concerned with the classification of organisms into an ordered hierarchical system of groups reflecting their natural relationships and similarities. In the Prometheus projects we are investigating

H. Williams and L. MacKinnon (Eds.): BNCOD 2004, LNCS 3112, pp. 150–164, 2004.

tools and techniques to aid plant taxonomists to capture and interact with their data. In particular we have developed database models for storing multiple classifications [1, 2] and data visualisation tools for exploring multiple overlapping classifications [3]. Currently we are developing tools for allowing plant taxonomists to describe the specimens used during the classification process. This classification process is based upon the identification and description of variation between different plant specimens. A key task for taxonomic projects therefore involves describing the characteristics of a number of specimens. Currently taxonomists capture these specimen descriptions using paper forms that are designed specifically for particular projects, to reflect the characteristics of importance for differentiating specimens in the plant group under study. These characteristics will vary between plant groups. Some electronic data formats have been developed for capturing taxonomic characteristic data [4,5,6], but do not address the semantic standardisation and quality of data stored [7].

During our research it became apparent that there was no agreed vocabulary used by taxonomists when describing their specimens. This meant that although specimen descriptions were comparable within one project, it was impossible to compare descriptions across projects undertaken by different taxonomists and possibly even by the same taxonomist at different times. This led us to develop a data model of plant descriptions and an associated ontology that defines the terms used in describing plants [7]. Taxonomy, as a traditional discipline, is resistant to changing working practices where extra time requirements to record higher quality data would be imposed on the individual taxonomist. This is emphasised by the fact that any improvement in data, tends not to benefit the taxonomist capturing it, as much as other taxonomists who interpret it later. We therefore wanted to improve the semantics and rigour of the recorded data whilst minimizing the burden of data capture and still allowing taxonomists to adequately describe their specimens. Although we describe our work in the context of plant taxonomy, we believe our approach is applicable to any domain where the capture of the semantics of the data in the database is important.

Creating appropriate, good quality data entry interfaces (DEIs) for databases is traditionally a difficult and time-consuming process for an IT expert. This mirrors the situation in GUI development in general. Two relevant strands of research do however continue to address the problem of improving the generation of UI. In one strand, research into model based (and other) user interface development environments [e.g. 8-11] attempt to combine abstract modelling with a more systematic approach to interface development. In these methods the UI developer investigates and models their understanding of the domain (as well possibly the task, presentation and layout models), to specialise the interface design for that domain. Abstraction in itself does not free the UI developer of the need to select appropriate interaction objects (although they may only be selecting abstract versions, with the details of the concrete coding being done automatically [12]). A convergent strand of research concerns automatic UI generation. Automatic UI generation is often based upon some form of model based solution or abstract design, which uses a presentation model to control the selection and layout of DEIs, based on the modelled tasks and/or domain (e.g. Janus [8] and Mecano [13] primarily use a domain model whereas Trident [14] and Modest [15] primarily use a task model). These approaches still require substantial investment by a UI developer, particularly if they are to be successful in creating a useful domain specific interface, and as Novak has observed 'Nobody will create applications using *specifications (models), if they can do it faster directly editing'* [16]. This is doubtless one of the reasons that model based approaches have so far failed to achieve wide-spread commercial adoption, despite a strong research base [17].

Database interface research tends to lag in regard to general database research [18] so whilst there have been advances in database applications and data modelling to effectively store complex data, there have not been equivalent advances in approaches which promote the ability to capture rigorous data for such applications. Ontologies are increasingly used to describe and define complex data. Using an ontology to control the data entry for a database has the potential to ensure that better quality data is captured and that data from differing data providers will be compatible. It may also allow a DEI to be created that allows domain users to enter data using terms with which they are familiar but which are clearly defined semantically. Existing ontology based approaches for data entry are, however, generally still limited to using automatically generated forms-based data entry interfaces, unless manual editing is used (e.g. [19]). These systems are designed to populate a knowledge base describing relationships between described instance items of interest, rather than regulating the capture of the description of a complex concept. An alternative approach for UI generation involves using an ontology to provide domain knowledge to a system that can automatically generate a user interface based on a presentation model to capture data. An ontology-based approach of this kind has been proposed in regard to universal UI design [20] but the approach has not been widely investigated, nor has it addressed the needs of rigorous data entry.

This paper presents an ontology-based approach to semi-automatically generate data entry interfaces to databases. The remainder of the paper is organised as follows: section 2 provides an overview of the conceptual approach and introduces the domain of biological taxonomy. The process of defining data requirements for the data entry interface is described in section 3. Section 4 considers the models and processes involved in generating the data entry interface. Section 5 concludes the paper.

2   Overview of the Approach – Concept and Application

Our basic approach for generating data entry interfaces to databases, for the capture of descriptive data about concepts of interest, is shown in fig.1. In the design of our system we have adopted a model based approach in that we have task, domain and presentation models. The task model is pre-determined to be the general task of data entry for a database. The *data entry task model* (see fig.1) is encapsulated within the system. The only modifiable aspect of the task model is the order in which the data entry task is completed (see Section 3).

2.1 Domain Models

We use a series of domain models to represent domain knowledge (see fig.1). The *abstract domain model* is transformed into a *concrete domain model* by mapping an existing domain ontology to it. A domain expert specialises this *concrete domain model* to create a *specialised domain model* for a given project of work (see Section 3).

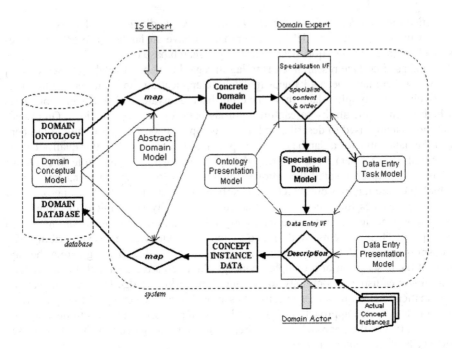

Fig. 1. Ontology Driven Automated Generation of Data Entry Interfaces Approach

2.1.1 Abstract Domain Model. Our system is designed to capture data concerning any high level concept that may be sub-divided into a hierarchy of defined constituent sub-concepts ('*description objects*') that are themselves described by instantiating *attributes* that they possess. Each *attribute* of a *description object* can be instantiated within the limits of its *value constraints*. These *value constraints* might restrict entered data (such as the data type or numerical range of entered data), or define selection from a limited set of *value objects*. A *value object* represents a defined concept that can be used to instantiate an *attribute*. Additional entities (modifiers and units of measurement) allow more detailed description of *attributes* and their value constraints. This data format is captured in an *abstract domain model* (fig.2). This data format could be widely applicable, representing both physical and abstract concept domains (e.g. a control system process or academic department).

2.1.2 Domain Ontology. Initially, in order to instantiate the *abstract domain model* with actual domain knowledge, we map an appropriate domain ontology to it, to create a *concrete domain model* (see fig.1). Our approach assumes the existence of an appropriate domain ontology, which does not necessarily have to be created solely for this system. Ontology is a widely used term, with a variety of meanings [21]. The commonly quoted definition '*a specification of a conceptualisation*' [22] is generally appropriate for our usage. Specifically, the domain ontology is a semi-formal, constrained and structured form of natural description language, with defined terms and possible relationships between them. Even so defined, ontologies can contain many different objects and relationships with various semantics.

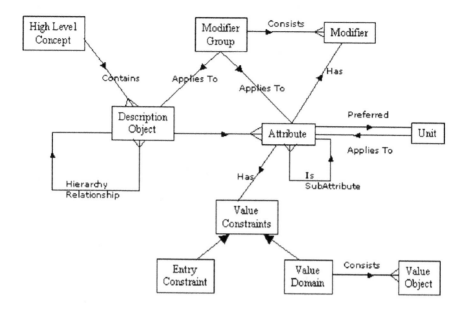

Fig. 2. Abstract Domain Model: the conceptual model for controlling domain knowledge in the system. The hierarchy of *description objects* is formed using the Hierarchy Relationship. Some details, such as synonym relationships, are not shown for clarity

In our example domain, an ontology to control the description of a set of plant specimens is being used as a domain ontology. Classical plant taxonomists describe plant specimens in terms of their observable characteristics, and interpret patterns of shared characteristics to evaluate relatedness between specimens in order to define taxonomic groups and compose a hierarchical tree (taxonomy) of relationships between these groups. As part of a project which attempts to standardize the composition of taxonomic descriptions, a defined terminology for the description of flowering plants (angiosperms) has been created in collaboration with taxonomists from the Royal Botanic Garden Edinburgh [7]. The ontology is composed of 'Defined Terms' (terms with associated definitions and citations) and relationships between these terms. As shown in fig.3, there are three major subclasses of defined terms used to create descriptions of biological specimens: Structure terms representing all the possible anatomical structures of a given specimen (e.g. petal, stamen); Property terms, which represent aspects of a structure that might be described (e.g. length, shape); and State terms which represent the actual values for a qualitative property of a given structure (e.g. round, yellow). In our description model 'quantitative properties' are scored by numerical values. 'State Group' relationships in the ontology capture permitted relationships between groups of States and the set of Structures that they may be used to describe. 'Is-part-of' forms the central organising relationship for the ontology, and allows representation of a hierarchy of all the possible structural relationships found on any given specimen (e.g. a blade is part of a leaf, or part of a leaflet, which itself is part of a leaf).

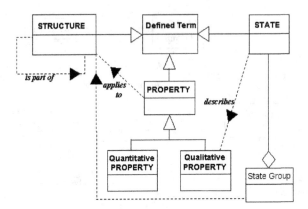

Fig. 3. Major terms and relationships represented in the angiosperm domain ontology

2.1.3 Concrete Domain Model. The potential variation in composition of domain ontologies makes their automatic adaptation for a domain model a nontrivial task [23] that defies automatic mapping of the domain ontology, thus requiring the intervention of an IT expert actor. The IT expert makes a mapping between the *abstract domain model* and the particular domain ontology's conceptual model. This allows the system to derive the *concrete domain model* from the imported domain ontology. It is only necessary to perform this mapping once for a given domain conceptual model. Where the database schema and ontology conceptual model are based on the same domain conceptual model, this mapping also allows the system to format the entered data for transfer to the database application. Where this is not the case, a second expert mapping would be required for each database schema

In order, to perform the domain ontology mapping, a number of key objects and relationships need to be identified or derived. At the fundamental level, *description object*s need to be identified along with a primary description object hierarchy interrelationship and root *description object*(s) (to form a *description object hierarchy*). *Attribute* objects must be identified or derived from ontology terms and/or relationships between *description object*s and possible *value object*s. In addition, the applicability of *attributes* to *description object*s is identified. *Value object*s must be identified from the descriptive terms that could form possible values of a *description object* via an *attribute* relationship (*value object*s can also be *description object*s themselves or instances of *description object*s). Beyond these basic terms and relationships, the *abstract domain model* can have modifiers, units, synonym relationships and various other aspects mapped to it (see section 3 for examples).

In mapping the angiosperm domain ontology (fig. 3) to the *abstract domain model* (fig. 2), specimens represent the *high-level concepts* that are described. Their constituent structures map to *description object*s, and their is-part-of relationships form the *description object hierarchy* relationship. Properties and state group relationships form the *attributes* of a *description object*. States form *value object*s, which belong to an *attribute* and which are constrained over a *'value domain'* defined by the permitted grouping relationships between structures and states.

2.1.4 Specialised Domain Model. A data entry interface based on the whole angiosperm domain ontology would be too large for usability and would cover a much larger number of structures and characteristics than a taxonomist would utilise in any one taxonomic project. Individual projects would typically be restricted to only a small subset of the angiosperm group of plants. Additionally, taxonomists are interested in different sets of specimen characteristics dependent on the focus of their work. The exact data requirements of a given taxonomic project must therefore be established. Normally, taxonomists do this by creating paper-based templates for each project, which have entries for the major describable characteristics of the specimens that they wish to record. Our system provides an equivalent to this process by allowing taxonomists to create *specialised domain models* based on the angiosperm domain model, which enables the system to present them with data entry forms based solely on the data and semantics relevant for their particular project.

2.2 Presentation Model

There are two presentation models in the system one for ontology presentation and one for data entry (see fig.1). In order to allow the expert taxonomist to create a *specialised domain model*, the system uses a modelling tool (the *specialisation interface*) which presents the entire angiosperm domain model for exploration and editing. The ontology presentation model is used in this tool, to provide a general layout presentation for displaying ontologies based on the *abstract domain model*. This presentation model is also utilised to display aspects of the *specialised domain model* in the final data entry interface. The *ontology presentation model* was derived by user requirement and evaluation testing and is now captured within the system. The *data entry presentation model* determines the layout and selection of interaction objects for the data entry interface. Different *data entry presentation models* could be utilised as plug-ins. User testing has been used to develop one such model.

3   Specialising the Data Entry Requirements

3.1 Domain and Task Model Specialisation Tool

This section describes the process by which domain experts specialise the data requirements for a particular project. The result of this process is the *specialised domain model* and the default task ordering of the *task model*. The specialisation tool consists of an interface (fig. 4) that allows users to interact with the domain model and task order. A domain expert can determine which *description objects* (i.e. plant structures) they wish to include in the Data Entry Interface, the *attributes* of those *description objects* they wish to use, and the specification (constraints) of those *attributes*. The system interprets the *task* and *concrete domain models* (Table 1) using its *ontology presentation model* to determine the layout and interface interaction objects, including the use of colour or icons to indicate summary information (e.g. greying out excluded elements or warning icons for *attributes* with no possible values).

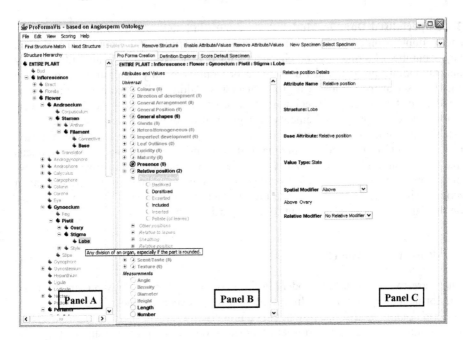

Fig. 4. Specialisation Interface Screenshot: 4A represents the *description object hierarchy*. 4B represents the potential *attributes* and their related possible *value objects* for a selected *description object*. 4C allows specification of the selected *attribute* details

3.1.1 Specialising the Description Object Hierarchy. A view of all the *description objects* (i.e. plant structures) is presented in a *description object hierarchy* (fig. 4A), through which the user can select description objects for inclusion in the DEI. The *description object hierarchy* view is primarily based upon an interpretation of elements of the *concrete domain model* as summarised in Table 1.

In addition to interpreting the *concrete domain model*, the *task model* is interpreted to provide the order of the *description objects* (presented as the order they appear in the *description object hierarchy*) which can be modified by the user. Any alterations to the default task order are captured in the *task model*. This functionality is provided to reflect the working practice of taxonomists, who, within the general task of describing specimens, may want to specify the order in which they describe the particular characteristics of the specimen, to fit with traditional biological description methodologies.

3.1.2 Specialising Description Objects. By selecting *description objects* in the hierarchy, the user can access its potential *attributes*. A second hierarchical view is presented for the selected *description object*, (fig.4B), which allows users to select *attributes* for inclusion and alter *value constraints* by specifying the set of possible *value objects*. This *attribute-value* hierarchy accesses the *attributes* and their potential *value objects* by interpreting the *concrete domain model* (Table 1). The details of a selected *attribute* can be further specified (fig. 4C), such as adding spatial modifiers to accurately represent where in a *description object*, an *attribute* is being measured. *Attributes* can also be more radically varied by adding relative modifiers which can change the nature of an *attribute* by relating it to another *description object* and *attribute* (e.g. to capture the ratio of leaflet-length to leaflet-width). Other *attribute* specification is aimed at affecting the data entry interface without modifying the fundamentals of the data that will be exported to the database. This includes influencing the selection of interaction objects (e.g. by varying the importance of multi-media display), or affecting presentation aspects (e.g. changing the display name of the *attribute*).

Description objects can also be declared to be concrete. Normally data entered about a *description object* is generalised data reflecting all actual instances of the *description object*, however sometimes it is preferable to enter data about individual actual instances of the *description object*. This allows taxonomists to record a volume of related numerical data suitable for later statistical analysis, if desired.

Table 1. This table shows the mapping of the *concrete domain model* to the *specialisation interface* using the *ontology presentation model*. The *task model* controls node ordering

Specialisation Interface Element	Ontology Presentation Model **INTERPRETS** Concrete Domain Model Element
Description Object Hierarchy (fig. 4A)	
Node Identities	*Description Object*s
Node Presentation	*Description Object* Fixed Data Elements (e.g.name)
Node Presentation /Interaction	*Description Object* DEI Inclusion Status
Tree Structure	*Description Object* Hierarchy Relationships
Attribute-Value Hierarchy (fig. 4B)	
Attribute Node Identities	*Attributes* (of selected *description object*)
Value Nodes	*Attribute* to *Value Object* Constraints
Node Presentation	*Attribute* Fixed Data Elements (e.g. name)
Node Presentation /Interaction	*Attribute* and *Value Object* DEI Inclusion Status
Tree Structure	*Sub-attribute* and *Attribute-Value* Relationships
Attribute Details Specification (fig. 4C)	
Element Presentation	*Attribute* Fixed Data Elements (e.g. value type)
Element Presentation /Interaction	*Attribute* Modifiable Data Elements (e.g. relative modifier)
Element Presentation /Interaction	*Attribute* Modifiable Display Elements (e.g. name)

3.1.3 Specialisation Restrictions. The domain expert in this specialisation process cannot transform the domain model in such a way as to make it inconsistent with the original domain ontology, for example, they cannot use an *attribute* for a *description object* that does not have an appropriate relationship in the domain model. This ensures the data exported by the system is compatible with the data model underlying the original ontology. The domain expert cannot directly alter the *data entry presen-*

tation model (for example by choosing the actual data entry abstract interaction objects, although they can alter the data in the *specialised domain model* upon which determinations are made by the *data entry presentation model*). This ensures a modelling split between data determination and presentation, thus avoiding confusion between the two different processes.

3.2 Domain Expert User Considerations

Editing domain models in model-based approaches is usually a task reserved for IT experts. In our case, a domain expert is performing this operation, so the interface must be configured towards a user who is not necessarily familiar with modelling or ontological terminology. The *ontology presentation model* in the system attempts to aid ease of understanding by using appropriate domain terms based on the domain ontology mapping (e.g. referring to structures instead of *description object*s). In addition, the *ontology presentation model* generally interprets the ontology to attempt to allow easy navigation and feedback, with easy access to related domain knowledge (e.g. access to definitions). Object definitions drawn from the domain ontology provide users with the knowledge to make informed editing choices, thus supporting the eventual capture of semantically good quality data. Definitions are provided in a variety of means, including mouse over pop-up summaries (see fig 4A) and a definition viewer gives additional details of selected terms on request. Evaluation by taxonomists from the Royal Botanical Garden Edinburgh showed that the *description object hierarchy* captured in the domain model allows users to navigate the potentially large description space, using their own domain knowledge.

4   Data Entry Interface

This section describes how data is captured based on the *specialised domain* and *task models*. As the details of the data to be entered have been determined by a domain expert actor, there is no further direct intervention by an IT expert before the *data entry interface* (DEI) is generated. Some fixed design decisions (such as basic architecture layout) are captured in the system, the DEI being generated by interpretation of the *specialised domain, task* and two presentation models. Working with one high-level concept instance (i.e. plant specimen), a domain actor enters data for the *attributes* of one *description object* (i.e. structure) at a time.

4.1 Navigating the Data Entry Interface

The DEI provides a view of the *description object hierarchy* (fig. 5A) and presents a series of windows with groups of interaction objects for data entry (fig. 5B). The default order of the *description object*s and *attributes* presented by the system to users for data entry is interpreted from the task model and can be overridden by the data entry user by selecting *description object*s directly from the *description object hierarchy* display (fig. 5A). This display is controlled by the *ontology presentation model*, as described in the previous section, although in this case it interprets the *specialised domain model* and is not editable. In the DEI context, the display uses colour, icons and mouse-over text to indicate summary data about the data entry status of the current specimen (e.g. to represent whether a structure has been skipped over in normal task order). By providing navigation context and summary data for each *description object*, the user is assisted in making informed data entry decisions.

For each *description object*, the DEI generates a grouped set of *attribute* presentation units (fig. 5B), which are complex data entry interaction objects that contain all the data and interaction capability required to enter data for one *attribute* of the *description object*. The *data entry presentation model* controls the level of grouping. In taxonomy, we group all *attributes* for one plant structure in one window, which fits with their observational methodology. An appropriate grouping, combined with the hierarchy view and the nature of the pre-determined task, offsets one of the traditional drawbacks of automatic generation, that users require information from multiple objects in one window [24], as all the required information to make an informed data entry decision should be available. The layout of the presentation units within the grouped screen is controlled by a 'place one below the other strategy'. More complex layout strategies could be defined by the *data entry presentation model*.

Where a *description object* is concrete (see section 3), the group of presentation units refer to one actual instance of a *description object*. Multiple instances of the one *description object* are often captured in this case. The DEI generates multiple grouped sets of presentation units for the *description object*, as required by the DEI user.

4.2   Entering Data in Attribute Presentation Units

The user enters data for individual *attributes* of a *description object* using a presentation unit. A presentation unit consists of four major components to support data entry: three data entry interaction objects; and a display with the *attribute* data required for the user to make meaningful data entry choices (such as *attribute* name, current entry status). This data is interpreted from the domain model; the presentation is fixed and captured in the system.

The primary data entry interaction object controls selection or entering of the values. The implementation of this interaction object varies. The abstract implementation is determined by the *data entry presentation model*, which selects abstract interaction objects (AIO) from a system library. These AIOs are internally specialised by the relevant *attribute* and related data captured in the domain model to create the concrete interaction objects. This specialisation controls aspects such as internal layout management (for example the number and layout of checkboxes), the display of names and icons, etc. In order to determine an appropriate AIO the *data entry presentation model* accesses various defined criteria of the underlying *attribute* object data. One criterion used to determine this AIO, is value type, of which there are two basic choices – *value object* selection and text entry. Selection involves choosing from a set of *value object*s, whereas text entry allows the user to enter data as desired. As this approach is based on an ontology for ensuring quality of collected data, text entry is usually limited to numerical data entry, as free text entry would allow recording of data not compliant with the domain ontology. Data type is generally used as a criterion for making automatic IO selection choices; in this case, the data type of the allowed values of the *attribute* is used. Multi-media representation of descriptive terms is very important in taxonomy, as in many other domains. The presence of multi-media definition representations is thus another criterion that can be used by the presentation model. The importance of the multi-media representations may also vary from *attribute* to *attribute*, and a tag can be assigned to an *attribute* to specify this in the *specialisation interface*. Other common criteria, which can be accessed by the presentation model, include data cardinality, data precision, numerical range constraints, etc.

4.3 Controlling Nuances of Entered Data

The remaining two interaction objects in a presentation unit control the adding of semantic nuances to the data. The first is an interaction object for adding applicable modifiers to the entered data (e.g. frequency modifiers like 'rarely', 'usually', *etc.*). The available modifiers are based on the *attribute* links captured in the domain model (see fig. 2) and allow users finer control of the entered data; a second interaction object controls the interpretation of multiple values. Initially one presentation unit is displayed for each *attribute* requiring instantiation. The data entry process however might require additional presentation units being generated to capture nuances of description. A common example of this situation is in distinguishing 'AND-ing' from 'OR-ing'. This applies where a number of values for the same *attribute* are applicable to every individual physical instance of the *description object*, as opposed to the situation where the instantiated *attribute* has different values on different individual *description object*s (e.g. to distinguish between a specimen whose individual petals are white *and* purple versus a specimen whose individual petals are *either* white petals *or* purple petals). As the permutations of this situation can be quite complex, the user is required to instantiate one *attribute* presentation unit for every permutation of individual *description object* instances. The system can replicate presentation units to allow entry of these different permutations as required by the domain actor using the DEI. This process is made less intrusive by not basing the grouping of presentation units upon the available screen space, but instead allowing the expansion of effective screen space using scrolling. For example (as in Fig. 5B) a taxonomist entering data for a specimen which had some purely white petals and some petals that were both white and purple would select white in the petal colour presentation unit, and click on 'Enter Another Score' button. This would generate a copy of the petal colour presentation unit, where the taxonomist would select both white and purple in a single presentation unit.

4.4 Exporting Data

Once a user has entered the data for one *high-level concept* instance (i.e. plant specimen), they can enter data for other instances of the concept. The data for each specimen can be exported to the database. This exported data is formatted using the mapping between the domain ontology conceptual model and the *concrete domain model*. The interface could also be reloaded from the database by a reverse procedure.

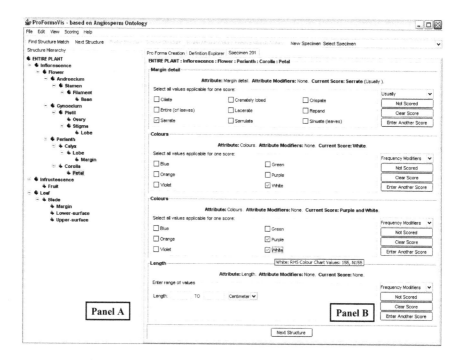

Fig. 5. Data Entry Interface: 5A is the *description object hierarchy* view providing both compositional context and a means of overriding the default data entry ordering. 5B is a group of *attribute* presentation units for the selected *description object*

5   Conclusions

The system described in this paper utilises domain knowledge from a domain ontology and domain experts to specify the data requirements of an automatically generated data entry interface to databases. This approach aims to improve the quality of data entered by users, without overburdening users or interface developers. In Szekely's retrospective [24], this work would fall into the model-based automatic interface generation approaches, specifically those that primarily allow users to access and specify a domain model. This system's domain model however, is based on an existing ontology to ensure that the semantics of the data are maintained. By tying the entered data to a domain ontology, semantically high quality data can be generated and be entered into a database based on a data model related to the original ontology.

Despite their potential benefits, model-based automatic generation approaches have not been widely adopted commercially and have been criticised as being unable to produce quality, appropriate interfaces [24]. Our approach, however, offers access to a modelling tool for domain experts to specialise the domain model rather than for interface developers. This specialisation can be done for individual projects, thus improving the appropriateness of the generated interface. An appropriate, good quality interface is a useful element for ensuring that captured data is an accurate representation of the intent of both the data entry user, and the project designer in a multi-user system. Furthermore, by limiting our approach to a descriptive data entry task, we have already gone some way to limiting the possible permutations of the interface, allowing the presentation model to be more appropriate. Focussed approaches also tend encourage wider adoption of new approaches than universal approaches that attempt to solve all problems at once [25]. Another contributory factor to the lack of quality in traditional automatically generated interfaces, lies with the difficulties of automatically selecting appropriate AIOs using a predetermined presentation model. By focussing on data entry tasks and allowing tailoring of the *data entry presentation model* to particular domains, this approach supports a more appropriate AIO selection.

By using the domain ontology and domain experts to create the *specialised domain model*, the approach provides benefits in the avoidance of time consuming and possibly distorted domain knowledge acquisition by a UI expert from a domain expert who must possess or acquire this knowledge to support their work in any case. A modelling tool has been developed for the system which has been tailored for easy and informed use by domain experts who are not familiar with modelling techniques.

Initial informal user evaluation for our approach has been positive. It has shown for example that taxonomists are able to navigate and interact with the *concrete domain model* in the *specialisation interface* to create effective *specialised domain models*; that taxonomists appreciate the value of access to the exact semantics of the domain terminology being used; and that data semantically consistent with the angiosperm ontology can be collected and exported to a database. More extensive user testing is planned, both in depth with the existing angiosperm ontology and with other domain ontologies. Our approach has been applied to the instance field of specimen description in plant taxonomy. We, however, believe the approach can be more widely applied in data entry applications, particularly where semantically high quality data capture is important and where there are variations in the data requirements for different projects. The provision of supporting tools for use by IT experts in mapping from *domain conceptual models* to the system's *abstract domain model*, and for generating alternative *data entry presentation models* will ease expansion of this approach beyond biological taxonomy applications.

We would like to acknowledge and warmly thank BBSRC for funding of this research, and the Royal Botanical Garden Edinburgh for their help in evaluation and development.

References

1. Raguenaud, C., Kennedy, J., Barclay, P.J.: The Prometheus Database for Taxonomy, 12th International Conference on Scientific and Statistical Database Management, (2000) 250-252
2. Pullan, M., Watson, M., Kennedy, J., Raguenaud, C., Hyam, R.: The Prometheus Taxonomic Model: A Practical Approach to Representing Multiple Taxonomies. Taxon **49** (2000) 55-75
3. Graham, M., Watson, M.F., Kennedy, J.: Novel Visualisation Techniques For Working With Multiple, Overlapping Classification Hierarchies. Taxon **51**(2) (2002) 351-358
4. Dallwitz, M.J.: A general system for coding taxonomic descriptions. Taxon **29** (1980) 41-46
5. Maddison, D.R., Swofford, D.L., Maddison, W.P.: NEXUS: An extensible file format for systematic information. Systematic Biology **46** (1997) 590-621

6. CBIT: Lucid, developed by The Centre for Biological Information Technology: University of Queensland, Australia. (2003) URLs: www.cpitt.uq.edu.au; www.lucidcentral.com
7. Paterson, T., Kennedy, J., Pullan, M. R., Cannon A. J., Armstrong, K., Watson M. F., Raguenaud C., McDonald S. M., Russell G.: A Universal Character Model and Ontology of Defined Terms for Taxonomic Description, DILS 2004, LNBI 2994 (2004) 63-78
8. Balzert, H., Hofmann, F., Kruschinski, V., Niemann, C.: The JANUS Application Development Environment-Generating More than the User Interface. In Proceedings of CADUI'96, Namur: Presses Universitaires de Namur (1996) 183-207
9. Elwert, T., Schlungbaum, T.: Modelling and Generation of Graphical User Interfaces in the TADEUS Approach. In Palangue, P., Bastide, R., (Eds.), Designing, Specification and Verification of Interactive Systems, Wien, Springer (1995) 193-208
10. Szekely, P., Sukaviriya, P., Castells, P., Muhktumarasamy, J., Salcher, E.: Declarative Interface Models For User Interface Construction Tools: The MASTERMIND Approach, In Engineering for Human-Computer Interaction (1996).
11. Butler, K.A.: Designing Deeper: Towards a User-Centered Development Environment Design in Context. In Proceedings of ACM Symposium on Designing Interactive Systems: Processes, Practices, Methods, & Techniques DIS'95 (1995) 131-142
12. Zloof, M.M.: Selected Ingredients in End-User Programming. In Proceedings of the Working Conference on Advanced Visual Interfaces (1998)
13. Puerta, A.R., Eriksson, H., Gennari, J.H., and Mussen, M.A.: Beyond Data Models For Automated User Interface Generation. In People and Computers IX HCI'94 (1994) 353-366
14. Vanderdonckt, J.: Automatic Generation of a User Interface for Highly Interactive Business-Oriented Applications. In Companion Proceedings of CHI'94 (1994) 41 & 123-124
15. Hinrichs, T., Bareiss, R., Birnbaum, L., Collins, G.: An Interface Design Tool based on Explicit Task Models. In Companion Proceedings of CHI' 96 (1996) 269-270
16. Novak, G.S.: (2003) Novak's rule: http://www.cs.utexas.edu/users/novak/
17. Traeteberg, H., Molina, P.J., Nunes, N.J.: Making Model-Based UI Design Practical: Usable and Open Methods and Tools. In Proceedings of the 9th international conference on Intelligent user interface (2004) 376-377
18. Carey, M., Haas, L., Maganty, V., Williams, J.: PESTO: An Integrated Query/Browser for Object Databases. In Proceedings of the 22nd International Conference on Very Large Data Bases (1996)
19. Gennari, J., Musen, M.A., Fergerson, R.W., Grosso, W.E., Crubézy, M., Eriksson, H., Noy, N.F., Tu, S.W.: The Evolution of Protégé: An Environment for Knowledge-Based Systems Development (2002) URL: http://www.smi.stanford.edu/pubs/SMI_Reports/SMI-2002-0943.pdf, http://protege.stanford.edu/index.html
20. Furtado, E., Furtado, J.J.V., Bezerra Silva, W., Tavares Rodrigues, D.W., da Silva Taddeo L., Limbourg, Q., Vanderdonckt, J.: An Ontology-Based Method for Universal Design of User Interfaces, In Proceedings of Workshop on Multiple User Interfaces over the Internet: Engineering and Applications Trends, Lille (2001)
21. Guarino, N., Giaretta, P.: Ontologies and Knowledge Bases: Towards a Terminological Clarification. In Mars, N.J.I. (ed.), Towards Very Large Knowledge Bases, IOS Press (1995)
22. Gruber, T.R.: A Translation Approach to Portable Ontology Specification. Knowledge Acquisition 5 (1993) 199-220
23. Wang, X., Chan, C.W., Hamilton, H.J.: Design Of Knowledge-Based Systems With The Ontology-Domain-System Approach. SEKE 2002 (2002) 233-236
24. Szekely, P.: Retrospective and Challenges for Model-Bases Interface Development. In Computer-Aided Design of User Interfaces, Namur University Press (1996) xxi--xliv
25. Myers, B., Hudson, S. and Pausch, R.: Past, Present, and Future of User Interface Software Tools, ACM Transactions on Computer-Human Interaction 7 (2000) 3-28

Incremental Observer Relative Data Extraction

Linas Bukauskas[1] and Michael H. Böhlen[2]

[1] Department of Computer Science, Aalborg University, Denmark
linb@cs.aau.dk
[2] Faculty of Computer Science, Free University of Bozen-Bolzano, Italy
boehlen@inf.unibz.it

Abstract. The visual exploration of large databases calls for a tight coupling of database and visualization systems. Current visualization systems typically fetch all the data and organize it in a scene tree that is then used to render the visible data. For immersive data explorations in a Cave or a Panorama, where an observer is data space this approach is far from optimal. A more scalable approach is to make the observer-aware database system and to restrict the communication between the database and visualization systems to the relevant data.

In this paper VR-tree, an extension of the R-tree, is used to index visibility ranges of objects. We introduce a new operator for incremental Observer Relative data Extraction (iORDE). We propose the Volatile Access STructure (VAST), a lightweight main memory structure that is created on the fly and is maintained during visual data explorations. VAST complements VR-tree and is used to quickly determine objects that enter and leave the visibility area of an observer. We provide a detailed algorithm and we also present experimental results that illustrate the benefits of VAST.

1 Introduction

Typical visualization systems extract data from the database and construct a scene tree that keeps track of all data points. The scene-tree is used to compute the data to be rendered and observer actions (movement, rotations, etc.) to be mapped to operations on the scene-tree. To get a feel for the possibilities and limitations of such an approach let us consider a concrete 3D visualization system. Assume, the system visualizes 80'000 customers (objects). Each object is displayed as a tetrahedron. Although the original database size is only 2 MB the visualization system uses 150 MB of memory. The reason is that visualization systems are highly optimized to operate at the frame rate required by state-of-the-art display systems. This requirement is met by constructing advanced scene trees that are optimized for speed, but require a significant amount of memory. This simple example shows that visualization systems do not scale well as the amount of data grows. In contrast, database systems have been designed to scale up to huge amounts of data stored on disks. However, visualization systems are only loosely coupled to database systems and they do not exploit database functionality. Most visualization systems simply fetch the complete dataset to

H. Williams and L. MacKinnon (Eds.): BNCOD 2004, LNCS 3112, pp. 165–177, 2004.
© Springer-Verlag Berlin Heidelberg 2004

construct scene-trees. At best, simple selection and projection operations are performed. To limit the memory consumption it is necessary to advance the integration of the database and visualization systems such that the scene-tree does not have to store all the data.

In this paper we focus on how to make the database system aware of the observer position. As a running example we assume an observer who navigates in a virtual data space to analyze the data. Our solution eliminates the data bottleneck at the visualization system by tightly coupling database and visualization systems. Instead of communicating large data sets we propose to exchange $\Delta^\pm$ slices. The extraction of $\Delta^\pm$'s is called incremental observer relative data extraction (iORDE). We introduce a lightweight memory structure called VAST. VAST complements VR-tree, which is a refined R-tree that indexes visibility ranges. The combination of VAST and VR-tree supported by an efficient expiration policy for invisible objects, yields an incremental observer relative data extraction. VAST is a structured cache that minimizes the number of disk operations when extracting $\Delta^\pm$ slices.

We run a set of experiments to confirm the effectiveness if extracting the visible objects incrementally. The number of I/O operations as well as the size of result sets is reduced dramatically. The experiments are based on a synthetic dataset that simulates an environment where the observer explores dense and sparse regions, respectively, and transitions between these regions.

Many spatial database access structures are based on the R-tree [1,2] and various extensions [3,4,5]. R-tree based structures use minimum bounding rectangles (MBRs) to hierarchically group objects and they support fast lookups of objects that overlap a query point/window. Another family of access structures is based on space partitioning, such as Quad-trees [6] and kdB-Trees [7,8]. Common to all these structures is a spatial grouping. In our case the visible objects are not located in the same area. Each object has its own visibility factor, and the visible objects may be scattered and located anywhere in the universe. Besides the lack of a spatial grouping of visible objects the above mentioned access structures do not support the incremental extraction of visible objects.

Song and Roussopoulos [9] have investigated k-nearest neighbor search for a moving query point. The basic idea is to refine the nearest neighbor query results when the point is moving. The set of new nearest neighbors for the new query point is extracted using the previous query result and pre-fetched results. The algorithm reuses the previous results for the new search. However, the distance to the objects cannot be used in our case because we are interested in the visible and not the nearest objects.

Kofler et. al. [10,11] and Shou et al. [12] investigated a walk through of large datasets. They extended the R-Tree to index objects with different levels of detail. Nodes within the view frustum are cached in main memory. A distance based metric is used to expire nodes. The focus of their approach is different in that they introduce three types of visibility levels—the level of detail. The distance identifies the visibility level. In contrast, we use the visibility range of objects to update VAST and always assume the precise visibility level.

Section 2 defines the problem. VAST the supplementary structure that enables visible object extraction incrementally is introduced in Sect. 3. In Sect. 4 we give experimental results that quantify the benefits of VAST. We finish the paper with conclusions and future work in Sect. 5.

2   Problem Definition

Throughout we assume that the observer movement is specified as a set of path points. The next path point determines where the observer is moving to. Figure 1 shows a part of an unbounded universe. Each dot represents an object, and the line represents the path along which the observer moves. The observer positions are given only on corner points.

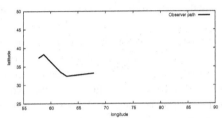

Fig. 1. Data Universe, Observer Path

During a data exploration the observer will not usually see all objects at the same time. Instead the observer will focus on selected parts of the universe and explore these areas in detail. Figure 2(a) illustrates the basic step during a data exploration. The observer is moving within the relatively short distance. Here, dots denote points that are visible from both positions. Step points are interconnected with the solid line. Objects that appear are marked with a +. Visible objects are scattered through out the universe and are not clustered in the same area. Thus, near objects might be invisible or far away visible. In Fig. 2(b) we show the example where the observer makes a larger step. The number of incoming objects is 3 times more than in the previous step. If the distance between the two positions is chosen appropriately then most objects remain (in)visible and only a small number of objects appear and disappear. This sequence of the figures illustrate that it is attractive to only extract objects that become visible and disappear, respectively.

The incremental observer relative data extraction (iORDE) operator returns a pair consisting of newly visible and disappearing objects, respectively. As arguments it takes the next observer position Pos' and the universe of objects r. $(\Delta^+, \Delta^-) \leftarrow \sigma_{iORDE}(Pos', r)$ We assume that R is a relation with schema $r ::= (x, y, s)$. x and y are spatial coordinates of the object of size s. The visibility of objects is given by the visibility factor function $VF(O, Pos) = \frac{O[s]}{\|O - Pos\|} \cdot c$, i.e., the object size $O[s]$ divided by the Euclidean distance between object O and

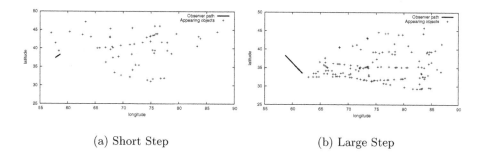

(a) Short Step   (b) Large Step

Fig. 2. Appearing Objects

observer position *Pos*. Throughout the paper we use the notation $\|A - B\|$ to denote the Euclidean distance between positions A and B. The iORDE selection operator selects objects with a visibility factor (VF) above a certain threshold ρ: $\{\mathcal{V}_{Pos} ::= \{o|o \in r \land VF(o, Pos) > \rho\}$.

The output is the set of visible objects. It is easy to notice that the visibility factor of an object changes when the observer is moving. Thus, the entire database (or VF based access structure) has to be recomputed each time the observer moves. To minimize the number of updates and avoid the calculation of visibility factors we associate visibility ranges with each object. The visibility range defines the distance where the object is visible. The simplest way to calculate the visibility range is to treat it proportional to the size of the object: $VR(O_i) = O_i[s] \cdot c$. Here, $VR(O_i)$ is the visibility range of object O_i, $O_i[s]$ is the size of the object, and c is a constant. Thus, object O_i will be visible in the circular or hyper-spheric area of size $VR(O_i)$. Parameters such as color, brightness, transparency, shape, etc. can easily be incorporated into the formula.

To index visibility ranges we use VR-tree, which is based on R-Tree. The VR-tree models visibility ranges as Minimal Bounding Squares (MBS) an approximation of the visibility range of an object. To index MBSs we use three types of nodes. Internal nodes use minimal bounding rectangles (MBR) to create a hierarchical structure. Leaf nodes use MBSs to efficiently approximate visibility ranges. Data nodes store the properties of an object. By introducing leaf nodes with MBSs we increase the fanout.

3   Volatile Access STructure

To efficiently determine appearing and disappearing objects an additional structure is needed. We propose the **V**olatile **A**ccess **ST**ructure (VAST). VAST is a tree like main memory structure and it provides a fast and scalable technique to compute Δ^+ and Δ^- when the observer is moving. The tree is called volatile because it is initialized and created when the observer starts to move. When the observer stops VAST structure is destroyed.

3.1   Structure of VAST

A node of the VAST consists of a number of entries. Each entry contains a value and a pointer to its child. If the node is a leaf-node, the child pointer is NULL. The number of entries in a VAST node is dynamic, but not larger than the number of entries in a node of the VR-tree.

When an observer relative query is issued a number of leaf-nodes of the VR-tree will satisfy the search condition. The traces from the root node to the data pages are added to VAST. A trace is a sequence of pointers from the root to the leaf. Each pointer in a trace is an address of a disk page. The disk page address is stored in the value field of VAST. VAST mirrors VR-tree traces. It caches the visible objects for the current observer position. Our goal is to not query VR-tree when doing local explorations. Thus, VAST should report appearing and disappearing objects, without accessing the VR-tree. We extend VAST to support lazy deletions and introduce a node expiration policy.

We add dynamic content to VAST node entries. Each entry in a VAST node stores the distance d to the observer position Pos, the angle α, and the VR of the object. The observer position is the center of the polar coordinate system and the angle is calculated with the respect to zero axis of the universe, i.e., North is equal to $0°$. The same idea is applied to internal and leaf-nodes of VAST. The formula to calculate d and α is

$$\begin{cases} d = \sqrt{(Pos_x - O_x)^2 + (Pos_y - O_y)^2} \\ \alpha = \arctan\left(\frac{Pos_x - O_x}{Pos_y - O_y}\right) \end{cases} \tag{1}$$

The distance is calculated to the center of the MBS or MBR. The enhanced VAST also mirrors a subset of VR-tree, but it mirrors all entries for each loaded node. Each node in VAST requires an update whenever the observer moves. Figure 3 shows an enhanced VAST structure that mirrors a subset of the VR-tree. Figure 3(a) illustrates a lookup on the VR-tree that returns a trace (cf. Fig. 3(b)) to node $N2$. Enhanced VAST (cf. Fig. 3(c)) creates an exact trace that consist of pointers. Each node stores a distance d, angle α, and $VR(O_i)$. To identify whether the observer is outside or inside of the object's visibility range we check $d - VR(O_i)$. The difference gives the distance to the visibility range border. If $d - VR(O_i) > 0$ then object is invisible. If $d - VR(O_i) \leq 0$ then the observer is inside the visibility range and the object is visible. For example, $7; 90; 10$ means that the observer is inside the MBS. In distance 3 in direction 90 degrees the observer will be leaving the object's visibility range. In contrast $7; 15; 2$ means that in distance 5 and direction 15 degrees the object will become visible. The visibility range of the object is 2.

The size of internal and leaf node entry in VAST is the same $SE = 2 \cdot |Ptr| + |d| + |\alpha| + |VR|$. However, the number of entries per node differs. VAST internal node uses $\lfloor \frac{b}{2 \cdot D \cdot |p| + |Ptr|} \rfloor \cdot SE$ bytes of memory. It is the number of VR-tree entries in a node multiplied by the size of an entry. A VAST leaf node uses $\lfloor \frac{b}{D \cdot |p| + |s| + |Ptr|} \rfloor \cdot SE$ bytes. Here b is a disk page size, $D \cdot |p|$ is a D-dimensional point p, where $|p|$ denotes the size of the value, $|d|$, $|\alpha|$, and $|VR|$ are sizes of values and $|Ptr|$ denotes size of a disk pointer.

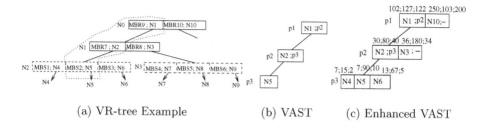

(a) VR-tree Example   (b) VAST   (c) Enhanced VAST

Fig. 3. Structure of VAST

VAST supports the selection of the currently visible objects if the observer has not moved. In order to find all visible objects the structure has to be traversed. For each leaf node we add all visible entries to the set of visible objects.

3.2   Function σ_{iORDE}

We implemented σ_{iORDE} as a recursive descent function (cf. Algorithm 3.1). It takes the new observer position Pos' and a VAST node as parameters. Initially the VASTNode parameter is set to the root. The algorithm processes each entry

---

Algorithm 3.1 Producing $\Delta^{\pm}$ (Function σ_{iORDE})

Require: In: Observer Pos', VASTNode $node$
Require: Out: (Δ^+, Δ^-)
  Expiration $exp \leftarrow$ MAX_DISTANCE_TO_MOVE
  for all entries $e \in node$ **do**
    $\ell \leftarrow$ updateEntry(Pos, e, Pos')
    if $\ell > 0$ **then**
      $\Delta^+ \leftarrow \Delta^+ \cup$ insertSubTree(VRTreePtr(e),Pos', newChild(e))
    else if $\ell < 0$ **then**
      $\Delta^- \leftarrow \Delta^- \cup$ pruneSubTree(Pos', exp, getChild(e))
    else
      $(\Delta^+, \Delta^-) \leftarrow (\Delta^+, \Delta^-) \cup \sigma_{iORDE}(Pos'$, getChild($e$))
    end if
  end for
  if hasNoVisibleEntries($node$) **then**
    deleteNode($node$)
  end if

---

in the node and updates the distance from the previous to the current position. Based on the result of updateEntry the insertion or deletion of a subtree is triggered. If the returned distance is $\ell > 0$ insertSubTree is called. This call returns a set of newly visible objects and creates a trace in VAST. If $\ell < 0$ the pruneSubTree is called. Finally, if $\ell = 0$ the observer did not leave or enter the visibility range.

VAST Insertions. The pseudocode in Algorithm 3.2 shows the implementation of the insertion algorithm. The insertSubTree function is called with the next observer position, the node the insertion shall start from, and a pointer to the node in the VR-tree. First, we load the VR-tree node. Each entry in the VR-tree

Algorithm 3.2 Insertion of Sub-tree (Function *insertSubTree*)

Require: In: VRTreePtr *r_ptr*, Observer *Pos*, VASTNode *node*
Require: Out: Δ^+
  VASTEntry $e \leftarrow nil$
  $r\_node \leftarrow$ VRTree_load(r_ptr)
  for all entries $re \in r\_node$ **do**
    $e \leftarrow$ mirrorEntry(re, pos)
    $visible \leftarrow$ addEntry($node, e$)
    if $visible$ is $true \wedge$ isNotLeaf($node$) **then**
      $\Delta^+ \leftarrow \Delta^+ \cup$ insertSubTree(VRTreePtr(re), Pos, newChild(e))
    else if $visible$ is $true \wedge$ isLeaf($node$) **then**
      $\Delta^+ \leftarrow \Delta^+ \cup e$
    end if
  end for
  if hasNoVisibleEntries($node$) **then**
    deleteNode($node$)
  end if

node is mirrored to VAST node. We calculate the distance d, angle α, and the VR to the center of the MBR. We also assign disk addresses of VR-tree entries which point to children. To identify which child node to load from VR-tree we compare the distance $d \le VR$. If it is true then the MBR is visible and the lower subtree shall be loaded. Else, when equality is false the MBR is invisible yet and a corresponding entry of VAST node is stored empty. However, VAST has a VR-tree disk address that enables us to load exactly a missing subtree from the disk when it becomes visible.

In Fig. 4 the insertion example is illustrated. Visible objects are marked with a solid line. Entries marked with the dashed line are invisible. When the observer moves from position P2 to P3 the entries are updated. σ_{iORDE} traverses VAST from the root. At the leaf it finds a new incoming object. The VR-tree pointer of the entry is used to load the requested data page.

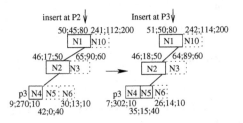

Fig. 4. Insertion into VAST

VAST Updates. When the observer moves we update the distance and angle stored in VAST. The update is done by descending from the root. In Fig. 5 observer moves from position *Pos* to position *Pos'* in distance k. Since MBRs and MBSs are not stored in the VAST we use the previous observer position to calculate the new distance from the observer to the object. From the previous observer position we, first, reconstruct the original location of the object. Next, the distance and angle from the new observer position to the original object position can be calculated. This yields the formula (2).

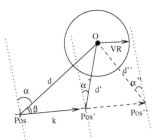

Fig. 5. Moving Observer and the Distance

$$d' = \sqrt{(Pos'_x - Pos_x + d \cdot \cos \alpha)^2 + (Pos'_y - Pos_y + d \cdot \sin \alpha)^2}. \qquad (2)$$

α' is calculated from the newly calculated d', the previous observer position, and d with angle α.

$$\sin \alpha' = \frac{Pos'_y - Pos_y + d \cdot \sin \alpha}{d'}. \qquad (3)$$

Before updating the entry we have to check if the object is visible. We use d' and α' to check if the object became visible.

VAST Deletions. A node expiration policy is introduced when pruning VAST entries. A node is checked for expiration when the distance from the observer to the invisible object is larger than a threshold. While updating node entries, the algorithm checks if one of the following conditions is satisfied.

– Descend to the children of entries that change the distance sign from the − to + when updating. That means the respective object has become invisible. Descend to the leaf node and mark all objects as invisible. If a leaf-node entry is changing the sign the disk page pointer is added to Δ^-.
– Look for expired nodes or entries. If the leaf-node contains only invisible objects it is deleted from the VAST tree.

In Fig. 6 the deletion of the subtree is illustrated. Leaf nodes that will be deleted contain entries with positive $d - VR(O_i)$ only. If a node or node entry has expired the whole subtree has to be deleted as soon as it becomes invisible. Note, that for the expiration the lookup in the VR-tree is not needed.

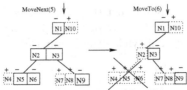

Fig. 6. Pruning Invisible Objects

4 Experiments

We evaluate the performance and effectiveness of VAST. VAST and the VR-tree have been integrated into the Generalized Search Tree package, GiST, [13] to support iORDE queries for the R-tree like structures.

The first experiment compares the I/O operations of the VR-tree and VAST. We expect that the implementation of observer relative data extraction on the VR-tree with uniformly distributed data points leads to a constant number of I/O. In contrast, we will access only new nodes on the disk based on the informations stored in VAST. We expect that the first observer movement using VAST leads to the same number of input operations as the VR-tree. However, the number of I/Os of further steps will be close to zero. When increasing the observer step size the number of I/O will increase.

The experimental data consist of 1 million of uniformly distributed objects. We generate five paths of observer movement with the same movement trajectory. The observer starts at a point (0,50) and moves to (100,50). Each path has fixed step sizes. We generate paths with step sizes proportional to the sizo of the universe: 0.5%, 1%, 2%, 5%, and 7%.

In Fig. 7 the experimental results show the I/O operations along the path of the moving observer. As expected the number of I/O operations of the VR-tree is high. It is not constant because the observer is moving from the boundary where the number of visible objects is less. It is marked with the solid line. Using VAST, the number of I/O operations is reduced close to zero. Enlarging the step size VAST scales up well and the number of I/O operations remains fairly low.

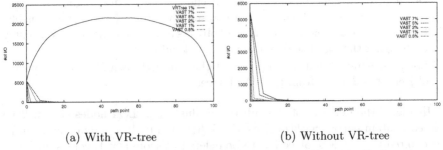

(a) With VR-tree   (b) Without VR-tree

Fig. 7. Comparison of I/O Operations Moving Along the Path

The second experiment is conducted on a torus dataset. In Fig. 8(a) a two dimensional torus with center (50,50) is shown. The torus consists of 10.000 objects distributed in a region of 100x100 according to the normal distribution. The inner border of the torus is more dense than the outer. The visibility ranges vary from 0–5% of the universe and are distributed according to the normal distribution. The dataset models rapid changes in the density of objects and allows to move inside dense regions. In Fig. 8(a) we also plot the paths the observer will follow. The first path is constructed of 100 path points and the observer is moving through the space from 0 to 100. The path is constructed such that the observer visits low and high density areas, and empty space.

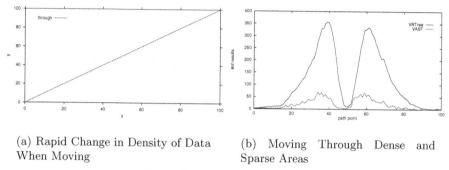

(a) Rapid Change in Density of Data When Moving

(b) Moving Through Dense and Sparse Areas

Fig. 8. Rapid Change in Density

The comparison of the result-set size when the observer is moving along the path is shown in Fig. 8(b). The upper line shows the size of results extracted when doing full re-select at each observer position. The lower line shows the number of results extracted incrementally. When the observer is approaching the dense inner ring the large number of results is produced twice. When the extraction is handled incrementally the number of objects extracted at each time is much less than doing full reselect.

The second path is when the observer is almost stationary (see Fig. 9(a)) (15, 30). The result is always the same or varies just a little bit (see Fig. 9(b)). The result shows that full re-select at each step returns 76 visible objects. However, when doing incremental extraction the almost stationary observer extracts initially 76 visible objects and later only small deltas of 1 or 2 objects.

The third path is a circular trajectory walk inside the torus in the distance of 20 from the center (see Fig. 10(a)) (50,50). This path keeps the observer within a high density area. The first query generates more than 350 visible objects (see Fig. 10(b)). If the observer extracts objects incrementally the number of visible objects is reduced. Otherwise, the average of 300 of visible objects is extracted at each position.

The next experiment investigates how VAST improves when the dataset has holes and high density regions as well. The purpose of the experiment is to

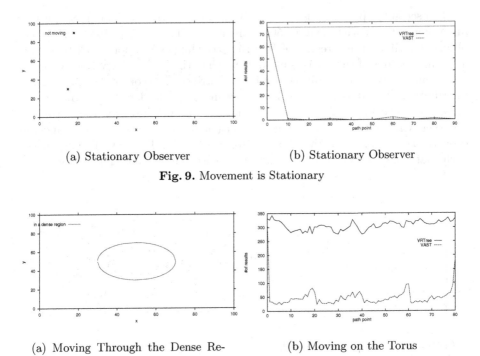

(a) Stationary Observer   (b) Stationary Observer

Fig. 9. Movement is Stationary

(a) Moving Through the Dense Region   (b) Moving on the Torus

Fig. 10. Moving Inside Dense Region

measure the number of I/O operations used per object for the given data. In Fig. 11(a) we construct the observer path such that observer moves along the cluster crosses the empty rectangular area (data were intentionally cut out), and further moves around the cluster. The step size is constant and is equal to 2% of the universe size. Solid line shows the movement path. Labels represent the path point and query points. We expect that the ratio using the VR-tree will be higher than with VAST. VAST incrementally extracts visible objects. On the contrary the VR-tree extracts all visible objects at any given observer position.

In Fig. 11(b) the results of an experiment confirm that number of I/O per object using VAST is lower than using full re-select on the VR-tree.

5   Conclusions and Future Work

In this paper we have proposed a unique way to combine visualization and database subsystems. The combination permits visual fly-through investigations of massive data sets. We introduced the VAST structure. Together with the VR-tree it enables incremental observer relative data extraction. VAST caches the visible objects and returns only relevant $\Delta^{\pm}$ slices. We give an intuition of how the tree operates and explain in detail how the VAST structure is created

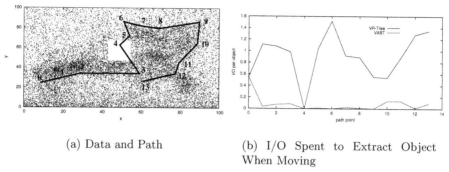

(a) Data and Path   (b) I/O Spent to Extract Object
                                When Moving

Fig. 11. Moving Observer in Non-uniform Environment

and maintained. Algorithms for insertion, deletion, and update of VAST are presented.

To validate our solution we ran experiments on synthetically generated datasets. The experiments confirm our expectations. VAST significantly reduces the number of I/O operations. By introducing appearing and disappearing objects the performance is boosted.

In the future it is interesting to investigate the optimization of the observer's fly-through path. The incremental extraction depends on the distance the observer moves. It would be valuable to have methods that support incremental extraction without overstepping objects along the path.

References

1. Guttman, A.: R-trees: A dynamic index structure for spatial searching. In: Proc. of Annual Meeting SIGMOD'84. (1984) 47–57
2. Beckmann, N., Kriegel, H.P., Schneider, R., Seeger, B.: The r*-tree: An efficient and robust access method for points and rectangles. In: Proc. of Int. Conference on Management of Data. (1990) 322–331
3. Berchtold, S., Keim, D.A., Kriegel, H.P.: The x-tree : An index structure for high-dimensional data. In: Proc. of Int. Conference on Very Large Data Bases. (1996) 28–39
4. White, D.A., Jain, R.: Similarity indexing with the ss-tree. In: Proc. of Int. Conference on Data Engineering. (1996) 516–523
5. Katayama, N., Satoh, S.: The sr-tree: An index structure for high-dimensional nearest neighbor queries. In: Proc. of Int. Conference on Management of Data. (1997) 369–380
6. Tzouramanis, T., Vassilakopoulos, M., Manolopoulos, Y.: Overlapping linear quadtrees: A spatio-temporal access method. In: Proc. of Int. Symposium on Advances in Geographic Information Systems. (1998) 1–7
7. Robinson, J.T.: The k-d-b-tree: A search structure for large multidimensional dynamic indexes. In: Proc. of Int. Conference on Management of Data. (1981) 10–18

8. Henrich, A.: The lsd^h-tree: An access structure for feature vectors. In: Proc. of Int. Conference on Data Engineering. (1998) 362–369
9. Song, Z., Roussopoulos, N.: K-nearest neighbor search for moving query point. In: Proc. of Int. Symposium on Advances in Spatial and Temporal Databases. (2001) 79–96
10. Kofler, M., Gervautz, M., Gruber, M.: R-trees for organizing and visualizing 3d gis databases. Journal of Visualization and Computer Animation **11** (2000) 129–143
11. Koefler, M.: R-Trees for Visualizing and Organizing Large 3D GIS Databases. PhD thesis, Technichen Universit at Graz (1998)
12. Shou, L., Chionh, J., Huang, Z., Tan, K.L., Ruan, Y.: Walking through a very large virtual environment in real-time. In: Proceedings of Int. Conference on Very Large Data Bases. (2001) 401–410
13. Hellerstein, J.M., Naughton, J.F., Pfeffer, A.: Generalized search trees for database systems. In: Proc. of Int. Conference on Very Large Data Bases. (1995) 562–573

Performing Colour-Based Similarity Searches in Multimedia Database Management Systems Augmented with Derived Images

Leonard Brown[1] and Le Gruenwald[2]

[1] The University of Texas at Tyler, Department of Computer Science, Tyler, TX, 75799
Leonard_Brown@UTTyler.edu
[2] The University of Oklahoma, School of Computer Science, Norman, OK, 73069
ggruenwald@ou.edu

Abstract. In order to improve the robustness of systems that perform similarity searching, it may be necessary to augment a collection of images in a Multimedia DataBase Management System (MMDBMS) with an additional set of edited images. Previous research has demonstrated that space can be saved in such a system by storing the edited images as sequences of editing operations instead of as large binary objects. The existing approaches for performing similarity searching in an MMDBMS, however, typically assume that the data objects are stored as binary objects. This paper proposes algorithms for performing colour-based similarity searches of images stored as editing operations and provides a performance evaluation illustrating their respective strengths and weaknesses.

1 Motivation

Because images and other types of multimedia data objects are different than traditional alphanumeric data, a MultiMedia Database Management System (MMDBMS) has different requirements from a traditional database management system. For example, multimedia data is typically larger than traditional data, so an MMDBMS should utilize efficient storage techniques. In addition, users interpret the content of images and other multimedia data objects when they view or hear them, so an MMDBMS should facilitate searching in those systems utilizing that content. Also, the binary representation of two images of the same objects may be very different, so an MMDBMS must perform similarity searching of images as opposed to searching for exact matches.

To facilitate similarity searching, systems typically extract features and generate a signature from each image in the database to represent its content in order to search those features in response to a user's query. For searching a heterogeneous collection of images, systems will often compare images utilizing a combination of low-level features including colour, texture, and shape as in [1]. When searching images under a specific domain, such as searching a set of facial images, systems will often extract more complex features for searching such as the shape and location of noses, eyes, mouths, and hair outline [2, 3]. Irrespective of whether the features are low-level or

H. Williams and L. MacKinnon (Eds.): BNCOD 2004, LNCS 3112, pp. 178–189, 2004.

high-level, the underlying system typically searches for images that are similar to a query image Q by first extracting the desired features from Q and then comparing them to the previously extracted features of the images in the database.

One of the limitations of the above approach for performing similarity searching is that it is dependent upon having the binary representations of all of the images that are stored in the database so that features can be extracted or a signature can be generated. To illustrate why this can be a limitation, consider the problem of facial recognition in an example application of a crime database containing a collection of suspects' faces. It is difficult enough to match images of the same faces under varying lighting conditions [2], but the current research does not appear to sufficiently address the problem of matching a facial image from a person intentionally trying to disguise themselves utilizing either simple techniques such as adding or removing facial hair or extensive technique such as undergoing plastic surgery.

One technique for addressing the above problem is to expand a given query image Q into several query images. Each query image is created by image by editing Q using common disguises and then submitted to the database as a separate query. The results from all of the query images are combined together to form one result. This technique is analogous to text retrieval systems that augment terms in a user's query utilizing a manually produced thesaurus before searching a collection of documents. The problem with this approach for searching images is that the features must be extracted from each query image in order to search the underlying MMDBMS. Because this is a very expensive process, the time needed to respond to the query will dramatically increase.

Instead of utilizing the above technique, the system may simply augment the collection of images stored in its underlying database with edited versions of the images. So, for each image object O in the database, the system will store O along with a set of images created by transforming O with editing operation sequences representing common disguises. Thus, the system augments its database with a set of edited images derived from its original collection.

As an alternative to storing all images in such a database in a binary format, previous research [4] proposed to save space by storing the images derived from an original base image object O in a virtual format, meaning that they are each stored as a reference to O along with the sequence of editing operations that were used to create it. Displaying an image stored virtually can be accomplished by accessing the referenced image and sequentially executing the associated editing operations on it, which is a process called instantiation [4].

The use of virtual images can be beneficial in numerous application areas in addition to law enforcement. Specifically, they are useful in any applications in which users create and store new objects by editing existing ones. For example, this approach will be useful in multimedia authoring environments where several versions of various images created by a user can be archived [5] such as publishing and web design. Virtual images will also be useful in the area of medicine where plastic surgeons can illustrate the changes they intend to make to their patients by editing their photo. Finally, virtual images can be useful for business applications where users order customized objects by selecting from a list of external features and enhancements, such as ordering clothes, class rings, or other types of apparel.

As a first step in investigating approaches for searching databases augmented with derived images, this paper focuses on searching a heterogeneous collection of images by colour. Systems that search by colour typically extract features from each image to represent its content and then search those features in response to a user's query. When extracting colour features, one common method is to generate a histogram for each image stored in the database where each bin contains the percentage of pixels in that image that are of a particular colour. These colours are usually obtained by quantizing the space of a colour model such as RGB or Luv into an equal number of divisions. To search for images that are similar to a query image Q, the MMDBMS can compare the histograms stored in the database to the histogram of Q. Common functions used to evaluate the similarity between two n-dimensional histograms $<x_1, ..., x_n>$ and $<y_1, ..., y_n>$ include (1) the Histogram Intersection [6] and (2) the L_p Distances [7].

$$\sum_{i=1}^{n} \min(x_i, y_i) \qquad (1)$$

$$\sqrt[p]{\sum_{i=1}^{n}(x_i - y_i)^p} \qquad (2)$$

The above distance functions allow the system to process nearest-neighbor queries of the type "*Retrieve the k images that are the most similar to Q*". Systems that perform similarity searches using methods involving histogram-based techniques include [1, 8, 9, 10].

The above histogram techniques are used for colour-based searching in systems that assume all of the images, including any derived ones, are stored in a binary format. New colour-based searching algorithms and techniques are needed for systems that save space by storing derived images virtually. The purpose of this paper is to present three such techniques and compare their respective performances to the above approach of storing all images in a binary format. The remainder of this paper has the following format. Each of Sections 2, 3, and 4 presents a different approach for searching virtual images by colour. Section 5 presents the results of a performance evaluation comparing these three approaches to the conventional approach. Finally, Section 6 summarizes the paper and describes the future work.

2 Virtual Storage That Instantiates During Searching (VSIS)

The previous section described the conventional approach to searching images using colour-based features, which stores all images in a binary format. This paper refers to this approach as Binary Storage with Histograms (BSH), and algorithms for it are presented in Figures 2 and 3. The insertion process for BSH is displayed in Figure 1, and in it, histograms are extracted from all images as they are inserted into the system. The histogram of an image is stored in the database along with the object ID of the image. The BSH algorithm for processing similarity searches of the type "*Retrieve the k images that are the most similar to Q*" is provided in Figure 2. In the algorithm, a histogram is extracted from the query image Q and compared to the histograms stored in the database to identify the k most similar images.

1.	Extract histogram from the image
2.	Store the image in database with an image ID
3.	Store histogram and image ID together in the database

Fig. 1. BSH Algorithm for Inserting Images

1. Identify the query image Q and the number of desired images k from the given query
2. Extract the histogram from Q and call it HQ
3. For each histogram, H, stored in the database
    3.1 Compute the distance between H and HQ
    3.2 Remember the k images corresponding to the histograms that are the smallest distances from HQ
4. Return the identifiers of the images stored in Step 3.2

Fig. 2. BSH Algorithm for Sequentially Processing Similarity Searches

Elements of BSH are used as part of the first strategy for processing similarity searches in MMDBMSs that store edited images virtually. The strategy is based upon instantiating the virtual images into a binary format during the searching and then using conventional histogram techniques to search them. Since instantiation is performed during searching, this paper refers to these algorithms as the Virtual Storage that Instantiates while Searching (VSIS) approach. In this approach, the images that are stored virtually are directly inserted into the database without any feature extraction processing, while histograms are extracted from the images stored in a binary format. This process for inserting images using the VSIS strategy is listed in Figure 3.

1. If image is binary
    1.1 Extract the histogram from the image
    1.2 Store the image in the database using its ID
    1.3 Store histogram and image ID together in the database
2. Else
    2.1 Store the virtual image in the database using its ID

Fig. 3. VSIS Algorithm for Inserting Images

When performing a similarity search, the VSIS algorithm begins in the same manner as the BSH algorithm described earlier. Specifically, a histogram is extracted from the query image and then compared to the histograms previously extracted from the binary images. The difference is that the VSIS algorithm must determine the distances from the query image to the images stored virtually. This is accomplished by accessing the virtual images, instantiating them, and then extracting histograms from them. When this process is complete, these newly extracted histograms can be compared to the histogram of the query image in order to determine the images that correspond to the smallest distances. The algorithm is presented in Figure 4.

1. Identify the query image Q and the number of desired images k from the given query
2. Extract the histogram from Q and call it HQ
3. For each histogram, H, stored in the database
    3.1 Compute the distance between H and HQ
    3.2 Remember the k images corresponding to the histograms that are the
    smallest distances from HQ
4. For each virtual image, V, stored in the database
    4.1 Instantiate V
    4.2 Extract Histogram H from the Instantiated Image
    4.3 Compute the distance between H and HQ
    4.4 Update the list of k images with histograms that are the smallest distances
    from HQ

Fig. 4. VSIS Algorithm for Sequentially Processing Similarity Searches

3 Virtual Storage That Instantiates During Inserting (VSII)

The second strategy to performing similarity searches with virtual images avoids image instantiation during searching. Instead, the virtual images are instantiated at the time they are inserted into the database. Thus, this paper refers to this strategy as the Virtual Storage that Instantiates during Inserting (VSII) approach.

1. If image is binary
    1.1 Extract the histogram from the image
    1.2 Store the image in the database using its ID
    1.3 Store histogram and image ID together in the database
2. Else
    2.1 Instantiate the virtual image
    2.2 Extract the histogram from the instantiated image
    2.3 Store histogram and image ID together in the database
    2.4 Discard the instantiated image
    2.5 Store the virtual image in the database using its ID

Fig. 5. VSII Algorithm for Inserting Images

Figure 5 displays the details of the VSII insertion algorithm. After a virtual image is instantiated, the system extracts and stores its histogram. Once the histogram is saved, the instantiated image is then discarded leaving only the virtual image to be added to the database. Also, since the VSII algorithm generates a histogram from both binary and virtual images when they are inserted, VSII can use the same searching algorithm as BSH. Thus, the algorithm in Figure 2 can be used to perform similarity searches for VSII.

A disadvantage of both VSIS and VSII is that instantiation is a slow process. Consequently, VSIS will quickly insert images, but perform poorly when performing similarity searches. Alternatively, VSII will perform similarity searches as quickly as BSH, but it will perform poorly when inserting virtual images. The next section will present a third strategy that is able to process similarity searches without instantiating images, thus saving time over both VSIS and VSII.

4 Virtual Storage with Rules (VSR)

The VSR algorithm processes similarity searches in systems that store edited images virtually without instantiating the virtual images. This means that VSR uses the same insertion algorithm as VSIS, which inserts virtual images directly into the database as shown in Figure 3.

The VSR algorithm for processing similarity searches is shown in Figure 6, and it consists of two major tasks. The first task is to identify the distances from the binary images in the database to the query image Q, and the second task is to identify the distances of the virtual images to Q. In the first three steps, the binary images' distances are computed using the same technique as in BSH, which is to compare histograms. The remaining steps compute the distance from Q to each virtual image based upon the Histogram Intersection [6]. Thus, the distance from Q to a virtual image V is computed the sum of the minimum values of their corresponding bins. Since the minimum values are desired, Step 4 of the algorithm determines the bins that are nonzero in the histogram of Q. The next step is a loop that executes once for each bin identified in the previous step, where the purpose of this loop is to determine the minimum values of the corresponding bins.

---

1. Identify the query image Q and the number of desired images k from the given query
2. Extract the histogram from Q and call it HQ
3. For each histogram, H, stored in the database
    3.1 Compute the distance between H and HQ.
    3.2 Remember the k images corresponding to the histograms that are the smallest distances from HQ
4. Enumerate the colours in the query image using the histogram HQ
5. Loop until there are no more colours in Q or all virtual images are eliminated
    5.1 Identify the histogram bin HB corresponding to the next colour in HQ
    5.2 Let match equal the value in bin HB of HQ
    5.3 Using rules, eliminate the virtual images that do not have a value in bin HB within δ of match, where δ is the distance from Q to the kth most similar image.
    5.4 For each remaining virtual image V
        5.4.1 Increase V's distance from Q by the minimum of match and its value in bin HB.
    5.5 Update the list of k images that are closest to Q using the distances of the remaining virtual images

---

Fig. 6. Rule-Based Algorithm for Processing Similarity Searches

The following steps are performed during each iteration of the above loop. First, the current bin is denoted as bin HB. Next, the algorithm identifies the value of the histogram of Q in bin HB and stores it in *match*. Given match, the algorithm must identify the value in bin HB for each virtual image. Once this value is identified for a virtual image V, the distance from Q to V is increased by that value to comply with the histogram intersection.

The key step in the above algorithm is the identification of the value in bin HB for a virtual image. Since the proposed approach never instantiates the virtual images, no histograms are stored for them. Thus, this algorithm must estimate the value that would be in bin HB for a virtual image if it were instantiated. This estimation is accomplished using rules establishing the effects of editing operations on the percentages of colours that are contained in an image. The rules used are dependent upon the editing operations that may appear in the virtual images, which are restricted to the set of operations listed in [4], Define, Combine, Modify, Mutate, and Merge. The reason why this set is used is that it can be used to perform any image transformation by manipulating a single pixel at a time [11].

The Define operation selects the group of pixels that will be edited by the subsequent operations in the list, and the parameters to the operation specify the coordinates of the desired group of pixels, called the Defined Region (DR). The Combine operation is used to blur images by changing the colours of the pixels in the DR to the weighted average of the colours of the pixels' neighbors, and the parameters to the operation are the weights (C_{11}, ..., C_{33}) applied to each of the neighbors. The Modify operation is used to explicitly change the colours of the pixels in the DR that are of a certain colour, RGB_{old}, and the parameters of the operation specify that old colour as well as the new colour, RGB_{new}. The Mutate operation is used to move pixels within an image, and the parameters specify the matrix (M_{11}, ..., M_{33}) used to shift the locations of the pixels. Finally, the Merge operation is used to copy the current DR into a target image, and the parameters specify the target image, *target*, and the coordinates specifying where to copy the DR (x_p, y_p).

The purpose of each rule is to determine how its corresponding editing operation can change a given histogram bin HB. Thus, each rule is expressed as an adjustment to the minimum and maximum bounds on the percentage of pixels that may be in bin HB when the virtual image is instantiated. The percentages are adjusted by repeatedly updating the total number of pixels that are in the image as well as the minimum and maximum number of pixels that are in bin HB for each editing operation listed in the virtual image.

Both the Combine and Modify operations only change the colours of the pixels in the current DR. Because of this, one rule for both operations is that the total number of pixels in the image will neither increase nor decrease after their application. In addition, the number of pixels that may change colour is bounded by the number of pixels in the DR, denoted |DR|. So, depending on whether RGB_{old} or RGB_{new} maps to bin HB, the number of pixels in bin HB may increase or decrease by at most |DR| as a result of the Modify operation. While |DR| also serves as a bound for the number of pixels that may change as a result of the Combine operation, note that pixels within homogeneously coloured regions will not change because the operation determines a new colour for a pixel based on the average colour of its neighbors. As a result, the rule for the Combine operation is that the adjustment to the number of pixels that are in bin HB will be so small that it can be ignored.

The Mutate operation can scale the pixels in the DR to overwrite other locations in the image, which means that it can dramatically alter the distribution of colours within an image. Consequently, the rules for the Mutate operation are based on specific instances of its parameters. One such rule is that if the current DR contains the whole image, then the distribution of colours in the image should remain the same. Another rule is that if the parameters imply a rigid body transformation [12], then the DR will simply be moved without any scaling. Thus, the total number of pixels that may change colour is bounded by $|DR|$ as in the Modify operation.

The rules for the Merge operation adjust the percentage of pixels in bin HB based on the combination of the pixels in the DR and the colours in the target image. Table 1 provides the formulae for computing these adjustments based on the parameters of the operation, along with a summary of the rules for the Combine, Modify, and Mutate operations presented previously. In the table, $|V|$ represents the number of pixels in the virtual image, $|T|$ represents the number of pixels in the target image of the Merge operation, $|T_{HB}|$ represents the number of pixels in the target that are in bin HB, $|HB|_{min}$ represents the minimum number of pixels in bin HB, and $|HB|_{max}$ represents the maximum number of pixels in bin HB.

Table 1. Rules for Adjusting Bounds on Numbers of Pixels in Bin HB

Editing Operation	Conditions	Minimum Number in bin HB	Maximum Number in bin HB	Total Number of Pixels in Image
Combine $(C_{11}, ..., C_{33})$	All	No change	No change	No change
Modify (RGB_{old}, RGB_{new})	RGB_{new} maps to HB	No Change	Increase by $|DR|$	No Change
	RGB_{old} maps to HB	Decrease by $|DR|$	No Change	No Change
Mutate $(M_{11}, M_{12}, M_{13}, M_{21}, M_{22}, M_{23}, M_{31}, M_{32}, M_{33})$	DR contains image	Multiply by $|M_{11} \times M_{22}|$	Multiply by $|M_{11} \times M_{22}|$	Multiply by $|M_{11} \times M_{22}|$
	Rigid Body	Decrease by $|DR|$	Increase by $|DR|$	No Change
Merge $(Target, x_p, y_p)$	Target is NULL	$|DR| - (|V| - |HB|_{min})$	$MIN[|HB|_{max}, |DR|]$	$|DR|$
	Target is Not NULL	$|DR| - (|V| - |HB|_{min}) + |T_{HB}| - |DR|$	$MIN(|HB|_{max}, |DR|) + MIN(|T_{HB}|, |T| - |DR|)$	$[MAX((x_p+x_2- x_1), \text{height of Target}) - MIN(x_p,0)+1] \times [MAX((y_p+y_2- y_1), \text{width of Target}) - MIN(y_p,0)+1]$

5 Performance Evaluation

The proposed algorithms presented in this paper have been implemented as part of a web-enabled prototype virtual image retrieval system [13] accessible from the URL http://www.cs.ou.edu/~lbrown. Modules in the above prototype were used to conduct tests to evaluate the performance of the algorithms proposed in this paper in terms of permanent storage space required, insertion time, searching time, and searching accuracy. The data set consists of 5 groups of images, where each group contains one binary image and 99 edited images stored virtually yielding a total of 500 images. The parameters of the evaluations are listed in Table 2. The binary images in the random data set were taken from a combination of various collections of images representing different application areas including law enforcement, space exploration, business, and weather [14]. Each virtual image in the data set was created by randomly selecting a binary image as the base image and randomly generating editing operations from [4] for it. Table 3 summarizes the results of the evaluation, and it illustrates the strengths and weaknesses of each of the proposed approaches.

Table 2. Parameters Used in Evaluation

Description	Default Value
Number of Images in the Database	500
Number of Binary Images in the Database	5
Number of Virtual Images in the Database	495
Average Number of Operations within a Virtual Image	2.11
Average Size of Binary Images in the Database (in bytes)	11396.60
Average Size of Virtual Images in the Database (in bytes)	70.27
Average Size of Histogram Extracted From Binary Images (in bytes)	190.40

Table 3. Summarized Results of Performance Evaluation

Approach	Storage Space (MB)	Insertion Time (sec)	Searching Time (sec)	Searching Accuracy
BSH	14.36	876.90	2.29	83%
VSR	0.09	6.54	2.33	73%
VSIS	0.09	6.54	12174.96	83%
VSII	0.15	13049.23	2.29	83%

BSH has the advantage of being simple. All images can be stored in the same format so the underlying database management system only needs to manipulate one type of image. Also, one of the main reasons of using features or signatures to search images is that it will be much faster than analyzing the images themselves during searching, so the BSH approach is as fast as the other approaches in terms of searching time. The disadvantage of BSH is that it consumes the most space of the four approaches since no images are stored virtually. Because the virtual approaches stored 99% of the images virtually, they used 99.35% less space than BSH. In addition, BSH extracts histograms from all images during insertion, so it was also 99.95% slower than VSR and VSIS when inserting the images.

One of the advantages of VSIS is that is saves space by storing images virtually. In addition, the approach does not store or extract any information from virtual images when they are first inserted, so it is as fast as VSR when inserting images. Another advantage of VSIS is that it produces the same results as BSH since it is histogram-based. The main disadvantage of VSIS is that it is extremely slow when processing retrieval queries since it instantiates all of the virtual images and extracts their histograms. Both VSR and BSH were 99.98% faster than VSIS when searching the images.

VSII extracts histograms from all images like BSH, so it shares some of the same advantages. Specifically, VSII searches as quickly as BSH, and the searches produce the same results. In addition, VSII used 98.91% less space than BSH in the tests due to it storing images virtually. The main disadvantage of VSII is that it is slow when inserting virtual images into the underlying database management system since it instantiates the images before extracting their features. In the tests, VSR and VSIS were 99.95% faster when inserting images.

VSR has the advantage that it required 99.35% less space than BSH. It also required 40.79% less space than the VSII approach since it does not store histograms for all images. The main contribution of VSR, however, is that it does not instantiate while inserting virtual images or searching them. The result is that in the tests, it was 99.98% faster than the VSIS approach when searching and 99.95% faster than the VSII approach when inserting. A disadvantage of VSR is that it does not produce the same results as the other approaches. During the tests, it was 12.3% less accurate.

Considering the above discussion, BSH is best suited for applications that are most dependent on retrieval time and not space or insertion time. Thus, the approach is the most appropriate for applications with static data sets that are searched frequently, such as medical diagnostic applications where an image taken from a patient may be compared with images of known diseases. BSH is also appropriate for data sets that do not contain sets of images that are similar; otherwise, they will waste space. VSIS is not suitable for applications that allow users to frequently perform content-based searches. Thus, VSIS is best suited for applications in which users may constantly create and add new images to the database but rarely retrieve them, such as applications that archive data. VSII is not appropriate for applications in which users will frequently update the database by adding new images. Instead, VSII is most appropriate for many of the same applications as BSH, which include applications with static data sets that are frequently searched. The difference is that VSII should be used with those applications that store edited images, such as one that displays standard automobile models that differ only in colour. Finally, VSR is best suited for applications where users frequently edit existing images and add them to the underlying database with the intention that those images will also be searched frequently. Applications with these characteristics that also need to reduce the amount of space by storing the edited images virtually include web-based stores where users want to browse similar images of products that are updated quickly.

6 Summary and Future Work

MultiMedia DataBase Management Systems (MMDBMSs) focus on the storage and retrieval of images and other types of multimedia data. In data sets that contain derived images, storing them virtually allows the images to be stored using a smaller amount of space when compared to storing them in conventional binary formats. This paper presented three different strategies for searching derived images stored virtually.

This paper focused on searching a heterogeneous collection of images utilizing colour features. As a result, the rules used in the VSR approach focused on identifying the effects of editing operations on colour features. In order to continue with the VSR approach, it will be necessary to identify rules for retrieving images using other features besides colour, such as texture and shape. Ultimately, rules must be identified for identifying the effects of editing operations on more complex features within a set of images from a specific domain, such as the effects of common disguises on the hair colour, eye colour, eye shape, and nose length on an image of a face.

It is also worth noting that the rules presented in this paper attempt to estimate the effect of editing operations on colour histograms. So, if the rules were perfect, a system using VSR would retrieve images with the same accuracy as the histogram or feature-based approaches. An alternative approach would be to develop rules that ignore the features extracted from images altogether. Such an approach would be based on the transformation approach [15] which computes the similarity between two images as the cost required to transform one into the other. This cost could be computed directly from the editing operations listed within the semantics of a virtual image. Such an approach would allow the VSR approach to potentially be more accurate than the feature-based approaches.

Another open research area is to evaluate the effect of using algorithms that are hybrids of the VSR and VSII algorithms presented in this paper. For example, one such hybrid approach could store histograms corresponding to some of the virtual images in order to optimize both the permanent storage space and retrieval time. An open issue, then, in creating such a hybrid approach is how to determine which histograms to store that optimize those metrics.

Finally, an area of future work is to construct and compare indexes for each of the three proposed strategies for searching virtual images. While many multidimensional indexes exist for arranging histograms extracted from images, new methods are needed to efficiently arrange the data for VSIS and VSR, which do not store extracted histograms.

References

1.   Ortega, M. et al.: Supporting Ranked Boolean Similarity Queries in MARS. IEEE Transactions on Knowledge and Data Engineering 10(6) (1998) 905-925.
2.   Zhao, W. et al.: Face Recognition: A Literature Survey. ACM Computing Surveys 35(4) (2003) 399-458

3. Hsu Rein-Lien, Jain, A. K.: Semantic Face Matching. Proceedings of the 2002 IEEE International Conference on Multimedia and Expo (2002) 145-148

4. Speegle, G. et al.: Extending Databases to Support Image Editing. Proceedings of the IEEE International Conference on Multimedia and Expo (2000)

5. Gibbs, S., Breiteneder, C., Tsichritzis, D., Modeling of Time-Based Media. The Handbook of Multimedia Information Retrieval, Chapter 1, Grosky, Jain, and Mehrotra (Eds.), Prentice-Hall (1997) 13-38.

6. Swain, M. J., Ballard, D. H.: Color Indexing. International Journal of Computer Vision 7(1) (1991) 11-32

7. Jagadish, H. V.: Content-Based Indexing and Retrieval. The Handbook of Multimedia Information Management, Chapter 3, Grosky, Jain, and Mehrotra (Eds.), Prentice Hall (1997)

8. Stehling, R. O., Nascimento, M. A., Falcão, A. X.: A Compact and Efficient Image Retrieval Approach Based on Border/Interior Pixel Classification. Proceedings of 11th International Conference on Information and Knowledge Management (2002) 102-109

9. Oria, Vincent, et al.: Similarity Queries in the DISIMA Image DBMS. Proceedings of 9th ACM International Conference on Multimedia (2001) 475-478

10. Park, Du-Sik et al.: Image Indexing using Weighted Color Histogram. Proceedings of 10th International Conference on Image Analysis and Processing (1999)

11. Brown, L., Gruenwald, L., Speegle, G.: Testing a Set of Image Processing Operations for Completeness. Proceedings of 2nd International Conference on Multimedia Information Systems (1997) 127-134

12. Gonzales, R. C., Woods, R. E.: Digital Image Processing, Addison-Wesley Publishing Company, Reading, MA (1993)

13. Brown, L., Gruenwald, L.: A Prototype Content-Based Retrieval System that Uses Virtual Images to Save Space. Proceedings of 27th International Conference on Very Large DataBases (2001)

14. Binary Images obtained from the Internet at http://nix.nasa.gov/browser.html, http://www.cs.ou.edu/~database/members.htm, http://www.weathergallery.com/tornado-gallery.shtml, http://c2.com/~ward/plates/, http://www.toyota.com, last accessed January 7, 2002.

15. Subrahmanian, V. S.: Principles of Multimedia Database Systems. Morgan Kaufmann Publishers Inc., San Francisco, CA (1998)

Bulk Loading the M-Tree to Enhance Query Performance

Alan P. Sexton and Richard Swinbank

School of Computer Science, University of Birmingham
Edgbaston, Birmingham, B15 2TT, UK
{A.P.Sexton, R.J.Swinbank}@cs.bham.ac.uk

Abstract. The M-tree is a paged, dynamically balanced metric access method that responds gracefully to the insertion of new objects. Like many spatial access methods, the M-tree's performance is largely dependent on the degree of overlap between spatial regions represented by nodes in the tree, and minimisation of overlap is key to many of the design features of the M-tree and related structures. We present a novel approach to overlap minimisation using a new bulk loading algorithm, resulting in a query cost saving of between 25% and 40% for non-uniform data.

The structural basis of the new algorithm suggests a way to modify the M-tree to produce a variant which we call the SM-tree. The SM-tree has the same query performance after bulk loading as the M-tree, but further supports efficient object deletion while maintaining the usual balance and occupancy constraints.

1 Introduction

The expansion of database systems to include non-alphanumeric datatypes has led to a need for index structures by which to query them. Tree-based index structures for traditional datatypes rely heavily on these datatypes' strict linear ordering; this is unsurprising as it is this same property that we use naturally in discussing ordered data, using notions such as 'before', 'after' and 'between'.

Newer datatypes such as images and sounds possess no such natural linear ordering, and in consequence we do not attempt to exploit one, but rather evaluate data in terms of their relative *similarities*: one image is 'like' another image but is 'not like' another different image. This has led to the notion of *similarity searching* for such datatypes, and the definition of queries like *k Nearest Neighbour*: find the k objects in the database at the shortest distance from a query object, where *distance* is some measure of the dissimilarity between objects.

Spatial access methods such as the R-tree [3] can support similarity queries of this nature by abstracting objects as points in a multidimensional vector space and calculating distance using a Euclidean metric. A more general approach is to abstract objects as points in a metric space, in which a distance function is known, but absolute positions of objects in a Cartesian space need not be. This

H. Williams and L. MacKinnon (Eds.): BNCOD 2004, LNCS 3112, pp. 190–202, 2004.

renders consideration of dimensionality unnecessary, and so provides a single method applicable to all (and unclear or unknown) dimensionalities.

The first paged, dynamically balanced metric tree was the M-tree [2]. The M-tree preserves the notion of objects' *closeness* more perfectly than in earlier structures (e.g. [6]) by associating a *covering radius* with pointers above the leaf level in the tree, indicating the furthest distance from the pointer at which an object in its subtree might be found. This, in combination with the triangle inequality property of the metric space, permits branches to be pruned from the tree when executing a query.

For a query result to be found in a branch rooted on a pointer with reference value O_n, that result must be within a distance $r(Q)$ (the *search radius*) of the query object Q. By definition, all objects in the branch rooted on O_n are also within $r(O_n)$ (the covering radius) of O_n, so for a result to be found in the branch rooted on O_n, the regions defined by $r(Q)$ around Q and $r(O_n)$ around O_n must intersect. This is a statement of the triangle inequality: For an object answering query Q to be found in the subtree rooted on O_n, it must be true that

$$d(Q, O_n) \leqslant r(Q) + r(O_n)$$

so when O_n is encountered in descending the tree, $d(Q, O_n)$ can be calculated in order to decide whether to prune or to descend the branch rooted on O_n. Figures 1 and 2 illustrate the two possibilities.

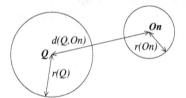
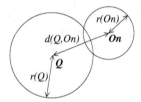

Fig. 1. The branch rooted on O_n can be pruned from the search.

Fig. 2. The branch rooted on O_n cannot be pruned.

An alternative to loading a tree by a series of object insertions was presented in [1]. This *bulk loading* algorithm selects a number of "seed" objects around which other objects are recursively clustered to build an unbalanced tree which must later be re-balanced. This provides construction cost saving of up to 50%, with query costs very similar to those of insertion-built trees.

Like many spatial access methods, the M-tree's performance is largely dependent on the degree of overlap between spatial regions represented by nodes in the tree. Minimisation of overlap is key to many of the design features of the M-tree and related structures; some approaches are discussed later. In this paper we present an alternative approach: that of pre-clustering an existing data set in a way that reflects the performance requirements of the M-tree before bulk loading the data into a tree. Unlike conventional bulk loading algorithms, the objective here is not efficient *loading* of the tree, but rather a subsequent tree organisation that maximises query performance. The structural basis of the new algorithm suggests a way to modify the M-tree to produce a variant which we call the SM-tree. The SM-tree has the same query performance after bulk loading as the M-tree, and supports efficient object deletion within the constraints of node balance and occupancy.

2   Insertion into the M-Tree

Insertion of an object O_i into an M-tree proceeds as follows. From the root node, an entry pointing to a child node is selected as the most appropriate parent for O_i. The child node is retrieved from disk and the process is repeated recursively until the entry reaches the leaf level in the tree.

A number of suggestions have been made as to how the 'best' subtree should be chosen for descent. The original implementation of the M-tree selects, if possible, a subtree for which zero expansion of covering radius is necessary, or, if not possible, the subtree for which the required expansion is least. The Slim-tree [4] further offers a randomly selected subtree or a choice based on the available physical (disk) space in the subtree. In all of these variations, in the event that the covering radius of the selected node entry O_n must be expanded to accommodate the entry, it is expanded to $d(O_n, O_i)$ as O_i passes O_n on its way to the leaf level. This is the smallest possible expansion that maintains a correct covering radius, and thus increases overlap the least.

Having reached a leaf, O_i is inserted if it fits, otherwise the leaf node is split into two with leaf entries being partitioned into two groups according to some strategy, referred to as the *splitting policy*. Pointers to the two leaves are then promoted to the level above, replacing the pointer to the original child. On promotion, the covering radius of each promoted node entry O_p is set to:

$$r(O_p) = \max_{O_l \in \mathcal{L}} \{d(O_p, O_l)\}$$

where $\mathcal{L}$ is the set of entries in the leaf. If there is insufficient space in the node to which entries are promoted, it too splits and promotes entries. When promoting internally, the covering radius of each promoted entry is set to:

$$r(O_p) = \max_{O_n \in \mathcal{N}} \{d(O_p, O_n) + r(O_n)\}$$

where $\mathcal{N}$ is the set of entries in the node. This applies the limiting case of the triangle inequality property of the metric space as an upper bound on $\max_{O_l \in \mathcal{L}} \{d(O_p, O_l)\}$ where $\mathcal{L}$ is the set of all leaf node entries in the subtree rooted on O_p. Use of this upper bound avoids the requirement for an exhaustive search of the subtree on every promotion.

The splitting policy offers a second opportunity to minimise overlap, albeit within the constraint of balanced node occupancy. The M-tree offers a number of heuristically-developed alternatives, the best of which selects the partitioning for which the larger of the two covering radii is minimal. The Slim-tree constructs a minimal spanning tree across the entries to be partitioned, and selects the longest edge of this as being the point at which the set of entries most closely resembles two clusters, and is thus likely to suffer least from overlap between the resulting node pair.

3   A Clustering Technique for Bulk Loading

As we have seen, the process of insertion attempts to locate new objects in nodes that contain other objects that are in close spatial proximity. After an M-tree has been constructed by the insertion of a set of objects, we may therefore observe that the set has been partitioned into a number of clusters of objects, each of which is contained in a leaf node of the tree. The degree of overlap between the regions represented by these leaf nodes is an indicator of the quality of the clustering obtained by M-tree insertion.

This observation suggests an alternative approach: cluster a pre-existing data set directly into a set of leaf nodes to minimise overlap globally across the data set, then construct an M-tree upwards from the leaf level. When building an M-tree from the bottom up, we set *all* covering radii at the limit of the triangle inequality, in a similar way to the case of entry promotion after node splitting, to avoid the requirement for an exhaustive search of each node entry's subtree. Our optimisation is to provide better organisation of the data than that achieved by the M-tree, replacing the M-tree's optimisation of limiting covering radii expansion at insertion, and offering significant performance benefits.

3.1   Desirable Features

In this section we discuss clusters in the context of M-tree nodes: a cluster is a collection of points that may be accomodated within a single disk page. A cluster's location is considered to be that of its medoid, as its centroid cannot be calculated exactly in a purely metric, non-Cartesian space. The cluster *radius* is the distance between the medoid and its furthest neighbour in the cluster. The cluster *boundary* falls at this distance from the medoid.

An unusual consideration of clustering algorithms for bulk-loading is the overriding importance of cluster size, even at the expense of cluster quality. All clusters produced for bulk loading must be sufficiently small to fit into a disk page while also being sufficiently large to exceed its underflow limit, typically 50%.

Another consideration is that of outlying points that do not clearly belong to any cluster. Figure 3(a) shows a group of points that we perceive as being in four clusters, in addition to another four points that do not clearly belong anywhere. The page underflow limit is unlikely to permit each outlier to occupy a node alone, although merging each outlier into its nearest cluster has the effect of making all clusters' M-tree representations mutually overlap, as in Fig. 3(b). In this situation, a better effect on the global cluster population might be achieved by retaining the four good clusters and making one (extremely!) bad cluster, as in Fig. 3(c). In this case, rather than each cluster overlapping three others, as in Fig. 3(b), each good cluster solely overlaps the single bad cluster.

3.2   The Clustering Algorithm

We present below a clustering algorithm that achieves the two objectives described above: guaranteed cluster size of between n and $2n$ points for disk pages

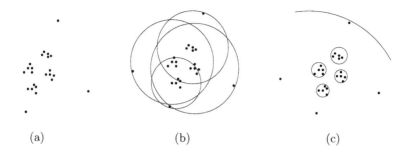

(a)   (b)   (c)

Fig. 3. The effect of outlying points on cluster overlap. The boundary of the bad cluster in (c) is shown only in part.

that can contain a maximum of $2n$, and a tendency to find good clusters first, leaving outlying points to be grouped into poorer clusters later.

We make use of the following definitions:

- A cluster medoid is any point m in the cluster for which there exists no other point p in the cluster that, if nominated as a medoid, would give the cluster a radius less than that given by m.
- A cluster may have multiple medoids. We impose an arbitrary linear order on points in the metric space and define the primary medoid of a cluster to be the least medoid of the cluster in this order.
- The distance between two clusters is that between their primary medoids.
- Given a cluster c, a nearest neighbour of c in a set of clusters $\mathcal{C}$ is a cluster c' such that there is no other cluster in $\mathcal{C}$ whose distance to c is less than that between c and c'. (c may have multiple nearest neighbours in $\mathcal{C}$.)
- A *closest pair* of clusters in $\mathcal{C}$ is a pair of clusters $c_1, c_2 \in \mathcal{C}$ such that $d(c_1, c_2) \leqslant d(c_i, c_j)$ for all $c_i, c_j \in \mathcal{C}$.

```
Function Cluster (
    CMAX: maximum acceptable cardinality of a cluster,
    C_in: a set of at least  CMAX/2  points
)
Returns a set of clusters, each of cardinality in [CMAX/2, CMAX].

Let C_out = {} ;
Let C = {} ;
For each p ∈ C_in
    Add {p} to C ;

While |C| > 1
    Let c_1, c_2 be a closest pair of clusters in C such that |c_1| ⩾ |c_2| ;
    If |c_1 ∪ c_2| ⩽ CMAX
        Remove c_1 and c_2 from C ;
        Add c_1 ∪ c_2 to C ;
    Else
        Remove c_1 from C ;
        Add c_1 to C_out ;
```

```
Let c be the last remaining element of C ;
If |C_out| > 0
    Let c' be a nearest neighbour of c in C_out ;
    Remove c' from C_out ;
Else
    Let c' = {};
If |c ∪ c'| ≤ CMAX
    Add c ∪ c' to C_out ;
Else
    Split c ∪ c' into c_1 and c_2 using the insertion splitting policy;
    Add c_1 and c_2 to C_out ;
Return C_out ;
```

The first phase of the clustering algorithm converts the input set of points into a set of singleton clusters, while the work of clustering occurs almost entirely within the loop structure of the second phase. In the final phase, if the last remaining element of C contains fewer than $\frac{CMAX}{2}$ points, its points and those of its nearest neighbour are redistributed to ensure that no cluster breaks the minimum size bound.

3.3   Bulk Loading

Preliminaries. The bulk load algorithm makes use of the clustering algorithm and definitions given above, and the following definitions:

- An M-tree leaf node entry is a pair (p, d) where p is a point and d is the distance from the point p to its parent, *i.e.* a distinguished point of the current node.
- An M-tree internal node entry is a tuple (p, d, r, a) where p is a point, d a parent distance (as in the case of a leaf node entry), r is the covering radius of the subtree, *i.e* a value that is at least as large as the maximum distance from p to any point in the subtree rooted at this entry, and a is the disk address of the child page identified by this internal node entry.

Furthermore, in the bulk load algorithm we call subroutines for writing leaf and internal node pages to disk. These are as follows:

```
Function OutputLeafPage(
    C_in: a set of points of cardinality no
        greater that will fit into a disk page
)
Returns a tuple (m, r, a) where:
    m is the primary medoid of C_in,
    r is called the covering radius,
    a is the disk address of the page output.
```

```
Let m = primary medoid of C_in;
Let r=0;
Let C = {};
For each p ∈ C_in
    Add (p, d(m,p)) to C ;
    Let r = Max(r, d(m,p));
Allocate new disk page a ;
Output C as a leaf page to disk address a ;
Return (m,r,a) ;
```

```
Function OutputInternalPage (
    C_mra: a set of (m,r,a) tuples as returned from OutputLeafPage
)
Returns (M,R,A) where:
    M is the primary medoid of the set of
        points C_in = {m|∃(m,r,a) ∈ C_mra},
    R is called the covering radius,
    A is the disk address of the page output.
```

```
Let C_in = {m|∃(m,r,a) ∈ C_mra} ;
Let M = primary medoid of C_in ;
Let R=0;
Let C = {};
For each (m,r,a) ∈ C_mra
    Add (m, d(M,m), r, a) to C ;
    Let R = Max(R, d(M,m) + r);
Allocate new disk page A ;
Output C as an internal page to disk address A ;
Return (M,R,A) ;
```

The Bulk Loading Algorithm. This bulk load algorithm uses the clustering algorithm to obtain a set of clusters suitable for writing to disk as one complete cluster per page. As each level of the tree is fully written to disk, entries for the level above are accumulated. The algorithm terminates when the set of entries to be written into the next level fit into a single page; the root of the M-tree.

```
Function BulkLoad(
    C_in: a set of points in a metric space,
    CMAX: maximum number of node entries that will fit into a disk page
)
Returns disk address of root page of constructed M-tree
```

```
If C_in ≤ CMAX
    Let (m,r,a) = OutputLeafPage(C_in);
    Return a ;
```

```
Let C_out = Cluster(C_in, CMAX) ;
```

```
Let C = {};
For each c ∈ C_out
    Add OutputLeafPage(c) to C ;

While |C| > CMAX
    Let C_in = {m|(m,r,a) ∈ C} ;
    Let C_out = Cluster(C_in, CMAX) ;
    Let C_mra = {};
    For each c ∈ C_out
        Let s = {(m,r,a)|(m,r,a) ∈ C ∧ m ∈ c} ;
        Add s to C_mra ;
    Let C = {} ;
    For each s ∈ C_mra
        Add OutputInternalPage(s) to C ;

Let (m,r,a) = OutputInternalPage(C);
Return a ;
```

We present BulkLoad here as using Cluster as a subroutine for reasons of clarity. An optimisation for implementation is to interleave the two to save distance computations used in clustering. This avoids re-computation of parent distances and covering radii during BulkLoad.

The clustering algorithm produces clusters containing between $\frac{CMAX}{2}$ and $CMAX$ points and (experimentally) on average $0.8 * CMAX$ points. This produces trees with an average page occupancy of 80%. Note that in the above algorithm we refer to cluster size merely in terms of numbers of points, however a change to reflect physical (on-disk) cluster size would permit consideration of variable-sized tree entries.

4   Experimental Evaluation

4.1   Details of Implementation

For experimental evaluation, a series of M-trees were constructed by bulk loading and by serial insertion of a set of 25 000 objects in 2, 4, 6, 8, 10, 15 and 20 dimensions. Data objects were implemented as points in a 20-dimensional vector space, enabling dimensionality of experiments to be varied simply by adjusting the metric function to consider a fewer or greater number of dimensions, while maintaining a constant object size. Trees built by insertion used the original M-tree's *MinMax* split policy and an underflow limit of 50%. All trees were built on 4kB pages and used the d_2 (Euclidean) metric for n dimensions:

$$d_2(x, y) = \sqrt{\sum_{i=1}^{n} (x_i - y_i)^2}$$

for $x = (x_1, x_2, ..., x_n), y = (y_1, y_2, ..., y_n)$.

Experiments were performed using an artifically clustered data set, produced by distributing randomly-generated points around other, also randomly-generated, seed points. A trigonometric function based distribution was chosen to produce a higher point density closer to seed points, although each vector component was produced independently, resulting in regions of higher point density parallel to coordinate axes (see Fig. 4; dimensions 1 and 2 of the 20-dimension data set).

Each tree was required to process a series of 1, 10 and 50 nearest-neighbour queries. Query performance is measured in terms of page-hits (IOs) assuming an initially empty, infinite buffer pool, and in all cases is averaged over 100 queries.

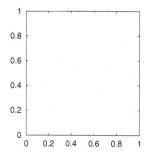

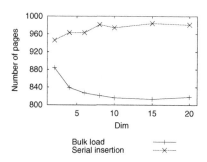

Fig. 4. Experimental data distribution

Fig. 5. Comparative tree sizes

4.2   Results and Discussion

Figure 5 indicates the comparative sizes of the trees built by bulk load and serial insertion. As remarked previously, the bulk load clustering algorithm produces page occupancies of around 80%, compared to 70% produced by the M-tree's insert algorithm. The higher occupancy of bulk loaded pages is reflected in the requirement for fewer pages to contain the full tree.

Figures 6 and 7 show very similar pictures of query performance in the two types of tree for 1-NN and 50-NN queries. In both cases the bulk loaded tree outperforms the insertion-built tree, making a query cost saving of between 25% and 40% in terms of absolute number of page hits. Even when normalised to take account of the more heavily occupied bulk loaded tree, we find that (for example) in 20 dimensions a 50-NN query is answered by reading fewer than 15% of the bulk-loaded tree's pages compared to 20% in the insertion-built M-tree.

These performance figures are readily understood in terms of reduced overlap by considering the leaf radii distributions of bulk loaded and insertion-built M-trees. Figure 8 shows the distribution of leaf node covering radii in M-trees in 2 dimensions. As one might expect from the clustering algorithm, explicitly outputting good clusters first leads to a higher number of low-radius clusters and a distribution which appears to tail off sooner. Not shown in the figure for reasons of scale however is the intermittent *longer* tail-off of the bulk-loaded

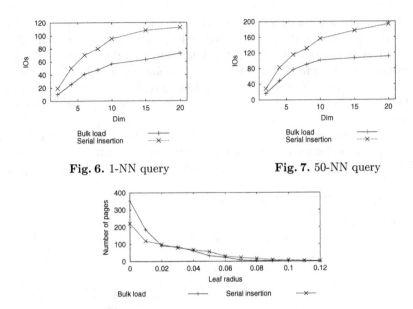

Fig. 6. 1-NN query   **Fig. 7.** 50-NN query

Fig. 8. Leaf radii distribution in 2 dimensions

tree's radius distribution. This is a direct consequence of allowing outliers to form unusually bad clusters.

5   A Symmetric M-Tree (SM-Tree)

5.1   Asymmetry in the M-Tree

Although the M-tree grows gracefully under Insert, there has, to date, been no algorithm published for the complementary Delete operation. The authors of [4] explicitly state in their discussion of the Slim-tree that neither their structure nor the original M-tree yet support Delete. We find that implementation of the delete algorithm is non-trivial as a direct consequence of an aspect of asymmetry introduced by the M-tree's overlap minimising optimisation at insertion.

A critical observation, with respect to the Delete problem, is that in a bulk loaded tree, the covering radius of *any* node entry in the tree is dependent solely on the distance from its immediate children, and the covering radii of those children. In an insertion-built M-tree this is only true in node entries newly-promoted from a lower-level node split. Ordinarily, when an object for insertion O_i passes a node entry and expands its covering radius to $d(O_n, O_i)$, the new covering radius depends on the entire contents of the node entry's subtree, and can only be specified exactly as:

$$r(O_n) = \max_{O_l \in \mathcal{L}} \{d(O_n, O_l)\}$$

where $\mathcal{L}$ is the set of *all* leaf entries in the subtree rooted on O_n.

This effect is illustrated in Fig. 9, which shows three levels of an M-tree branch. Figure 9(a) shows leaf entries **B** and **C**, under a subtree pointer with reference value **B**. This subtree's covering radius is currently contained within that of its own parent, **A**. In Fig. 9(b), insertion of point **D** causes a slight expansion of the radius around **A**, but expands the child's radius *beyond* that of its parent. Thus the correct covering radius around **A** is no longer calculable from the distance to, and the radii of, **A**'s immediate children. The decision to

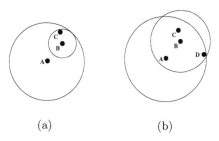

(a)   (b)

Fig. 9. The effect of the M-tree's Insert algorithm on covering radii

expand the covering radius only as far as is immediately necessary and no further therefore introduces asymmetry between the Insert and (unimplemented) Delete operations: Insert adds an object and may expand covering radii, but conversely Delete cannot contract a node entry's covering radius without reference to *all* objects at the leaf level in its subtree, thus requiring an expensive subtree walk for correct implementation.

5.2   Maintaining Symmetry After Bulk Loading

Given that, after bulk loading with our algorithm, the covering radii of all node entries are dependent solely on their immediate children, we may observe that the tree is symmetric with respect to Insert and Delete. Maintenance of this symmetry permits support of object deletion, but requires modification of the tree's insert algorithm to fully expand covering radii to the limit of the triangle inequality on further insertion. We refer to trees whose symmetry is maintained in this way as symmetric M-trees (SM-trees). Full algorithms and analysis of the SM-tree are presented in [5] but are omitted here for lack of space.

The principal modification of the insertion algorithm is this: in cases when insertion does not induce a node split, any expansion of node radius must propagate back up the tree from the leaf level towards the root. This is achieved by returning, from a call to Insert, the resulting radius of the node into which the insertion was made. At the leaf level this is simply the M-tree leaf radius:

$$\max_{O_l \in \mathcal{L}} \{d(O_p, O_l)\}$$

where $\mathcal{L}$ is the set of entries in the leaf, while at higher levels the node radius is:

$$\max_{O_n \in \mathcal{N}} \{d(O_p, O_n) + r(O_n)\}$$

where $\mathcal{N}$ is the set of entries in the node. This is exactly the node radius propagated from an internal node split in the M-tree, however in the SM-tree it is maintained as an invariant. Node entry and radius propagation at a node split is managed in exactly the same way as in the M-tree. The disk I/O cost of the modified Insert algorithm is therefore still $O(h)$, where h is the height of the tree.

The choice of subtree for insertion is made by finding the node entry closest to the entry being inserted O_i (i.e. the entry $O_n \in \mathcal{N}$ for which $d(O_n, O_i)$ is a minimum), rather than by attempting to limit the expansion of existing covering radii, because it is no longer possible while descending the tree to make any assertions about the effect of that choice on the radius of the selected subtree.

The choice made in the original M-tree was based on the heuristic that we wish to minimise the overall volume covered by a node N. In the SM-tree, unlike the original M-tree, all node entry covering radii entirely contain their subtrees, suggesting that subtrees should be centred as tightly as possible on their root (within the constraint of minimising overlap between sibling nodes) to minimise the volume covered by N.

5.3   Deletion from the SM-Tree

After bulk loading, maintenance of insert/delete symmetry in the SM-tree using the modified insert algorithm permits support of the delete operation. Covering radii may now be returned by an implementation of the delete operation in the same way that they are by the modified insert algorithm, and permit node entry covering radii to contract as objects are deleted. Furthermore, as a node entry's covering radius is no longer directly dependent on the distance between itself and leaf-level entries in its subtree, node entries can be distributed between other nodes, permitting underflown internal nodes to be merged with other nodes at the same level.

The deletion algorithm proceeds in a similar manner to an exact match query, exploiting the triangle inequality for tree pruning, followed by the actions required to delete an object if it is found, and handle underflow if it occurs. In the simple (non-underflowing) case, calls to Delete, like those to Insert, return the (possibly contracted) covering radius of the subtree.

When a node underflows, the full set of entries from the underflown node is returned from Delete, and must be written into alternative nodes. Although not explored here, this suggests the possibility of a *merging policy* analogous to the splitting policy used at node overflow. Our implementation of underflow handling is relatively simple, merging returned entries with those contained in the child of the nearest neighbour of the underflown node's parent. If the merged collection fits into a single node, that node remains, otherwise the insertion splitting policy is used to redistribute the entries appropriately. As in the B-tree, the Delete algorithm's complexity is $O(h)$, where h is the height of the tree.

5.4   Evaluation of the SM-Tree

The performance of a bulk-loaded SM-tree matches that of a bulk-loaded M-tree, indeed they are structurally identical, while unlike the M-tree, the SM-tree is also able to support object deletion. As might be expected however, insertion-built SM-trees suffer rather from losing the optimisation of limited expansion of covering radii. In [5] we show results that suggest (for insertion-built trees only) an average query cost increase of 15% for the SM-tree compared to the M-tree. In order to take advantage of the fully dynamic behaviour offered by the SM-tree, we suggest bulk loading a tree first wherever possible.

6   Conclusions and Further Work

In this paper we presented a clustering algorithm designed specifically to meet the requirements of a bulk load algorithm for the M-tree. Unlike conventional bulk loading algorithms our objective was not to efficiently load the tree, but rather to maximise its subsequent query performance. We have shown that the performance of bulk loaded trees exceeds that of insertion-built M-trees by between 25% and 40% for non-uniform data. We further observe that bulk loaded trees have a particular property with respect to the symmetry of the insert and delete operations, which, if maintained, permits support of both.

The clustering algorithm seeks out concentrations of points in the data set while protecting clusters from the effect of outlying points. One direction for future work is the extension of the algorithm to handle near-uniform data with the same degree of success. Another avenue is suggested by the observation that our approach to bulk loading is simply an alternative optimisation to improve the tree's query performance: we are currently searching for a way to avoid the need for such opportunistic optimisations altogether, and rely solely on a tree's intrinsic properties to provide efficient search.

References

1. P. Ciaccia and M. Patella. Bulk loading the M-tree. In *Proceedings of the 9th Australasian Database Conference (ADC'98)*, pages 15–26, Perth, Australia, 1998.
2. P. Ciaccia, M. Patella, and P. Zezula. M-tree: An efficient access method for similarity search in metric spaces. In *Proceedings of the 23rd VLDB Conference*, pages 426–435, Athens, Greece, 1997.
3. A. Guttman. R-trees: A dynamic index structure for spatial searching. *SIGMOD Record*, 14(2):47–57, June 1984.
4. C. Traina Jr., A. Traina, C. Faloutsos, and B. Seeger. Fast indexing and visualization of metric data sets using Slim-trees. *IEEE Transactions on Knowledge and Data Engineering*, 14(2):244–260, March/April 2002.
5. Alan P. Sexton and Richard Swinbank. Symmetric M-tree. Technical Report CSR-04-2, University of Birmingham, UK, 2004. Available at URL `www.cs.bham.ac.uk/~rjs/research`.
6. J. K. Uhlmann. Satisfying general proximity/similarity queries with metric trees. *Information Processing Letters*, 40(4):175–179, November 1991.

A Fast Filter for Obstructed Nearest Neighbor Queries

Chenyi Xia, David Hsu, and Anthony K.H. Tung

National University of Singapore,
{xiacheny,dyhsu,atung}@princeton.edu

Abstract. In this paper, we study the Obstructed Nearest Neighbor (ONN) problem: given a set of points and a set of polygonal obstacles in two dimensions, find the k nearest neighbors to a query point according to the length of the shortest obstacle-avoiding path between two points. ONN query is useful both as a stand-alone tool in geographical information systems and as a primitive for spatial data analysis such as clustering and classification in the presence of obstacles. We propose an efficient ONN algorithm that processes only the data points and obstacles relevant to the query in an incremental way and thus filters out a large number of points and obstacles. Experiments on spatial data sets show the algorithm scales well with respect to the input data size and the number of nearest neighbors requested.

1 Introduction

Nearest neighbor (NN) queries are a fundamental primitive for spatial databases. It has numerous applications in geographical information systems, wireless communication, facility location planning, and virtual environment walk-through. It also serves as a useful tool for spatial data mining algorithms such as clustering [10,19] and classification [18]. Hence, the problem has received much attention in the past decades [6].

Most NN algorithms measure the distance between two points using a simple metric, *e.g.*, the Euclidean distance. This is not always adequate. Two nearest cities under Euclidean metric may not be nearest according to the travel distance due to the blocking of mountains and lakes; troops may have to take detours to avoid enemy's ground. In these settings, a more suitable measure of the distance is ℓ (the obstructed distance), the length of the shortest obstacle-avoiding path between two points. This leads to the *Obstructed Nearest Neighbor* (ONN) problem, in which we find nearest neighbors under the shortest-path metric ℓ. Furthermore, ONN queries can also be combined with well-known clustering algorithms such as Chameleon [19] and DBSCAN [10] as a tool for spatial clustering in the presence of obstacles [26] and provide more meaningful clusters in some applications.

In this paper, we study the spatial ONN query problem: given a set of points and a set of polygonal obstacles, find the k nearest neighbors to a query point under the shortest-path metric ℓ. The new metric ℓ makes ONN queries substantially different from the usual NN queries. Two points close under the Euclidean metric may be far apart under ℓ, due to obstruction by obstacles. There is no simple way to convert ONN into NN queries.

H. Williams and L. MacKinnon (Eds.): BNCOD 2004, LNCS 3112, pp. 203–215, 2004.

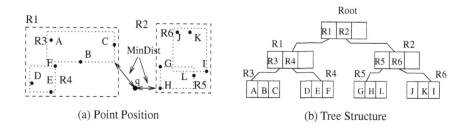

(a) Point Position   (b) Tree Structure

Fig. 1. An R-tree Example

Apart from the usual difficulties with NN queries in large data sets, a new challenge with ONN queries is to compute ℓ, the length of the shortest obstacle-avoiding path between two points efficiently. The lower bound for the problem is $\Omega(n \log n)$ by reduction from sorting, where n is the total number of obstacle vertices. An asymptotically optimal algorithm exists [15], but it is very complex and has a large hidden constant, which makes it impractical. A more practical algorithm [9] is based on the notion of *visibility graph* [26]. It runs in $O(n^2 \log n)$ time and uses $O(n^2)$ space in the worst case.

This paper is the first in-depth study of the ONN problem. The contributions of our work are:

1. We formulate the interesting ONN problem which is important to geographical information systems, location-based services, spatial-related decision support systems and spatial data mining.
2. We propose an efficient incremental method to compute the obstructed distance which filters out a large number of obstacles.
3. We present the ONN search algorithm with the R-tree employing the *best-first* search algorithm [17].

Our extensive experimental study on spatial data sets shows our algorithm scales well with the number of obstacles and points and the number of nearest neighbors. We thus envision our algorithm used as an efficient filter.

The rest of the paper is organized as follows: 2 overviews related work. 3 formulates and analyzes the ONN problem, while Section 4 describes the ONN search algorithm with the R-tree. Finally, we report the experimental findings in 5 and conclude the paper in 6.

2   Related Work

NN problems have been studied extensively (see, *e.g.*, [7,14,16,17,22]). Most of the proposed algorithms use spatial indexes, among which R-tree and its variants [5,3,13,23] are very popular. An R-tree is a height-balanced tree, in which each node v corresponds to a *minimum bounding rectangle* (MBR) that contains all data objects in the subtree rooted at v. Using MBRs, one can infer the spatial relationship between a query point and a data object in an MBR to approximate the minimum distance between them. Figure 1 shows an R-tree which indexes a set of points.

Queries based on R-trees are performed in a branch-and-bound manner. For NN search algorithms, they fall into two categories, the depth-first and the best-first, depending on how they traverse the R-tree. The depth-first algorithm [22,7] starts from the root of the tree and visits the entry whose minimum distance (MinDist) from the query point is smallest. When it reaches a leaf node, it finds the candidate nearest neighbor and traces back. In the procedure of back-tracing, the algorithm only visits entries whose minimum distance is smaller than the distance of the candidate nearest neighbor. For example, given a query point q in Figure 1, the depth-first algorithm will follow the path R1, R3 (find C as the first potential nearest neighbor) and R2, R5 (find H as the result).

The best-first nearest neighbor search [17], also known as the incremental nearest neighbor search, maintains a priority queue with entries being visited. The queue elements are sorted in increasing order of their minimum distance from the query point. The entry with the smallest minimum distance is visited first. In the example of Figure 1, the content of the priority queue Q changes as follows: $Q=\{\text{Root}\} \rightarrow \{R_1, R_2\} \rightarrow \{R_2, R_3, R_4\} \rightarrow \{R_5, R_3, R_6, R_4\} \rightarrow \{\text{H, G}, R_3, R_6, \text{L}, R_4\}$. H then pops out of the priority queue as the nearest neighbor. The best-first nearest neighbor search is proved to be optimal in terms of the number of node accesses [6]. In addition, it has the advantage that we can obtain successive nearest neighbors incrementally without re-computing the query from the scratch. If we ask for the second nearest neighbor in above example, G pops out of the priority queue immediately.

Variants of nearest neighbor search (see, *e.g.*, [20,11,25,4,24]) have been an increasing interest in the recent years. A parallel work can be found in [27], while our paper gives a more detailed study of the ONN query. ONN query is more difficult than the classic NN queries due to the presence of obstacles. Nevertheless, ideas developed in the classic settings are valuable.

3 The ONN Query

3.1 Problem Formulation

Definition 1. (Obstructed Distance) [26]: *The obstructed distance between any two points p_1, p_2 from point data set P, denoted as $\ell(p_1, p_2)$, is the length of the shortest Euclidean path from p_1 to p_2 without cutting through any obstacles from the obstacle data set B.*

Definition 2. (ONN query): *Let P be a finite set of points and B be a finite set of obstacles. Given a query point q and an integer k, an ONN query returns $ONN(q, k) = \{p_1, p_2, \ldots, p_k \in P \mid \forall p \in P \setminus \{p_1, p_2, \ldots, p_k\}, \ell(p, q) \geq \max_{1 \leq i \leq k} \ell(p_i, q)\}$.*

The ONN query finds k nearest neighbors of a query point q under the shortest-path metric ℓ. The obstacles in our discussion are n-vertex polygons in the plane represented by a sequence of vertices $< v_0, \ldots, v_{n-1} >$. We constrain our discussion in the 2-dimensional space, while the proposed method can be extended to higher-dimensional spaces. $\ell(p, q)$

is the obstructed distance from p to q, i.e., the length of the shortest obstacle-avoiding path between two points p and q.

The challenge with ONN queries is to compute ℓ, the length of the shortest obstacle-avoiding path between two points efficiently. Computation of ℓ requires the shortest path search on the *visibility graph*. The lower bound for the problem is $\Omega(n \log n)$ by reduction from sorting, where n is the total number of obstacle vertices. Therefore, it is not feasible to compute ℓ for each data point.

The difficulty of the ONN problem may be alleviated by the pre-construction of the visibility graph. While one can pre-materialize the visibility graph, it has several disadvantages. First, the space requirement is usually not acceptable when n is large, since it uses $O(n^2)$ space. Second, the visibility graph may not fit in the main memory, resulting in many expensive disk accesses. And third, the update cost is high, if obstacles or data points are inserted and deleted frequently.

We focus on solving the ONN query problem without any pre-computed information. Efficient method for the computation of ℓ and the selection of candidate points for the obstructed distance computation are discussed in the following two sections.

3.2   Incremental Computation of ℓ

We first introduce the *incremental* computation of shortest path. A shortest path can be found based on the visibility graph [9]. The visibility graph G of the union of B and $\{p, q\}$ is an undirected graph such that a node of G is p, q, or an obstacle vertex, and there is an edge between two nodes if the straight-line segment between the nodes does not intersect the obstacles. See 2 for an illustration.

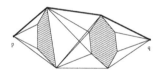

Fig. 2. A visibility graph example. Shaded areas indicate obstacle. The thick line indicates the shortest path between p and q.

Lemma 1. *Let B be a set of polygonal obstacles. The shortest path between two points p and q lies in the visibility graph of B and $\{p, q\}$.*

Lemma 1 [9] indicates although there can be infinitely many paths between p and q, it can be shown that the shortest one must be a path in G. A shortest-path algorithm proceeds in two steps [9]. It first computes a visibility graph G, and then searches G for the shortest path using Dijkstra's algorithm. The first step takes time $O(n^2 \log n)$ using the *rotational plane sweep* [21] and can be optimized to $O(l + n \log n)$ time using an output-sensitive algorithm [12], where l is the number of edges in G. In the second step, Dijkstra's algorithm [8] takes time $O(n \log n + k)$, where k is the number of edges in G and n is the total number of obstacle vertices. Generally, the entire algorithm runs in $O(n^2 \log n)$ time and uses $O(n^2)$ space, hence is prohibitive for a large number of obstacles.

A key observation that it may be unnecessary to build the entire visibility graph and search it to process a shortest-path query. We propose to compute a *local workspace* W by introducing obstacles incrementally, as needed, and build in W a small visibility graph that is relevant to the query. Initially the *local workspace* W contains only the start and end points and the *core obstacles* (Definition 3). We compute a candidate shortest path γ in W and check whether γ intersects any obstacles outside of W. If so, we expand W by adding these obstacles to W and recompute γ. The algorithm repeats until no more obstacles outside of W intersect the shortest path. By ignoring the obstacles outside of W, the Dijkstra's algorithm runs more efficiently on a much smaller visibility graph.

Definition 3. (Core Obstacles) *Core Obstacles of two points p and q, denoted as $CO(p, q)$, are a set of obstacles that intersect the line segment $\overline{pq}$.*

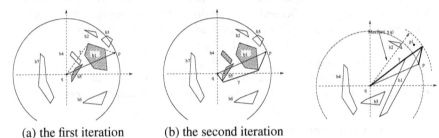

(a) the first iteration	(b) the second iteration

Fig. 3. An example of incremental computation of shortest path. The shaded obstacles are in the local workspace.

Fig. 4. Illustration of $MaxDist(\gamma, q)$.

For example, in Figure 3, $CO(p, q) = \{b_1, b_5\}$. The initial *local workspace* $W = \{p, q, b_1, b_5\}$. In the first iteration, we find the dashed line as the shortest path γ based on W. Because γ intersects b_4, we insert b_4 into W and re-compute the shortest path. The thick line is then found as the shortest path γ. Because γ doesn't intersect any obstacles outside of W, it is output as the shortest path between p and q.

Lemma 2. *The incremental computation of the shortest path finds the true shortest path the that goes from point p to point q and avoids all obstacles in B.*

Proof. Let $\ell_W(p, q)$ ($\ell_B(p, q)$) be the length of shortest path between p and q over W (B). Since $W \subseteq B$, we have $\ell_W(p, q) \leq \ell_B(p, q)$, because adding obstacles can only increase the length of the shortest path. When the algorithm terminates, we have the shortest path γ over W that is clear of all obstacles in B, and thus $\ell_W(p, q) = \ell_B(p, q)$.

3.3   Choice of Candidate Points

Since the computation of the obstructed distance is expensive, we should limit such computation to the most promising points. Despite the difference between the shortest-path metric ℓ and the Euclidean distance d, they are related. An immediate observation is that $\ell(p, q) \geq d(p, q)$ for all points p and q. Furthermore, points that are close under d are likely close under ℓ. After all, if one stands in the middle of San Francisco and looks for a hospital with the shortest walking distance, it is much better to look a few blocks away than to look in New York. So, to process an ONN query, we find successively points close to the query point q under d as candidates and compute their obstructed distances to q to check whether any candidate answers the query. Then, when can we stop?

Algorithm ONN

Input: R-tree T_{pt}, R-tree T_{obs}, Point q, int k
Output: $ONN(q,k)$
1. Initialize priority queue $Q1(Q2)$ with root of T_{pt} (T_{obs});
2. **for** $i = 1$ to k $C[i].\ell = \infty$;
3. Initialize obstacle list $L_{obs}=\emptyset$;
4. $nn = \textbf{INN}(T_{pt}, Q1, q)$;
5. **while** (nn!=NULL) **and** $(C[k].\ell > d(nn,q))$,
6. $\ell(nn,q) = \textbf{OBSTRUCT-DISTANCE}(nn, q, Q2, L_{obs})$;
7.   **if** $(\ell(nn,q) < C[k].\ell)$ insert nn into C;
8. $nn = \textbf{INN}(T_{pt}, Q1, q)$;
9. **return** C;

Fig. 5. ONN query algorithm: points and obstacles are indexed by separate R-trees.

Lemma 3. (Termination Condition) *Let q be a query point and $p_1, p_2, p_3 \ldots$ be the data points in P ordered so that $d(p_1,q) \leq d(p_2,q) \leq d(p_3,q) \leq \cdots$. Suppose that $c_1, c_2, \ldots c_k$ are k candidate points with the smallest shortest path lengths to q among the first m points $p_1, p_2, \ldots, p_m$. If $d(p_m,q) \geq \max_{1 \leq i \leq k} \ell(c_i,q)$, then $c_1, c_2, \ldots, c_k$ are the k nearest neighbors to q among all points in P under the shortest-path metric ℓ.*

The lemma indicates, suppose that we have examined the first m nearest points $p_1, p_2, \ldots, p_m$ and have k candidate points $c_1, c_2, \ldots, c_k$. We can stop if $d(p_m,q) \geq \max_{1 \leq i \leq k} \ell(c_i,q)$. The reason is that for all $i \geq m, d(p_i,q) \geq d(p_m,q)$ and thus $\ell(p_i,q) \geq d(p_i,q) \geq d(p_m,q) \geq \max_{1 \leq i \leq k} \ell(c_i,q)$.

4   ONN Algorithm with R-Trees

Now we introduce the ONN search algorithm with R-trees. With the R-tree, we can retrieve candidate points and obstacles in a branch-and-bound manner to reduce the search space. In geographic information systems, different types of objects are usually stored in separate data files and have individual indexes built for them. We assume that two R-trees are built for data points and obstacles separately.

4.1   ONN Search Algorithm

The ONN search algorithm retrieves successively points close to the query point q as candidates using conventional NN search and then computes their obstructed distance and inserts them into the candidates array C. It terminates when the maximum obstructed distance of the candidates is smaller than the Euclidean distance of the next nearest neighbor from the query point. We adopt the best-first algorithm INN because it has the optimal I/O cost and the best-first approach can retrieve successive nearest neighbors based on previous computing without restarting the query from the scratch. Figure 5 depicts the algorithm.

It employs following data structures: (1) Two priority queues - $Q1$ for the R-tree indexing data points T_{pt} and $Q2$ for the R-tree indexing obstacles T_{obs}. They have the

---

Function OBSTRUCT-DISTANCE(Point p, Point q, Priority Queue $Q2$, LinkList L_{obs})

1. **INN-R**(T_{obs}, $Q2$, q, $d(p,q)$, L_{obs});
2. **for** every obstacle b in L_{obs}
3.   **if** b intersects $\overline{pq}$, **insert** b **into** CO;
4. **if** CO is empty, **return** $d(p,q)$; /*p and q are not obstructed */
5. **else**
6.   Add p, q and CO into local workspace W and build the visibility graph G over W.
7.   **repeat**
8.   Search G for the shortest path γ using Dijkstra's algorithm.
9.   **INN-R**(T_{obs}, $Q2$, q, $MaxDist(\gamma, q)$, L_{obs});
10.   **for** every obstacle b in L_{obs} and out of W
11.   **if** b intersects γ, **insert** b **into** W;
12.   **if** no obstacle intersects γ, **return** the length of γ.

Fig. 6. Computation of the obstructed distance between two points.

same function as the priority queue of the best-first nearest neighbor algorithm [17]. The queue elements are sorted in increasing order of their Euclidean distances from the query point. (2) A link list L_{obs}. It is used to store obstacles having been retrieved so far by the incremental range query INN-R when computing the obstructed distance. (3) An array C of size k. This stores candidate points in increasing order of their obstructed distances from the query point.

Function OBSTRUCT-DISTANCE computes the obstructed distance $\ell(p,q)$ in an incremental way as we introduced in Section 3.2. Figure 4.1 presents the algorithm. It is composed of two phases: (1) Initialization of the *local workspace* W (Line 1-6). It first uses incremental range query INN-R to retrieve obstacles within range $d(p,q)$ and then determines the core obstacles CO. p, q and CO is inserted into *local workspace* W and the visibility graph is build over W. (2) Refinement of the shortest path (Line 7 -12). It computes the shortest path γ and checks whether γ intersects obstacles out of W. Obstacles intersecting γ are inserted into W. The procedure repeats until γ doesn't intersect any obstacles out of W. Length of γ is then returned.

Function INN-R is a range query and used to retrieve obstacles from T_{obs} for the construction of the *local workspace* and store them in L_{obs} (Figure 6 Line 1 and 9). We design the incremental range query INN-R (Figure 7) in order to prevent the range query from searching from the R-tree root every time. It is similar to the incremental nearest neighbor search algorithm and stops when the requested query range is smaller than the range it has already searched. Therefore, when the query range is enlarged, it doesn't need to process the query from the scratch. Figure 7 presents the detail of the algorithm.

An ONN query includes a nearest neighbor search of the data point tree T_{pt} and a range search of the obstacle tree T_{obs}. The traversal of the R-trees from the root to the leaf accesses $O(\log N)$ R-tree nodes. So the total number of node accesses of an ONN query is $O(\log N_{pt} + \log N_{obs})$, where $N_{pt}(N_{obs})$ is the number of data points(obstacles). CPU cost is dominated by the computation of the obstructed distance. Let m be the average number of obstacles involved in the computation of the obstructed distance and ν be the average number of obstacle vertices. Utilizing the *rotational plane sweep* for visibility graph construction [21] and Dijkstra's algorithm for shortest path computation, a com-

---

Function INN-R(R-tree T, Priority Queue Q, Point q,Float r, LinkList $oList$)

---

1.   **while** (Q is not empty) **and** (the distance of the first element of Q to q is smaller than r),
2. e = Dequeue(Q);
3.   **if** e is an obstacle, **insert** e **into** L_{obs};
4.   **elseif** e is the MBR of an obstacle b,
5.   Get the description of obstacle b;
6.   **Enqueue**($Q, b, MinDist(b, q)$);
7.   **elseif** e is a leaf node,
8.   **for** each entry N, **Enqueue**($Q, N, MinDist(N, q)$);
9.   **else** /*e is an internal node*/
10.   **for** each entry N, **Enqueue**($Q, N, MinDist(N, q)$);

Fig. 7. Incremental retrieval of obstacles within radius r.

putation of the obstructed distance runs in $O(m^2 \nu^2 \log m\nu)$ time and uses $O(m^2 \nu^2)$ space in the worst case.

Theorem 1. (Correctness of ONN algorithm) *The ONN algorithm finds correct obstructed nearest neighbors.*

Proof. The algorithm returns answers set when the maximum obstructed distance of the candidates is smaller than the Euclidean distance of the successive nearest neighbor from the query point. According to Lemma 3, it returns correct answers.

4.2   ONN Search with Unified R-Tree

Data points and obstacles can also be stored in a single unified R-tree. As searching a unified R-tree are more efficient than using two separate R-trees, it is useful when the data points and obstacles are static and the query efficiency is important. Here, we deploy the ONN query to the case when data points and obstacles are indexed by one unified R-tree.

The algorithm is similar but needs following modifications. (1) Data structure: It employs only one priority queue Q and needs another link list L_{pt} for data points being retrieved by INN-R during the computation of the obstructed distance. For example, in Figure 4, data point p_1 will be retrieved by INN-R when OBSTRUCT-DISTANCE verifying γ. (2) Function INN-R: If an element dequeued from Q is a data point, it inserts the data point into the link list L_{pt}. (3) Algorithm ONN search. It needs two modifications: (i) Before it dequeues an element from the priority queue Q, it checks whether L_{pt} is empty. For each point in the L_{pt}, it computes its obstructed distance and inserts it into C. (ii) If an element dequeued from Q is an obstacle, it inserts the obstacle into L_{obs}. If an element dequeued is the MBR of an obstacle, it gets the description of the obstacle and inserts the obstacle into the priority queue.

5   Experimental Study

We conducted an extensive experimental evaluation to prove the efficiency of the proposed techniques. We implemented the algorithms in C++ and used the disk-based implementation of the R-tree [2].

The experiments were conducted on a Sun Enterprise 450 server with Sun SPARCII 480 MHz CPU and 4GB memory, running Solaris 7. The data sets used for the experiments are the Greek [2] (contains locations of 5,922 cities and villages in Greece and 24,650 MBRs of rivers in Greece) and the CA [1] (62,556 locations in California and 98,451 MBRs of rivers in California). The default R-tree node size is 4 KB and the number of nearest neighbors (k) is 30. The performance is evaluated by the CPU time and the number of R-tree node accesses. The presented results are the average of 100 queries of points randomly selected from the data sets. Unless otherwise stated, data points (cities or locations) and obstacles (MBRs of rivers) are indexed by two R-trees. Note that although we use the MBRs as obstacles in our experiments, the algorithm can be applied to arbitrary polygon-shaped obstacles generally. The experimental results give a good indication of how the algorithm is influenced by various factors such as input data set size and the number of nearest neighbor requested.

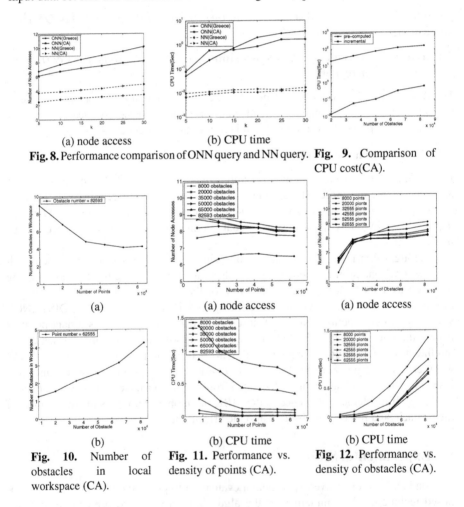

(a) node access   (b) CPU time

Fig. 8. Performance comparison of ONN query and NN query.

Fig. 9. Comparison of CPU cost(CA).

(a)

(b)

Fig. 10. Number of obstacles in local workspace (CA).

(a) node access

(b) CPU time

Fig. 11. Performance vs. density of points (CA).

(a) node access

(b) CPU time

Fig. 12. Performance vs. density of obstacles (CA).

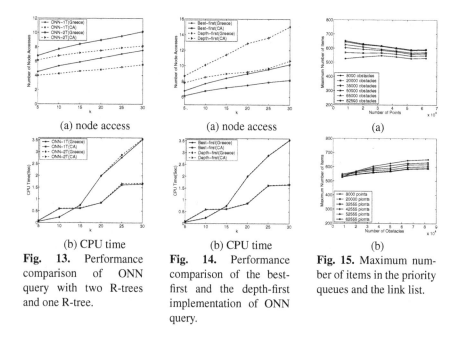

(a) node access   (a) node access   (a)

(b) CPU time   (b) CPU time   (b)

Fig. 13. Performance comparison of ONN query with two R-trees and one R-tree.

Fig. 14. Performance comparison of the best-first and the depth-first implementation of ONN query.

Fig. 15. Maximum number of items in the priority queues and the link list.

– **Comparison of ONN Queries and NN Queries.** We first compare the ONN query with the NN query in Figure 8. The ONN query is much more costly and requires two times of the node accesses of the NN query because it need access two R-trees to retrieve points and obstacles and its search radius is usually greater than the NN query. Moreover, we observed while the NN query is I/O bounded, the ONN query is CPU bounded because of the heavy CPU cost for the obstructed distance computations. So, the ONN query has very different characteristic from the NN query.

– **Efficiency of Incremental Computation of the Obstructed Distance.** Figure 9 presents the CPU time for the computation of the obstructed distance and compares the incremental approach (incremental) with the method that has the visibility graph pre-computed (pre-computed). It proves the efficiency of the incremental method. The graph shows the incremental approach outperforms the pre-computed approach significantly by orders of magnitude. The efficiency comes from the low selectivity of the obstacles involved in the computation of the obstructed distance. As shown in Figure 10, a limited number of obstacles are in the local workspace when the shortest path is confirmed.

– **Effect of Densities.** Now, we study how the densities of data points and obstacles affect the query performance. We fix the number of data points (or obstacles) and then vary the number of obstacles (or data points). Figure 11 shows as the density of points increases, the number of node accesses and the CPU time decrease. The reason is, the denser the points, the shorter the distances between the query point and its ONNs. Therefore, fewer obstacles will be involved in the computation of the obstructed distance (see Figure 10 (a)), which reduces the I/O cost and the CPU time.

Figure 12 studies the effect of the density of obstacles. The increase of node access is sharp at the beginning (from 0.8×10^4 to 2×10^4) but turns moderate after that. The CPU time is more affected by the increase of the number of obstacles because the computation of the obstructed distance runs in $O(n^2 logn)$ time with respect to the total number of obstacle vertices.

- **ONN Query with Two R-trees and One R-tree.** Figure 13 presents the query performances when the data sets are indexed by two R-trees (2T) and when they are indexed by one single R-tree (1T). It shows 1T is more efficient with regard to the node access. The reason is when both data points and obstacles are indexed by one R-tree, only one traversal of the unified R-tree is required. Nearby data point and obstacles could be found in the same leaf node of the R-tree. For the 2T case, two R-tree should be traversed and at least two leaf nodes should be accessed to retrieve the data point and the obstacles nearby. Based on this result, when we perform expensive spatial data mining tasks, we can build a single R-tree for both data points and obstacles to obtain better performance.

- **Effect of Number of Nearest Neighbors.** From Figure 13, we also observe that the query cost goes up with the increase of the number of nearest neighbors, k. A greater k leads to the larger query radius and more number of obstructed distance computations, and ultimately more node accesses and CPU time. The Query cost of the Greek data set increases more rapidly because its obstacles are denser with respect to its data points.

- **Best-first vs. Depth-first Implementation.** We compare two implementations of the ONN query, the best-first NN search (best-first) and depth-first NN search (depth-first) in Figure 14. We optimize the depth-first approach by that in the first iteration, it retrieves $k + 1$ NNs (the first k NNs are candidates and the $(k + 1)$th NN is used to check whether the ONN search can be terminated). It shows the depth-first approach needs much more R-tree node accesses. The reason is first, the best-first approach is optimized for node access. Second, when we need to retrieve more candidate points, the depth-first approach has to search from scratch. The CPU time for both methods is similar since CPU cost is dominated by the computation of the obstructed distance, which is same for both approaches.

- **Size of Auxiliary Data Structures.** At last, we study the size of the auxiliary data structures used by the ONN query. The ONN query algorithm requires two priority queues and one link list to store entries having been visited during the traversing of the R-trees. The size of these data structures affects the query performance and if it is too big, a disk-based implementation is required, which increases both CPU and I/O cost. Figure 15 plots the maximum total number of items in these data structures. The study shows that with either the variation of the number of data points and obstacles or the number of nearest neighbors, the total size of these data structures remains modest. The size of the local visibility graph is $O(n^2)$, where n is the total number of obstacle vertices in the *local workspace*. Since only a small number of obstacles are involved in computation (see Figure 10), the size of the local visibility graph is modest as well.

6 Conclusion

In this paper, we propose an efficient ONN algorithm with R-tree that processes only the data points and obstacles relevant to the query in an incremental way and thus filters out a large number of points and obstacles. We conduct extensive experimental study to evaluate our proposed algorithm. Experiments on real-life data sets show the algorithm scales well with respect to the input data size and the number of nearest neighbors requested.

References

1. http://epoch.cs.berkeley.edu/sequoia/benchmark/.
2. http://www.rtreeportal.org/.
3. N. Beckmann, H.-P. Kriegel, R. Schneider, and B. Seeger. The R*-tree: An efficient and robust access method for points and rectangles. pages 322–331, 1990.
4. R. Benetis, C. Jensen, G. Karciauskas, and S. Saltenis. Nearest neighbor and reverse nearest neighbor queries for moving objects. 2002.
5. S. Berchtold, D.A. Keim, and H.-P. Kriegel. The X-tree: An index structure for high-dimensional data. pages 28–39, 1996.
6. C. Böhm, S. Berchtold, and D.A. Keim. Searching in high dimensional spaces: index structures for improving the performance of multimedia databases. *ACM Computing Surveys*, 33(3):322–373, 2001.
7. K.L. Cheung and A.W.C. Fu. Enhanced nearest neighbor search on the R-tree. *SIGMOD Record*, 27(3):16–21, 1998.
8. T.H. Cormen, C.E. Leiserson, R.L. Rivest, and C. Stein. *Introduction to Algorithms. Second Edition*. MIT Press, 2nd edition, 2001.
9. M. de Berg, M. van Kreveld, M. Overmars, and O. Schwarzkopf. *Computational Geometry: Algorithms and Applications*. Springer, Berlin, 2nd edition, 2000.
10. M. Ester, H. Kriegel, J. Sander, and X. Xu. A density-based algorithm for discovering clusters in large spatial databases with noise. pages 226–231, 1996.
11. H. Ferhatosmanoglu, Ioanna Stanoi, Divyakant Agrawal, and Amr El Abbadi. Constrained nearest neighbor queries. pages 257–278, 2001.
12. S.K. Ghosh and D.M. Mount. An output sensitive algorithm for computing visibility graphs. pages 11–19, 1987.
13. A. Guttman. R-trees: A dynamic index structure for spatial searching. pages 47–57, 1984.
14. A. Henrich. A distance scan algorithm for spatial access structures. pages 136–143, 1994.
15. J. Hershberger and S. Suri. An optimal algorithm for euclidean shortest paths in the plane. *SIAM J. on Computing*, 28(6):2215–2256, 1999.
16. G. Hjaltason and H. Samet. Ranking in spatial databases. pages 83–95, 1995.
17. G. Hjaltason and H. Samet. Distance browsing in spatial databases. *ACM Transactions on Database Systems*, 24(2):265–318, 1999.
18. M. James. *Classification Algorithms*. John Wiley & Sons, 1985.
19. G. Karypis, E.H. Han, and V. Kumar. Chameleon: Hierarchical clustering using dynamic modeling. *Computer*, 32(8):68–75, 1999.
20. F. Korn and S. Muthukrishnan. Influence sets based on reverse nearest neighbor queries. pages 201–212, 2000.
21. J. O'Rourke. *Computational geometry: algorithms and applications. Second Edition*. Springer-Verlag, 2000.

22. N. Roussopoulos, S. Kelley, and F. Vincent. Nearest neighbor queries. pages 71–79, 1995.
23. T. Sellis, N. Roussopoulos, and C. Faloutsos. The R^+-tree: A dynamic index for multi-dimensional objects. pages 507–518, 1987.
24. Y. Tao and D. Papadias. Time-parameterized queries in spatio-temporal databases. pages 334–345, 2002.
25. Y. Tao, D. Papadias, and Q. Shen. Continuous nearest neighbor search. pages 287–298, 2002.
26. A.K.H. Tung, J. Hou, and J. Han. Spatial clustering in the presence of obstacles. pages 359–367, 2001.
27. J. Zhang, D. Papadias, K. Mouratidis, and M. Zhu. Spatial queries in the presence of obstacles. 2004.

Language Bindings for Spatio-Temporal Database Programming in Tripod

Tony Griffiths, Norman W. Paton, Alvaro A.A. Fernandes, Seung-Hyun Jeong, and Nassima Djafri

Department of Computer Science, University of Manchester,
Oxford Road, Manchester M13 9PL, United Kingdom
{griffitt,norm,a.fernandes,jeongs,djafrin7}@cs.man.ac.uk

Abstract. While there are many proposals for spatio-temporal data models and query languages, there is a lack of research into application development using spatio-temporal database systems. This paper seeks to redress the balance by exploring how to support database programming for spatio-temporal object databases, with specific reference to the Tripod spatio-temporal OODBMS.

1 Introduction

Spatio-temporal databases provide facilities for capturing and querying changes that have taken place to the spatial and aspatial properties of data over time. Applications for spatio-temporal databases are potentially numerous, and significant work has been undertaken to develop spatio-temporal data types (e.g. (1)), data models (e.g. (2)), storage structures (e.g. (3)) and algorithms (e.g. (4)). However, to date, few proposals have been worked through to yield complete spatio-temporal database systems, and thus work on application development languages and environments tends to lag behind that on models and algorithms.

There are several techniques that can be used to develop spatio-temporal applications, including bespoke development where the database schema and application programs are developed on a per-application basis, or versioning systems, where transaction time is used to create snapshots of the system data. Perhaps the most straightforward approach to the development of a spatio-temporal database system involves defining spatio-temporal data types, and adding these as primitive types to a relational database system using abstract data type (ADT) mechanisms (also known as "cartridges" or "data blades"). Although spatio-temporal ADTs are not yet commercially available, commercial spatial extensions to relational systems from database and geographical information system vendors are in widespread use.

If adopted to support spatio-temporal data, ADTs would make operations for querying and updating spatio-temporal data available from within a query language, but have a number of limitations for wider application development.

H. Williams and L. MacKinnon (Eds.): BNCOD 2004, LNCS 3112, pp. 216–233, 2004.

For example, impedance mismatches between a programming language and a database system are increased in the presence of database type extensions. It may therefore not be straightforward for an application to manipulate transient spatio-temporal data using the same types as are stored in the database without creating temporary tables, and casting analysis operations over such data as queries over the database. This damages programmer productivity by increasing the extent to which the application developer is conscious of programming using two loosely integrated languages, which encourage different programming paradigms, and may well have performance implications. Although work on open standards for representing geospatial data (e.g. www.opengis.org) could lead to the development of consistent representations in multiple language environments, standard representation for spatio-temporal data are certainly some way off.

As a result, there is a need to explore how best to support database programming for spatio-temporal data. This includes issues such as how database types relate to programming language types, how query language operations relate to those provided in a programming language setting, and what impact the use of imperative language constructs may have for declaratively defined spatio-temporal models. This paper discusses such issues in the context of the Tripod (6) spatio-temporal object database system. The Tripod system is an extension of the ODMG object model (7) to support spatial, timestamp and historical data representation. As illustrated in Figure 1, Tripod not only extends the ODMG object model, but also the OQL query language and the programming language bindings. This paper discusses the design of the Tripod programming language bindings, and illustrates them in use in a simple cadastral application. We know of no previous work that explicitly addresses programming language support for spatio-temporal application development.

The remainder of the paper is structured as follows. Section 2 provides an overview of the Tripod system. Details of the Tripod architecture are presented in Section 3, focussing on how to create a database, and on the mapping between the object model's type system and that of the language bindings. Section 4 illustrates how developers can use the language bindings to program spatio-historical database applications. Finally Section 5 draws some conclusions.

2   Tripod Overview

Tripod is a spatio-historical object database system that orthogonally extends the ODMG standard for object databases. By orthogonality we mean that users can model the spatial, or the temporal aspects of modelled types and their properties, or both, or neither. Figure 1 illustrates the relationships between the different components in Tripod. At the core is the ODMG object model, which is extended with primitive spatial and timestamp types.

The ODMG Object Model provides a set of object and literal types – including collection types, (e.g., Set, Bag and List) and atomic types (e.g., long and string) – with which a designer can specify their own object types, and thus construct a particular database schema. Each user-defined type has a structure (a collection of attributes and binary relationships with other user-defined types) and a behaviour (a collection of methods whose implementation is specified using the language binding).

Tripod's spatial data types (SDTs) are based on the ROSE (RObust Spatial Extensions) approach described in (5). The ROSE approach defines an algebra over three SDTs, namely Points, Lines and Regions, and an extensive collection of spatial predicates and operations over these types. Every spatial value in the ROSE algebra is set-based, thus facilitating set-at-a-time processing. Roughly speaking, each element of a Points value is a pair of coordinates in the underlying geometry, each element of a

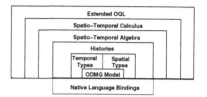

Fig. 1. Tripod Components

Lines value is a set of connected line segments, and each element in a Regions value is a polygon containing a (potentially empty) set of holes.

Tripod extends the set of ODMG primitive types with two timestamp types, called Instants and TimeIntervals. The timestamp types are one-dimensional specialisations of the spatial types, thus inheriting all the functionality of the spatial types, but extending these with timestamp-specific notions such as a calendar and ordering predicates. For further details see (8).

Figure 2 illustrates timestamps in graphical form, where timestamp A is a TimeIntervals value, and timestamps B and C are Instants values. Notice that B happens to be a singleton. Tripod's timestamps benefit from the collection-based nature of their spatial counterparts, as they are allowed to contain gaps. This facility is used to good effect in the maintenance of histories as shown in Section 4.

The Tripod history mechanism provides functionality to support the storage, management and querying of entities that change over time. A history models the changes that an entity (or its attributes, or the relationships it participates in) undergoes as the result of assignments made to it. In the Tripod object model, a request for a history to be maintained can be made for any construct to which a value can be assigned, i.e., a history

Fig. 2. Example Tripod Timestamps

is a history of changes in value and it records episodes of change by identifying these with a timestamp. Each such value is called a *snapshot*. As a consequence of the possible value assignments that are well defined in the Tripod model, a history can be kept for object identifiers, attribute values, and relationship instances. In other words, any construct denoted by the left hand side of an assignment operation (i.e., an *l-value*) can have a record kept of the different values assigned to it over time, no matter the type of the value assigned.

3   The Tripod Architecture

Figure 3 details the various components of the Tripod architecture, and in particular how these components interact with each other in the specification of spatio-historical database applications. There are three main components in the Tripod architecture: a Persistent Store that is responsible for loading and saving persistent objects to and from the database and also for maintaining metadata about a particular database schema; a Query Processor that is responsible for optimizing and executing database queries; and a Programming Language Binding that is responsible for providing programming language access to the database, and which is the principal focus of this paper.

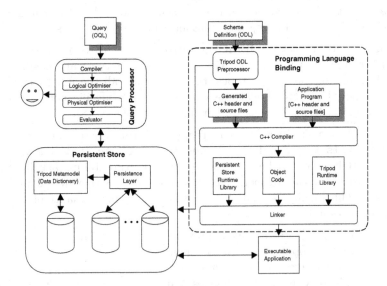

Fig. 3. Tripod Architecture

3.1   Creating a Tripod Database

Developers specify a Tripod database by defining a schema definition using an extension to ODMG's object definition language (ODL). Figure 4 provides a Tripod ODL specification of a simple cadastre schema that utilises two historical types `Person` and `LandParcel` with a 1:M binary relationship `owns` between them, and a non-historical type `FlagPole`. For each historical property (attribute or relationship) Tripod maintains a history of the values of that property (primitive values or collections of primitive values for attributes, and object values or collections of object values for relationships) with timestamps (`instants` or `timeIntervals`) at the specified granularity (i.e., `DAY`). When applied to the keyword `class`, the keyword `historical` tells Tripod to maintain an implicit, i.e., system-maintained, attribute called `lifespan`, whose purpose is to record when instances of this class were valid or invalid in a database.

```
forward class Person; forward class LandParcel; forward class FlagPole;

historical<timeIntervals, DAY> class Person ( extent Persons ) {
    historical<timeIntervals, DAY> attribute string name;
    historical<timeIntervals, DAY> relationship set<LandParcel> owns inverse LandParcel::owned_by;
    void purchase(in state<timeIntervals, LandParcel> aParcel);
    void sell(in state<timeIntervals, LandParcel> aParcel); };

historical<timeIntervals, DAY> class LandParcel ( extent Parcels ) {
    attribute string postcode;
    historical<timeIntervals, DAY> attribute regions boundary;
    historical<timeIntervals, DAY> relationship Person owned_by inverse Person::owns; };

class FlagPole ( extent FlagPoles) { attribute points location; };
```

Fig. 4. Example Schema

3.2   Model Mapping

Once a schema has been specified, developers must send the ODL file to Tripod for processing. There are several outputs from this process, namely: An empty Tripod database whose structure corresponds to that of the schema; A separate metadata database (data dictionary) populated with metadata corresponding to the schema (Tripod's metamodel is an orthogonal extension of the ODMG metamodel to accommodate histories); a collection of C++ header files, each of which is a mapping from an ODL class to a corresponding C++ class; and a collection of C++ source files, each of which contains implementations of methods to set and get the class's properties.

Each of these outputs is automatically generated by Tripod from an ODL schema specification. The ODMG standard allows for the functionality provided by these C++ classes to be made available to the language bindings through two mechanisms: the mapped types and embedded queries, both of which are available in Tripod. Figures 5 and 6 show the mapping from the ODL of Figure 4 to the C++ class `LandParcel`. This will be explained in the following sections.

Mapping Classes. In conformance with the ODMG standard, Tripod maps each ODL class to a corresponding C++ class. For each historical class Tripod generates an additional, private and system-maintained, historical attribute

```
1  #include "Person.h"
2  #include "LetterBox.h"
3  #include "ODMG.h"
4
5  // forward declarations
6  class Person;
7  class LetterBox;
8
9  extern const char __Person_owns[];
10
11 class LandParcel : public Object {
12 // Automatically generated constructor stubs.
13 public: // These must be written by the programmer in a corresponding .cpp file
14 LandParcel();
15 ~LandParcel();
16
17 public: // Automatically generated initialiser stubs
18 LandParcel(const LandParcel&);
19
20 d_History<d_TimeIntervals, DAY, d_Boolean> __lifespan; // lifespan attribute
21
22 private:  // attributes
23 d_String postcode;
24 d_History<d_TimeIntervals, DAY, d_Regions> boundary;
25
26 public: // relationships
27 d_Historical_Rel_Set<Person, __Person_owns, LandParcel, d_TimeIntervals, DAY> owned_by;
28
29 public:  // operations
30 void merge_with(d_Ref<State<d_TimeIntervals, LandParcel> > aLandParcel);
31 void sell_to(d_Ref<State<d_TimeIntervals, Person> > aPerson);
32
33 // Access methods omitted
34 public: //Extent
35 static d_Ref<d_Set<d_Ref<LandParcel> > > Parcels; // reference to the class extent
36 static const char* extent_name;  };
```

Fig. 5. ODL to C++ mapping for class `LandParcel`

called `lifespan` (Figure 5, line 20), whose purpose is to record when objects of this type exist in a database. For example the lifespan: $\{\langle[1-8, 17-27), \texttt{true}\rangle\}$ records that the object existed during two distinct time periods (and by inference did not exist at any other times). As per the ODMG standard, Tripod also generates a collection-based and system-maintained attribute (Figure 5, line 35) to represent the extent of all instances of the class.

Mapping Attributes. Non-historical attributes are mapped to a corresponding (private) class property with a type from the ODMG C++ type system: i.e., ODL boolean maps to d_Boolean, whereas ODL string maps to d_String. Historical attributes, however, map to a new Tripod C++ template type called d_History (i.e., LandParcel :: boundary (Figure 5, line 24)). This type takes as its template arguments the timestamp type, granularity, and snapshot type of the history, and in turn provides facilities to populate, maintain and query itself. Since histories record states, Tripod provides a further C++ template type State which takes as arguments the snapshot and timestamp types, and whose purpose is to assist in the process of inserting new states to a history. In conformance with the ODMG standard, Tripod only allows access to attributes via *set* and *get* methods, which it automatically generates (as shown in Section 4.2).

Mapping Relationships. Tripod maps ODL relationships to template types whose purpose is to allow the population of the binary relationship, and to ensure that the objects participating in its roles are automatically maintained. The ODMG C++ binding specifies the types d_Rel_Ref, d_Rel_Set, and d_Rel_List to represent to-one and to-many (unordered and ordered) relationships. Tripod extends the ODMG type system with the types d_Historical_Rel_Ref, d_Historical_Rel_Set, and d_Historical_Rel_List. These types serve the same general purpose as their non-historical counterparts, but instead of an assignment to such a property causing the previous value to be overwritten, they instead add a new state to their internal data structure (a history).

Although it is possible to create spatio-historical schemas using techniques such as bespoke development, versioning or ADT type extensions (i.e., "cartridges"), each of these techniques have their own difficulties. For example: bespoke development requires developers to do all the work themselves without any database kernel or programming language support; versioning depends on the transaction time of any database commits, with valid time being difficult, or impossible, to support; and while ADT extensions to DBMSs provide the necessary kernel database types, the extended models are less expressive than that of Tripod, and require programmers to write explicit code for database maintenance.

4   Programming in Tripod

It is preferable for a historical DBMS to support DBMS functionality over spatial and historical data both orthogonally and synergistically (9). By synergy we mean that if a user makes use of either only spatial or only historical or both spatial and historical facilities, the system responds positively (e.g., by making available specific syntax, by providing additional behaviour, by seeking optimisation opportunities, etc.). This section presents how the language bindings support synergy.

The primary use of the language bindings is to act as an OML for an object database. Although it is entirely possible to query the state of a database through these language bindings, this is not the preferred method. The language bindings do not have full access to the index structures and optimization strategies utilised by Tripod's query language interface (OQL) (10). The preferred method of querying data via the language bindings is to create a d_OQL_Query class, and then use the results of this query within an application program. For example:

```
d_Bag<d_Ref<LandParcel> > someParcels;
d_OQL_Query q1("select l from l in Parcels
               where l.boundry.vt.before($1) and l.boundry.value.overlaps($2)");
q1 << aTimeInterval << aSpatialValue;
d_oql_execute(q1, someParcels);
```

```
d_Ref<LandParcel> aParcel; // iterate over results of q1
d_Iterator<d_Ref<LandParcel> > it = someParcels.create_iterator();
while(it.next(aParcel)) {
  cout << "Parcel: " << aParcel->get_postcode() << endl;
  cout << "Area: " << aParcel->get_boundary().CurrentValue().area() << endl;
}
```

This simple example shows how spatial and historical operations can be utilised both within an embedded query and also within the language bindings (see (6) for further details of Tripod OQL).

4.1 Object Creation

The ODMG language bindings specify a syntax and semantics for the creation of both transient and persistent objects. For example, a new persistent `FlagPole` can be created in the database `bncod04` using the following syntax:

```
d_Ref<FlagPole> aFlagPole = new(bncod04, "FlagPole") FlagPole;
```

Tripod extends this syntax with a further overloading of the C++ `new` operator to allow developers to specify an initial valid time for historical objects. Note that in accordance with our aim of synergy, the non-historical version of the `new` operator is available for historical objects, but the valid time of the object will default to a `timeIntervals` value starting at the current system time until it is changed, as returned by the Tripod function `now2uc()`.

```
d_Ref<Person> elizabeth = new(bncod04, "Person",
                        "21/4/1926 - until_changed") Person("Elizabeth");
d_Ref<Person> philip = new(bncod04, "Person", "10/6/1921 - until_changed") Person("Philip");
d_Regions r1("regions{[1:3_4:5,4:5_6:3,6:3_3:1,3:1_1:3]}"); // simple rectangle
d_Ref<LandParcel> buckPalace = new(bncod04, "LandParcel",
                        "1/1/1761 - until_changed") LandParcel("SW1A 1AA", r1);
```

Each of the above historical objects will therefore have a system-maintained `lifespan` historical attribute whose initial values will be the following histories:

1. `elizabeth`: $\{\langle[21/4/1926 - uc), \text{true}\rangle\}$
2. `philip`: $\{\langle[10/6/1921 - uc), \text{true}\rangle\}$
3. `buckPalace`: $\{\langle[1/1/1761 - uc), \text{true}\rangle\}$

where `true` indicates that the object was valid in the database at that time.

4.2 Object Manipulation

Accessing and Assigning Values to Attributes. In addition to generating the structure of the C++ class, Tripod automatically generates methods to access an object's properties. So, for example, a non-historical attribute `location : d_Points` will have two methods: `void set_location(d_Points)`,

and d_Points get_location(). The signatures for the access methods for the
LandParcel class are shown in Figure 6.

Since instances of historical attributes are no longer primitive values (they are
histories – essentially collections of states), any attempt to access such attributes
through their access methods will result in a (possibly empty) history. For example, the operation buckPalace− > get_boundary() will result in the complete
history of Buckingham Palace's boundary, and
buckPalace− > set_boundary(State⟨d_TimeIntervals, d_Regions⟩(t1, r1))
(where r1 is a timeInterval and r1 is a d_Regions value) will result in the
assignment of a new state to the boundary history. While this operation is more
laborious than simply assigning a primitive value, as would happen in a non-
historical setting, the nature of a historical domain means that more precision
is required. For historical attributes, Tripod generates an overloaded collection
of set and get methods. For example, the attribute LandParcel :: boundary has
two set_boundary, and three get_boundary methods as shown in Figure 6.

```
1  // Access methods - postcode access omitted for space reasons
2  void set_boundary( const State<d_TimeIntervals, d_Regions >& ) throw(d_Error);
3  void set_boundary( const d_Regions& ) throw(d_Error);
4
5  const d_History<d_TimeIntervals, DAY, d_Regions > get_boundary( );
6
7  const d_History<d_TimeIntervals, DAY, d_Regions > get_boundary( const d_TimeIntervals&,
8              d_Boolean (d_TimeIntervals::*pred_func) (const d_TimeIntervals*) const  );
9
10 const d_History<d_TimeIntervals, DAY, d_Regions > get_boundary( const d_TimeIntervals&,
11             d_Boolean (d_TimeIntervals::*pred_func) (const d_TimeIntervals*,
12                                        Quantifier=TPD_FORALL) const,
13             Quantifier=TPD_FORALL  );
14
15 protected: // lifespan attribute
16 void set_lifespan(const d_History<d_TimeIntervals, DAY,  d_Boolean>& _in);
17 const d_History<d_TimeIntervals, DAY,  d_Boolean>& get_lifespan(void) const;
```

Fig. 6. Attribute Access Methods for class Person

The first of the set methods (line 2 of Figure 6) allows a new state to be added
to the boundary history, whereas the method (line 3) allows a regions value to
be added to the history with a defaulted valid time of now2uc(). The first of the
get methods (line 5 of Figure 6) simply returns a copy of the entire history of an
object's boundary attribute. The remaining two get methods (lines 7 to 8 and
lines 10 to 13) have quite complex signatures, but these belie the simple manner
in which they are used. Example of these use are shown below.

```
h1 = buckPalace->get_boundary(t1, &d_TimeIntervals::before);
h2 = buckPalace->get_boundary(t2, &d_TimeIntervals::during, TPD_FORALL);
```

Both of these get methods filter the historical attribute based on the timestamp
predicate function supplied as the input parameter. The difference between the
two variants lies in the non-convex nature of Tripod's timestamps. Since a non-
convex timestamp can be composed of several component convex timestamps
(with gaps between them) it may be that part of the argument timestamp satis-

fies the predicate, but not all of it. Tripod's get methods therefore accept the optional arguments `TPD_FORALL` and `TPD_EXISTS` to allow developers finer-grained control over the semantics of the get operation.

Accessing and Assigning values to Relationships. The ODMG language bindings handle relationships in a different manner to attributes. There are no set and get methods per se, rather the syntax uses direct assignment to get/set relationship values. In addition, since relationships are bi-directional, any assignment to one role in the relationship will automatically result in an assignment to the inverse role. In a non-historical setting this is exemplified as follows:

```
// Assume a now non-historical relationship Person::owns
buckPalace->owned_by = elizabeth; // Assignment - automatically updates elizabeth->owns
// The above is equivalent to: (automatically updates buckPalace->owned_by)
// elizabeth->owns.insert_element(buckPalace);
```

Just as historical attributes are no longer simple-valued, historical relationships are themselves collections of states, with each snapshot being either an object identifier or a collection of object identifiers. Since relationships must automatically maintain the integrity of the inverse role, this raises additional complexities for the DBMS in terms of maintaining the integrity of the underlying histories. These complexities should of course be hidden from the user. The code shown below adds a new state to the 1:M `owned_by` relationship of the object `buckPalace`:

```
// Assignment - automatically updates elizabeth->owns
buckPalace->owned_by = State<timeIntervals, Person> \
                   (timeIntervals("21/5/1952 - until_changed"), elizabeth);
// The above is equivalent to:
// elizabeth->owns.insert_element(State<timeIntervals, LandParcel> \
//                    (timeIntervals("21/5/1952 - until_changed"), buckPalace));
```

Figure 7 illustrates the result of the above operation, showing that the object called `elizabeth` has an `owns` history that currently contains a single state whose snapshot is a collection containing a single object `buckPalace`. `buckPalace` has a relationship called `owned_by`, whose single state is the object `elizabeth`.

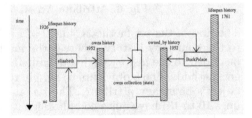

Fig. 7. DBMS Maintenance of Historical Relationships

Manipulating Histories. Once a history has been accessed, developers can use the `History` class's API to manipulate the history: i.e., querying, manipulation, performing set-based operations on two histories. Full details of the functionality found in this API can be found in (8). Examples of this functionality in use are:

```
d_History h1 = philip->get_name(); // Retrieve a (copy) of a historical attribute
d_History h2 = elizabeth->get_name();
// Delete all states before 1/1/1960 (beginning is the earliest data supported by Tripod)
h1.DeleteTimestamp(d_TimeIntervals("beginning - 1/1/1960"));
// Does history contain a particular snapshot value?
d_Boolean b = h2.ContainsSnapshot(State<d_TimeIntervals,d_String>(t1,"Princess Elizabeth"));
d_History h3 = h1 + h2; // Merge two histories: + is overloaded to indicate union
```

In addition to providing functionality to create and populate a history, Tripod provides functionality to query (i.e., isEmpty, Equals, ContainsTimestamp), merge (i.e., Union, Difference, Intersection) and mutate (i.e., Dissect) a history (for full details see (8)). Such functionality is available in both the language bindings and the OQL.

Specifying Historical Containment Constraints. Tripod's object model enforces temporal containment constraints on the states within a history (i.e., a historical attribute cannot contain states whose timestamps lie outside the scope of the containing object's lifespan (8)). The question therefore arises of what to do if a program attempts to invalidate these constraints. Tripod allows developers to state a policy for such occurrences. They can choose either to: Throw an exception; automatically update the timestamp associated with the new state so that it does not violate the containment constraint; automatically update the lifespan of the containing object so that it now includes the new state's timestamp. Developers can either specify their preference in the Tripod database options file, or can explicitly override these defaults within a program. For example, they can write:

```
TripodPolicy::setHistoricalConstraintPolicy(TripodPolicy::update_lifespan);
// other options are: abort_operation and update_state
```

If an exception is caught then Tripod provides facilities to allow programs to temporarily override the containment constraint policy to, for example, update the containing object's lifespan; alternatively they can update the input state's timestamp or reject the operation.

While the data models that underlie many (spatio-) temporal systems also specify such containment constraints (e.g., (11)), they do not specify what should happen if a violation occurs in any implementation of their model. In a purely temporal setting TSQL2 (12) returns an error code if an attempt is made to inconsistently update temporal tuples, whereas (13) provides greater flexibility by allowing finer-grained spatio-temporal constraints to be specified for moving objects.

4.3   Object Deletion

Semantics of Delete. In a non-historical object database, when an object is deleted all references to that object are removed from the database. In the case of a historical database this is not necessarily the case. For example, a user may want to delete an object so that it only exists before or after a certain date, or for only a certain portion of its valid time. They may however want to permanently delete the object. Each of these types of deletion is a valid operation in terms of a historical database, and as such is supported by Tripod.

Deleting an object for a portion of its valid time affects its system maintained lifespan attribute. This, in turn can affect the object's historical attributes, since a object cannot have attributes whose valid time is not contained by the valid time of the object's lifespan.

The consequences of deleting an object may also have ramifications for other objects in a database, through the relationships that the deleted object participated in. For example, if we deleted buckPalace from our database, we would want this to be propagated through to its owner, since logically they could not be said to own the land when it did not exist. This type of propagation is also required if only a portion of an object's valid time is deleted, for the same reasons.

The deletion of an object's period of validity in the universe of discourse can be seen to be an operation on its lifespan attribute, since it is this (DBMS maintained) property that records when the object exists (and by implication, does not exist) in the database. For example, we could delete buckPalace from the database for all valid times after 03/05/2010, if it were demolished on that date. We could also delete a portion of its period of validity if it were destroyed and subsequently rebuilt, i.e., if during the second world war it had been bombed and then rebuilt in 1946. The original valid time of buckPalace (as created in Section 4) is realised by its lifespan attribute as:

$$lifespan_{\texttt{buckPalace}} = \{\langle [1/1/1761 - \texttt{uc}), \texttt{true}\rangle\}$$

The first of the above operations (demolishment) would result in a lifespan of:

$$lifespan'_{\texttt{buckPalace}} = \{\langle [1/1/1761 - 03/05/2010), \texttt{true}\rangle\}$$

It can be seen that this has the effect of updating the object's lifespan from being *quasi*-closed at until_changed to being fully closed; whereas the second of the above operations (bombing and rebuilding) results in:

$$lifespan''_{\texttt{buckPalace}} = \{\langle [1/1/1761 - 03/04/1942, \ 03/05/1946 - \texttt{uc}), \texttt{true}\rangle\}$$

This second operation shows the utility of collection-based timestamps when maintaining Histories. The above operations do not however delete buckPalace from the database. If this were the case then buckPalace.isnull()[1] would be true.

The question then arises: what if someone attempts to build a visitor centre at buckPalace (requiring annexation of land from surrounding areas) on 6/12/2020? Logically, they should not be allowed to undertake this operation since the house no longer exists as it has been demolished. These detailed se-

---

[1] Note that since Tripod uses a 'smart pointer' to reference persistent objects, then the smart pointer itself will never be NULL, however the object that it references can be NULL, as detected by the isnull() function.

mantics are dependant on the requirements of the particular application. In this case, the operation should be rejected, whereas another application may reactivate `buckPalace` so that it merely has a gap in its history (the interpretation of this gap is again application-dependent). Tripod supports both these options.

Effects on an Object's Historical and non-Historical Attributes. If an object has a portion of its valid time deleted then this will effect its lifespan property. The affect of any update to an object's lifespan should also be propagated to its attributes. Since Tripod only allows attributes to be simple-valued (i.e., Tripod does not allow object-valued attributes), changes to such attributes need not be propagated to other objects in a database. Figure 8(a) shows the object called `elizabeth` after having it's `name` history populated by two states, as shown in Section 4.2. If this initial system state is updated by deleting a portion of `elizabeth`'s lifespan, then the effect of deleting this portion of `elizabeth`'s lifespan is shown in Figure 8(b), where the corresponding histories have been updated to show the cascading effect of such an update.

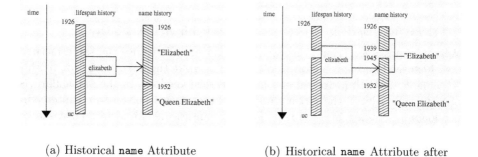

(a) Historical **name** Attribute   (b) Historical **name** Attribute after Object Deletion

Fig. 8. Updating Historical Attributes

Effects on an Object's Historical and non-Historical Relationships. As already stated, if an object has all or portion of its valid time deleted, this can have ramifications for objects that have relationships with the deleted object.

An example of the relationship between two objects has been shown in Figure 7. If we were to delete `buckPalace` during the time period 03/04/1960 to 03/05/1965, then this would have implications for its owners at that time. Figures 9(a) to 9(b) show how the deletion of this portion of `buckPalace`'s lifespan is first propagated to the history that maintains its owners, and then to the inverse of `buckPalace`'s `owned_by` relationship, `Person :: owns`.

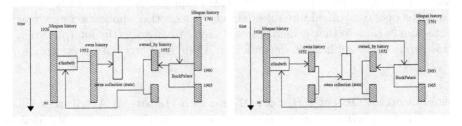

(a) Cascading to buckPalace's owned_by history

(b) Cascading to related Person's owns history

Fig. 9. Updating Historical Relationships

Language Bindings Extensions to Support Deletion. The ODMG 3.0 standard states that an object is deleted by calling the delete_object() method on a 'smart pointer' (a d_Ref) to that object, i.e.:

```
d_Ref<FlagPole> fp = new(bncod04, "FlagPole") FlagPole();
fp.delete_object();
```

will cause the Flag Pole object fp to be deleted from the database.

Wherever possible, Tripod developers should be able to use the same methods over historical and non-historical objects. Therefore the delete_object method is available on both historical and non-historical versions. In the particular case of historical objects, the delete_object operation can have several interesting overloadings, taking in several possible semantics, including (amongst many): Delete the object so that it does not exist *during* a specifie timestamp; delete the object so that it does do not exist *before* a specified timestamp; delete the object so that it does not exist *after* a specified timestamp.

These operations can be combined into the following generalised form:

d_Ref⟨T⟩ :: delete_object(τ, ω);

where T is the object type, ω is a Tripod timestamp predicate operation, and τ is a timestamp used in conjunction with ω. For example, this can be instantiated on the object elizabeth as:

```
elizabeth.delete_object(d_TimeIntervals("03/04/1960 - 03/05/1965"), &d_TimeIntervals::equals);
elizabeth.delete_object(d_TimeIntervals("03/04/1960 - 03/05/1965"), &d_TimeIntervals::after);
```

Each of these operations will map down to calls on the histories that are being deleted. For a historical object obj, this will take the form:

obj.delete_object(τ, ω) ≡ obj− > lifespan.DeleteTimestamp(τ, ω)

In addition, the delete_object operation ensures that the lifespans of each of the object's historical attributes and relationships, and the lifespans of the inverses of these relationships are updated so that they satisfy Tripod's historical containment constraints.

Since each class has a different collection of properties, the `delete_object` operation is implemented by extending the ODMG d_Ref type with an operation:

```
template<class T, class TS> virtual void d_Ref<T>::delete_object(const TS* timestamp,
                              d_Boolean(TS::*predicate_func)(const TS*) const) {
    pointed_to_object->delete_object(timestamp, predicate_function);
}
```

that invokes a class-specific `delete_object` operation that Tripod automatically generates from each class's metadata.

Previous database research has identified the delete operator as being of special importance in a temporal setting. However, to the best of our knowledge, such research has been limited to a relational setting rather than an object one. Here, temporal extensions to the relational algebra's delete operator have been proposed (e.g., (14)), allowing access to delete functionality through an extended SQL DELETE operation. Examples of such functionality can be found in the TSQL2 language specification (12), and also in (15) where the authors recognise the semantic problems associated with updating (spatio-) temporal data and propose algebraic operators to enforce the consistency of a database. In addition, (16) have developed a temporal RDBMS that takes as input a TSQL2 schema and automatically generates constraints to enforce the temporal consistency of TSQL2 update operations – it is not surprising to note that these constraints are complex in nature.

4.4   Iterating over Historical Properties

Since a history is a collection of states, it exhibits many of the general features of other collection types. One of the important facilities specified by the ODMG language bindings is the ability to iterate over its collection types in ways that are natural to these types. There are two essential properties of such an iteration, namely the type of each element in the collection, and the order in which each element is returned during the iteration.

There are several properties that all ODMG iterators over collection types exhibit as embodied by the base class `Iterator`. Tripod extends these facilities with a new iterator class that provides facilities targeted at a history's specific properties, i.e. such as to: Read or write from or to a History; access a state; move to the next or previous state; move to the Nth state; move forward or backwards N states; test if the iterator is at the beginning or end state.

The adopted approach is to provide an iterator class called `RandomAccessIterator` as described by the interface shown in Figure 10. Tripod's language bindings wrap many of the operations provided by the `RandomAccessIterator` to make them appear more like the interface provided by other iterators found in the C++ standard template library. For example, goto_nth_position() is wrapped to appear like the subscript ([]) operator, and forward_Npositions is wrapped to appear like the increment (+ =) operator.

```
interface RandomAccessIterator : BidirectionalIterator {
  exception InvalidInde x{ };
  void goto_nth_position(unsigned long index) raises(InvalidIndex);
  void forward_Npositions(unsigned long index) raises(InvalidIndex);
  void reverse_Npositions(unsigned long index) raises(InvalidIndex);
  unsigned long current_position();
};
```

Fig. 10. The `RandomAccessIterator` Interface

It is the responsibility of the d_History type to specify methods to create an appropriate iterator. The History ADT provides a family of iterator types: `StateIterator`, `SimpleStateIterator` and `InstantStateIterator`, as exemplified by:

$$\mathbf{boundary} = \{\langle[t_1 - t_3, t_9 - t_{11}], r_1\rangle, \langle[t_5 - t_7], r_2\rangle, \langle[t_{15} - t_{16}], r_3\rangle\}$$

as follows: `StateIterator` produces elements such as those shown in table 11(a), `SimpleStateIterator` produces elements such as those shown in table 11(b) (i.e., each state has its timestamp decomposed from a non-convex interval to a convex one [2]), and `InstantStateIterator` produces elements as those shown in table 11(c) (i.e., each state is decomposed to a convex instant). An example of the `StateIterator` in use is shown below:

State	value
1	$\langle[t_1 - t_3, t_9 - t_{11}], r_1\rangle$
2	$\langle[t_5 - t_7], r_2\rangle$
3	$\langle[t_{15} - t_{16}], r_3\rangle$

(a) Iterating over $\langle TimeIntervals, snapshot\rangle$ pairs

State	value
1	$\langle[t_1 - t_3], r_1\rangle$
2	$\langle[t_5 - t_7], r_2\rangle$
3	$\langle[t_9 - t_{11}], r_1\rangle$
4	$\langle[t_{15} - t_{16}], r_3\rangle$

(b) Iterating over $\langle TimeInterval, snapshot\rangle$ pairs

State	value
1	$\langle t_1, r_1\rangle$
2	$\langle t_2, r_1\rangle$
3	$\langle t_5, r_2\rangle$
4	$\langle t_6, r_2\rangle$
5	$\langle t_9, r_1\rangle$
6	$\langle t_{10}, r_1\rangle$
7	$\langle t_{15}, r_3\rangle$

(c) Iterating over $\langle Instant, snapshot\rangle$ pairs

Fig. 11. Results of Different Forms of Iteration over a History

---

[2] Tripod provides the simple timestamp types d_Instant and d_TimeInterval for this purpose

```
RandomAccessIterator iter = buckPalace->get_boundary().create_StateIterator(true);
while(!iter.at_end()) {
  try {
    State<d_TimeIntervals, d_Regions> tmp = (State<d_TimeIntervals, d_Regions>)iter.get_element();
    iter.next_position(); // to next state
    iter.previous_position(); // reverse again
    iter.forward_Npositions(3); // forward 3 states
    iter.goto_nth_position(7); // go directly to state 7
  } catch(const InvalidIndex& error) { std::cerr << error.what() << std::endl; }
}
```

5   Summary and Conclusions

OODBMSs provide OML facilities through an imperative programming language interface, and APIs for such interfaces are well documented by standards bodies such as the ODMG. Spatio-historical OODBMSs must provide programming language extensions to accommodate their extended type system and enhanced semantics in ways that facilitate the exploitation of these features by developers migrating from existing OODBMS platforms.

We have previously contended that a historical DBMS should support DBMS functionality over spatial and historical data both orthogonally and synergistically (9). In a relational setting, languages such as TSQL2 reinforce this opinion as in their language features for creating, and maintaining, the temporal aspects of data are optional. In addition, their temporal OML statements frequently provide optional syntax elements assuming temporal default values.

Tripod supports orthogonality by providing an intuitive declarative mechanism that allows developers to create database schemas containing the spatial features of types and properties, or the temporal aspects of modelled types and properties, or both, or neither. This ability provides a high degree of flexibility to the types of systems that can be modelled. In addition, Tripod uses consistent extensions to the existing ODMG 3.0 programming language bindings that allow developers to create, update and delete historical objects and their (spatio-) historical properties. We also provide explicit facilities to ensure that developers can set system policy for determining what should happen if values violate the integrity of the application.

In accordance with our aim of synergy, Tripod provides a specialised syntax to allow the update of (spatio-) historical values. If developers do not use these specialised operations then we provide default semantics for such operations. We have also shown how the complexity of operations such as delete in a temporal setting can be hidden from developers, allowing them to focus on the process of developing their applications.

Although many proposals have been made for temporal and spatio-temporal data models and query languages, we know of no other proposal that follows through from these and also considers close integration of DML functionality in a programming language setting.

Acknowledgments. This research is funded by the UK Engineering and Physical Sciences Research Council (EPSRC - grant number GR/L02692) and the Paradigm EPSRC platform grant. Their support is gratefully acknowledged.

References

[1] Erwig, M., Guting, R., Schneider, M., Vazirigiannis, M.: Abstract and Discrete Modeling of Spatio-Temporal Data Types. Geoinformatica **3** (1999) 269–296

[2] Parent, C., Spaccapietra, S., Zimanyi, E.: Spatio-Temporal Conceptual Models: Data Structures + Space + Time. In: Proc. ACM GIS. (1999) 26–33

[3] Saltenis, S., Jensen, C.S.: Indexing of moving objects for location-based services. In: Proc ICDE02, IEEE Computer Society (2002) 463–472

[4] Lema, J.A.C., Forlizzi, L., Güting, R.H., Nardelli, E., Schneider, M.: Algorithms for moving objects databases. The Computer Journal **46** (2003) 680–712

[5] Güting, R., Schneider, M.: Realm-Based Spatial Data Types: The ROSE Algebra. VLDB Journal **4** (1995) 243–286

[6] Griffiths, T., Fernandes, A.A.A., Paton, N.W., Mason, T., Huang, B., Worboys, M., Johnson, C., Stell, J.: Tripod: A Comprehensive System for the Management of Spatial and Aspatial Historical Objects. In Proc. ACM-GIS, ACM Press (2001) 118–123

[7] Cattell, R.G.G., ed.: The Object Database Standard: ODMG 3.0. Morgan Kaufmann (2000)

[8] Griffiths, T., Fernandes, A., Paton, N., Barr, R.: The Tripod Spatio-Historical Data Model. Data & Knowledge Engineering **49** 1 (2004) 23–65

[9] Paton, N.W., Fernandes, A.A., Griffiths, T.: Spatio-Temporal Databases: Contentions, Components and Consolidation. In: Proc. DEXA 2000 (ASDM 2000), IEEE Press (2000) 851–855

[10] Griffiths, T., A.A.A. Fernandes, Djafri, N., N.W. Paton: A Query Calculus for Spatio-Temporal Object Databases. In: Proc. TIME, IEEE Press (2001) 101–110

[11] Bertino, E., Ferrari, E., Guerrini, G., Merlo, I.: Extending the ODMG Object Model with Time. In: Proc. ECOOP'98. (1998) 41–66

[12] Snodgrass, R.T., ed.: The TSQL2 Temporal Query Language. Kluwer (1995)

[13] Forlizzi, L., Güting, R., Nardelli, E., Schneider, M.: A data model and data structures for moving objects databases. In: ACM SIGMOD Conf. (2000) 319–330

[14] McBrien, P.: Principles of implementing historical databases in RDBMS. In: Proc.BNCOD93, LNCS, Vol. 696, Springer Verlag (1993) 220–237

[15] Lorentzos, N.A., Poulovassilis, A., Small, C.: Manipulation operations for an interval-extended relational model. Data and Knowledge Engineering **17** (1995) 1–29

[16] Detienne, V., Hainaut, J.L.: CASE Tool Support for Temporal Database Design. In Proc. ER 2001. LNCS Vol. 2224, Springer (2001) 208–224

Gauging Students' Understanding Through Interactive Lectures

Helen C. Purchase, Christopher Mitchell, and Iadh Ounis

Department of Computing Science, University of Glasgow
(hcp,mitchell,ounis)@dcs.gla.ac.uk

Abstract. The Personal Response System (PRS) enables audience responses to multiple choice questions to be collected quickly, and for a summary of all the answers to be displayed to the whole group immediately, making it a useful tool for promoting classroom discussion. This paper describes its use as a means for assessing students' understanding of previously learned material, in the context of two consecutive database modules. The PRS was used in the areas of Entity-Relationship diagrams, Relational Algebra, and SQL, and proved to be useful in assessing students' current level of understanding.

1 Introduction

It is often difficult for a lecturer to know the extent of students' knowledge outside of formal summative assessment, particularly if prerequisite material is presented in a different module taught by another lecturer. The aim of this paper is to describe our use of the Personal Response System for eliciting timely feedback from students in two large database classes.

1.1 The Personal Response System (PRS)

The PRS allows for responses to multiple choice questions to be submitted by each person in a large group, and then present the responses as a bar chart immediately after all responses are collected. Each student has a handset (with buttons 0 to 9) with which to indicate their answer (Fig. 1).

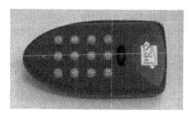

Fig. 1. A PRS Handset

H. Williams and L. MacKinnon (Eds.): BNCOD 2004, LNCS 3112, pp. 234–243, 2004.

2   Context

Computing Science students at the University of Glasgow are taught Database material in first, second and third year, typically by different lecturers. In the first year, they have three weeks of database material (data modeling, relations, Access, simple SQL) within a general Computer Systems module. In the second year Information Management module they have five weeks of database material (relational algebra, query optimization, normalization, transaction processing). The third year is the first time the students have a module entirely devoted to Databases (advanced SQL, integration with applications, implementation).

2.1   Not-knowing

While this arrangement ensures that database material is a continual thread through the students' studies, there are two main problems:

- As the lecturers are different, the second and third year lecturers do not ne-cessarily know the extent to which the topics in the previous years have been covered and understood. They can look at the defined curriculum, lecture notes and assessed exercises, but they will not necessarily know the extent of understanding of the relevant material. The problem is further complica-ted by the fact that the focus of the second year Information Management module is different to that of the more advanced third year Database module.
- Students easily forget material from one year to the other. They often do not recognize the extent of what they have forgotten, and resent having revision lectures at the start of the year. In particular, while recalling overall concepts (e.g. entities and relations), they tend to have forgotten finer details (e.g. cardinality and participation). This is further complicated by the fact that not all students continue from first to second year Computing Science and from second to third year Computing Science, so their focus tends to be on the immediate assessment, not on what might be required in future. The forgotten details are crucial for understanding the more advanced material in subsequent years.

Outside of summative assessment, lecturers only know the extent of students' understanding through small group tutorials and labs (typically only part of the class), and through informal interaction with individual students. It is hard to get a big picture view of the overall extent of understanding within the class. Students too have to rely on summative assessment and infrequent interactions with the lecturer to check their understanding is complete and correct.

2.2   Not-understanding

The other problem we have found with database teaching is the students' diffi-culty with relational algebra, and its connection to SQL. Students are introduced to this in second year, and they need a firm and secure understanding for the more advanced material covered in third year. Their performance in second year examples classes and examinations in 2002/3 revealed that they struggled with understanding the theoretical concepts, and that they start third year knowing some SQL syntax, but have little knowledge of its theoretical basis.

3   Addressing the Problems: PRS

We wished to increase the interaction between lecturers and students in large classes, with the aim of:

- increasing the lecturer's knowledge of students' understanding;
- increasing the students' knowledge of their own understanding;
- increasing the students' knowledge of lecturer's expectations;
- increasing the students' understanding of difficult material.

Laurillard[4] emphasises the importance of frequent communication between students and lecturers. Various methods of holding interactive lectures have been shown to enhance student understanding within mechanics courses [3]. Non technical solutions to the problem of communication between a large group of students and the lecturer include simple voting by hands, volunteered verbal answers, written tests, small group discussions, and Flashcards (students hold up a coloured piece of card, the colour representing their answer [5]).

These methods tend not to be anonymous, favour the confident student, and do not enable the immediate calculation of quantitative data that enables students to see their standing amongst their peers. Written tests are costly and time consuming, and, if they are not summative, are seldom taken seriously by students.

Benefits of using the PRS system include:

- less costly than a written test;
- students can see how they stand in relation to their peers;
- students get immediate feedback on a problem that is fresh in their mind;
- stimulates discussion about student misconceptions;
- easier to get representative, quantitative data than simple 'hands-up' voting;
- students know the extent of understanding required of them, at a particular time in the module;
- encourages lecturer-student interaction, even within large classes.

We chose to use PRS three times in database lectures: for ER diagrams, for SQL queries, and for Relational Algebra (RA) expressions.

For our particular goals, PRS allowed us to:

- reinforce material covered in the previous year;
- reassure students about what they do remember from the previous year;
- reveal students' misunderstandings of material covered in the previous year, including highlighting material they may be feeling complacent about.

The PRS system has successfully been used elsewhere (statistics [7], mechanics [1]). The main educational advantages stated for the use of PRS are to enhance the feedback from learners to teachers, allowing for the lecturer to better prepare subsequent material, and for the initiation of class discussion [2]. PRS has been used to reinforce or redeliver recently presented material, focusing on revealed misunderstandings [7], and at the end of a module to assist students in preparing for examinations.

4   Method: Using PRS for Learning Database Material

Our use of PRS for ER diagrams and for SQL queries was aimed at assisting the lecturer in establishing how much the students' remembered from the previous year. The Relational Algebra (RA) PRS exercise aimed to reinforce material students typically found difficult.

4.1   Not-knowing

The ER and SQL PRS exercises were held at the start of the term in both the second and third year modules. In both cases, the aim was for the lecturer to find out the extent of the students' knowledge of the previous years' material, and for the students to find out the extent of what they were expected to know.

In second year, the exercise entailed giving students a textual description of a domain (in this case, the information stored by a video shop), and each question presented four possible ER diagrams for representing information within the domain. The students needed to indicate which one of the ER diagrams was correct (Figs. 2 & 3). The students had studied ER diagrams in first year.

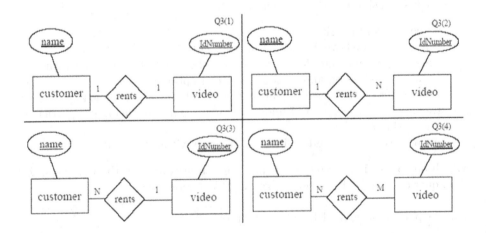

Fig. 2. A question from the Entity-Relationship exercise

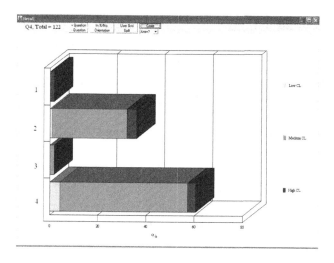

Fig. 3. The display of responses for the Entity-Relationship question in Fig. 2

In third year, the exercise entailed giving the students two SQL queries (A and B), and asking them to indicate whether the answers to these queries were identical, the answer to A contained within B, the answer to B contained within A, or different (Fig. 4). The students had studied SQL extensively, and its relation to relational algebra in second year.

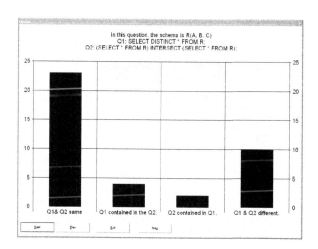

Fig. 4. A Question from the SQL exercise, together with its responses

4.2   Not-understanding

The RA PRS exercise was held in week three, after the lectures in which relational algebra and its relation to SQL were presented. The aim was to:

- demonstrate to the students the extent of the understanding required;
- demonstrate practical application of the concepts presented;
- reinforce material that students typically find difficult.

Students were presented with an SQL query, and four RA expressions: they needed to indicate which of the expressions matched the query (Figs. 5 & 6). In some cases, more than one answer was correct, thus allowing for discussion of expression equivalence.

SELECT * FROM person, animal
WHERE person.houseNum = animal.houseNum

1. $person \bowtie_{(person.houseNum=animal.houseNum)} animal$

2. $\sigma_{(person.houseNum=animal.houseNum)} person \times animal$

3. $\prod_{(houseNum=houseNum)} person, animal$

4. $\prod_{(houseNum=houseNum)} person \bowtie animal$

5. Don't Know

Fig. 5. A question from the Relational Algebra exercise

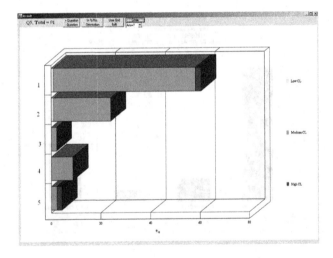

Fig. 6. The display of responses for the Relational Algebra question in Fig. 5

5   Practical Details

The PRS hardware consists of a set of infrared handsets (Fig. 1) and receivers
(Fig. 7), connected to a computer that has its screen displayed to the audi-
ence(Fig. 8), usually through a data projector. The handsets have 10 number
buttons and 2 'confidence' buttons. A student can use these extra two buttons to
modify their response to show either higher or lower confidence in their answer
(The handset defaults to 'normal confidence'). This is then shown on the bar
chart (for example, as can be seen in Fig. 3).

Fig. 7. A PRS Receiver

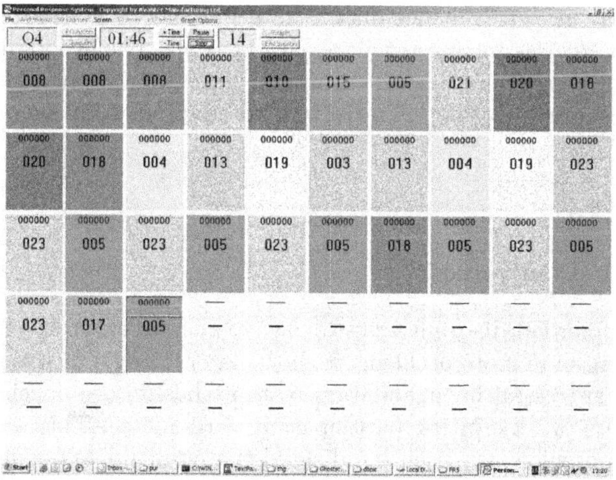

Fig. 8. Screen display while the students are registering their answers

5.1   Considerations for Use

Time to vote. When a button on the handset is pressed, this is transmitted to the computer, but the signal may be lost (it may be blocked by other signals or not in line of sight of a receiver). Since the registering of a vote is not guaranteed, the unique ID for each handset that registers a response is displayed to the whole audience (the IDs on the screen are colour coded by the last digit of the ID to ease identification). Any student who sees that their response has not been successfully received must revote. Students quickly become adept at voting and revoting, and by the end of their first session 100 students' responses can be collected in less than a minute.

Time to set up. The equipment (receivers and computer) requires less than 5 minutes to setup. This is usually done as the class are coming into the lecture theatre.

Cost. If the handsets are bought in bulk the price can be reduced to about £20 per handset; the receivers cost approximately £150 each. The recommended ratio of handsets to receivers is 50 to one. While the cost of handsets and receivers for one class may be prohibitive, sharing this cost over several departments throughout the university makes the purchase justifiable.

Handset Distribution. Since the equipment is used by many classes the handsets are distributed to students during each lecture. The simplest distribution method is to give each student a random handset as they walk in the door. This means that any data collected across more than one lecture cannot later be aggregated by student.

Other Equipment. The reliance on the data projector to display the computer screen is not ideal as technical failures are possible though infrequent. The receiver equipment requires that the computer have a serial port. Modern laptops only have USB ports, and not all serial to USB adapters work completely reliably.

6   Results

6.1   Learning Outcomes

The first, simpler ER diagrams questions were answered well by the second year students; there were more problems with the later, more difficult questions. The exercise was successful in highlighting to the students the deficiencies in their knowledge (e.g. weak entities, participation, cardinality). This was particularly important as previous experience indicated that students felt complacent about ER diagrams at the start of second year, having learnt them in first year. This PRS exercise has run for both years that this second year module has run, so no learning comparisons can be made; however, the lecturer reports that the majority of students are very careful about the production of their ER diagrams, even for unassessed problems.

The easier SQL questions were answered well by the third year students, and, like the second years, the performance deteriorated with the more difficult later questions. The exercise was considered very useful for the lecturer in determining the extent of what had been covered in theoretical aspects of SQL in second year. It was also a clear indicator to the students of the extent of knowledge that may be expected of them in their summative assessment. The lecturer reports that the performance of the students is higher than previous years, and (independently of the second year lecturer) reports that students are more careful in their use of SQL.

As the RA exercise covered material that had been recently presented in the second year class, the pattern of responses was different: the first, easier, questions were poorly answered, and the lecturer discussed and explained the correct answers to these questions. The students' performance on the later, more difficult, questions was better, indicating that the students were correcting their misunderstandings, and applying their new knowledge immediately. The lecturer reports that their understanding of relational algebra is markedly improved when compared with students last year (who did not have this PRS exercise, and who had learned some relational algebra in first year).

As the aim of the ER and SQL exercises was primarily to reveal the students' knowledge of material that they had covered in the previous year (to both the students and the lecturers), the responses to these questions did not influence the subsequent delivery of material. As the RA exercise was used to determine students' understanding of recently presented material, the students' responses indicated to the lecturer which aspects of RA needed further immediate explanation.

6.2   Student Responses

Students' responses to the use of the PRS are generally positive: they see the benefits of the exercise in consolidating their understanding, in identifying where their knowledge deficiencies are and where they need to revise or catch up material, and in assisting them in their preparation for summative assessment. Students report that they are more likely to attempt to answer the question using PRS than if the lecturer requests a volunteered response by a 'hands-up' or verbal method.

7   Conclusions

Using PRS to support large class teaching is clearly effective for both students and lecturers in assisting students in achieving the level of understanding of recently taught material required for summative assessment. Our approach is to use PRS in a timely manner, concentrating on informing both the lecturer and student of current knowledge status at an important point during the semester.

By integrating our use of PRS within the Database materials covered in different year levels, we hope to enhance the students' understanding, address the problems of student complacency, and assist the lecturers in providing continuity in the database curriculum.

Acknowledgements. We are grateful for the contribution and enthusiasm of the database students at the Department of Computing Science at the University of Glasgow. The use of the PRS system is supported by the EPSRC funded GRUMPS project (GR/N38114), and is partly funded by the University of Glasgow, and the Department of Computing Science.

References

1. Boyle, J,T. and Nicol, D.J. (2003) "Using classroom communication systems to support interaction and discussion in large class settings." Assocation for Learning Technology Journal, 11(3), pp43-57.
2. Draper, S.W. Cargill, J. and Cutts, Q (2002), "Electronically enhanced classroom interaction", Austrailian Journal of educational technology, vol 18 no.1 pp13-23.
3. Hake, R.R. (1998), "Interactive engagement v. traditional methods: A six-thousand-student survey of mechanics test data for introductory physics courses." American Journal of Physics, 66, pp64-74.
4. Laurillard, D. (2002), "Rethinking university teaching : a conversational framework for the effective use of learning technologies", Routledge.
5. Pickford, R. and Clothier, H. (2003), "Ask the Audience: A simple teaching method to improve the learning experince in large lectures", Proceedings of the Teaching, Learning and Assessment in Databases conference, LTSN ICS.
6. Stuart, S. and Brown, M.I. Draper, S.W. (2004), "Using an electronic voting system in logic lectures: One practitioner's application", Journal of Computer Assisted Learning, 20, pp95-102.
7. Wit, E. (2003), "Who wants to be... The use of a Personal Response System in Statistics Teaching," MSOR Connections, Vol 3, no. 2, pp5-11.

Teaching SQL — Which Pedagogical Horse for This Course?

Karen Renaud[1] and Judy van Biljon[2]

[1] Department of Computing Science, University of Glasgow
[2] School of Computer Science, University of South Africa

Abstract. A student with a Computing Science degree is expected to have reached a reasonable level of expertise in writing SQL. SQL is a non-trivial skill to master and is taught with different degrees of success at different institutions. When teaching any skill we have to take both previous learning and experience into consideration as well as the best possible way of teaching the skill.

When learning a new skill humans form mental models of particular problems and formulate internal patterns for solving these problems. When they encounter the same problem later they apply these previously internalised patterns to solve the problem. This reality has to be taken into account when selecting a teaching approach because changing an existing mental model is difficult and much more difficult than encoding the correct model in the first place.

This paper considers two different pedagogical approaches to teaching SQL and compares and contrasts these in terms of mental models and cognition. We conclude by making recommendations about the tools that should be used in teaching SQL if the afore-mentioned mental models are to be constructed to support a coherent and correct understanding of SQL semantics and not merely the syntax thereof.

1 Introduction

It is an indisputable fact that many students have difficulty learning SQL. Database educators have been teaching SQL for many years and this problem tends to persist throughout the years. This is partly due to the nature of SQL, and the fact that it is fundamentally different from the other skills students master during their course of study. However, we feel it will be beneficial to take a closer look at different pedagogical paradigms involved in teaching SQL to see whether we can come up with some recommendations about how SQL ought to be taught and the tools that should be used in teaching it.

In this investigation the results obtained from two completely different paradigms used for SQL teaching are discussed. When contemplating issues such as these we need to consider mental models and cognition. Humans form mental models, or previously internalised patterns, in order to understand common problems, and apply these patterns to solve previously encountered problems. In comparing these paradigms we want to identify effectual and efficient ways of teaching SQL and also find explanations for the failure of paradigms that are not as effective.

It is not easy to draw comparisons between teaching paradigms at different institutions because student dynamics differ not only between institutions but in the same

H. Williams and L. MacKinnon (Eds.): BNCOD 2004, LNCS 3112, pp. 244–256, 2004.

institution in successive years as well. There are also other factors, such as different teaching styles and concepts being taught at different levels to students with varying abilities. However, it is still useful to examine these teaching paradigms to draw valuable lessons from them and, in the end, to find out how best to teach SQL.

Before considering the different teaching paradigms we introduce, in Section 2, the idea of pedagogical patterns, a way of formulating specific teaching approaches which enables educators to share and publish effective teaching practices. Section 3 will explore human mental models and learning in general. Section 4 will compare and contrast the teaching of SQL at the different institutions. Section 5 considers the connection between the teaching paradigm, the mental model support and the results attained by students at the two institutions. Section 6 concludes and identifies further research in this area.

2   Pedagogical Patterns

A notion which is emerging in teaching circles is the use of pedagogical patterns to formulate teaching of a particular concept [1]. Pedagogical patterns attempt to focus the educator on important parts of the pedagogical process, and on finding the best possible way of teaching a particular concept, with a view to sharing this knowledge.

The concept of a pattern as being a perennial solution to a recurring problem originated in the field of architecture, based on the work of Alexander [2]. Patterns have been taken up in various fields, including software engineering and human-computer interaction. Each particular field has their own specialized vocabulary and structure. However, the notion of a pattern as a generalised, core solution, which can be applied to resolve the forces in the recurring problem, is pervasive. A related concept is that of *anti-patterns*, which are commonly used solutions that yield undesirable results. Coplien describes an anti-pattern as something that looks like a good idea, but which backfires badly when applied [3]. Thus some pedagogical patterns may actually be anti-patterns without the educator realising it.

Pedagogical patterns commonly consist of *issues, strategies* and *implementation*. The issues in these patterns are concerned with the transfer of knowledge of a particular type. The strategy is the design which aims to transfer that knowledge in a particular way and the implementation delivers material in the way specified by the strategy.

It would be helpful to database educators if tried and tested pedagogical patterns to teach SQL were formulated. There are many approaches that can be taken and the educator does not initially know whether a particular pedagogical pattern is a true pattern or an anti-pattern. To better understand the efficacy of two particular approaches Section 4 will compare and contrast the teaching of SQL at two institutions. However, before doing this we need to discuss relevant issues pertaining to human cognition and learning in the following section.

3   Mental Models and Learning

Mental models are *small-scale models of reality* constructed to anticipate events, to reason and to underlie explanation [4]. Models can represent abstract notions such as negation and ownership. Mental models are not the only psychological knowledge representation [5], but for the purpose of this discussion we will focus on the mental model as knowledge representation.

The mind constructs mental models as a result of perception, imagination, knowledge and the comprehension of discourse [6]. These models can engender thoughts, inferences and emotions. When a person encounters a new problem and is presented with a solution to the problem, a pattern(solution) is encoded in memory. This pattern needs to be reinforced so that it will persist for later usage. Once the pattern is well established by frequent application, the person will have little difficulty in retrieving it when they encounter the problem again as the knowledge has been integrated into the user's mental model.

There are at least two ways in which this process can fail. The first can be referred to as the *incorrect encoding* problem, and the second as the *incorrect paradigm* problem. The incorrect encoding problem can be caused by the learner being taught incorrectly or by a failure to correctly understand the solution which should be applied to the problem. This is not a problem if the incorrect solution is eradicated before it has been established, but continuous *reinforcement* of the incorrect solution will make this much harder. If the learner establishes an incorrect pattern of solving a problem, he/she will have to work very hard to unlearn the "bad" solution and to respond to problems with the correct solution [7]. It appears that the "bad" solution is not replaced but merely supplanted — it will always remain, and will emerge at times of stress or tiredness.

The incorrect paradigm problem occurs when a learner has been taught or has assimilated a way of solving a problem that ranges from merely ill-advised to detrimental. For a skill-based subject such as Maths or Computing, for example, where one concept builds upon another, an incorrect understanding of any particular concept will negatively influence the learning and assimilation of all further concepts. Skill-based learning is based on the learning theory of *constructivism*, where the emphasis is on setting up nodes of information and establishing links between related nodes [8]. Constructivism recognises that items of knowledge build on previously learnt items, referred to as *nodes*, and new learning is thus not independent of other nodes [9]. Learners build on both previous experience *and* on previously assimilated knowledge. Failure of constructivism, where new learning attempts to build on nodes that are simply not there, has been observed in the New Maths Movement of the 1970s [10]. During this time the way Maths was taught was changed radically. Children's initial success with the New Maths was misleading since in later years it was found that they could not grasp more advanced mathematical concepts, having missed out on the required grounding (the required nodes did not exist). It ill-behoves educators in other disciplines to ignore this lesson.

These concepts are extremely important in the development of pedagogical patterns, and may play an important role in turning an erstwhile pedagogical pattern into a pedagogical anti-pattern. By concentrating on teaching the right concepts at the right time it may be possible to prevent the unwitting use of pedagogical anti-patterns. The following section will discuss the application and observations of the pedagogical paradigms used by two institutions to determine their efficacy.

4   Teaching SQL

Understanding and writing SQL is a crucial skill for Computing Science students to master. It is the most widely-used database querying language in industry and it is expected that graduates will have mastered this skill [11]. SQL needs to be taught incrementally, with each concept building on the previous one, to construct a full understanding of the language, building from the specific to the general [12] to teach required concepts. SQL is one of those languages that is deceptively difficult to master. The syntax is very simple and it is all too easy to think that an understanding of the syntax reflects an understanding of the underlying semantics. However, more advanced querying capabilities of SQL are much harder to master, something which appears to take learners by surprise. The SQL competency list consists of the following concepts, in increasing order of difficulty:

1. Select (syntax)
2. Use of distinct and ordering
3. Grouping
4. Having
5. Joining
6. Aggregation
7. Nesting
8. Set operators (not in, in, any)
9. Predicate operators (exists)
10. Some programming interface to databases, such as JDBC.
11. Constraints and triggers
12. PL/SQL - stored procedures
13. Recursive SQL based on Datalog

A student who has mastered all of these concepts has mastered the intricacies of the SQL language. It is important to bear in mind that a superficial understanding or misunderstanding at any of these levels will provide an insufficient structure upon which to build further concepts, and inevitably lead to frustration and poor grades.

4.1   Where Is the Problem?

Despite its deceptively simple syntax, SQL is not a simple language to master. It is counter-intuitive [13], and totally unlike the procedural or object-oriented languages students are familiar with, because SQL is essentially a declarative language, which allows us to specify *what* we want and not *how* to get it.

SQL writers have to work with sets and reason about values. The concept of a group of values within a set not being ordered in any particular fashion, even though the underlying tables being queried are ordered in some way, is confusing. Students must understand concepts like joins, grouping structures and deep nesting. SQL also extends the traditional binary logic of True and False, by adding a NULL, which is neither. This is completely unlike anything else they have done before and many students find it challenging [11].

It is essential for students to have a good understanding of what exactly is happening when a SQL query is executed if they are going to have any chance of progressing up the competency list to master all the concepts [12]. A student with only a superficial knowledge of SQL may, for example, be unable to progress to complicated queries using predicate logic.

Since SQL is a skill, and we can reasonably conclude that SQL learning is essentially constructivist, we need to identify the foundations upon which SQL needs to build. The absence or insufficient understanding of these concepts will inevitably lead to a failure to truly understand SQL. The foundations are made up of an understanding of:

- relational data models;
- relational algebra;
- set theory;
- logic.

The common pedagogical issue can therefore be formulated as follows:

- to ensure that the required grounding of required fundamental concepts has been provided;
- to give students an understanding of the syntax and semantics of SQL;
- to make them aware of the differences between SQL and procedural programming;
- to give them enough practice to ensure that the concepts are fully assimilated.

The following section presents the pedagogical paradigms used at each institution.

4.2   Institution A

Strategy. Students are first taught SQL in a discovery-based manner using a visual interface. By the end of the first year students will have been exposed to the concepts up to and including step (5) in the competency list. In the second year they are encouraged to formulate their own SQL to carry out simple queries. By the end of the second year students will have been exposed to the concepts up to and including step (8) in the competency list. In the third year they are required to use a command-line based client to write their own queries. The queries are complex and require students to master some of the most challenging aspects of SQL such as those numbered 9 to 13 in the competency list. By the end of the third year students will have been exposed to all the concepts in the competency list.

With respect to the required foundations, students are taught about relational data models and set theory in their first year before they learn SQL. They are taught relational algebra in their second year, after they have first been exposed to SQL.

Implementation. Students' first exposure to SQL at Institution A is the Microsoft Access query interface — mostly using the Wizard and the Visual Query Builder is as shown on the left in Figure 1. Students specify the tables involved in the query, the columns to be displayed, and the criteria which limit results. This corresponds directly to the query shown in the SQL query view on the right in Figure 1. However, the students do not have to be concerned with the joining of the two tables, with the syntax of SQL, or with the mechanism for constraining the resulting output. They only have to specify what they

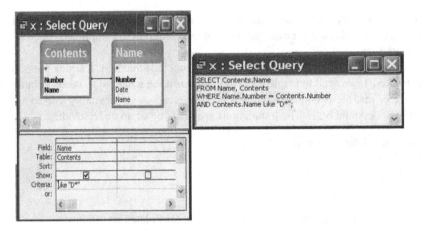

Fig. 1. *Visual Query Builder(left) and SQL View (right)*

want, which tables to use, and what should be displayed — in a graphical format. Joins are done automatically and Access uses a non-standard SQL in its "SQL view" window.

In their second year an attempt is made to wean students from the Visual Query Builder. To this end, they are strongly encouraged to use the SQL view to formulate their queries.

Third year students are given only a command-line client interface to the Oracle DBMS. The third year team spends a great deal of time revising previously-taught concepts, and students are given challenging queries to write which encompass many of the concepts in the competency list. The third-year course is split into three sections — the first part is SQL, the second JDBC and PHP, and the third consists of basic database theory such as transactions, recovery etc. During the year students submit two assessed exercises — one requires them to write substantial queries in SQL and the other requires them to write two programs to query the database: one using JDBC and the other using PHP. At the end of the year the students take an exam which consists of two questions — one covers SQL and the other covers the rest of the syllabus. An example of a typical SQL exam question is:

```
Articles (ID, dateline, headline, author, text)
Keywords (ID, keyword)
```

```
The purpose of the first relation is that each tuple represents a
news article, a unique ID for the article, the day written, the
headline of the article, the author, and the text of the article.
The second relation gives zero or more keywords for each article.
```

```
i) If we declare Articles, we might want to enforce the constraint
that dateline author -> ID: that is, no one can write more than
one article in one day. Show how to write this constraint in SQL
using a tupled-based check.
```

ii) Write an SQL query to find all the authors who never wrote an article with the keyword 'Clinton'. You must use the EXCEPT set operator.

iii) Write an SQL statement giving, for each author and for each keyword of three or more of that author's articles, the earliest dateline among this set of articles (i.e., the set of articles by this author and with this keyword).

4.3   Institution B

Strategy. Students are first exposed to SQL at the third year level. SQL is introduced by an algorithmic approach in which generic SQL syntax is introduced first. The students are then introduced to the command-line like, SQL window of MS Access. They are not encouraged to use the Design View and no tutoring is given to that end. This means that they are focused on formulating queries independently. The queries range from easy to moderately complex and include some of the more challenging aspects of SQL. By the end of the third year students will have been exposed to the concepts up to and including step (10) in the competency list.

At this institution students have a wide choice of modules and thus not all students have the same background. A course which includes set theory can be taken in the first year but it is not a pre-requisite for the database module. They do not learn relational algebra before they learn SQL.

Implementation. Students first write SQL statements without any computer aids, submitting a paper-based solution for assessment. They then use MS Access to design and implement a database and write the accompanying SQL to execute queries on it. The second assessed exercise requires students to implement a complete database system using Delphi or Microsoft Access. Forms, reports and more complicated queries form part of this exercise. An example of a typical SQL exam question is:

```
Consider the following  relations and then write the SQL:

BOOK(ISBN-Number, Book-Title, Publisher-Code, Book-Type,
     Book-Price, Paper-Back)
AUTHOR(Author-Number, Author-Last, Author-First)
BRANCH(Branch-Number, Branch-Name, Branch-Location,
       Number-Employees)
INVENT(ISBN-Number, Branch-Number, Units-On-Hand)
PUBLISHER(Publisher-Code, Publisher-Name,
          Publisher-City, Publisher-State)
WROTE(ISBN-Number, Author-Number, Sequence-Number)

i) Create a new table called FICTION using the data in the ISBN
number, book title and book price columns in the BOOK table.
The primary key is the ISBN number. The price cannot be null.
```

The book title column should be a text column with a maximum
length of 30 characters and the ISBN column should be a text
column with a maximum length of 4 characters. Select only
those books of type FIC and insert them into the new table.

ii) List every pair of ISBN numbers that have the same branch
number.

iii) Find the number of units on hand, book title, and author's
last name for all paperback books in branch number 4.

iv) Find the titles of all books written by Howard Rheingold.
Use a sub-query to get the result.

v) Calculate and display the average price for each type of book.

4.4 Synopsis

The two institutions have very different approaches to teaching SQL. At Institution A,
students experience success relatively quickly in querying their database without having
to master the intricacies of SQL itself. They have extended exposure to SQL syntax and
concepts with increasing difficulty as they progress through the system. At Institution B,
students learn to formulate queries on paper before progressing to using a tool, and then
move on to more difficult queries during the year. They have only one year's exposure
to SQL. In Section 5 we discuss the results attained by students at the two institutions.

5   Discussion

It is impossible to directly compare the examination results from the two institutions as
there are too many variables involved. The syllabus, teaching, study material, examination paper, examination procedures and student selection are some of the many variables
that could influence the results. What does make sense is to compare how well students
master SQL compared to the other concepts taught in the database module. At Institution A there is some concern about students' performance in the SQL component of the
course while at Institution B students' performance is considered to be satisfactory. We
now examine these differences more closely.

5.1   Differences Between Institutions

In the second year, when students at Institution A are encouraged to switch over to
writing their own SQL, rather than using the Visual Query Builder, they resist the move.
They tend to formulate their queries using the Visual Query Builder and then submit the
generated SQL in their assessed coursework. Educators are able to detect this because
Microsoft Access generates copious numbers of brackets and students often do not

remove these. Even in the third year a number of students still express a preference for the Visual Query Builder.

The third year lecturers find that the students do not understand the semantics of SQL and demonstrate difficulty in formulating queries at the beginning of the year — although they have a superficial understanding of SQL's syntax.

This is somewhat surprising, given that it is effectively their third year of exposure to the same concepts. The exam results are disappointing. Students often perform worse in the SQL question than in the other one.

By the time students start using Microsoft Access, at Institution B, however, their approach to SQL appears to be one of writing their own queries. This process seems to be already internalised and although they use Microsoft Access Visual Query Builder view to get the field names their previous exposure to the algorithmic approach leads them to use the SQL view window and not the Visual Query Builder window.

The results shown in Table 1 show the difference between the students' performance in the SQL question and their overall exam performance.

Table 1. Comparison between SQL mark and full exam mark

	Institution A SQL Mark	Institution B SQL Mark
Year End 2002	-36.5%	Unavailable
Resit 2002	+10%	+5%
Year End 2003	+0.01%	+22.56%
Resit 2003	-30.0%	+21.68%

There could be many reasons for this. The student body composition cannot be compared, student motivation may differ, and teaching practices will differ too. However, we believe that a strong factor in influencing the performance of students at Institution A is the pedagogical paradigm being applied. We will explore this idea further in the following section.

5.2   Explanation

One would have thought that longer exposure to the SQL teaching material would ensure that the students understood the concepts more thoroughly and that the results at Institution A would be better than those at Institution B. The students at Institution A clearly have more trouble mastering the intricacies of SQL. This is evidenced both by the exam results as shown above, and also from student feedback forms, of which a majority have some comment about the difficulty of SQL.

We believe this is due to the fact that students first exposed to SQL via MS Access Visual Query Builder base their mental model of SQL on this tool. The teaching (encoding) and use (reinforcement) of this model for a year establishes the mental model in the students' minds. When they are later required to write SQL without this tool they have to change their mental model. The tool-introduced approach as followed at institution A is visual, provides instant results and boosts the confidence of students — perhaps falsely. The tool provides a basis for discovery-based learning as syntax and semantics can easily be verified against the results. Students appear not to do this. They appear to be satisfied with the Visual Query builder, and are focused on the task of querying the database so that they do not examine the generated SQL. Even if students are interested enough to look at the generated SQL they may find the unique Microsoft Access-defined syntax difficult to reconcile with the standard syntax being taught in the lectures.

Hence the previous exposure hinders the learning process, resulting in the learner feeling that they need to 'unlearn' previous concepts and habits in order to make way for new ones. Negative transfer from the exposure to the Visual Query Builder in Microsoft Access could provide students with habits/concepts that they need to unlearn in order to assimilate concepts required to formulate SQL queries without the assistance of the tool.

At institution B, on the other hand, an algorithmic approach is followed. This is a tool-independent approach which supports the understanding of common problems, and uses internalised patterns to solve recognised problems. This approach provides more support for the mental model as the student's algorithmic abilities are developed. Students are taught to be self-sufficient and algorithmically oriented in approaching the problem as tool support is only made available after they have mastered the basic syntax and semantics of SQL.

5.3   Related Findings

We believe that the problems experienced by institution A are related to the way students are first exposed to database querying. This corresponds with the finding of Halland [14] who noted the negative transfer effects resulting from exposure to a conceptually different paradigm in teaching programming. In a study on the effect of transfer between different mental models Hyyppä [15] found that users' pre-existing mental models can be quite strong and should be taken into account.

The first exposure to a particular paradigm of usage appears to have an unexpected effect on usage of other applications later on. For example, Windows-based word processors provide a large measure of external cognitive support, easing memory retrieval while other applications the user often has to rely on his/her internal mental model of the system. According to van Biljon [16] it is possible that people whose expectations are first formed by word processors are most comfortable with the support provided by such a system, unlike people who prefer to rely on their own internal mental model rather than using the support system. This could explain why people who are introduced to SQL using the visual, supportive Microsoft Access interface find it hard to adapt to the command-line paradigm. The visual approach does not prepare them to formulate their own queries, which they have to do when they have to develop any serious interface to the database.

There is anecdotal evidence that experienced writers of SQL switch to the Visual Query Builder with difficulty [17]. This appears to suggest that a completely different paradigm of querying the database is being learnt in the Visual Query builder. It seems that once learners have internalised either of the these querying paradigms they resist using the other.

5.4   Recommendations

Microsoft Access is ubiquitous and tempting to use in an educational setting. However, there are clearly problems with using it as a teaching tool. The experienced problems may be related to its interface usability. Dringus and Terrell [18] point out that learners need to focus on the exploration of knowledge (learning SQL) rather than the performance of their task — querying or updating the database. If the interface makes the task too easy, as the Visual Query builder does, it does not allow users to explore SQL and to master the language itself. The Microsoft Access interface makes it simple and easy to query and update data, and applies a user-centred approach. However, this software may be unsuitable for *teaching* SQL-writing skills. Learners are learning how to use *Microsoft Access* rather than learning how to write SQL. Mayes and Flower [19] appear to confirm this argument, by arguing that a good, usable interface may be counter-productive in terms of learning.

When we consider the differences between the two institutions a new need emerges in the study of the use of patterns and anti-patterns in pedagogy. An important context which clearly needs to be considered in the use of patterns in pedagogy and instruction is the user's context. This context — the user's previous exposure to a proposed solution to the design problem for which the current pattern is being offered as a solution — is of vital importance.

It seems that if a learner is taught using a certain paradigm, and has internalised this mechanism, later exposure to other, less optimal paradigms do not compromise the internalised schema for problem solving and SQL query formation. However, if the learner learns by means of an incorrect paradigm, it is very difficult to remedy it by even prolonged exposure to the accompanying correct paradigm. The use of a high-level assistant such as the Wizards in Microsoft Access, as the first exposure to a particular concept, leads to a specific mental model which is not compatible with the abilities required later. It influences the user's mental model of the system and creates expectations about the support provided which can hardly be fulfilled in other applications. Students who form a mental model of using SQL as a written language adapt to the use of tools without losing their basic ability to write SQL. The problems occur when students start with the tool. In this scenario the student's ability to form a mental model of the SQL language is encumbered by their pre-existing mental model formed during usage of the visual tool.

6   Conclusion

Understanding the effects and implications of the initial use of high-level tools is essential so that they do not prove counter-productive to the learning process and the functioning of the mental model. If our interpretation of these pedagogical paradigms is correct, it has implications for the use of high-level tools in pedagogy. If the designer being exposed to the tool is an experienced SQL writer, then the tool will probably have a positive effect by carrying out mundane tasks for the database queryer. If, on the other hand, the designer has not yet internalised the semantics of SQL, the tool's faciliation of the querying process may be taken and internalised as the schema or pattern which should be applied to querying the database — and it will be very difficult to eradicate this and to replace it with the SQL-writing ability.

We conclude that the pedagogical paradigm being used by Institution A is potentially flawed. Institution B does not expose students to the full competency list, and indeed it would be difficult to do this in a single year. Considering the scenarios presented, the paradigm based on fundamental SQL knowledge acquisition before tool support, as used by Institution B, emerges as the better approach. This approach could easily be applied at Institution A merely by replacing the use of Microsoft Access at the first and second year levels with a command-line SQL query tool.

This study is too small to be conclusive. What emerged does appear interesting enough to require a larger and more substantial study in order to confirm or deny our assertions about the value or detriment of an approach where the existing mental model is rendered invalid over time and where a discovery-based visual approach is followed by a more command-driven tool-less approach. This knowledge should be used to develop pedagogical patterns for teaching SQL using tools which foster learning and do not unwittingly hinder it.

Acknowledgements. Our thanks to Paula Kotzé, Ruth de Villiers, Iadh Ounis and Rebecca Mancy for their extremely helpful comments and inputs.

References

1. Bergin, J.: Fourteen pedagogical patterns. Web Document (February 2004) http://csis.pace.edu/ bergin/PedPat1.3.html.
2. Alexander, C.: A Pattern Language: towns, buildings, construction. Oxford University Press (1977)
3. AntiPatterns: Portland pattern repository. Web Document (2004) http://c2.com/cgi/wiki.
4. Johnson-Laird, P.N., Girottoa, V., Legrenzi, P.: Mental models: a gentle guide for outsiders. Web document (2003) http://www.si.umich.edu/ICOS/gentleintro.htm.
5. Johnson-Laird, P.N., Byrne, R.M.J.: Precis of deduction. Behavioural and Brain sciences **16** (1993) 323–334
6. Byrne, R.: Mental models website. Web Document (2003) http://www.tcd.ie/Psychology/Ruth_Byrne/mental_models/theory.html.
7. Halland, K., Malan, K.: Reflections by teachers learning to program. In Eloff, J., Kotze, P., Engelbrecht, A., Eloff, M., eds.: SAICSIT 2003, IT Research in Developing Countries. (2003)
8. Kettanurak, V., Ramamurthy, K., Haseman, W.D.: User attitude as a mediator of learning performance improvement in an interactive multimedia environment: an empirical investigation of the degree of interactivity and learning styles. International Journal Human-Computer Studies **54** (2001) 541–583
9. Draper, S.: Constructivism and instructional design. Web Document (2004) http://www.psy.gla.ac.uk/ steve/constr.html.
10. Kananoja, T.: Teacher training in technological education in finland. In: Proc. Conference on Pupil's Attitudes towards Technology, Linköping (1996) 10.5–14.5

11. Kearns, R., Shead, S., Fekete, A.: A teaching system for SQL. In: Proceedings of the second Australasian conference on Computer Science education, Melbourne, Australia (1997) 224–231

12. Gennick, J.: On the importance of mental model. Web Document (12/2/2004) (2004) http://gennick.com/mental_models.html.

13. Matos, V.M., Grasser, R.: A simpler (and better) SQL approach to relational division. Journal of Information Systems Education **13** (2002) 85–88

14. Halland, K., Malan, K.: Bad examples for teaching programming. In: Proceedings of the 33 rd annual conference of the South African Computer Lecturers' Association. (2003)

15. Hyyppä, K., Tamminen, S., Hautala, I., Repokari, L.: The effect of mental models guiding user's action in mobile phone answering situations. In: Proceedings from Design vs. Design, 1st Nordic Conference on Human-Computer Interaction, Nordichi 2000, Stockholm, Sweden (2000)

16. van Biljon, J.A., Renaud, K.V.: Investigating the difference between interaction approaches in advisory support systems for curriculum planning. In Rauterberg, M., Menozzi, M., Wesson, J., eds.: Proceedings Interact 2003. (2003)

17. Experts: Exchange. Microsoft Graph — What is datasheet view all about? Web Document (2004) http://www.experts-exchange.com/Databases/MS_Access/Q_20822093.html.

18. Dringus, L.P., Terrell, S.: A framework for directed online learning environments. Internet and Higher Education **2** (1999) 55–67

19. Mayes, J.T., Fowler, C.J.: Learning technology and usability: a framework for understanding courseware. Interacting with Computers **11** (1999) 485–497

Computer-Based Assessment Strategies in the Teaching of Databases at Honours Degree Level 1

Gill Harrison

School of Computing
Leeds Metropolitan University
g.harrison@leedsmet.ac.uk

Abstract. The first-year database module for degree students at Leeds Metropolitan University provides a useful case study in the introduction of "blended" learning, particularly with respect to the module's assessment. A computer-based test, delivered using WebCT, now accounts for a substantial proportion of this. In the 2003 delivery to a cohort of 200 students, a sample test was used formatively, to provide detailed feedback to the students, and then a summative version was used. Logistical and technical problems in the staging of the test for the first time were encountered and overcome. Evaluation of the results has enabled such issues as question design and marking strategy to be analysed. The problems encountered and issues considered, including the security and practicality of testing large groups and the use of automated question analysis, will be of interest to those seeking to incorporate elements of computer-based assessment in their teaching of databases, and others.

Keywords: Computer-Based Assessment (CBA), VLE, Databases, Security

1 Introduction

In October 2002 the School of Computing at Leeds Metropolitan University introduced a new undergraduate degree scheme, which included a first-year module delivered in the second semester entitled Data Modelling and Database Design. The syllabus for this module comprised the usual topics of entity-relationship modelling and logical design, together with some background on the historical development of databases, and the ethical and legal aspects of their use. A brief introduction to SQL was also included.

The assessment strategy for this new module was carefully considered. In the previous degree scheme the assessment of corresponding material had taken two forms:

- a summative assignment involving the creation of an entity-relationship diagram
- an unseen 2-hour examination, heavily based on work done in a formative assignment that required the design and building of a database.

H. Williams and L. MacKinnon (Eds.): BNCOD 2004, LNCS 3112, pp. 257–264, 2004.

(The terms "summative" and "formative" are used here and throughout to mean respectively contributing to and not contributing to the total module mark achieved by the student.)

Many students did not choose to engage with the formative practical assignment, and it was felt to be desirable to give the building of a database summative status. The creation of an entity-relationship diagram was retained as a summative assignment, and, using an approach similar to that advocated by Gearing [4], extensive feedback ensured that all students could then move on to design and build the database. Although students had clearly expressed, in their module feedback questionnaires, dislike of the examination, it was still felt to be desirable to set a written test of some kind, to ensure that all of the module outcomes (of which some were more practically and some more theoretically orientated) were adequately covered. This also minimised the plagiarism problems arising when assessment is wholly coursework based.

As Leeds Metropolitan had by now adopted the use of a Virtual Learning Environment (WebCT) and the School of Computing was encouraging its use throughout all modules to at least level 1 or 2 of the Harmon and Jones classification [5], a decision was made that it would be appropriate to set a computer-based test and to present it through WebCT. The principal issues considered before arriving at this decision were:

- The main assessment of these first-year students was to be at levels 2 (Comprehension) and 3 (Application) in terms of Bloom's taxonomy [1], in other words their understanding and application of the principles that they had learned in the module. Although it may be possible to write questions to test the higher levels, it becomes increasing difficult and time-consuming to devise suitable questions, whereas at the lower levels devising robust questions is more straightforward. (Excellent guidance on writing questions at whatever level is available for example from the CAA Centre [10].)

- The students, being enrolled on a computing-related degree course, were highly IT-literate, and would have no difficulty in using computers for testing purposes.

- Marking of examination papers would be eliminated, although a considerable amount of time would need to be expended initially in the writing of the new questions.

- A formative test with feedback could be made available to provide much better preparation for the summative test than had been possible using old examination papers in previous years. There are indications that related formative testing improves student scores on summative tests [3].

The balance of assessment was set at 50% for the practical database assignment and 50% for the summative end-of-module computer-based test.

2 Constructing the Test

Questions were created for each of the topics in the module, though fewer questions were presented on the topic areas that were felt to be heavily tested by the practical assignment. Different question types were used, including true/false, "matching" from a list of options, multiple-choice with a single correct answer and multiple-choice with several correct options. The facility to include diagrams in either questions or answers was found to be useful. Publicly available sources of questions [6] were investigated, and proved helpful for ideas about suitable questions, though generally the questions needed to be re-thought in the context of the way that material had been presented in the module.

It was found to be particularly difficult to formulate questions on normalisation, since although this essentially involves the Application level of Bloom's taxonomy, it is most easily assessed by simply asking students to normalise a given table or tables. Providing students with alternatives to choose from seems to be taking away their opportunity to show that they can perform, on their own initiative, the normalisation process. This topic would perhaps lend itself to the use of more complicated types of question style [9], for example where attributes from an un-normalised table could be moved into other tables. Only a limited range of fairly simple question types was available within WebCT, so it was not possible to try this out. In this section of the test only, it was felt necessary to write linked series of questions, generally beginning with an un-normalised table and suggesting possibilities for its normalisation in stages. However, this proved difficult to do as later questions in a series might pre-suppose or suggest the answers to earlier ones. An example of a series of questions based around the same initial table is shown below. Clearly question 3 could imply part of the answer to question 2, so VEHICLE had to be included in each of question 2's options.

```
1. A Car Hire Bureau records the hiring out of cars
to clients in a table: HIRE (Hire#, Vehicle_Reg,
Vehicle_Model, Client#, Client_Name,
Client_Company, Date_Hired, Daily_Cost, Bureau#,
Bureau_Address).
Is this table:

        a. un-normalised?
        b. in First Normal Form (but not second)?
        c. in Second Normal Form (but not Third)?

2. In normalising the table HIRE what would you
choose as new tables?

        a. BUREAU, TYPE, VEHICLE
        b. BUREAU, VEHICLE, CLIENT
        c. VEHICLE, COST, CLIENT
```

3. A new table, VEHICLE, is to be defined. Which of
the following statements is/are true?

    a. Attributes Vehicle_Reg and Vehicle_Model
should appear in the new VEHICLE table
    b. Neither of the attributes Vehicle_Reg and
Vehicle_Model should now appear in the
original HIRE table
    c. Hire# should appear as a foreign key in
VEHICLE
    d. Vehicle_Reg should appear as a foreign key
in HIRE

All the questions of the test were reviewed against accepted guidelines [2] for setting computer-based questions in an attempt to improve the standard of assessment. Consideration was given to the effect that guessing might have on the student scores; for example a test in which every question requires the selection of one option from 4 could theoretically award a 25% score to a student on the basis of guesswork. To guard against this some multiple-choice questions with a single correct answer had 5 or more options to choose from, and other multiple-choice questions required a number of options to be selected (how many being unspecified), with marks only being awarded for fully correct answers. Negative marking for wrong answers - "a controversial topic, widely seen as unpopular among students and hotly debated amongst practitioners" [8] - was contemplated but not adopted at least in this initial stage.

Had it been possible to run the test for all candidates at the same time (see next section) then a single version of the test would have sufficed, although workstations are fairly close together in computer laboratories and it may be rather easier for students to view a neighbour's screen than to view another student's script in an examination hall. However, as one single sitting for the test was impractical, a decision was made to write variations of each question in the test, and to arrange for the Virtual Learning Environment to select one of the variations of each question at random. This would reduce the likelihood of copying from a neighbour's screen. It was planned that there would be 4 versions of each question to select from in the summative test, though only 3 were finally written because there was insufficient time to write more. In addition, another version of each question was written and inserted into a formative test that was made available to students about 6 weeks before their final test. This formative test was thus very similar in style and content to the real test, and contained extensive feedback on individual choices made by the student.

3   Practicalities of Test Delivery

The cohort to be tested consisted of about 200 students. Leeds Metropolitan is at a fairly early stage in its adoption of large-scale computer-based summative assessment, and it is currently in the process of working towards the provision of appropriate facilities and administrative procedures. This case study may indicate to those whose institutions are at a similar stage what might be done in the intervening period of transition.

There are as yet no assessment halls containing large numbers of workstations, nor "secure" browsers [7] available in the laboratories that allow access only to the summative test and to no other material, nor a secure server dedicated to providing summative tests with a backup server that could be switched into use in the event of failure of the main server. There are no variations (yet) of the examination regulations to cater for computer-based tests, and the test described here was not designated a formal examination. Thus the best use of the facilities available had to be made, and the spirit of the regulations followed.

The first possibility considered was to run the test in parallel in 10 or 11 separate laboratories. However, this was eventually decided against for the following reasons:

- Although 200 is not a very large number, there was no absolute certainty that simultaneous access to the same test within WebCT would proceed smoothly and without technical difficulties. As far as was known, such a test had not been given on our campus before, and there was no way of performing a large-capacity "stress test" on the system beforehand
- Authentication of student identity would be easier if the students were supervised by the tutor who had taught them for this module during the semester, and who therefore knew them well. The test was not subject to examination regulations with formal lists of student names and the requirement to show identity cards. (The possibility of allowing the students to take the test wherever and whenever they liked was also ruled out for this reason, though some expressed a wish to take the test at home in the middle of the night!)
- Having only three laboratories in use, in close proximity to one another, would make communication and trouble-shooting far easier. An additional staff member, preferably expert in WebCT and its assessment features, could be used to circulate between the laboratories to keep the three tutors in touch and to report any problems. This would be far harder to manage with 11 laboratories widely spread over the campus.

The decision to use only three tutors and laboratories meant that 4 separate deliveries of the test were needed, each of one hour and all on the same day. Minimal breaks between these were scheduled, but it was still felt that if exactly the same test were presented each time, then it was possible that the last students to sit the test might have an unfair advantage by learning the content from some of the earlier students. This led to the writing of variants of each question, as mentioned in the previous section.

The issue of student identity has been referred to above: each tutor was asked to take a register of students attending the test, which could later be cross-checked if necessary with the results list, and every student also had his/her own login ID and password to gain access to WebCT. The test could only be taken under the eye of the tutor, because a password was required to access it and this password, different for each delivery, was issued by the tutor only to the students present in the laboratory. Impersonation of one student by another was therefore thought to be unlikely.

Issues of question security were addressed as follows: the development of all questions was done off-campus and offline, using a development tool called Respondus, which is designed to assist in the creation of computer-based questions that can subsequently be uploaded to a Virtual Learning Environment such as WebCT. Testing of the questions was carried out by uploading them to a separate WebCT server, accessible only to staff (though the inaccessibility of this server to a determined student had to be relied upon). The uploading of the questions to the live WebCT server was delayed until the last possible moment, and the tests were given settings that specified a release time and a password.

The question of whether a secure browser was needed, to ensure that students could not access anything other than the test itself (for example course material or the Internet) was not thought to be particularly important in the given context. Where questions are based on understanding and application of principles rather than on recall of facts simple look-up will not help very much. There is also the question, in a time-limited (one hour) test such as this, of whether the student will be wasting precious time searching for answers.

The possibility of technical problems was anticipated and sufficient paper-based versions of the test were printed to provide for the whole student body.

On the morning of the test, a technical problem did arise, in that the module containing the test (WebCT is organised on a module basis) exhibited access difficulties. However, it proved possible to reconstruct the test fairly rapidly within another WebCT module to which the students also had access, and everything then proceeded as planned without recourse to the paper backup.

Students taking the test appeared in general fairly relaxed. They were in a familiar small computer laboratory with about 20 other students of their regular tutorial group and supervised by their usual module tutor, rather than in an examination hall of several hundred students being patrolled by a dozen invigilators. They all finished within the allotted hour, and a small number commented, while leaving, on how similar many of the questions were to those in the Practice Test.

The test proceeded smoothly, and all marking was completed by WebCT immediately on completion. Full marks lists were thus instantly available.

4   Evaluation of Results

One of the strengths of a computer-based assessment system lies in its ability to provide detailed statistical feedback on the performance of a test as a whole and of individual questions within it.

The individual student scores ranged from 26% to 92%, with an average mark of 58% and a failure rate of just under 10%. This was satisfactory, though perhaps the results were a little high, and the influence of guessing may need to be considered in the longer term.

Detailed analysis of individual questions was provided by the Virtual Learning Environment. This information included:

- the average score for each question
- a summary of which individual options were chosen for multiple-choice questions

- a discrimination figure, giving an indication of whether the question had been answered proportionally better or worse by the top and bottom 25% of students (i.e. a poor discriminator would be answered better by the weaker students than by the stronger students)

These statistics allowed for reflection upon and improvement of the test for the second presentation of the module in 2004. The average scores were reviewed, and the small number of questions that seemed either too easy (average score near 100%) or too difficult (average score near 0%) were removed or reworded. The options for multiple-choice questions were reviewed and improved where possible. Most questions showed a positive value for discrimination, and those that did not were reworded or removed. The questions on normalisation were particularly scrutinised, and some were re-worded to improve their clarity, as results seemed to indicate a poor understanding of the question. All questions will be evaluated again after the 2004 delivery.

5 Conclusion

Computer-based assessment can play a useful part in the assessment of first-year database courses, reducing marking load greatly though requiring considerable initial effort in the preparation of suitable questions. It is likely to be no more stressful than a conventional examination from the students' point of view. Anyone seeking to incorporate such assessment should consider carefully, within the context of their institution, the design of questions, the practicalities of running the test, the question of student authentication, and the possibility of technical problems arising. The assessment process should be reviewed and where possible improved upon year by year.

References

1. Bloom, B.S. (Ed.) (1956) Taxonomy of educational objectives: The classification of educational goals: Handbook I, cognitive domain. New York, Longmans, Green
2. Bull, J. and McKenna, C. (2004) Blueprint for Computer-Assisted Assessment. London and New York, RoutledgeFalmer
3. Charman, D. (1999) Issues and impacts of using computer-based assessments (CBAs) for formative assessment In: Brown, S., Race, P. and Bull, J. Computer-assisted Assessment in Higher Education. London, Kogan Page, 85-93
4. Gearing, L. (2003) Break it up for Success in Assessment In: O'Reilly, U., James, A. and Jackson, M. (eds) Proceedings of the Teaching Learning and Assessment of Databases conference, July 14 2003, LTSN-ICS, 34-38
5. Harmon, S. and Jones, M. (1999) The five levels of web use in education: Factors to consider in planning online courses. Educational Technology 39(6) 28-32
6. Companion website to Hoffer J., Prescott M. & McFadden F. (2002) Modern Database Management 6th ed. Prentice Hall [Internet] Available from: <http://www.prenhall.com/hoffer> [Accessed February 2003] The companion website to the 6th edition is no longer available, but a companion website to the 7th edition is due in April 2004.

7.   Questionmark Perception Secure Browser [Internet] Available from:
      <http://www.questionmark.com/perception/help/v2/securebrowser/> [Accessed 7 March 2004]
8.   University of Derby centre for interactive assessment development (TRIADS),
      Assessment marking strategies [Internet] Available from:
      <http://www.derby.ac.uk/ciad/dev/logical.htm> [Accessed 7 March 2004]
9.   University of Derby centre for interactive assessment development (TRIADS), summary
      of question styles [Internet] Available from: <http://www.derby.ac.uk/ciad/ciastyles.html>
      [Accessed 7 March 2004]
10.   UK CAA Centre, Guide to Objective Tests [Internet] Available from
      <http://www.caacentre.ac.uk/resources/objective_tests/index.shtml> [Accessed 7 March 2004]

Author Index